"I immediately went to my nurse manager after I failed the NCLEX® and she referred me to ATI. I was able to discover the areas I was weak in, and focused on those areas in the review modules and online assessments.

I was much more prepared the second time around!"

Terim Richards
Nursing student

Danielle Platt

Nurse Manager • Children's Mercy Hospital • Kansas City, MO

"The year our hospital did not use the ATI program, we experienced a 15% decrease in the NCLEX® pass rates. We reinstated the ATI program the following year and had a 90% success rate."

"As a manager, I have witnessed graduate nurses fail the NCLEX® and the devastating effects it has on their morale. Once the nurses started using ATI, it was amazing to see the confidence they had in themselves and their ability to go forward and take the NCLEX® exam."

Mary Moss

Associate Dean of Nursing - Service and Health Division • Mid-State Technical College • Wisconsin Rapids, WI

"I like that ATI lets students know what to expect from the NCLEX®, helps them plan their study time and tells them what to do in the days and weeks before the exam. It is different from most of the NCLEX® review books on the market."

Editor

Jeanne Wissmann, PhD, RN, CNE
Director Nursing Curriculum and Educational Services
Assessment Technologies Institute®, LLC

Associate Editors

Audrey Knippa, MS, MPH, RN, CNE
Curriculum Project Coordinator

Susan Adcock, MS, RN
Consulting Associate Editor

Michele Hinds, PhD, RN
Consulting Associate Editor

Brant Stacy, BS Journalism
Product Developer

Erika A. Knoblock, BS Education
Product Developer

Copyright Notice

Important Notice to the Reader of this Publication

Assessment Technologies Institute®, LLC is the publisher of this publication. The publisher reserves the right to modify, change, or update the content of this publication at any time. The content of this publication, such as text, graphics, images, information obtained from the publisher's licensors, and other material contained in this publication are for informational purposes only. The content is not providing medical advice and is not intended to be a substitute for professional medical advice, diagnosis, or treatment. Always seek the advice of your primary care provider or other qualified health provider with any questions you may have regarding a medical condition. Never disregard professional medical advice or delay in seeking it because of something you have read in this publication. If you think you may have a medical emergency, call your primary care provider or 911 immediately.

The publisher does not recommend or endorse any specific tests, primary care providers, products, procedures, processes, opinions, or other information that may be mentioned in this publication. Reliance on any information provided by the publisher, the publisher's employees, or others contributing to the content at the invitation of the publisher, is solely at your own risk. Health care professionals need to use their own clinical judgment in interpreting the content of this publication, and details such as medications, dosages or laboratory tests and results should always be confirmed with other resources.

This publication may contain health or medical-related materials that are sexually explicit. If you find these materials offensive, you may not want to use this publication.

The publishers, editors, advisors, and reviewers make no representations or warranties of any kind or nature, including, but not limited to, the accuracy, reliability, completeness, currentness, timeliness, or the warranties of fitness for a particular purpose or merchantability, nor are any such representations implied with respect to the content herein (with such content to include text and graphics), and the publishers, editors, advisors, and reviewers take no responsibility with respect to such content. The publishers, editors, advisors, and reviewers shall not be liable for any actual, incidental, special, consequential, punitive or exemplary damages (or any other type of damages) resulting, in whole or in part, from the reader's use of, or reliance upon, such content.

Preface

Overview

The overall goal of this Assessment Technologies Institute®, LLC (ATI) Content Mastery Series module is to provide nursing students with an additional resource for the focused review of "Nursing Care of Children" content relevant to NCLEX-RN® preparation and entry level nursing practice. Content within this review module is provided in a key point plus rationale format in order to focus recall and application of relevant content. Unit and chapter selections are reflective of the nursing care of children nursing-relevant content categories and explanations of the NCLEX-RN® test plan, the ATI "Nursing Care of Children Nursing" assessment test plans, and standard nursing curricular content. Each chapter begins with an overview of some of the topic-relevant nursing activities outlined by the NCLEX-RN® test plan in an effort to guide the learner's review and application of chapter content.

Contributors

ATI would like to extend appreciation to the nurse educators and nurse specialists who contributed content for this review module. The names of contributors are noted in the chapter bylines. We would also like to thank those talented individuals who reviewed, edited, and developed this module. In the summer and fall of 2005, two focus groups of committed nurse educators gave invaluable input and feedback regarding the format and purposes of review modules. Their input and ideas were instrumental to the development of this review module, and we are very appreciative. Additionally, we would like to recognize and extend appreciation to the multiple nursing students and educators who have contacted us in the past year with comments and ideas regarding the content of this review module. And finally, we want to recognize and express appreciation to all of the contributors, reviewers, production developers, and editors of previous editions of this Content Mastery Series module.

Suggestions for Effective Utilization

Δ   Understanding the organizational framework of this review module will facilitate focused review. Each unit focuses on a specific aspect of nursing care of children. Unit 1 focuses on "Basic Concepts;" Unit 2 focuses on "Nursing Care of Children with System Disorders;" and Unit 3 focuses on "Nursing Care of Children with Emergencies, Developmental Disorders, or Psychosocial Issues." The chapters are organized with headings to include Key Points, Key Factors, Assessment, NANDA Nursing Diagnoses, Nursing Interventions, and Complications and Nursing Implications.

Δ   Some suggested uses of this review module include:

  •   As a review of NCLEX-RN® relevant nursing care of children content in developing and assessing your readiness for the NCLEX-RN®.

  •   As a focused review resource based on the results of an ATI "Nursing Fundamentals" or "Comprehensive Predictor" assessment. "Topics to Review" identified upon completion of these assessments can be used to focus your efforts to a review of content within specific chapter(s) of this review module. For example, an identified "Topic to Review" of "Dermatitis: Interventions to Manage Pruritus" suggests that a review of chapter 34, "Dermatitis and Acne," and completion of the application exercises at the end of the chapter would be helpful.

Δ   To foster long-term recall and development of an ability to apply knowledge to a variety of situations, learners are encouraged to take a comprehensive approach to topic review. Using this review module along with other resources (class notes, course textbooks, nursing reference texts, instructors, ATI DVD series), consider addressing questions for each aspect of nursing care of children.

  •   For **basic concepts,** ask questions such as:

    ◊   What are the basic concepts of the content area of nursing care of children?

◊ What key points should you know? What are the differences/similarities between nursing care of children and nursing care of adults in relation to cultural awareness, physical assessment findings, safe medication administration, pain management, hospitalization and issues surrounding death and dying?

- For **each specific disorder,** ask questions such as:

    ◊ What are the presenting signs and symptoms? Which ones are classic? What are the differences/similarities between signs and symptoms seen in children and those seen in adults? What techniques are used to assess?

    ◊ What are relevant diagnostic and therapeutic procedures? For altered laboratory values, what are expected findings in comparison to normal values? What are the interventions used prior to, during, and following the procedure?

    ◊ What are appropriate nursing diagnoses and interventions (including medication administration)?

    ◊ What are the overarching desired client outcomes or goals? Which ones are priorities? Explain.

    ◊ What are client findings that need to be reported immediately to the primary care provider?

    ◊ What are possible complications associated with the disorder? What are signs and symptoms of the complication? How should the nurse respond (in order of implementation) to identification of a complication?

    ◊ How would you evaluate the client's response to interventions and progress toward recovery?

    ◊ Does the child/family have educational needs (e.g., appropriate dietary alterations, symptoms to report, and appropriate use of medications)?

- For **emergencies**, ask questions such as:

    ◊ What emergencies are common in children? How do they relate to developmental levels? What primary prevention is needed to prevent them from occurring? What are the assessment findings for each and how does the nurse intervene?

- For **developmental disorders and psychosocial issues**, ask questions such as:

    ◊ How does the developmental disorder and/or psychosocial issue impact the child's normal growth and development? What impact does it have on the child's family? Are the implications short or long term? What interventions can the nurse implement to assist the child/family?

△ Complete application exercises at the end of each chapter after a review of the topic. Answer questions fully and note rationales for answers. Complete exercises initially without looking for the answers within the chapter or consulting the answer key. Use these exercises as an opportunity to assess your readiness to apply knowledge. When reviewing the answer key, in addition to identifying the correct answer, examine why you missed or answered correctly each item – was it related to ability to recall, recognition of a common testing principle, or perhaps attention to key words?

Feedback

All feedback is welcome – suggestions for improvement, reports of mistakes (small or large), and testimonials of effectiveness. Please address feedback to: comments@atitesting.com.

Section: Nursing Care of Children with Neurosensory Disorders

Section: Nursing Care of Children with Musculoskeletal Disorders

Unit 3 Nursing Care of Children with Emergencies, Developmental Disorders, or Psychosocial Issues

Unit 1:   Basic Concepts

Chapter 1:   Family-Centered Nursing Care
               Contributor: Candyce F. Antley, MN, RN

 NCLEX-RN® Connections:

Learning Objective: Review and apply knowledge within "**Family-Centered Nursing Care**" in readiness for performance of the following nursing activities as outlined by the NCLEX-RN® test plan:

Δ   Initiate and maintain the client-nurse relationship with children and their families.

Δ   Recognize what roles family members play within the structure of the family.

Δ   Assess the family for stressors and how they adapt to alterations in health, illness, and/or disease.

Δ   Plan and provide care for the family to assist with adaptation.

Δ   Present health information and teach families how to manage emergencies.

 Key Points

Δ   The family is the one group that should be constant in a child's life.

Δ   Components of family-centered care are respect, collaboration, and support.

Δ   Professionals collaborate with the family regarding hospitalization, home, and community resources.

Δ   A nurse must respect cultural diversity and incorporate cultural views in the plan of care.

Δ   A nurse must have an understanding of the growth and developmental needs of the child and the child's family.

Δ   A nurse must be aware that while the child is the priority concern, the child's family is also in need of care.

Δ   Various family compositions are common in society.

Δ   Positive family relationships are characterized by parent-child warmth and respect.

Δ   Family assessment tools are used to gather information about the family.

Key Factors

Δ   Family-centered care includes:

- The primary care provider providing medical care.

- The family serving as the expert regarding the child's health condition, the child's usual behavior in different situations, and the child's routine needs.

- The nurse as the expert regarding specific health care needs.

- A mutually beneficial partnership between the child's family, the nurse, and the primary care provider.

- Promoting family-centered care

    ◊   The nurse should perform a comprehensive family assessment to identify strengths and weaknesses.

    ◊   The nurse should pay close attention when a family member states that the child "isn't acting right."

    ◊   The child's opinions should be considered when providing care.

    ◊   Recognition and respect should be given to different methods of the child's coping. Support should also be provided as needed.

Δ   Family Composition

Type	Members
Nuclear family	Two parents and their children (e.g., biologic or adoptive)
Single-parent family	One parent and one or more children
Blended family	At least one stepparent, stepsibling, or half-sibling
Extended family	At least one parent, one or more children, and other individuals either related or not related
Same-sex family	A common-law tie between two members of the same sex who may or may not have children
Foster family	A child or children that have been placed in an approved living environment away from the family of origin – usually with one or two parents

Δ   Changes that occur with the birth (or adoption) of the first child include:

- Parents sense of self and how families work.

- Division of labor and roles within the couple's relationship.

- Relationships with grandparents.

- Work relationships.

Δ   Positive parental influences include:

- Parents who are in good mental health.

- Maintained structure in the household.

- Parents' engagement in activities with their children.

- Communication that validates the child's feelings.

- Monitoring of children for safety with special consideration for their developmental needs.

Δ   Parenting Styles

Type	Description	Example
Dictatorial or authoritarian	Parents try to control their children's behaviors and attitudes through unquestioned rules and expectations.	Children may not watch TV on school nights.
Permissive or laissez-faire	Parents exert little or no control over their children's behaviors.	Children may watch TV whenever they want to watch it.
Authoritative or democratic	• Parents direct children's behavior by setting rules and explaining the reason for each rule setting. • Parents also negatively reinforce deviations from the rules.	• Children may watch TV for an hour if their homework is completed. • If homework is not completed and children are watching TV, then the privilege will be taken away for a specified time, because the children did not follow the rule.

Δ   Guidelines for promoting healthy behavior in children include:

- Setting realistic limits and expectations based on developmental tasks.

- Validating the child's feelings.

- Providing reinforcement for appropriate behavior.

- Focusing on the child's behavior when disciplining the child.

- Explaining expectations to a child in a manner the child can understand.

Δ Family assessment includes:

- Genogram – medical history for parents, siblings, aunts, uncles, and grandparents.

- Structure – members in the family, such as mother, father, and son.

- Developmental tasks – tasks families work on as children grow, such as families with school-age children helping those children develop peer relations.

- Family functions/roles – ways in which family members interact with each other, such as mother being the disciplinarian.

- Family stressors – events that cause stress, such as illness of a child

Δ Evaluation outcomes for family-centered nursing care includes:

- The family assuming the role of case manager, or working effectively with an assigned case manager.

- The family providing care to a child with disabilities within identified guidelines.

Primary Reference:

Hockenberry, M., Wilson, D., Winkelstein, M. (2005). *Wong's essentials of pediatric nursing care.* (7th ed.). St. Louis, MO: Mosby.

Additional Resources:

NANDA International (2004). *NANDA nursing diagnoses: Definitions and classification 2005-2006.* Philadelphia: NANDA.

Chapter 1: Family-Centered Nursing Care

Application Exercises

Scenario: A 5-year-old child with autism lives with her mother, two brothers, and grandmother. The child was recently hospitalized with a respiratory infection and has special needs because of her autism.

1. Which of the following describes this family's composition?

    A. Nuclear family

    B. Blended family

    C. Extended family

    D. Same-sex family

2. What would be the best approach for the nurse to take when first assessing this child?

    A. Ask the child's family to step out of the room.

    B. Ask the child's mother what approach would work best.

    C. Ask the child if she is allergic to anything.

    D. Ask the child's grandmother to interpret the child's behaviors.

3. Match the parenting style to the statement that most reflects that style.

_____ Democratic   A. "Your curfew is 10 p.m. You know that."

_____ Dictatorial   B. "As long as you have your homework done, I don't care when you come home."

_____ Permissive   C. "Tonight is a school night, so you need to come home by 10 p.m."

4. Which of the following should be included in a family assessment? (Select all that apply.)

    _____ Genogram

    _____ Structure

    _____ Child's physical growth

    _____ Developmental tasks

    _____ Family functions/roles

    _____ Family stressors

5. True or False: When providing care to a child, the nurse should not be concerned about what the child thinks about the care.

6. List three guidelines for promoting healthy behaviors in children.

7. True or False: When a child is admitted to the pediatric unit, the nurse should keep in mind that the family of the child also needs nursing care.

Chapter 1: Family-Centered Nursing Care

Application Exercises Answer Key

Scenario: A 5-year-old child with autism lives with her mother, two brothers, and grandmother. The child was recently hospitalized with a respiratory infection and has special needs because of her autism.

1. Which of the following describes this family's composition?

   A. Nuclear family

   B. Blended family

   C. Extended family

   D. Same-sex family

   An extended family includes one or more parents, one or more children, and other family members, such as a grandmother. A nuclear family includes two parents and their children. A blended family includes at least one step parent, step sibling, and/or half sibling. A same-sex family includes a common-law tie between two members of the same sex who may or may not have children.

2. What would be the best approach for the nurse to take when first assessing this child?

   A. Ask the child's family to step out of the room.

   B. Ask the child's mother what approach would work best.

   C. Ask the child if she is allergic to anything.

   D. Ask the child's grandmother to interpret the child's behaviors.

   The family is the expert regarding the child's usual behaviors and routine needs, especially when a child has special needs.

3. Match the parenting style to the statement that most reflects that style.

   C Democratic   A. "Your curfew is 10 p.m. You know that."

   A Dictatorial   B. "As long as you have your homework done, I don't care when you come home."

   B Permissive   C. "Tonight is a school night, so you need to come home by 10 p.m."

4. Which of the following should be included in a family assessment? (Select all that apply.)

   _X_   **Genogram**

   _X_   **Structure**

   _____ Child's physical growth

   _X_   **Developmental tasks**

   _X_   **Family functions/roles**

   _X_   **Family stressors**

Genogram, structure, developmental tasks, family functions/roles, and family stressors should all be included in a family assessment. The child's physical growth is part of that child's individual assessment.

5. True or False: When providing care to a child, the nurse should not be concerned about what the child thinks about the care.

False: The child's opinion should be considered when providing care.

6. List three guidelines for promoting healthy behaviors in children.

Set realistic limits and expectations based on developmental tasks.

Validate the child's feelings.

Provide reinforcement for appropriate behavior.

Focus on the child's behavior when disciplining the child.

Explain expectations to a child in a manner the child can understand.

7. True or False: When a child is admitted to the pediatric unit, the nurse should keep in mind that the family of the child also needs nursing care.

True: Although the child is the priority, the family also needs nursing care.

Unit 1:	Basic Concepts
Chapter 2:	**Cultural Awareness**
	Contributors: Candyce F. Antley, MN, RN
	Carole A. Shea, PhD, RN, FAAN
	Susan Adcock, MSN, RN

 NCLEX-RN® Connections:

Learning Objective: Review and apply knowledge within "**Cultural Awareness**" in readiness for performance of the following nursing activities as outlined by the NCLEX-RN® test plan:

Δ   Recognize the impact of cultural, spiritual, and psychosocial factors when providing care to children and their families.

Δ   Assess the child for needs related to culture (e.g., language barriers, education, personal space).

Δ   Provide written teaching materials in the child/family's language.

Δ   Assign appropriate interpreters to assist in helping the child/family/significant others understand health care.

Δ   Serve as an interpreter for primary care providers per agency protocol.

Δ   Plan/provide care that is sensitive to the child's culture (e.g., space and time orientation, care of the dying).

Δ   Evaluate and document how care was adapted to meet the child/family's cultural needs.

 Key Points

Δ   **Culture** is a collection of learned, adaptive, and transmitted social values and beliefs that form the context from which a group interprets the human experience.

Δ   These values and beliefs can be shared by members of an ethnic, racial, social, or religious group.

Δ   Communication, dietary preferences, and dress are influenced by culture.

Δ   Being a multicultural society, nursing care of children in the United States requires transcultural nursing care that is **culturally competent**. Effectiveness depends on the nurse's understanding of both her and the child/family's culture.

Δ   Culture influences health beliefs, manifestation of symptoms, response to illness, health practices, and treatment of disease.Cultural awareness and competence from nurses will improve communication, foster mutual respect, promote sensitive and effective care, and increase compliance as a family's needs are met.

Δ   Differences in language, habits, customs, attitudes, and beliefs can lead to feelings of isolation and loneliness in children.

Δ   Language and cultural barriers may impede the support structure needed by families during illness or death of a child.

Δ   Coping abilities are influenced by the perceptions of an illness or disability, treatment interventions, use of alternative therapies, and the cultural history of the family.

Δ   Children that cannot resolve their grief issues because of cultural barriers may develop signs of posttraumatic stress disorder or depression.

Key Factors

Δ   The nurse should understand her own cultural background and biases and the effect on the care provided to those from different cultures.

Δ   Nurses must be aware of, sensitive to, and appreciative of cultural differences to provide culturally competent family-centered nursing care.

Δ   The goal of the culturally competent nurse is to adapt family-centered nursing care to the child's needs and preferences.

Δ   The culturally competent nurse communicates with the child/significant other/family with respect for and understanding of different cultural verbal and nonverbal behaviors.

Δ   Barriers to providing culturally sensitive care include:

- Language and communication differences.

- Culturally inappropriate tests and tools that lead to misdiagnosis.

- Ethnic variations in medication metabolism related to genetics.

Assessment

Δ   In order to meet the child's cultural needs, a nurse must first perform a **cultural assessment** on the child to identify those needs.

Δ   The nurse must perform the cultural assessment in a language that is common to both her and the child. Otherwise, the nurse should employ an interpreter.

Δ **Nonverbal Behaviors**

Nonverbal Behavior	Culture	Variation
Tone of voice	• Asian • Italian and Middle Eastern	• Asians use a soft tone of voice to convey respect. • Italian/Middle Eastern individuals typically use a loud tone of voice.
Eye contact	• American • Middle Eastern • Asian • Native American	• Americans use direct eye contact. Lack of direct eye contact implies the person is lying or embarrassed. • Middle Eastern individuals usually avoid making direct eye contact with nonrelated members of the opposite gender. Direct eye contact can be seen as rude, hostile, or sexually aggressive. • Asians may believe direct eye contact is seen as disrespectful. • Native Americans may believe direct eye contact may lead to soul loss or soul theft.
Tactile/touch	• American • Italian and Latin American	• Americans may use touch during conversation between intimate partners or family members. • Italian/Latin American individuals may view frequent touch as a sign of concern, interest, and warmth.
Use of space	• Anglo American/North Europeans (English, Swiss, Scandinavian, German) • Italian, French, Spanish, Russian, Latin American, Middle Eastern	• Anglo American/North Europeans tend to keep their distance during communication except in intimate or family relationships. • These cultures tend to like closer, personal contact, and less distance between individuals during communication.

Δ Cultural Characteristics of Family Structure

• Communication and decision-making patterns depend on the family structure and cultural values.

Hierarchical – Asian, Middle Eastern, Latin American	Egalitarian – American, Northern European
• Family/community oriented • Oldest (male) is usually authority figure and makes decisions for child. • Parents direct children. • Parents/children may be reluctant to share honest thoughts and feelings. • Family wants to provide physical care for child. • Self-help groups convey a lack of respect for authority and violate family's sense of privacy.	• Individual/self oriented • Less respect for authority figures, and the parents makes decisions. • Parents consult with children. • Parents/children may share honest thoughts and feelings. • Family wants others to provide care if necessary. • Children and family value self-help groups.

Δ Use careful observation to identify cultural influences on health beliefs.

Δ Ask parents about their understanding and perception of:

• The cause of illness.

• The impact of the illness on their child.

• The severity of the illness.

• How long the illness will last.

• Preferred treatments to use.

• Expected results of the treatments.

• Concerns or worries regarding the condition.

Δ Identify key members of the child's family.

NANDA Nursing Diagnoses

Δ Interrupted family processes

Δ Risk for relocation stress syndrome

Δ Social isolation

Δ Spiritual distress

Δ Impaired verbal communication

Nursing Interventions

△ **Religion/spirituality/death rituals**

- Respect the religious/spiritual practices of the child.

- Death rituals vary among cultures and the nurse must be prepared to facilitate such practices whenever possible.

△ **Pain**

- Recognize the way pain is reacted to and displayed among different cultures.

- Use an alterative to the pain scale (1 to 10) as it may not appropriately reflect pain evaluations of all cultures.

- Explore religious beliefs that may influence the meaning of pain.

△ **Nutrition**

- Provide and prepare food choices that are consistent with cultural beliefs.

- As possible, allow the child to consume foods that may be viewed as a treatment for illness.

- Communicate food intolerances/allergies that are related to ethnicity to dietary staff.

△ **Communication**

- Improve nurse-client communication when cultural variations exist.

- Use interpreters when the communication barrier is great enough to impact the exchange of information between the nurse, child, and family.

- Cautiously use nonverbal communication as it may have very different meanings for the child, family, and the nurse.

△ **Family patterns and gender roles** – Include and communicate with the person who has the authority to make decisions in the family.

△ **Repatterning**

- Accommodate the child's and family's cultural beliefs and values as much as possible, making sure they are in their best interest.

- When a cultural value/behavior is a direct hindrance to the child's health/wellness, the nurse should attempt to repattern that belief to one that is compatible with health promotion.

- With knowledge of cultural differences, the nurse can plan and implement appropriate interventions.

- The nurse needs to respect the family structure and communicate with the appropriate decision maker in planning care.

Δ   **Using an Interpreter**

- Information for the interpreter – Allow the interpreter to know the reason for, and type of questions, that will be asked; expected response (brief or detailed); and with whom to converse.

- Allow time for the interpreter and the family to be introduced and become acquainted before starting the interview.

- Refrain from making comments about the family to the interpreter, as the family may understand some English.

- Ask one question at a time.

- Direct the questions to the family, not the interpreter.

- Use layman's terminology if possible, knowing that some words may not have an equivalent word in the child/family's language.

- Inquire about the child's father rather than the mother's husband when asking questions about pregnancy, marriage, and/or sex.

- Do not interrupt the interpreter and family as they talk.

- Do not try to interpret answers.

- Following the interview, ask for any additional information from the interpreter regarding thoughts on the interview and the family's responses, both verbal and nonverbal.

Primary Reference:

Hockenberry, M., Wilson, D., Winkelstein, M. (2005). *Wong's essentials of pediatric nursing care.* (7th ed.). St. Louis, MO: Mosby.

Additional Resources:

Campinha-Bacote, J. (2002). Cultural competence in psychiatric nursing: Have you "ASKED" the right questions? *Journal of the American Psychiatric Nurses Association, 8,* 183-187.

Galanti, G. A. (2006). Cultural diversity in healthcare. Retrieved November 1, 2006, from http://ggalanti.com/index.html

NANDA International (2004). *NANDA nursing diagnoses: Definitions and classification 2005-2006.* Philadelphia: NANDA.

Varcarolis, E. M., Carson, V. B., and Shoemaker, N. C. (2006). *Foundations of psychiatric mental health nursing* (5th ed.). St. Louis, MO: Saunders.

Chapter 2: Cultural Awareness

Application Exercises

1. Differences in language, habits, customs, attitudes, and beliefs can lead to feelings of _____ and _____ in children.

2. True or False: The need for an interpreter may inhibit the support that families need during the illness of a child.

3. Which of the following is appropriate when using an interpreter? (Select all that apply.)

   _____ Talk to the interpreter about the family while the family is in the room.

   _____ Ask the family one question at a time.

   _____ Look at the interpreter when asking the family questions.

   _____ Use lay terms if possible.

   _____ Do not interrupt the interpreter and family as they talk.

4. When working with a child from a culture different from the nurse's, what nonverbal actions should the nurse take to promote culturally sensitive interactions?

5. True or False: Children are not affected by cultural barriers.

Chapter 2: Cultural Awareness

Application Exercises Answer Key

1. Differences in language, habits, customs, attitudes, and beliefs can lead to feelings of _____ and _____ in children.

   Isolation and loneliness

2. True or False: The need for an interpreter may inhibit the support that families need during the illness of a child.

   True: Language and cultural barriers may impede the support structure that families need during the illness or death of a child.

3. Which of the following is appropriate when using an interpreter? (Select all that apply.)

   _____ Talk to the interpreter about the family while the family is in the room.

   __X__ **Ask the family one question at a time.**

   _____ Look at the interpreter when asking the family questions.

   __X__ **Use lay terms if possible.**

   __X__ **Do not interrupt the interpreter and family as they talk.**

   Asking the family one question at a time, using lay terms, and not interrupting will promote communication between the family and the nurse/interpreter. Talking to the interpreter about the family while the family is in the room, and looking at the interpreter instead of the family will hinder communication between the family and the nurse/interpreter.

4. When working with a child from a culture different from the nurse's, what nonverbal actions should the nurse take to promote culturally sensitive interactions?

Observe for clues regarding appropriate use of eye contact; determine whom to address information or questions; allow the family to determine the distance between parties in the room; take time and do not appear rushed; actively listen; and determine the meaning of pauses, silence, and interruptions for different cultures.

5. True or False: Children are not affected by cultural barriers.

False: Children may not be able to work through their worries or grief if cultural barriers are present.

Unit 1:	Basic Concepts

Chapter 3:	Physical Assessment Findings

Contributor: Sally Swenson, MA, RN

 NCLEX-RN® Connections:

Learning Objective: Review and apply knowledge within "**Physical Assessment Findings**" in readiness for performance of the following nursing activities as outlined by the NCLEX-RN® test plan:

Δ   Use effective communication to collect history assessment data from the child and parents.

Δ   Perform appropriate assessment of the child within the nursing role, including:

- Preparation of the child for the procedure.

- Client teaching (before and following the procedure).

- Using accurate equipment and technique based on the child's needs.

Δ   Assess the child's status by obtaining baseline data and comparing with subsequent findings.

Δ   Identify physical changes in the child's condition over time.

Δ   Implement interventions based on changes in the child's physical health.

Δ   Document baseline and subsequent findings according to facility protocol.

Δ   Maintain confidentiality of all client information.

 Key Points

Δ   Alter the exam to accommodate the child's developmental needs.

Δ   Perform an examination in a nonthreatening environment.

Δ   Involve the child and family member(s) in the examination. Adolescents may prefer to be examined without a family member present.

Δ   Use activities that can be perceived as games to engage the child.

Δ   Perform invasive portions of the exam last.

Δ   Praise the child for cooperation during the exam.

Key Factors

Δ   Keep the room warm and well lit.

Δ   Hide any threatening equipment prior to the exam.

Δ   Provide privacy for the child.

Δ   Tell the child what to expect as the physical exam is being performed.

Δ   Examine the child in a secure, comfortable position. A toddler may sit on a parent's lap if desired.

Δ   Allow the child and/or parents to ask questions during the physical exam.

Assessment

Δ   **Expected Vital Signs**

- Infants

  ◊   Temperature (axillary or rectal): 36.5 to 37.5° C (97.7 to 99.5° F)

  ◊   Pulse: 120 to 160/min

  ◊   Respirations: 23 to 50/min

  ◊   Blood pressure: BP reading for the 90th percentile taken by oscillometry is 110/71 mm Hg

- Children

  ◊   Temperature (oral): 36 to 38° C (96.8 to 100.4° F)

  ◊   Pulse: 75 to 100/min

  ◊   Respirations: 20 to 30/min

  ◊   Blood pressure:

      °   Age, height, and gender all influence BP readings. Readings should be compared with standard measurements (e.g., The National High Blood Pressure Program tables).

      °   For ages 2 to 5 years, BP reading for the 90th percentile taken by oscillometry is 112/66 BP. BP will continue to rise as the child grows. Normal BP is any reading that is less than the 90th percentile adjusted for height and weight.

- Adolescents

  ◊ Temperature (oral): 36 to 38° C (96.8 to 100.4° F)

  ◊ Pulse: 60 to 90/min

  ◊ Respirations: 16 to 19/min

  ◊ Blood pressure: BP continues to rise as the adolescent ages. Age, height, weight, and gender all influence BP readings. Readings should be compared with standard measurements (e.g., The National High Blood Pressure Program tables).

Δ **Expected Physical Assessment Findings**

- **General appearance**

  ◊ Growth – Growth can be evaluated using height, weight, head circumference, and body mass index (BMI). Growth charts have been developed by the National Center for Health Statistics (NCHS) and include:

    ° Weight-for-age percentiles – boys or girls, birth to 36 months, or 2 to 20 years.

    ° Length-for-age percentiles – boys or girls, birth to 36 months.

    ° Stature-for-age percentiles – boys or girls, 2 to 20 years.

    ° Weight-for-length percentiles – boys or girls, birth to 36 months.

    ° Weight-for-stature percentiles – boys or girls.

    ° BMI-for-age percentiles – boys or girls, 2 to 20 years.

    ° Head-circumference-for-age percentiles – boys or girls, birth to 36 months.

  ◊ Appears to be in no apparent distress

  ◊ Clean with a well-kept appearance

  ◊ No body odors

  ◊ Muscle tone

    ° Limp posture is expected in infants with extension of the extremities.

    ° Erect head posture is expected in infants after 4 months of age.

  ◊ Makes eye contact when addressed (except infants)

  ◊ Able to follow simple commands as age appropriate

  ◊ Spontaneous use of speech, language, and motor skills

- **Skin, hair, and nails**

  ◊ Skin

    ° Skin color may show normal variations based on race and ethnicity.

    ° Temperature should be warm or slightly cool to the touch.

    ° Skin turgor should demonstrate brisk elasticity with adequate hydration.

    ° Skin texture should be smooth and slightly dry.

    ° Lesions are not normal findings.

    ° Skin folds should be symmetrical.

  ◊ Hair

    ° Hair loss may be normal in infants where the head frequently comes in contact with the bed.

    ° Hair should be evenly distributed, smooth, and strong.

    ° Children approaching adolescence should be assessed for the presence of secondary hair growth.

  ◊ Nails should be pink over the nail bed and white at the tips; smooth and firm, but slightly flexible in infants; no clubbing.

- **Lymph nodes** should be nonpalpable, but may be small, palpable, nontender, and mobile in children and still be normal.

- Head and neck

  ◊ Head

    ° Shape of the head should be symmetrical.

    ° Fontanels should not be bulging. The posterior fontanel usually closes by 2 to 3 months; the anterior fontanel usually closes by 18 months.

  ◊ Face

    ° Symmetrical appearance and movement

    ° Proportional features

  ◊ Neck

    ° Short in infants

    ° No masses palpable

    ° Trachea is midline

    ° Full range of motion present whether assessed actively or passively

- Eyes
  - ◊ Visual acuity – may be difficult in children under 3
    - ° Infants' visual acuity can be assessed by holding an object in front of the infant's eyes and checking if they are able to fix on the object and follow it.
    - ° Older children should be tested using a Snellen chart or symbol chart. Vision less than 10/20 or 20/40 in either eye should be referred for further evaluation. Refer children 3 to 5 years old if vision is less than 10/20 or 20/40; refer children 6 years and older if vision is less than 10/15 or 20/30.
  - ◊ Color vision should be assessed using the Ishihara color test. Children should be able to correctly identify shapes.
  - ◊ Peripheral visual fields should be:
    - ° Upward 50°.
    - ° Downward 70°.
    - ° Nasally 60°.
    - ° Temporally 90°.
  - ◊ **Extraocular movements** may not be symmetrical in newborns.
    - ° **Corneal light reflex** should be symmetrical.
    - ° **Cover/uncover test** should demonstrate equal movement of the eyes, and strabismus needs to be detected no later than 6 years of age.
    - ° **Six cardinal fields of gaze** should demonstrate no nystagmus.
  - ◊ **Eyebrows** should be evenly distributed from the inner to the outer canthus and symmetrical.
  - ◊ **Eyelids** should close completely and open to allow the lower border and most of the upper portion of the iris to be seen.
  - ◊ **Eyelashes** should curve outward and be evenly distributed with no inflammation around any of the hair follicles.
  - ◊ **Conjunctiva**
    - ° **Palpebral** is pink.
    - ° **Bulbar** is transparent.
  - ◊ **Lacrimal apparatus** is without excessive tearing, redness, or discharge.
  - ◊ **Sclera** should be white.
  - ◊ **Corneas** should be clear.

◊ **Pupils** should be:

  ° **Round.**

  ° **Equal in size.**

  ° **Reactive to light.**

  ° **Accommodating** – can be tested in older children.

◊ **Irises** should be round with the permanent color manifesting around 9 months of age.

- **Internal exam**

  ◊ **Red reflex** should be present in infants.

  ◊ Arteries, veins, optic disc, and macula may be visualized in older children and adolescents.

- Ears

  ◊ Alignment – The top of the auricles should meet in an imaginary horizontal line that extends from the outer canthus of the eye.

  ◊ External ear

    ° Free of lesions and nontender

    ° Ear canal free of foreign bodies or discharge

    ° Cerumen is an expected finding

  ◊ Internal ear

    ° Tympanic membrane should be pearly gray.

    ° Light reflex should be visible.

    ° Umbo and manubrium landmarks should be visible.

    ° Ear canal is pink with fine hairs.

  ◊ Hearing

    ° Newborns should have an intact acoustic blink reflex to a sudden sound.

    ° Infants should turn toward sounds.

    ° Older children can be screened by whispering a word from behind to see if they can identify the word.

- **Nose**

  ◊ Position should be midline.

  ◊ Patency should be present for each nostril without excessive flaring.

  ◊ Internal structures

    ° Septum is midline and intact.

    ° Mucosa is deep pink and moist with no discharge.

  ◊ Smell can be assessed in older children.

- Mouth and throat
  - ◊ Lips
    - ° Darker pigmented than facial skin
    - ° Smooth, soft, moist
  - ◊ Gums – coral pink, tight against the teeth
  - ◊ Mucous membranes – without lesions, moist, and pink
  - ◊ Tongue
    - ° Infants may have a white coating on the tongue from milk that can be easily removed. Oral candidiasis coating is not easily removed.
    - ° Children and adolescents – Tongue should be pink, symmetrical, and the child should be able to move it beyond the lips.
  - ◊ Teeth
    - ° Infants will not have teeth.
    - ° Children and adolescents – Teeth should be white, smooth, with 20 deciduous and 32 permanent teeth.
  - ◊ Hard and soft palates – intact and firm, concave
  - ◊ Uvula – intact, should move with vocalization
  - ◊ Tonsils
    - ° Infants – may not be able to visualize
    - ° Children – barely visible to prominent, same color as surrounding mucosa, deep crevices that hold food particles
  - ◊ Speech
    - ° Infants – strong cry
    - ° Children and adolescents – clear and articulate
- Thorax and lungs
  - ◊ Chest shape
    - ° Infants – Shape is more round.
    - ° Children and adolescents – Transverse diameter to anteroposterior diameter changes to 2:1.
  - ◊ Ribs and sternum – more soft and flexible in infants, symmetrical, and smooth with no protrusions or bulges
  - ◊ Movement – symmetrical, no retractions
    - ° Infants – Irregular rhythms are common.
    - ° Children under 6 – More abdominal movement is seen during respirations.

◊ Breath sounds

° Infants – harsher and easier to hear than in adults; harder to differentiate between upper versus lower respiratory sounds

° Children and adolescents – vesicular sounds heard over the lung fields

◊ Breasts

° Newborns – Breasts may be enlarged during the first several months.

° Children and adolescents – Nipples and areolas are darker pigmented, symmetrical.

° Females – Breasts typically develop between the ages of 10 to 14. The breasts should appear asymmetrical, have no masses, and be palpable.

° Males may develop a firm, approximately 2 cm area of breast tissue or gynecomastia.

- Circulatory system

◊ Heart sounds – S_1 and S_2 heart sounds should be clear and crisp. Sinus arrhythmias that are associated with respirations are common. Physiologic splitting of S_2 and S_3 heart sounds are expected findings in children.

◊ Pulses

° Infants – Brachial, temporal, and femoral pulses should be palpable, full, and localized. Pedal pulses will be fainter and more difficult to palpate. Apical pulse may not be palpable.

° Children and adolescents – Pulse locations and expected findings are the same as those in adults.

- **Abdomen** – without tenderness, no guarding. Peristaltic waves may be visible.

◊ Shape – symmetrical; without protrusions around the umbilicus

° Infants and toddlers have rounded abdomens.

° Children and adolescents should have a flat abdomen.

◊ Bowel tones heard every 5 to 30 sec

◊ Liver – palpable 1 to 2 cm below the right lower border of the ribs

◊ Spleen – palpable 1 to 2 cm below the left lower border of the ribs in infants and children

◊ Descending colon – cylindrical mass possibly palpable in the lower left quadrant due to the presence of stool

- Musculoskeletal system
  - ◊ Length, position, and size – symmetrical
  - ◊ Joints – stable, symmetrical, full range of motion, and no crepitus or redness
  - ◊ Spine
    - ° Infants – Spine should be without dimples or tufts of hair, midline with an overall C-shaped lateral curve.
    - ° Toddlers appear squat with short legs and protuberant abdomen.
    - ° Preschoolers appear more erect than toddlers.
    - ° Children should develop the cervical, thoracic, and lumbar curvatures like that of adults.
    - ° Adolescents should remain midline (no scoliosis noted).
  - ◊ Gait
    - ° Toddlers and young children – Bowlegged or knock-knee appearance is a common finding; feet should face forward while walking.
    - ° Older children and adolescents – Steady gait should be noted with even wear on the soles of shoes.
- Neurological system

Primitive Reflexes in Infants		
Reflex	Expected Finding	Expected Age
Rooting reflex	Turns head to side when cheek of mouth is touched	Birth to 6 months
Palmar grasp	Will grasp object when palm is touched	Birth to 4 months
Plantar grasp	Toes will curl downward when sole of foot is touched	Birth to 8 months
Moro reflex (startle)	Legs flex, arms and hands extend when startled by loud noise	Birth to 6 months
Asymmetric tonic neck reflex (fencer position)	Extension of the arm and leg on the side when the head is turned to that side with flexion of the arm and leg of the opposite side	Birth to 3 to 4 months

Cranial Nerves		
Cranial nerve	Expected Findings: Infants	Expected Findings: Children/Adolescents
I Olfactory	Difficult to test	Identifies smells through each nostril individually
II Optic	Looks at face and tracks with eyes	Intact visual acuity, peripheral and color vision
III Oculomotor	Blinks in response to light, pupils reactive to light	No nystagmus, PERRLA intact
IV Trochlear	Looks at face and tracks with eyes	Able to look down and in with eyes
V Trigeminal	Rooting and sucking reflexes intact	Able to clench teeth together, detects touch on face with eyes closed
VI Abducens	Looks at face and tracks with eyes	Able to see laterally with eyes
VII Facial	Symmetrical facial movements	Able to differentiate between salty and sweet on tongue, symmetrical facial movements
VIII Acoustic	Tracks a sound, blinks in response to a loud noise	No vertigo, intact hearing
IX Glossopharyngeal	Intact gag reflex	Intact gag reflex, able to taste sour sensations on back of tongue
X Vagus	No difficulties swallowing	Speech clear, no difficulties swallowing
XI Spinal Accessory	Symmetrical movements of the shoulders	Equal strength of shoulder shrug against examiner's hands
XII Hypoglossal	No difficulties swallowing, opens mouth when nares occluded	Tongue is midline, able to move tongue in all directions with equal strength against tongue blade resistance

◊ Deep tendon reflexes should demonstrate the following:

  ° Partial flexion of the lower arm at the biceps tendon

  ° Partial extension of the lower arm at the triceps tendon

  ° Partial extension of lower leg at patellar tendon

  ° Plantar flexion of the foot at the Achilles tendon

◊ Cerebellar function (children and adolescents)

º Finger to nose test – rapid coordinated movements

º Heel to shin test – able to run the heel of one foot down the shin of the other leg while standing

º Romberg test – able to stand without swaying while eyes are closed

◊ Language, cognition, and fine and gross motor development can be screened using a standardized tool such as the Denver Developmental Screening Test – Revised (Denver II). Referrals for further evaluation should not be based solely on results of one tool but a combination of data collected from psychosocial and medical history and a physical examination.

- **Genitalia**

  ◊ Male

  º **Hair distribution** is diamond shaped after puberty in adolescent males. No pubic hair noted in infants and small children.

  º **Penis**

  º Penis should appear straight.

  º Urethral meatus should be at the tip of the penis.

  º Foreskin may not be retractable in infants and small children

  º Enlargement of the penis occurs during adolescence

  º **Scrotum**

  º Scrotum hangs separately from penis.

  º The skin on the scrotum has a rugated appearance and is loose.

  º Left testicle hangs slighter lower than the right.

  º Testes should be descended bilaterally (1.5 to 2 cm in infants and children).

  º The inguinal canal should be absent of swelling.

  º During puberty, testes and scrotum enlarge with darker scrotal skin.

  ◊ Female

  º **Hair distribution** over the mons pubis should be documented in terms of amount and location during puberty. Hair should appear in an inverted triangle. No pubic hair should be noted in infants or small children.

  º **Labia** – symmetrical, without lesions, moist on the inner aspects

  º **Clitoris** – small, without bruising or edema

- ° **Urethral meatus** – slit-like appearance with no discharge

- ° **Vaginal orifice** – The hymen may be absent, and completely or partially cover the vaginal opening prior to sexual intercourse.

- ◊ **Anus** – surrounding skin should be intact with sphincter tightening noted if the anus is touched. Routine rectal exams are not done with the pediatric population.

Primary Reference:

Hockenberry, M., Wilson, D., Winkelstein, M. (2005). *Wong's essentials of pediatric nursing care*. (7th ed.). St. Louis, MO: Mosby.

Additional Resources:

Bickley, L. S., & Szilagyi, P. G. (2003). *Bates' guide to physical examination and history taking.* (8th ed.). Philadelphia: Lippincott, Williams & Wilkins.

NANDA International (2004). *NANDA nursing diagnoses: Definitions and classification 2005-2006*. Philadelphia: NANDA.

Potter, P. A. & Perry, A. G. (2005). *Fundamentals of nursing*. (6th ed.). St. Louis, MO: Mosby.

Rush University Medical Center. (n.d.). High Blood Pressure. Retrieved March 20, 2007, from, http://www.rush.edu/rumc/page-1089887346062.html

Chapter 3: Physical Assessment Findings

Application Exercises

1. List five basic assessments that should be included in the physical assessment of a child over 3 years of age.

2. By what age should the anterior fontanel be closed?

     A. 2 weeks

     B. 6 months

     C. 12 months

     D. 18 months

3. Rank the following assessments in the order they should be performed on a 9 month old.

_____ Axillary temperature

_____ Respiratory rate

_____ Weight

_____ Heart rate

4. Match the following reflexes with their correct response.

_____ Rooting reflex   A. Extension of the arm and leg on the side when the head is turned to that side with flexion of the arm and leg of the opposite side

_____ Palmar grasp   B. Legs flex, arms and hands extend when startled by a loud noise

_____ Plantar grasp   C. Turns head to side when cheek or mouth is touched

_____ Moro reflex (startle)   D. Will grasp object when palm is touched

_____ Asymmetric tonic neck reflex   E. Toes will curl downward when sole of foot is touched

5. Match the cranial nerve with the expected finding for a 14-year-old adolescent.

_____ Olfactory   A. No vertigo

_____ Optic   B. Tongue is midline

_____ Oculomotor   C. No nystagmus

_____ Trochlear   D. Symmetrical facial movements

_____ Trigeminal   E. Speech is clear

_____ Abducens   F. Able to clench teeth together

_____ Facial   G. Intact visual acuity

_____ Acoustic   H. Intact gag reflex

_____ Glossopharyngeal   I. Equal strength of shoulder

_____ Vagus   J. Able to look laterally with eyes

_____ Spinal Accessory   K. Individually identifies smells through each nostril

_____ Hypoglossal   L. Able to look down with eyes

Chapter 3: Physical Assessment Findings

Application Exercises Answer Key

1. List five basic assessments that should be included in the physical assessment of a child over 3 years of age.

   Height, weight, temperature, respiratory rate, heart rate, and blood pressure

2. By what age should the anterior fontanel be closed?

   A. 2 weeks
   B. 6 months
   C. 12 months
   D. 18 months

   The posterior fontanel usually closes by 2 months, and the anterior fontanel usually closes by 18 months.

3. Rank the following assessments in the order they should be performed on a 9 month old.

   __4__ Axillary temperature

   __1__ Respiratory rate

   __3__ Weight

   __2__ Heart rate

   Perform a physical examination on a child starting with the least invasive, progressing towards the most invasive. Assessing the respiratory rate is the least invasive, followed by the heart rate, which requires touching the child with a stethoscope, followed by the weight, which requires picking up the child and placing him on a scale, followed by obtaining an axillary temperature.

4. Match the following reflexes with their correct response.

C Rooting reflex

D Palmar grasp

E Plantar grasp

B Moro reflex (startle)

A Asymmetric tonic neck reflex

A. Extension of the arm and leg on the side when the head is turned to that side with flexion of the arm and leg of the opposite side

B. Legs flex, arms and hands extend when startled by a loud noise

C. Turns head to side when cheek or mouth is touched

D. Will grasp object when palm is touched

E. Toes will curl downward when sole of foot is touched

5. Match the cranial nerve with the expected finding for a 14-year-old adolescent.

K Olfactory

G Optic

C Oculomotor

L Trochlear

F Trigeminal

J Abducens

D Facial

A Acoustic

H Glossopharyngeal

E Vagus

I Spinal Accessory

B Hypoglossal

A. No vertigo

B. Tongue is midline

C. No nystagmus

D. Symmetrical facial movements

E. Speech is clear

F. Able to clench teeth together

G. Intact visual acuity

H. Intact gag reflex

I. Equal strength of shoulder

J. Able to look laterally with eyes

K. Individually identifies smells through each nostril

L. Able to look down with eyes

Unit 1:   Basic Concepts

Chapter 4:   Health Promotion and the Infant (Birth to 1 year)
Contributors: Candyce F. Antley, MN, RN
               Sally Swenson, MA, RN

 NCLEX-RN® Connections:

Learning Objective: Review and apply knowledge within **"Health Promotion and the Infant (Birth to 1 year)"** in readiness for performance of the following nursing activities as outlined by the NCLEX-RN® test plan:

Δ   Assess an infant's physical, cognitive, and psychosocial development, and compare to expected growth and development for age.

Δ   Identify and report variances from expected growth and development.

Δ   Plan and/or provide care to assist the infant to achieve expected growth and development outcomes.

Δ   Plan and/or provide care appropriate to the infant's developmental level, inclusive of age-appropriate recreational/diversional activities.

Δ   Teach children/family expected normal growth and development and age appropriate health maintenance recommendations for the infant.

Δ   Teach accident prevention and health promotion activities for the infant.

 Key Points

Δ   **Stages of Development** – The infant (birth to 1 year)

Theorist	Type of Development	Stage
Erikson	Psychosocial	Trust vs mistrust
Freud	Psychosocial	Oral
Piaget	Cognitive	Sensorimotor

Expected Growth and Development

Δ   **Physical Development**

•   The infant's **posterior fontanel** closes at 2 to 3 months of age.

•   The infant's **size** is tracked by weight, height, and head circumference.

◊ **Weight**: The infant gains 0.7 kg (1.5 lb) per month the first 6 months, and 0.3 kg (0.75 lb) per month the last 6 months. The infant triples birth weight by the end of the first year.

◊ **Height**: The infant grows 2.5 cm (1 in) per month the first 6 months, and then 1.25 cm (0.5 in) per month the last 6 months.

◊ **Head circumference**: The circumference of the infant's head increases 1.25 cm (0.5 in) per month for the first 6 months.

- Following size, the infant develops **gross motor skills**.

  ◊ Holds head up (3 months)

  ◊ Rolls over (5 to 6 months)

  ◊ Holds head steady when sitting (6 months)

  ◊ Gets to sitting position alone and can pull up to standing position (9 months)

  ◊ Stands holding on (12 months)

  ◊ Stands alone (12 months)

- **Fine motor** development follows next in the sequence.

  ◊ Brings hands together

  ◊ Grasps rattle

  ◊ Looks for items that are dropped from view

  ◊ Transfers an object from one hand to the other (6 months)

  ◊ Rakes finger foods with hand (6 months)

  ◊ Uses thumb-finger to grasp items (9 months)

  ◊ Bangs two toys together (9 months)

  ◊ Can nest one object inside another (12 months)

Δ **Cognitive Development**

- **The sensorimotor** period for an infant (Piaget) is characterized by:

  ◊ Initial reflexes replaced by voluntary movements that are self-centered on having needs met.

    ° Object permanence – The infant realizes that an object still exists even when it is no longer in view (occurs between 6 to 12 months).

    ° The infant discriminates between persons.

    ° The infant comprehends word meanings.

- **Language** development follows the sensorimotor period.
  - ◊ Responds to noises
  - ◊ Vocalizes with "ooos" and "aahs"
  - ◊ Laughs and squeals
  - ◊ Turns head to the sound of a rattle
  - ◊ Pronounces single-syllable words
  - ◊ Begins speaking two and then three-word phrases

Δ **Psychosocial Development**

- **Personal-social** development occurs next in the sequence.
  - ◊ Regards faces
  - ◊ Smiles in response to others
  - ◊ Regards own hands
  - ◊ Works to reach toys
  - ◊ Feeds self by eating self finger foods
  - ◊ Waves goodbye
  - ◊ Plays pat-a-cake
  - ◊ Drinks from a cup with handles

- The infant begins to bond with its parents within the first month. The process is enhanced when both the infant and parents are in good health, have positive feeding experiences, and receive adequate rest.

- Separation recognition occurs during the first year as the infant learns his physical boundaries from that of other people. Learning how to respond to people in his environment is the next phase of development. Positive interactions with parents, siblings, and other caregivers help to establish trust (Erikson).

- Separation anxiety develops the latter half of the first year. Therefore, parents should be encouraged not to leave the infant for long periods of time.

Δ **Self-concept Development**

- By the end of the first year, infants will be able to distinguish themselves as being separate from their parents.

Δ **Body-image Changes**

- The infant discovers that his mouth is a pleasure producer (Freud: oral stage).

- Hands and feet are seen as objects of play.

- The infant discovers that smiling causes others to react.

Δ   **Age-appropriate activities**

- Infants have short attention spans and do not interact with other children during play (solitary play). Appropriate toys include those that stimulate the senses and encourage development. These toys include:

  ◊   Rattles.

  ◊   Mobiles.

  ◊   Teething toys.

  ◊   Nesting toys.

  ◊   Playing pat-a-cake.

  ◊   Playing with balls.

  ◊   Reading books.

Δ   **Nutrition**

- **Feeding alternatives** for an infant include:

  ◊   Breastfeeding (recommended).

  ◊   Iron-fortified formula (acceptable alternative to breast milk).

  ◊   Cow's milk (not recommended).

- **Solids** can be introduced around the time the infant doubles his birth weight (5 to 6 months).

  ◊   First, give the infant iron-fortified cereals.

  ◊   Next, give the infant puréed or strained foods one at a time to assess for food allergies.

  ◊   Finally, breast milk/formula should be decreased as intake of solid foods increases.

- **Weaning** can be accomplished when the infant is able to drink from a cup with handles (sometime after 6 months).

  ◊   Replace one of the infant's feedings to a cup with handles.

  ◊   The infant's bedtime feeding is the last one to be replaced.

Δ   **Health Promotion and Prevention**

- **Hyperbilirubinemia** (newborns) is commonly caused by immaturity of the liver and is observed as jaundice. Bilirubin levels are assessed, and if elevated, are treated with phototherapy. If left untreated, hyperbilirubinemia can cause brain damage.

- **Child abuse** is a potential risk and may be **manifested as:**

  ◊ **Physical neglect**: poor hygiene, failure to demonstrate adequate growth and development, injuries related to insufficient safeguards.

  ◊ **Emotional abuse and neglect**: failure to demonstrate adequate growth and development, poor social interactions, and fear of strangers.

  ◊ **Physical abuse**: bruising, welts, lacerations, burns, fractures, bite marks, fear of a parent(s) or lack of reactions, abdominal distension, vomiting, or missing hair.

  ◊ **Sexual abuse**: bruising; bleeding; abrasions around external genitalia, rectum, or mouth; STDs; and urinary tract infections.

- **Dentition** – 6 to 8 teeth erupt in the infant's mouth by the end of the first year.

  ◊ Teething pain can be eased using cold teething rings, over-the-counter teething gels, or acetaminophen (Tylenol) and/or ibuprofen.

  ◊ Clean the infant's teeth using a wet washcloth.

  ◊ Bottles should not be given to infants when they are falling asleep. This will help to avoid prolonged exposure to milk or juice that can cause dental caries (bottle mouth syndrome).

- 2007 Centers for Disease Control and Prevention (CDC) immunization recommendations for healthy **infants less than 12 months** include:

  ◊ **Birth** – hepatitis B (Hep B).

  ◊ **2 months** – Hep B, rotavirus vaccine (Rota), diphtheria and tetanus toxoids and pertussis (DTaP), *Haemophilus influenzae* type B (Hib), pneumococcal vaccine (PCV), inactivated poliovirus (IPV)

  ◊ **4 months** – Rota, DTaP, Hib, PCV IPV.

  ◊ **6 months** – Hep B (6 to 12 months) ,Rota, DTaP, PCV, IPV (6 to 18 months)

  ◊ Infants 6 to 12 months should receive a yearly **influenza** vaccination. The trivalent inactivated influenza vaccine (TIV) is available as an intramuscular injection, or the live, attenuated influenza vaccine (LAIV) is available as an intranasal spray.

- **Diaper rash treatment and prevention includes:**

  ◊ Changing the infant's diapers frequently.

  ◊ Cleansing the infant's skin with water and drying thoroughly at each change.

  ◊ Applying either A&D or zinc oxide ointment to the infant's rash before replacing the diaper.

  ◊ Exposing the infant's reddened skin to air during the day when possible.

Δ   **Injury prevention includes:**

- Suffocation.

  ◊   Plastic bags should be avoided.

  ◊   A firm crib mattress should fit tight.

  ◊   Crib slats should be no further apart than 6 cm (2.4 in).

  ◊   No pillows should be allowed in the infant's crib.

  ◊   The infant should be placed on the back for sleep.

  ◊   The infant should never be left alone in the bath.

- Falls.

  ◊   Rails should be up on the crib.

  ◊   Use restraints in infant seats.

  ◊   Place the infant seat on the ground or floor if used outside of the car, and do not leave it unattended or on elevated surfaces.

  ◊   Use safety gates across stairs.

- Poisoning.

  ◊   Avoid exposing the infant to lead paint.

  ◊   Keep toxins and plants out of the infant's reach.

  ◊   Keep safety locks on cabinets with cleaners and other household chemicals.

  ◊   Keep poison control number near the phone.

  ◊   Keep medications in childproof containers.

- Burns.

  ◊   Check temperature of bath water.

  ◊   Turn down the thermostat on hot water heater.

  ◊   Make sure smoke detectors are working at all times.

  ◊   Elevate hot objects.

  ◊   Use sunscreen during the infant's exposure to the sun.

  ◊   Cover electrical outlets.

- Motor vehicles.

  ◊   Use an approved rear-facing car seat in the back seat (away from air bags) to transport the infant. Infants should be in rear-facing car seats for the first year of life and until they weigh 9.1 kg (20 lb). It is recommended to have the infant ride rear facing until he has reached the height and weight limit allowed by the manufacturer of the car seat.

- Bodily damage.

  ◊   Keep sharp objects out of the infant's reach, and turn diaper pins away from the infant.

Primary Reference:

Hockenberry, M., Wilson, D., Winkelstein, M. (2005). *Wong's essentials of pediatric nursing care*. (7th ed.). St. Louis, MO: Mosby.

Additional Resources:

Centers for Disease Control and Prevention. (2007). *Recommended adult immunization schedule*. Retrieved January 17, 2007, from www.cdc.gov/

NANDA International (2004). *NANDA nursing diagnoses: Definitions and classification 2005-2006*. Philadelphia: NANDA.

Potter, P. A., & Perry, A. G. (2005). *Fundamentals of nursing*. (6th ed.). St. Louis, MO: Mosby.

Chapter 4: Health Promotion and the Infant (Birth to 1 year)

Application Exercises

1. A 9-month-old infant weighed 3.86 kg (8.5 lb) at birth. Currently, at his well-child check-up, he weighs 8.1 kg (18 lb). Is this infant's weight normal for his age?

2. The mother of an infant asks a nurse when she can expect her infant to begin walking. What gross motor skills should the infant develop before he begins walking?

3. A mother of an infant tells the nurse that her infant makes many sounds. What should the nurse tell the mother about the language development of an infant?

4. An 8-month-old infant is brought into the health facility by his parent. The nurse notes several bruises on the infant's abdomen, legs, and arms. The infant also has a cut on his scalp, his clothes are dirty, and he has areas of redness and skin breakdown around his buttocks and scrotum. When assessing this infant for abuse, the nurse should look for which of the following manifestations? (Select all that apply.)

    _____ Normal growth and development

    _____ Bruising, welts, and lacerations

    _____ Poor hygiene

    _____ Smiles at caregivers

    _____ Fear of strangers

5. Which of the following immunizations should be given to a 4-month-old infant?

    _____ Measles, mumps, rubella (MMR)

    _____ *Haemophilus influenzae* type B (Hib)

    _____ Polio (IPV)

    _____ Diphtheria and tetanus toxoids and pertussis (DTaP)

    _____ Pneumonococcal vaccine (PCV)

    _____ Varicella

    _____ Rotavirus vaccine (Rota)

6. Which of the following foods should be introduced into an infant's diet first?

      A. Strained yellow vegetables

      B. Iron-fortified cereals

      C. Puréed fruits

      D. Whole milk

Chapter 4: Health Promotion and the Infant (Birth to 1 year)

Application Exercises Answer Key

1. A 9-month-old infant weighed 3.86 kg (8.5 lb) at birth. Currently, at his well-child check-up, he weighs 8.1 kg (18 lb). Is this infant's weight normal for his age?

   Yes. An infant should gain 0.7 kg (1.5 lb) per month for the first 6 months, and 0.3 kg (0.75 lb) per month the last 6 months of the first year. The child has gained 4.3 kg (9.5 lb), which is within the normal range.

2. The mother of an infant asks a nurse when she can expect her infant to begin walking. What gross motor skills should the infant develop before he begins walking?

   Getting up to a sitting position and sitting alone

   Pulling up to a standing position

   Standing holding on and/or standing alone

   Development is cephalocaudal; therefore, before the infant can walk, he must develop the skills of sitting and standing.

3. A mother of an infant tells the nurse that her infant makes many sounds. What should the nurse tell the mother about the language development of an infant?

   The infant will first respond to noises and turn her head toward the sound. As she grows she will vocalize "ooos" and "aahs," laugh and squeal, pronounce single-syllable words, and then begin to speak two and then three-word phrases.

4. An 8-month-old infant is brought into the health facility by his parent. The nurse notes several bruises on the infant's abdomen, legs, and arms. The infant also has a cut on his scalp, his clothes are dirty, and he has areas of redness and skin breakdown around his buttocks and scrotum. When assessing this infant for abuse, the nurse should look for which of the following manifestations? (Select all that apply.)

_____ Normal growth and development

__X__ **Bruising, welts, and lacerations**

__X__ **Poor hygiene**

_____ Smiles at care givers

__X__ **Fear of strangers**

Bruising, welts, and lacerations, poor hygiene, and fear of strangers may be indications of abuse. A child who is abused does not usually demonstrate normal growth and development and positive interactions with caregivers.

5. Which of the following immunizations should be given to a 4-month-old infant?

_____ Measles, mumps, rubella (MMR)

__X__ *Haemophilus influenzae* **type B (Hib)**

__X__ **Polio (IPV)**

__X__ **Diphtheria and tetanus toxoids and pertussis (DTaP)**

__X__ **Pneumonococcal vaccine (PCV)**

_____ Varicella

__X__ **Rotavirus vaccine (Rota)**

Hib, IPIV, DTaP, PVC, and Rota are all given at 4 months of age. MMR and varicella are not recommended by the CDC until the child is at least 12 months old.

6. Which of the following foods should be introduced into an infant's diet first?

A. Strained yellow vegetables

B. Iron-fortified cereals

C. Puréed fruits

D. Whole milk

Cereal is the first solid food introduced to an infant. Maternal iron stores in the infant begin to diminish around 4 months; therefore, iron-fortified cereal should be used. Puréed yellow vegetables followed by puréed fruits are then introduced. Whole milk is not given to infants.

Unit 1:   Basic Concepts

Chapter 5:   Health Promotion and the Toddler (12 months to 3 years)
Contributors: Candyce F. Antley, MN, RN
Sally Swenson, MA, RN

 NCLEX-RN® Connections:

Learning Objective: Review and apply knowledge within "**Health Promotion and the Toddler (12 months to 3 years)**" in readiness for performance of the following nursing activities as outlined by the NCLEX-RN® test plan:

Δ   Assess a toddler's physical, cognitive, and psychosocial development, and compare to expected growth and development for age.

Δ   Identify and report variances from expected growth and development.

Δ   Plan and/or provide care to assist the toddler to achieve expected growth and development outcomes.

Δ   Plan and/or provide care appropriate to the toddler's developmental level, inclusive of age-appropriate recreational/diversional activities.

Δ   Teach children/family expected normal growth and development and age appropriate health maintenance recommendations for the toddler.

Δ   Teach accident prevention and health promotion activities for the toddler.

 Key Points

Stages of Development – The toddler (12 months to 3 years)

Theorist	Type of Development	Stage
Erikson	Psychosocial	Autonomy vs shame
Freud	Psychosocial	Anal
Piaget	Cognitive	Sensorimotor transitions to preoperational

Expected Growth and Development

Δ   **Physical development**

•   **The toddler's anterior fontanel** closes by 18 months of age.

- **Weight:** At 30 months, the toddler should weigh 4 times his birth weight. Height: The toddler grows by 7.5 cm (3 in) per year.

Δ **Developmental skills** achieved by the toddler include:

- Development of steady gait.

- Climbing stairs.

- Jumping and standing on one foot for short periods.

- Stacking blocks in increasingly higher numbers.

- Drawing stick figures.

- Undressing and feeding self.

- Toilet training.

Δ **Cognitive Development**

- The concept of object permanence is fully developed.

- Toddlers demonstrate memory of events that relate to them.

- Language increases to about 400 words with the toddler speaking in 2- to 3-word phrases.

- Preoperational thought does not allow for the toddler to understand other viewpoints, but it does allow toddlers to symbolize objects and people in order to imitate activities they have seen previously.

Δ **Psychosocial Development**

- **Independence** is paramount for the toddler who is attempting to do everything for himself.

- **Separation anxiety** continues to occur when a parent leaves the child.

Δ **Moral Development**

- Moral development is closely associated with cognitive development.

- Egocentric – Toddlers are unable to see another's perspective; they can only view things from their point of view.

- The toddler's punishment and obedience orientation begins with a sense that good behavior is rewarded and bad behavior is punished.

Δ **Self-concept Development**

- Toddlers progressively see themselves as separate from their parents and increase their explorations away from them.

Δ **Body-image Changes**

- The toddler appreciates the usefulness of various body parts.

- Toddlers develop gender identity by age 3.

Δ **Age-appropriate Activities**

- Solitary play evolves into parallel play where the toddler observes other children and then may engage in activities nearby.

  ◊ Filling and emptying containers

  ◊ Playing with blocks

  ◊ Reading books

  ◊ Playing with toys that can be pushed and pulled

  ◊ Tossing a ball

Δ **Nutrition**

- Toddlers are picky eaters with repeated requests for favorite foods.

- The toddler should be switched to 3 or 4 glasses of cow's milk a day, and serving sizes should be kept small to avoid overwhelming the toddler.

Δ **Health Promotion and Prevention**

- Child abuse is a potential risk and may be manifested as

  ◊ **Physical neglect**: poor hygiene, failure to demonstrate adequate growth and development, injuries related to insufficient safe guards.

  ◊ **Emotional abuse and neglect**: failure to demonstrate adequate growth and development, poor social interactions, and fear of strangers.

  ◊ **Physical abuse**: bruising, welts, lacerations, burns, fractures, bite marks, fear of a parent(s) or lack of reactions, abdominal distension, vomiting, or missing hair.

  ◊ **Sexual abuse**: bruising; bleeding; abrasions around external genitalia, rectum, or mouth; STDs; and urinary tract infections.

- Upper respiratory tract infections and otitis media: Acetaminophen (Tylenol) and cool mist vaporizers may be useful. Antibiotics or decongestants may be prescribed by a primary care provider.

- Temper tantrums result when the toddler is frustrated with restrictions on independence. Providing consistent, age-appropriate expectations helps the toddler work through his frustration.

- Toilet training can begin when it is recognized that the child has the sensation of needing to urinate or defecate. Parents should demonstrate patience and consistency in toilet training their child. Nighttime control may develop last of all.

- Discipline should be consistent with well-defined boundaries that are established to develop appropriate social behavior.

- 2007 Centers for Disease Control and Prevention (CDC) immunization recommendations for healthy toddlers **12 months to 3 years** of age include:

    ◊ **12 to 15 months** – *Haemophilus influenzae* type B (Hib); pneumococcal vaccine (PCV); inactivated poliovirus (IPV) (6 to 18 months); measles, mumps, and rubella (MMR); and varicella.

    ◊ **12 to 23 months** – Hepatitis A (Hep A), given in two doses, at least 6 months apart.

    ◊ **15 to 18 months** – Diphtheria and tetanus toxoids and pertussis (DTaP).

    ◊ **12 to 36 months** – Yearly trivalent inactivated influenza vaccine (TIV).

- Injury Prevention

    ◊ **Drowning** – Do not leave the toddler unattended in the bathtub. Keep toilet lids closed. Closely supervise the child at the pool or any other body of water.

    ◊ **Falls** – Keep doors and windows locked. Keep crib mattress in the lowest position with the rails all the way up. Use safety gates across stairs.

    ◊ **Suffocation** – Keep toys with small parts out of reach. Make sure food items are cut into small pieces and are without seeds, small bones, nuts, or popcorn. Remove drawstrings from jackets and other clothing.

    ◊ **Poisoning** – Avoid exposing the toddler to lead paint, elevate toxins and plants, place safety locks on cabinets with cleaners and other chemicals. Keep poison control number near the phone. Keep medications in childproof containers.

    ◊ **Burns** – Check temperature of bath water, turn down thermostat on hot water heater, have working smoke detectors at all times, turn pot handles toward the back of the stove, cover electrical outlets, and use sunscreen when outside.

    ◊ **Motor vehicles** – Use an approved car seat in the back seat (away from air bags). The toddler should be in a rear-facing car seat until he weighs 9.1 kg (20 lb). It is recommended to keep the toddler rear facing until he has reached the height and weight limit allowed by the manufacturer of the car seat.

    ◊ Supervise children when playing outside.

    ◊ **Bodily damage** – Keep sharp objects out of the toddler's reach.

    ◊ Educate the toddler regarding what to do when he is approached by a stranger.

    ◊ Teach toddlers to avoid unknown animals.

Primary Reference:

Hockenberry, M., Wilson, D., Winkelstein, M. (2005). *Wong's essentials of pediatric nursing care*. (7th ed.). St. Louis, MO: Mosby.

Additional Resources:

Centers for Disease Control and Prevention. (2007). *Recommended adult immunization schedule*. Retrieved January 17, 2007, from www.cdc.gov/

NANDA International (2004). *NANDA nursing diagnoses: Definitions and classification 2005-2006*. Philadelphia: NANDA.

Potter, P. A., & Perry, A. G. (2005). *Fundamentals of nursing*. (6th ed.). St. Louis, MO: Mosby.

Chapter 5: Health Promotion and the Toddler (12 months to 3 years)

Application Exercises

1. List the immunizations that should be given to each of the age groups listed below.

> 12 to 15 months
>
> 15 to 18 months
>
> 12 to 23 months
>
> 12 to 36 months

2. A parent of a 20-month-old toddler is concerned about how often the child seems to be getting hurt. Why are toddlers prone to accidents?

3. A parent of a 17-month-old toddler is frustrated with the toddler's behavior. The parent tells the nurse that the child is "bad" but doesn't know how to make the toddler behave better. Which of the following responses should the nurse make to this parent?

> A. "Allow your child to learn by trial and error."
>
> B. "Consistently enforce well-defined limits, such as no climbing on the counters."
>
> C. "Reward your child's good behavior, but ignore the bad behaviors."
>
> D. "Punish your child when he behaves badly."

4. A 13-month-old toddler is being discharged from the hospital. Which of the following potential health risks should be addressed with the parents? (Select all that apply.)

> _____ Cholesterol screening
>
> _____ Poisoning
>
> _____ Peer pressure
>
> _____ Burns
>
> _____ When to leave the child at home alone
>
> _____ Falls

5. The parent of a 2-year-old toddler tells the nurse that she is frustrated with her child's behaviors. The child throws temper tantrums and says "No" every time she tries to help her. Although the parent knows toddlers do this, she cannot understand why. The nurse explains that toddlers are often negative, which is the normal expression of their desire to

> A. increase their independence.
>
> B. develop their sense of trust.
>
> C. gratify their oral fixation.
>
> D. finish a project they set out to do.

6. The parents of a 14-month-old toddler want to know why their daughter has not been responsive to toilet training. The toddler is standing by herself but still crawls for locomotion. Her vocabulary is developing, but she does not seem to understand what it means to go "potty." What skills will this toddler need to develop before she is able to achieve toilet training?

Chapter 5: Health Promotion and the Toddler (12 months to 3 years)

Application Exercises Answer Key

1. List the immunizations that should be given to each of the age groups listed below.

   12 to 15 months – **Hib, PCV, IPV (6 to 18 months), MMR, and varicella**

   12 to 18 months – **Hep A, given in two doses, at least 6 months apart**

   12 to 23 months – **DTaP**

   12 to 36 months – **Yearly TIV**

2. A parent of a 20-month-old toddler is concerned about how often the child seems to be getting hurt. Why are toddlers prone to accidents?

   Toddlers are still developing their fine and gross motor skills, while at the same time trying to exert their independence through movement. Developmental tasks include developing autonomy, independence, the desire to try things alone, wanting to explore more of the world away from parents, walking well, and beginning to run and climb.

3. A parent of a 17-month-old toddler is frustrated with the toddler's behavior. The parent tells the nurse that the child is "bad" but doesn't know how to make the toddler behave better. Which of the following responses should the nurse make to this parent?

   A. "Allow your child to learn by trial and error."

   B. **"Consistently enforce well-defined limits, such as no climbing on the counters."**

   C. "Reward your child's good behavior, but ignore the bad behaviors."

   D. "Punish your child when he behaves badly."

   Toddlers need to have consistent boundaries enforced for discipline to be effective. Behavior should not be enforced with only rewards or only punishments. Trial and error lacks consistent boundaries and may allow the toddler to experience unhealthy consequences.

4. A 13-month-old toddler is being discharged from the hospital. Which of the following potential health risks should be addressed with the parents? (Select all that apply.)

_____ Cholesterol screening

__X__ **Poisoning**

_____ Peer pressure

__X__ **Burns**

_____ When to leave the child at home alone

__X__ Falls

Poisoning, burns, and falls are all potential risks for this age group as the child gains independence and becomes more curious. A cholesterol screening may start as early as adolescence. Peer pressure usually begins during the school-age years, becoming more of a risk during adolescence.

5. The parent of a 2-year-old toddler tells the nurse that she is frustrated with her child's behaviors. The child throws temper tantrums and says "No" every time she tries to help her. Although the parent knows toddlers do this, she cannot understand why. The nurse explains that toddlers are often negative, which is the normal expression of their desire to

A. increase their independence.

B. develop their sense of trust.

C. gratify their oral fixation.

D. finish a project they set out to do.

The drive for independence is expressed by the toddler opposing the desires of those in authority and attempting to do everything for herself. Developing trust and gratifying oral fixation are developmental tasks for infants. Finishing a project is a developmental task of the school-age child.

6. The parents of a 14-month-old toddler want to know why their daughter has not been responsive to toilet training. The toddler is standing by herself but still crawls for locomotion. Her vocabulary is developing, but she does not seem to understand what it means to go "potty." What skills will this toddler need to develop before she is able to achieve toilet training?

Voluntary control of anal and urethral sphincters; gross motor skills of sitting, walking, and squatting; fine motor skills for removing clothing; communication skills to indicate toileting need; cognitive skills to follow directions; and the ability to recognize the urge for toileting

Unit 1:   Basic Concepts

Chapter 6:   Health Promotion and the Preschooler (3 to 5 years)

Contributors: Candyce F. Antley, MN, RN

Sally Swenson, MA, RN

 NCLEX-RN® Connections:

> **Learning Objective**: Review and apply knowledge within "**Health Promotion and the Preschooler (3 to 5 years)**" in readiness for performance of the following nursing activities as outlined by the NCLEX-RN® test plan:
>
> Δ   Assess a preschooler's physical, cognitive, and psychosocial development, and compare to expected growth and development for age.
>
> Δ   Identify and report variances from expected growth and development.
>
> Δ   Plan and/or provide care to assist the preschooler to achieve expected growth and development outcomes.
>
> Δ   Plan and/or provide care appropriate to the preschooler's developmental level, inclusive of age-appropriate recreational/diversional activities.
>
> Δ   Teach children/family expected normal growth and development and age appropriate health maintenance recommendations for the preschooler.
>
> Δ   Teach accident prevention and health promotion activities for the preschooler.

 Key Points

Stages of Development – The preschooler (3 to 5 years)

Theorist	Type of Development	Stage
Erikson	Psychosocial	Initiative vs guilt
Freud	Psychosocial	Phallic
Piaget	Cognitive	Preoperational

Expected Growth and Development

Δ   **Physical Development**

- **Weight**: The preschooler should gain about 2.25 kg (5 lb) per year.

- **Height**: The preschooler should grow 6.2 to 7.5 cm (2.5 to 3 inches) per year.

- **Developmental** skills typically acquired by the preschooler include:
  ◊ Alternating feet on stairs.
  ◊ Going up and down steps easily.
  ◊ Hopping.
  ◊ Walking heel-to-toe.
  ◊ Dressing without help.
  ◊ Drawing copies of shapes on paper.
  ◊ Drawing a more detailed stick figure.
  ◊ Playing on playground equipment.

Δ **Cognitive Development**

- Preschoolers develop two phases of **preoperational thinking**, which include:
  ◊ **Preconceptual** thought (2 to 4 years) – Preschoolers make judgments based on visual appearances. Misconception in thinking during this stage include:
    ° Artificialism – Everything is made by humans.
    ° Animism – Inanimate objects are alive.
    ° Imminent justice – A universal code exists that determines law and order.
  ◊ **Intuitive** thought (begins around age 4) – Preschooler can classify information and become aware of cause-and-effect relationships.

- **Language** – The preschooler's vocabulary continues to increase. The preschooler can now speak in sentences, is able to identify colors, and enjoys talking.

- **Time** – The preschooler begins to understand the concepts of the past, present, and future. By the end of the preschool years, the child may comprehend days of the week.

Δ **Psychosocial Development**

- A preschooler may take on many new experiences despite not having all of the physical abilities necessary to be successful at everything. Guilt may occur when children are unable to accomplish a task and believe they have misbehaved. Guiding preschoolers to attempt activities within their capabilities while setting limits is appropriate.

Δ **Moral Development**

- Preschoolers continue in the good/bad orientation of the toddler years but begin to understand behaviors in terms of what is socially acceptable.

Δ   **Self-concept Development**

- The preschooler feels good about self with regard to mastering skills, such as dressing and feeding, that allow independence. During stress, insecurity, or illness, a preschooler may regress to previous immature behaviors or develop habits such as nail biting or nose picking.

Δ   **Body-image Changes**

- Mistaken perceptions of reality coupled with misconceptions in thinking lead to active fantasies and fears. The greatest fear is that of bodily harm.

- Sex-role identification is also occurring.

Δ   **Age-appropriate Activities**

- Parallel play shifts to associative play during the preschool years. Play is not highly organized, but cooperation does exist between children. Appropriate activities include:

    ◊   Playing ball.

    ◊   Putting puzzles together.

    ◊   Riding tricycles.

    ◊   Pretend and dress-up activities.

    ◊   Role play.

    ◊   Painting.

    ◊   Sewing cards and beads.

    ◊   Reading books.

Δ   **Nutrition**

- A preschooler consumes about half the amount of an adult (1,800 kcal).

- Preschoolers may continue being picky eaters up to age 5.

- Parents need to ensure that their child is receiving a balance of nutrients.

Δ   **Health Promotion and Prevention**

- **Child abuse** is a potential risk and may be **manifested as:**

    ◊   **Physical neglect**: poor hygiene, failure to demonstrate adequate growth and development, injuries related to insufficient safe guards.

    ◊   **Emotional abuse and neglect:** failure to demonstrate adequate growth and development, poor social interactions, and fear of strangers.

    ◊   **Physical abuse**: bruising, welts, lacerations, burns, fractures, bite marks, fear of a parent(s) or lack of reactions, abdominal distension, vomiting, or missing hair.

    ◊   **Sexual abuse**: bruising; bleeding; abrasions around external genitalia, rectum, or mouth; STDs; urinary tract infections.

- **Otitis media**, in general, becomes less prevalent as a child grows.

- **Accidents** continue to be prevalent during this age and include the risk of poisoning and drowning.

Δ   **Health Promotion and Accident Prevention**

- **Sleep disturbances** frequently occur during early childhood, and problems range from difficulties going to bed to night terrors. Advise parents to:

    ◊   Assess whether or not the bedtime is too early if the child is still taking a nap. The average preschooler needs about 12 hr of sleep a day. Some preschoolers still require a daytime nap.

    ◊   Keep a consistent bedtime routine.

    ◊   Use a night light.

    ◊   Reassure the child who has been frightened, but avoid having the child sleep with the parents.

- **Vision screening** is routinely done in the preschool population as part of the prekindergarten physical exam. Myopia and amblyopia can be detected and treated before poor visual acuity impairs the learning environment.

- 2007 Centers for Disease Control (CDC) **immunization recommendations** for healthy preschool children **3 to 5 years** and children to **6 years** of age include:

    ◊   **4 to 6 years** – diphtheria and tetanus toxoids and pertussis (DTaP); inactivated poliovirus (IPV); measles, mumps, and rubella (MMR); and varicella.

    ◊   Yearly trivalent inactivated influenza vaccine (TIV) for preschoolers **36 to 59 months**.

- **Injury prevention**

    ◊   **Drowning** – Do not leave the child unattended in the bathtub. Closely supervise the child at the pool or any other body of water.

    ◊   **Poisoning** – Avoid exposure to lead paint, keep plants out of reach, place safety locks on cabinets with cleaners and other chemicals. Keep poison control number near the phone. Keep medications in childproof containers.

    ◊   **Motor vehicles** – Use an approved car seat in the back seat (away from air bags). Preschool children should be in car seats appropriate for weight and height. The child should be restrained in a car seat or booster chair until adult seat belts fit correctly. Laws may vary from state to state and requirements may be up to 80 lb and a height of 5 feet 9 inches.

Primary Reference:

Hockenberry, M., Wilson, D., Winkelstein, M. (2005). *Wong's essentials of pediatric nursing care.* (7th ed.). St. Louis, MO: Mosby.

Additional Resources:

Centers for Disease Control and Prevention. (2007). *Recommended adult immunization schedule.* Retrieved January 17, 2007, from www.cdc.gov/

NANDA International (2004). *NANDA nursing diagnoses: Definitions and classification 2005-2006.* Philadelphia: NANDA.

Potter, P. A., & Perry, A. G. (2005). *Fundamentals of nursing.* (6th ed.). St. Louis, MO: Mosby.

Chapter 6: Health Promotion and the Preschooler (3 to 5 years)

Application Exercises

1. A nurse is providing nutritional teaching to a group of parents whose children attend a local day care. Which of the following is the most effective way to encourage good nutritional habits for preschool children?

        A. Offer snacks if the child does not like what is served.

        B. Serve nutritious foods that all family members will eat.

        C. Allow the child to eat only what she asks for.

        D. Insist that the child eat all of the food that is served to her.

2. A parent asks the nurse at a well-child visit why his 4-year-old son is always talking about "George." The parent tells the nurse that the family does not even know anyone named George. The child tells his parents about George's escapades, such as climbing onto the counter to raid the cookie jar. What explanation can be given to the parent about his son's behavior?

3. The parents of a preschooler are worried because their child has so much trouble going to sleep at night. Which of the following are strategies that can be used to help a preschool child go to sleep? (Select all that apply.)

        _____ Let the child fall asleep in another room.

        _____ Place a night light in the child's room.

        _____ Keep a regular bedtime schedule.

        _____ Insist the child take a nap to make up for lost nighttime sleep.

        _____ Read a bedtime story to the child.

        _____ Allow the child to play quietly in her room.

4. True or False: Magical thinking can be the cause of a preschooler's feelings of guilt.

5. What immunizations should a preschool child receive if all immunizations have been kept up to date?

6. Vision screening is done on a preschool child to detect and possibly treat _____ and _____.

7. Which of the following statements made by the parent of a preschooler indicates that the parent understands the need her child has for injury prevention?

    A. "My child is able to watch his younger brother when they play outside."

    B. "Now that my child does not put everything in his mouth, I can remove the locks on my cabinets."

    C. "I programmed the number to the poison control center into my cell phone."

    D. "My child rides his bike in the street with the bigger kids."

Chapter 6: Health Promotion and the Preschooler (3 to 5 years)

Application Exercises Answer Key

1. A nurse is providing nutritional teaching to a group of parents whose children attend a local day care. Which of the following is the most effective way to encourage good nutritional habits for preschool children?

> A. Offer snacks if the child does not like what is served.
> **B. Serve nutritious foods that all family members will eat.**
> C. Allow the child to eat only what she asks for.
> D. Insist that the child eat all of the food that is served to her.

Preschoolers learn by example. Seeing family members eat healthy foods will encourage them to do the same. Offering snacks as alternatives and allowing the child to eat only what she asks for will not promote good nutritional habits. Insisting that the child eat all of the food served even if she is no longer hungry can lead to feelings of guilt and overeating.

2. A parent asks the nurse at a well-child visit why his 4-year-old son is always talking about "George." The parent tells the nurse that the family does not even know anyone named George. The child tells his parents about George's escapades, such as climbing onto the counter to raid the cookie jar. What explanation can be given to the parent about his son's behavior?

George is most likely an imaginary friend or playmate. Imaginary playmates help children in many ways. When the child is lonely, an imaginary playmate can be a companion. An imaginary friend also experiments with things that the child is afraid of trying.

3. The parents of a preschooler are worried because their child has so much trouble going to sleep at night. Which of the following are strategies that can be used to help a preschool child go to sleep? (Select all that apply.)

_____ Let the child fall asleep in another room.

__X__ Place a night light in the child's room.

__X__ Keep a regular bedtime schedule.

_____ Insist the child take a nap to make up for lost nighttime sleep.

__X__ Read a bedtime story to the child.

__X__ Allow the child to play quietly in her room.

Various strategies can be used to help a preschool child go to sleep. Placing a night light in her room will provide some light for reassurance. Reading a bedtime story and/or allowing the child to play quietly before sleep can help to calm the child down. Keeping a regular bedtime schedule is also important for regulating sleep-wake cycles. It is best if the child learns to fall asleep in her own room. If the child still needs an afternoon nap, it might be necessary to make the bedtime later.

4. True or False: Magical thinking can be the cause of a preschooler's feelings of guilt.

True: Words and thoughts are powerful to preschoolers. They believe that others can see the thoughts they have. Therefore, if something bad happens and the child thought bad thoughts, then the child believes he is responsible for the event.

5. What immunizations should a preschool child receive if all immunizations have been kept up to date?

Diphtheria and tetanus toxoids and pertussis (DTaP); inactivated poliovirus (IPV); measles, mumps, and rubella (MMR); and varicella. In addition, yearly trivalent inactivated influenza vaccine (TIV) for preschoolers 36 to 59 months.

6. Vision screening is done on a preschool child to detect and possibly treat _____ and _____.

Myopia and amblyopia

7. Which of the following statements made by the parent of a preschooler indicates that the parent understands the need her child has for injury prevention?

    A. "My child is able to watch his younger brother when they play outside."

    B. "Now that my child does not put everything in his mouth, I can remove the locks on my cabinets."

    C. "I programmed the number to the poison control center into my cell phone."

    D. "My child rides his bike in the street with the bigger kids."

Preschoolers are great imitators and may mimic others by taking medications or drinking colored liquids. Therefore, having the number to the poison control center available is vital. While preschool children are more independent than they were as toddlers, they still need to be supervised. They may be capable of helping adults with tasks but are not able to be in charge of siblings. Preschoolers do not have the judgment necessary to be riding a bicycle in the street unsupervised.

Unit 1:   Basic Concepts

Chapter 7:   Health Promotion and the School-Age Child (5 to 12 years)
Contributor: Sally Swenson, MA, RN

NCLEX-RN® Connections:

Learning Objective: Review and apply knowledge within "**Health Promotion and the School-Age Child (5 to 12 years)**" in readiness for performance of the following nursing activities as outlined by the NCLEX-RN® test plan:

Δ   Assess the school-age child's physical, cognitive, and psychosocial development, and compare to expected growth and development for age.

Δ   Identify and report variances from expected growth and development.

Δ   Plan and/or provide care to assist the school-age child to achieve expected growth and development outcomes.

Δ   Plan and/or provide care appropriate to the school-age child's developmental level, inclusive of age-appropriate recreational/diversional activities.

Δ   Teach children/family expected normal growth and development and age appropriate health maintenance recommendations for the school-age child.

Δ   Teach accident prevention and health promotion activities to the school-age child.

Key Points

Stages of Development – The school-age child (5 to 12 years)

Theorist	Type of Development	Stage
Erikson	Psychosocial	Industry vs inferiority
Freud	Psychosocial	Latency
Piaget	Cognitive	Concrete operations

Expected Growth and Development

Δ   **Physical Development**

- **Weight**: The school-age child will gain 2 to 4 kg (4.4 to 8.8 lb) per year.

- **Height**: The school-age child will grow by about 5 cm (2 inches) per year.

- There is typically a weight gain between 10 to 12 years of age prior to the changes in height that come after this age.

- Changes related to puberty begin to appear in females, which include:

  ◊ Budding of breasts.

  ◊ Appearance of pubic hair.

  ◊ Menarche.

- Changes related to puberty begin to appear in males, which include:

  ◊ Enlargement of testicles with changes in scrotum, such as increased looseness.

  ◊ Appearance of pubic hair.

- Permanent teeth erupt.

- Coordination improves.

- Visual acuity improves to 20/20.

Δ **Cognitive Development**

- **Concrete** thought

  ◊ Weight and volume seen as unchanging

  ◊ Is able to understand simple analogies

  ◊ Is able to understand time (days, seasons)

  ◊ Can define many words and understand rules of grammar

  ◊ Classifies more complex information

  ◊ Is able to understand various emotions people experience

Δ **Psychosocial Development**

- A sense of industry is achieved through achievements in learning.

- Children at this age prefer the company of same-sex companions.

- Most relationships come from school associations.

- Children at this age may rival the same-sex parent.

- Fears of ridicule by peers and teachers over school-related issues are common. Some children manifest nervous behaviors to deal with the stress, such as nail biting.

Δ **Moral Development**

- Early on, the school-age child may not understand the reasoning behind many rules and may try to find ways around them. Instrumental exchange is in place – "I'll help you if you help me." The child is out to make the best deal, and she does not really consider elements of loyalty, gratitude, or justice as she makes her decisions.

- In the later part of the school years, the child moves into a law-and-order orientation with more emphasis placed on justice being administered fairly.

Δ **Self-concept Development**

- School-age children strive to develop a healthy self-respect through finding out in what areas they excel.

- School-age children need parents to encourage them regarding educational or extracurricular successes.

Δ **Body-image Changes**

- This is the age at which solidification of body image occurs.

- Curiosity about sexuality should be addressed with education regarding sexual development and the reproduction process.

- School-age children are more modest and place more emphasis on privacy issues than preschoolers.

Δ **Age-appropriate Activities**

- Competitive and cooperative play is predominant.

- 6 to 9 year olds:

  ◊ Play simple board and number games.

  ◊ Hopscotch.

  ◊ Jump rope.

  ◊ Collect rocks, stamps, cards, or coins.

  ◊ Ride bicycles.

  ◊ Build simple models.

  ◊ Join organized sports – skill building.

- 9 to 12 year olds:

  ◊ Make crafts.

  ◊ Build models.

  ◊ Collect/engage in hobbies.

  ◊ Solve jigsaw puzzles.

  ◊ Play board and card games.

  ◊ Join organized competitive sports.

Δ **Nutrition**

- By the end of the school-age years, the child is eating an adult proportion of food. He needs quality nutritious snacks.

Δ   **Health Promotion and Prevention**

- **Child abuse** is a potential risk and may be **manifested as:**

  ◊   **Physical neglect**: poor hygiene, failure to demonstrate adequate growth and development, injuries related to insufficient safe guards.

  ◊   **Emotional abuse and neglect:** failure to demonstrate adequate growth and development, poor social interactions, and fear of strangers.

  ◊   **Physical abuse**: bruising, welts, lacerations, burns, fractures, bite marks, fear of a parent(s) or lack of reactions, abdominal distension, vomiting, or missing hair.

  ◊   **Sexual abuse**: bruising; bleeding; abrasions around external genitalia, rectum, or mouth; STDs; urinary tract infections.

- **Scoliosis** – School-age children should be screened for scoliosis by examining for a lateral curvature of the spine before and during growth spurts. Screening may take place at schools or at a health provider's office.

- **Obesity** is an increasing concern of this age group that predisposes them to low self-esteem, diabetes, heart disease, and high blood pressure. Advise parents to:

  ◊   Not use food as a reward.

  ◊   Emphasize physical activity.

  ◊   Make sure a balanced diet is consumed.

  ◊   Avoid frequent meals eaten in fast-food restaurants.

- **Cancers** such as leukemia are the second leading cause of death in children.

- **Respiratory infections** are still common at this age.

- **Asthma** accounts for many school absences. Parents, primary care providers, and school employees need to work together to manage the disease.

Δ   2007 Centers for Disease Control and Prevention (CDC) **immunization recommendations** for healthy school-age children **5 to 12** years of age include:

- If not given between ages **4 to 5,** then by **age 6**: diphtheria and tetanus toxoids and pertussis (DTaP); inactivated poliovirus (IPV); and measles, mumps, and rubella (MMR); and varicella.

- **11 to 12 years** – Tetanus and diphtheria toxoids and pertussis vaccine (Tdap); measles, mumps, and rubella vaccine (MMR); human papillomavirus vaccine (HPV) in 3 doses; and meningococcal vaccine (MCV4).

Δ   **Substance abuse** – teach children to say "no" when offered drugs or alcohol.

Δ   **Dental health** should be encouraged including:

- Brushing.

- Flossing.

- Regular check-ups

- Appropriate snacks.

Δ   **Injury Prevention**

- **Fracture prevention** – Helmets and/or pads should be used when rollerblading, skateboarding, bicycling, riding scooters, and snowboarding.

- Avoid trampolines.

- Teach children to swim.

- Teach fire safety.

- Keep firearms locked up.

- **Motor vehicles** – The child should be restrained in a car seat or booster chair until adult seat belts fit correctly. Laws may vary from state to state and requirements may be up to 36.3 kg (80 lb) and a height of 5 feet 9 inches. Children less than 13 years of age are safest in the back seat.

Primary Reference:

Hockenberry, M., Wilson, D., Winkelstein, M. (2005). *Wong's essentials of pediatric nursing care*. (7th ed.). St. Louis, MO: Mosby.

Additional Resources:

Centers for Disease Control and Prevention. (2007). *Recommended adult immunization schedule*. Retrieved January 17, 2007, from www.cdc.gov/

NANDA International (2004). *NANDA nursing diagnoses: Definitions and classification 2005-2006*. Philadelphia: NANDA.

Potter, P. A., & Perry, A. G. (2005). *Fundamentals of nursing*. (6th ed.). St. Louis, MO: Mosby.

Chapter 7: Health Promotion and the School-Age Child (5 to 12 years)

Application Exercises

1. When teaching a class about pubertal changes in girls, a question is asked about when development appears. Number the following changes in the order they occur.

    _____ Menarche

    _____ Breast buds

    _____ Appearance of pubic hair

2. The mother of a 9-year-old child reports that her son develops stomach cramping every Sunday night before school. How can the nurse assist this parent and child?

3. True or False: School-age children should be screened for scoliosis.

4. What immunizations should a school-age child receive between the ages of 11 and 12?

5. Which of the following activities demonstrates that a school-age child is working toward a healthy achievement of Erikson's developmental task of industry?

    A. The child brings home completed school work to show parents.

    B. The child prefers to watch cartoons on TV rather than practicing the piano.

    C. The child depends on older siblings to tell him what to wear to school.

    D. The child refuses to play by the rules of a board game.

6. What should be included in a course on safety during the school-age years?

    _____ Keeping stair gates closed

    _____ Wearing helmets when riding bicycles or skateboarding

    _____ Playing safely on trampolines

    _____ Firearm safety

    _____ Wearing seat belts

7. Identify three strategies parents can use to decrease the risk for obesity in school-age children.

Chapter 7: Health Promotion and the School-Age Child (5 to 12 years)

Application Exercises Answer Key

1. When teaching a class about pubertal changes in girls, a question is asked about when development appears. Number the following changes in the order they occur.

   __3__ Menarche

   __1__ Breast buds

   __2__ Appearance of pubic hair

2. The mother of a 9-year-old child reports that her son develops stomach cramping every Sunday night before school. How can the nurse assist this parent and child?

   The nurse can explore with the child's mother possible reasons for this behavior. The child may be experiencing difficulties with academics, peers, and/or teachers. The nurse can give the mother guidance as to how to talk with her child. Follow-up may be necessary to determine the need for referrals for additional help for the child.

3. True or False: School-age children should be screened for scoliosis.

   True: Scoliosis can be detected during the school-age years and will allow for early intervention.

4. What immunizations should a school-age child receive between the ages of 11 and 12?

   Tetanus and diphtheria toxoids and pertussis vaccine (Tdap); measles, mumps, and rubella vaccine (MMR); human papillomavirus vaccine (HPV) in 3 doses; and meningococcal vaccine (MCV4).

5. Which of the following activities demonstrates that a school-age child is working toward a healthy achievement of Erikson's developmental task of industry?

A. The child brings home completed school work to show parents.

B. The child prefers to watch cartoons on TV rather than practicing the piano.

C. The child depends on older siblings to tell him what to wear to school.

D. The child refuses to play by the rules of a board game.

School-age children are working on developing a sense of industry, which becomes inferiority when the child does not achieve the tasks. School-age children are proud of their academic achievements. While it may be easier to watch TV or to let others help decide what to wear, those activities do not demonstrate industry. Following the rules helps the child develop feelings of accomplishment and achievement.

6. What should be included in a course on safety during the school-age years?

_____ Keeping stair gates closed

X Wearing helmets when riding bicycles or skateboarding

_____ Playing safely on trampolines

X Firearm safety

X Wearing seat belts

School-age children are active and need to take precautions, such as wearing helmets and pads when skateboarding or bicycling, as well as wearing seat belts when in the car. They are also able to understand rules for fire arm safety. There is no safe play on trampolines. School-age children are coordinated enough to climb and descend stairs.

7. Identify three strategies parents can use to decrease the risk for obesity in school-age children.

Avoid or reduce fast-food meals

Encourage physical activities

Do not use food as rewards

Provide nutritious meals

Unit 1:   Basic Concepts

Chapter 8:   Health Promotion and the Adolescent (12 to 20 years)

Contributors: Candyce F. Antley, MN, RN

Sally Swenson, MA, RN

 NCLEX-RN® Connections:

Learning Objective: Review and apply knowledge within "**Health Promotion and the Adolescent (12 to 20 years)**" in readiness for performance of the following nursing activities as outlined by the NCLEX-RN® test plan:

Δ   Assess an adolescent's physical, cognitive, and psychosocial development, and compare to expected growth and development for age.

Δ   Identify and report variances from expected growth and development.

Δ   Plan and/or provide care to assist the adolescent to achieve expected growth and development outcomes.

Δ   Teach children/family expected normal growth and development and age appropriate health maintenance recommendations for the adolescent.

Δ   Plan and/or provide care appropriate to the adolescent's developmental level, inclusive of age-appropriate recreational/diversional activities.

Δ   Teach accident prevention and health promotion activities to the adolescent.

 Key Points

Stages of Development – The adolescent (12 to 20 years)

Theorist	Type of Development	Stage
Erikson	Psychosocial	Identity vs role confusion
Freud	Psychosocial	Genital
Piaget	Cognitive	Formal operations

Expected Growth and Development

Δ   **Physical Development**

• Acne may appear during adolescence.

• Females reach 95% of their adult height by age 13. Hips widen throughout these years.

- Males reach 95% of their adult height by age 15. Shoulders widen throughout these years.

- In males, sexual maturation occurs in the following order:

  ◊ Increase in the size of the testes.

  ◊ Appearance of pubic hair.

  ◊ Rapid growth of genitalia.

  ◊ Growth of axillary hair.

  ◊ Appearance of downy hair on upper lip.

  ◊ Change in voice.

- Sleep habits change with puberty due to increased metabolism and rapid growth during the adolescent years. Changes are characterized by staying up late, sleeping in later in the morning, and perhaps sleeping longer than during the school-age years.

Δ **Cognitive Development**

- The adolescent is capable of thinking at an adult level.

- Abstract thought is possible, and adolescents can deal with principles.

- The adolescent can evaluate the quality of his/her own thinking.

- Attention span becomes longer.

- **Language**: Adolescents develop jargon within the peer group. They are able to communicate one way with the peer group and another way with adults or teachers.

Δ **Psychosocial Development**

- The adolescent develops a sense of **personal identity** that is influenced by expectations of the family.

- **Group** identity – The adolescent may become part of a peer group that greatly influences his/her behavior.

- **Vocationally** – Work habits begin to solidify.

- **Sexually** – There is increased interest in the opposite sex.

- **Health perceptions** – Adolescents may view themselves as invincible to bad outcomes of risky behaviors.

Δ **Moral Development**

- Conventional law and order – Rules are not seen as absolutes. Each situation needs to be looked at, and perhaps the rules will need to be adjusted. Not all adolescents attain this level of moral development during these years.

Δ   **Self-concept Development**

- A healthy self-concept is developed by having healthy relationships with peers, family, and teachers. Identifying a skill or talent helps maintain a healthy self-concept. Participation in sports, hobbies, or the community can have a positive outcome.

Δ   **Body-image Changes**

- Adolescents seem particularly concerned with the lean bodies portrayed by the media. Changes that occur during puberty result in a great deal of comparisons among adolescents in the surrounding peer group. Parents also give their input as to hair styles, dress, and activity. Adolescents may require help if depression or eating disorders result due to poor body image.

Δ   **Age-appropriate Activities**

- Nonviolent video games
- Nonviolent music
- Sports
- Caring for a pet
- Career-training programs
- Reading
- Social events (e.g., going to the movies, school dances)

Δ   **Nutrition**

- Rapid growth and high metabolism require increases in quality nutrients. Nutrients that tend to be deficient during this stage of life are iron, calcium, and vitamins A and C.

- **Eating disorders** commonly develop during adolescence (more prevalent in girls than in boys) due to a fear of being overweight, fad diets, and/or as a mechanism of maintaining control over some aspect of life. Severe eating disorders include:

- **Anorexia nervosa** – extreme weight loss through severe dieting/extreme exercising or binging and purging.

- **Bulimia nervosa** – severe binging and purging in between intense dieting.

- **Obesity** – diet high in fat without adequate physical activity.

Δ   **Health Promotion and Prevention**

- 2007 Centers for Disease Control (CDC) recommendations for the healthy adolescent **12 to 20** years include the following vaccines if not given at age 11 to 12: tetanus and diphtheria toxoids and pertussis vaccine (Tdap); human papillomavirus vaccine (HPV) series; hepatitis B (Hep B) series; inactivated poliovirus (IPV) series; measles, mumps, and rubella (MMR) series; varicella series; and meningococcal (MCV4).

- **Scoliosis** – Screening for scoliosis should continue during the adolescent years by examining for a lateral curvature of the spine before and during growth spurts. Screening may take place at school or at a health provider's office.

- **Child abuse** is a potential risk and may be **manifested as:**

  ◊ **Physical neglect**: poor hygiene, failure to demonstrate adequate growth and development, injuries related to insufficient safe guards.

  ◊ **Emotional abuse and neglect:** failure to demonstrate adequate growth and development, poor social interactions, and fear of strangers.

  ◊ **Physical abuse**: bruising, welts, lacerations, burns, fractures, bite marks, fear of a parent(s) or lack of reactions, abdominal distension, vomiting, or missing hair.

  ◊ **Sexual abuse**: bruising; bleeding; abrasions around external genitalia, rectum, or mouth; STDs; urinary tract infections.

- Motor vehicle crashes **are the leading cause of death.**

- **Homicides are the second leading cause of death** and most prevalent among male adolescent acquaintances with a firearm. Violent media may influence this type of behavior.

- **Suicide is the third leading cause of death** among adolescents. Depressed and socially-isolated adolescents may demonstrate changes in behavior, which include:

  ◊ Poor school performance.

  ◊ Lack of interest.

  ◊ Tearfulness and not interacting with others.

  ◊ Disturbances in sleep or appetite.

  ◊ Expression of suicidal thoughts.

- **Substance abuse** – Adolescents are more likely to experiment with alcohol, tobacco, or illegal drugs to impress peers or because they believe it will help them feel better. Substance abuse is the leading contributor to motor vehicle fatalities. Drug Abuse Resistance Education (DARE) and other similar programs provide assistance in preventing experimentation.

- **Sexual experimentation** occurs in approximately 50% of adolescents. Abstinence is highly recommended. If sexual activity is occurring, the use of birth control is recommended.

- **Sexually transmitted diseases (STDs)** – Adolescents should undergo external genitalia examinations, Pap smears, and cervical and urethral cultures (specific to gender). Rectal and oral cultures may also need to be taken. The adolescent should be counseled about risk-taking behaviors and their exposure to STDs, as well as acquired immunodeficiency syndrome (AIDS), hepatitis. The use of condoms will decrease the risk of STDs.

- **Pregnancy** – Identification of pregnant adolescents should be done to ensure that nutrition and support is offered to promote the health of the adolescent and the fetus. Following infant delivery, education should be given to prevent future pregnancies.

Δ   **Injury Prevention**

◊   Encourage attendance at driver's education courses. Emphasize the need for compliance with seat belt use.

◊   Teach the dangers of combining substance abuse with driving (Mothers Against Drunk Driving – MADD).

◊   Insist on helmet use with bicycles, motorcycles, skateboards, roller blades, and snowboards.

◊   Screen for substance use.

◊   Teach the adolescent not to swim alone.

◊   Teach proper use of sporting equipment prior to use.

Primary Reference:

Hockenberry, M., Wilson, D., Winkelstein, M. (2005). *Wong's essentials of pediatric nursing care.* (7th ed.). St. Louis, MO: Mosby.

Additional Resources:

Centers for Disease Control and Prevention. (2007). *Recommended adult immunization schedule.* Retrieved January 17, 2007, from www.cdc.gov/

NANDA International (2004). *NANDA nursing diagnoses: Definitions and classification 2005-2006.* Philadelphia: NANDA.

Chapter 8: Health Promotion and the Adolescent (12 to 20 years)

Application Exercises

1. Identify the order of sexual maturation in males by numbering the changes from 1 to 6.

   _____ Voice changes.

   _____ Pubic hair appears.

   _____ Size of testes increase.

   _____ Downy hair appears on upper lip.

   _____ Axillary hair grows.

   _____ Rapid growth of genitalia occurs.

2. Sleep habits change with puberty due to _____ and _____.

3. Adolescents are likely to take risks because

   A. they are incapable of thinking at an adult level.

   B. they see themselves as invincible to bad outcomes.

   C. they have a short attention span.

   D. they have no respect for the rules.

4. An adolescent visits the school nurse because of pain in his shoulder. The nurse discovers that the adolescent has been lifting weights daily as he prepares for baseball. What should the nurse include in her discussion with the adolescent to help reduce the risk for further injury?

   A. Encourage the use of braces when lifting weights.

   B. Discourage the continuation of weight lifting.

   C. Instruct the adolescent to consult with his coach to make sure the proper technique is being used for weight lifting.

   D. Discuss the possibility of arthritis development due to shoulder injury.

5. Identify five behavioral changes that may indicate an adolescent is socially isolated or depressed.

Chapter 8: Health Promotion and the Adolescent (12 to 20 years)

Application Exercises Answer Key

1. Identify the order of sexual maturation in males by numbering the changes from 1 to 6.

   6 Voice changes.

   2 Pubic hair appears.

   1 Size of testes increase.

   5 Downy hair appears on upper lip.

   4 Axillary hair grows.

   3 Rapid growth of genitalia occurs.

2. Sleep habits change with puberty due to _____ and _____.

   Increased metabolism and rapid growth

3. Adolescents are likely to take risks because

   A. they are incapable of thinking at an adult level.

   B. they see themselves as invincible to bad outcomes.

   C. they have a short attention span.

   D. they have no respect for the rules.

   Adolescents may be able to recite the consequences of their behavior, but they believe that they are invincible; therefore, the consequences will not happen. Adolescents have a longer attention span than younger children and they are capable of thinking at an adult level. Although rules are not seen as absolute for some adolescents, they may still have respect for the rules.

4. An adolescent visits the school nurse because of pain in his shoulder. The nurse discovers that the adolescent has been lifting weights daily as he prepares for baseball. What should the nurse include in her discussion with the adolescent to help reduce the risk for further injury?

> A. Encourage the use of braces when lifting weights.
>
> B. Discourage the continuation of weight lifting.
>
> **C. Instruct the adolescent to consult with his coach to make sure the proper technique is being used for weight lifting.**
>
> D. Discuss the possibility of arthritis development due to shoulder injury.

Adolescents need to know how to properly use the sporting equipment to prevent injuries. Weight lifting can be continued if the equipment is properly used. Even if braces are used when lifting weights, if the equipment is not properly used, injury can occur. Discussing arthritis is not appropriate at this time since specific injuries have not been identified.

5. Identify five behavioral changes that may indicate an adolescent is socially isolated or depressed.

Poor school performance

Lack of interest in things that had been of interest to the adolescent in the past.

Not interacting with others

Disturbances in sleep or appetite

Expression of suicidal thoughts

Unit 1:   Basic Concepts

Chapter 9:   Nutrition
                   Contributor: Candyce F. Antley, MN, RN

 NCLEX-RN® Connections:

Learning Objective: Review and apply knowledge within "**Nutrition**" in readiness for performance of the following nursing activities as outlined by the NCLEX-RN® test plan:

Δ   Assess nutritional and hydration status of the child, including the child's diet history.

Δ   Assess the child's weight, length, and height.

Δ   Identify the child's nutritional preferences to assist the child to obtain adequate nutrition and maintain restrictions of diet.

Δ   Plan and provide nutritional care appropriate to the developmental level of the child.

Δ   Teach the child/family the required dietary modifications for the specific health alteration.

Δ   Evaluate impact of disease/illness on the child's nutritional status.

 Key Points

Δ   Nutritional assessment is an integral part of health care for children and adolescents.

Δ   Adequate nutrition is essential for normal growth and development.

Δ   Children with health care problems require additional nutritional support.

Δ   Common nutritional concerns in childhood include hunger, failure to thrive, obesity, foodborne illness, dietary deficiencies, and food intolerance/allergy.

Δ   Dehydration is a common concern in infants and children due to their body composition.

Δ   Eating disorders in adolescence include obesity, anorexia nervosa, and bulimia nervosa.

Δ   Enteral or parenteral feeding methods may be necessary for some children.

Key Factors

Δ   Nutritional Needs

- Preterm infant (less than 37 weeks gestation) and small for gestational age (weighs less than 2,500 g)

    ◊   These infants require 50 to 60 kcal/kg per day (parenteral) or 75 kcal/kg per day if fed orally.

    ◊   Breast milk is recommended.

    ◊   Needs are increased with illness.

- Infants – birth to 1 year

    ◊   Birth to 1 year: Breast milk or formula

    ◊   4 to 6 months: iron-fortified cereal, such as rice cereal

    ◊   6 to 8 months: yellow vegetables, fruits

    ◊   8 to 10 months: meat

    ◊   Usually delayed until after 12 months: whole milk, eggs, strawberries, wheat, corn, fish, and nut products

- Toddlers – 1 to 3 years

    ◊   Toddlers do well with finger foods. They may temporarily become a "picky eater" and will require three meals and two snacks per day.

    ◊   Give the toddler small portions that are healthy.

    ◊   Limit fruit juice to 4 to 6 oz/day due to sugar content.

- Preschool children – 3 to 5 years

    ◊   A preschool child may eat only certain foods for a period of time.

    ◊   A preschool child requires three meals and two to three snacks per day from all areas of the food pyramid.

- School-age children – 5 to 12 years

    ◊   Nutritional needs of the school-age child are dependent on activity level.

    ◊   A school-age child requires a balanced diet. A school-age child also likes to be included in meal planning and preparation.

- Adolescents – 12 to 20 years

    ◊   Growth spurts are associated with adolescents.

    ◊   Fast foods make maintaining healthy nutrition difficult.

    ◊   The adolescent requires 2,000 to 3,000 kcal/day.

Δ   Nursing assessment should include:

- Physical appearance.

- Anthropometry measurements, which include height/length, weight, and head and chest circumference.

- Behavioral patterns.

- Activity level and tolerance.

Δ   Nutritional assessment should include:

- Amount and frequency of formula intake for infants.

- Time and frequency of feedings, if breastfeeding.

- 24-hr diet and fluid recall for older children and adolescents.

NANDA Nursing Diagnoses

Δ   Activity intolerance

Δ   Ineffective breastfeeding

Δ   Deficient fluid volume

Δ   Delayed growth and development

Δ   Imbalanced nutrition: less than body requirements

Nursing Interventions

Δ   Assess/monitor for signs and symptoms of altered nutrition.

Δ   Teach/reinforce breastfeeding techniques.

Δ   Determine dietary preferences of the child.

Δ   Encourage frequent small meals/snacks.

Δ   Provide child choice of nutritional snacks.

Δ   Provide guidance for meal planning according to child's growth and developmental needs.

Primary Reference:

> Hockenberry, M. J., Wilson, D., & Winkelstein M. L. (2005). *Wong's essentials of pediatric nursing.* (7th ed.). St. Louis, MO: Mosby.

Additional Resources

Ball, J. W., Bindler, R. C. (2006). *Child health nursing: Partnering with children and families.* (1st ed.). Upper Saddle River, NJ: Prentice Hall.

NANDA International (2004). *NANDA nursing diagnoses: Definitions and classification 2005-2006.* Philadelphia: NANDA.

Chapter 9: Nutrition

Application Exercises

1. A mother of a 2-month-old infant asks a nurse when she should introduce solid foods into her infant's diet. Which of the following responses by the nurse is most appropriate regarding the mother's question?

    A. "Infants should only be given breast milk until they are 1 year old."

    B. "You may feed your baby rice cereal at 6 months."

    C. "You may feed your baby cereal now if he seems to be hungry after he eats."

    D. "Infants can be given yellow vegetables when they are 4 months old."

2. Which of the following foods are usually be introduced into an infant's diet after 1 year?

    _____ Iron-fortified oatmeal

    _____ Whole milk

    _____ Peas

    _____ Eggs

    _____ Applesauce

    _____ Peanuts

    _____ Chicken

    _____ Sweet potatoes

3. True or False: Toddlers should not be allowed to eat sandwiches.

4. True or False: Fruit juices should be limited to 4 to 6 oz per day for toddlers.

5. A nurse is teaching a class about nutrition to a high school health class. Which of the following foods selected by adolescents indicates an understanding of good nutritional practices? (Select all that apply.)

    _____ Cheeseburger from a fast food restaurant

    _____ Green salad with low-fat dressing

    _____ Peanut butter and apple slices

    _____ Packaged cookies

    _____ Pasta and tomato sauce

6. Which of the following strategies will help promote appropriate weight gain in children and adolescents? (Select all that apply.)

_____ Regular physical activity

_____ Elimination of all sugar from diet

_____ Eating low-fat dairy products

_____ Giving all children the same size servings

_____ Encouraging the child/adolescent to participate in shopping and meal preparation

Chapter 9: Nutrition

Application Exercises Answer Key

1. A mother of a 2-month-old infant asks a nurse when she should introduce solid foods into her infant's diet. Which of the following responses by the nurse is most appropriate regarding the mother's question?

   A. "Infants should only be given breast milk until they are 1 year old."

   B. "You may feed your baby rice cereal at 6 months."

   C. "You may feed your baby cereal now if he seems to be hungry after he eats."

   D. "Infants can be given yellow vegetables when they are 4 months old."

   Although breast milk is recommended for up to 1 year, infants may be given iron-fortified cereal, such as rice cereal, between 4 to 6 months. Iron-fortified cereal is the first solid food to be introduced, followed by vegetables and fruits.

2. Which of the following foods are usually introduced into an infant's diet after 1 year?

   _____ Iron-fortified oatmeal

   _X_ Whole milk

   _____ Peas

   _X_ Eggs

   _____ Applesauce

   _X_ Peanuts

   _____ Chicken

   _____ Sweet potatoes

   Foods that may be introduced during infancy include iron-fortified cereals, most green and yellow vegetables, most fruits, and meat. Whole milk is not given due to the infant's need for iron, which is not part of whole milk. Eggs may cause an allergic reaction; therefore, they are delayed and then introduced slowly. Nut products present a choking hazard.

3. True or False: Toddlers should not be allowed to eat sandwiches.

False: Toddlers enjoy eating finger foods. These foods provide them with a sense of autonomy.

4. True or False: Fruit juices should be limited to 4 to 6 oz per day for toddlers.

True: Fruit juices are high in sugar content and should be limited for toddlers.

5. A nurse is teaching a class about nutrition to a high school health class. Which of the following foods selected by adolescents indicates an understanding of good nutritional practices? (Select all that apply.)

_____ Cheeseburger from a fast food restaurant
_X_ Green salad with low-fat dressing
_X_ Peanut butter and apple slices
_____ Packaged cookies
_X_ Pasta and tomato sauce

Green salad with low-fat dressing, peanut butter and apple slices, and pasta and tomato sauce are all nutritious choices. Cheeseburgers from fast food restaurants are high in fat, and packaged cookies are usually made from processed flour and are high in fat.

6. Which of the following strategies will help promote appropriate weight gain in children and adolescents? (Select all that apply.)

_X_ Regular physical activity
_____ Elimination of all sugar from diet
_X_ Eating low-fat dairy products
_____ Giving all children the same size servings
_X_ Encouraging the child/adolescent to participate in shopping and meal preparation

Regular physical activity has many benefits. Eating low-fat dairy products will provide nutrients and will decrease the amount of fat consumed. Encouraging participation in meal preparation allows the child/adolescent to have some control and choice in what is eaten. It is not necessary to eliminate all sugar from the diet, as sugar can be a good source of energy. Children of different ages require different amounts of nutrients; therefore, serving sizes should reflect those needs.

Unit 1:   Basic Concepts

Chapter 10:   Play
Contributor: Candyce F. Antley, MN, RN

 NCLEX-RN® Connections:

Learning Objective: Review and apply knowledge within "**Play**" in readiness for performance of the following nursing activities as outlined by the NCLEX-RN® test plan:

Δ   Assess the child's ability to participate in activities.

Δ   Provide/assist the child in selecting activities that are appropriate according to age, development, preference, and physical capacity.

Δ   Use diversional activities that are appropriate for age or developmental level of the child.

Δ   Explain medications/treatments appropriately for age or developmental needs.

Δ   Evaluate and document the child's response to treatment.

 Key Points

Δ   Play is the work of children.

Δ   Children express feelings and fears through play.

Δ   Functions of play affect all areas of the child's development.

Δ   Play facilitates mastery of developmental stages and assists in problem solving.

Δ   Socially acceptable behavior is learned through play.

Δ   Play activities are specific to a child's stage of development.

Δ   Play can be used to teach children.

Δ   Play is a means of protection from everyday stressors.

Key Factors

Δ   **Content of Play**

  • Social-affective – taking pleasure in relationships

  • Sense-pleasure – objects in the environment catching the child's attention

  • Skill – demonstrating new abilities

  • Unoccupied behavior – focusing attention on something of interest

Δ   **Social Character of Play**

  • Onlooker – child observing others

  • Solitary – child playing alone

  • Parallel – child playing independently, but among other children, which is characteristic of a toddler

  • Associative – children playing together without organization, which is characteristic of preschoolers

  • Cooperative play – organized playing in groups, which is characteristic of the school-age child

Δ   **Functions of Play**

  • Sensorimotor development

  • Intellectual development

  • Socialization

    ◊   Creativity

    ◊   Self-awareness

    ◊   Provides therapeutic and moral value

Δ   **Play Activities Related to Age**

  • Infant

    ◊   Birth to 3 months – visual and auditory stimuli

    ◊   3 to 6 months – noise-making objects and soft toys

    ◊   6 to 9 months – teething toys and social interaction

    ◊   9 to 12 months – large blocks, toys that pop apart, and push and pull toys

  • Toddler

    ◊   1 to 3 years – cloth books, large crayons and paper, push-and-pull toys, riding a tricycle, tossing a ball, and puzzles with large pieces

    ◊   Watches educational TV and videos for children

- Preschool
  - ◊ Associative, imitative, and imaginative play
  - ◊ Likes to draw, paint, ride tricycle, swim, jump, and run
  - ◊ Watches educational television and videos
- School-age
  - ◊ Games that can be played alone or with another person
  - ◊ Team sports
  - ◊ Playing a musical instrument
  - ◊ Arts and crafts, collections
- Adolescent
  - ◊ Sports
  - ◊ School activities
  - ◊ Quiet activities
  - ◊ Peer interactions

Δ **Therapeutic Play**

- Dramatic play or symbolic play is an essential component of play therapy. It can take place with dolls and/or stuffed animals.

- Therapeutic play helps preschool and school-age children experiencing anxiety, stress, or other nonpsychotic mental disorders.

- Therapeutic play encourages the acting out of feelings of fear, anger, hostility, and sadness.

- Therapeutic play enables the child to learn coping strategies in a safe environment.

- Therapeutic play assists in gaining cooperation for medical treatment.

Assessment

Δ   Developmental level of child

Δ   Motor skills

Δ   Level of activity tolerance

Δ   Child's preferences

NANDA Nursing Diagnoses

Δ   Activity intolerance

Δ   Anxiety

Δ   Ineffective coping

Δ   Deficient diversional activity

Δ   Fear

Δ   Social isolation

Nursing Interventions

Δ   Select activities that enhance development.

Δ   Observe the child's play for clues to the child's fears or anxieties.

Δ   Encourage parents to bring one favorite toy from home.

Δ   Determine the child's play preferences.

Δ   Use dolls and/or stuffed animals to demonstrate procedure before it is done.

Δ   Provide play opportunities that meet the child's level of activity tolerance.

Δ   Allow the child to go to play room if able.

Δ   Encourage the adolescent's peers to visit.

Primary Reference:

Hockenberry, M. J., Wilson, D., & Winkelstein M. L. (2005). *Wong's essentials of pediatric nursing*. (7th ed.). St. Louis, MO: Mosby.

Additional Resources:

Ball, J. W., Bindler, R. C. (2006). *Child health nursing: Partnering with children and families*. (1st ed.). Upper Saddle River, NJ: Prentice Hall.

NANDA International (2004). *NANDA nursing diagnoses: Definitions and classification 2005-2006*. Philadelphia: NANDA.

Chapter 10: Play

Application Exercises

1. Match the following play activities with the appropriate age.

   _____ Watching black-and-white mobiles   A. 1 to 3 years

   _____ Playing peek-a-boo   B. 3 to 6 months

   _____ Holding a soft rattle   C. Birth to 3 months

   _____ Playing with cloth books   D. 9 to 12 months

   _____ Banging large blocks   E. 6 to 9 months

2. Before cleaning an abrasion on a 3 year old, what diversional activity could a nurse use to help decrease the child's anxiety?

   A. Give the child pain medication as prescribed.

   B. Tell the child what to expect.

   C. Allow the child to pick out a sticker.

   D. Have the child "clean the owie" on her doll.

3. True or False: When working with a child who is developmentally delayed, the nurse should use diversional activities appropriate for the child's age.

4. Which of the following play activities is expected for a preschooler?

   A. Playing on a soccer team

   B. Reading a book quietly

   C. Playing the violin

   D. Finger painting

5. What age group is most likely to engage in collecting trading cards?

   A. Toddler

   B. Preschooler

   C. School-age child

   D. Adolescent

6. In which of the following activities would an adolescent most likely engage?

     _____ Playing video games with peers

     _____ Playing in groups without structure

     _____ Participating in school sports

     _____ Drawing or coloring

     _____ Reading or listening to music

     _____ Creating art projects

7. A 5-year-old child is hospitalized and is in skeletal traction for a fractured femur. Which of the following is the most appropriate diversional activity for this child?

     A. Putting together a jigsaw puzzle

     B. Playing with puppets

     C. Watching TV

     D. Stacking blocks to build towers

Chapter 10: Play

Application Exercises Answer Key

1. Match the following play activities with the appropriate age.

   <u>C</u> Watching black-and-white mobiles   A. 1 to 3 years

   <u>E</u> Playing peek-a-boo   B. 3 to 6 months

   <u>B</u> Holding a soft rattle   C. Birth to 3 months

   <u>A</u> Playing with cloth books   D. 9 to 12 months

   <u>D</u> Banging large blocks   E. 6 to 9 months

2. Before cleaning an abrasion on a 3 year old, what diversional activity could a nurse use to help decrease the child's anxiety?

   A. Give the child pain medication as prescribed.

   B. Tell the child what to expect.

   C. Allow the child to pick out a sticker.

   D. Have the child "clean the owie" on her doll.

   Having the child perform a task on a comfort toy, such as a doll, helps reduce anxiety. Giving pain medication does not reduce anxiety, nor is it a diversional activity. Telling the child what to expect may not help a preschooler understand the procedure. Selecting a reward should happen after the procedure is completed.

3. True or False: When working with a child who is developmentally delayed, the nurse should use diversional activities appropriate for the child's age.

   False: The nurse should determine the developmental level of the child, and then select activities appropriate to that child's level of development.

4. Which of the following play activities is expected for a preschooler?

> A. Playing on a soccer team
> B. Reading a book quietly
> C. Playing the violin
> **D. Finger painting**

Finger painting is a creative activity for the preschooler. Playing on a sports team, reading, and/or playing a musical instrument are activities for older children.

5. What age group is most likely to engage in collecting trading cards?

> A. Toddler
> B. Preschooler
> **C. School-age child**
> D. Adolescent

School-age children enjoy collecting various things. Early school-age children may not have organization to their collections, while older school-age children are organized and specific with their collections.

6. In which of the following activities would an adolescent most likely engage?

> __X__ **Playing video games with peers**
> _____ Playing in groups without structure
> __X__ **Participating in school sports**
> _____ Drawing or coloring
> __X__ **Reading or listening to music**
> _____ Creating art projects

Peers are very important to adolescents. Therefore, any activity that includes peers, such as video games, sports, or listening to music are more appealing. Unstructured play, drawing, and coloring are more appropriate for preschoolers. School-age children enjoy completing art projects.

7. A 5-year-old child is hospitalized and is in skeletal traction for a fractured femur. Which of the following is the most appropriate diversional activity for this child?

        A. Putting together a jigsaw puzzle

        B. Playing with puppets

        C. Watching TV

        D. Stacking blocks to build towers

Playing with puppets provides the preschool child an avenue for expressing creativity, fears, anxieties, and pain. Putting together a jigsaw puzzle is an activity an older child might enjoy. Watching TV might provide diversion for a 5 year old, but would not be the best activity. Stacking blocks is an activity for toddlers.

Unit 1:   Basic Concepts

Chapter 11:   Safe Administration of Medications

Contributor: Ann H. Johnson, MSN, RN

 NCLEX-RN® Connections:

Learning Objective: Review and apply knowledge within "**Safe Administration of Medications**" in readiness for performance of the following nursing activities as outlined by the NCLEX-RN® test plan:

Δ   Use the six "rights" of medication administration when administering medications to children and adolescents.

Δ   Assess client data (e.g., vital signs, laboratory values, allergies) before medication preparation and administration.

Δ   Assess/monitor the child for physical and psychosocial factors that impact medication administration.

Δ   Calculate/verify the child's medication dosage.

Δ   Prepare and demonstrate safe administration of different routes of medications (e.g., oral topical, subcutaneous, intramuscular, intradermal, intravenous).

Δ   Demonstrate appropriate documentation of all medication administration.

Δ   Inform the child/family of the therapeutic effects and possible side/adverse effects of medications.

Δ   Assess the child's condition during intravenous administrations.

Δ   Evaluate and document the effects of medications on the child's alteration in health status.

 Key Points

Δ   Pediatric dosages are based on body weight, body surface area (BSA), and maturation of body organs. Neonates (< 1 month old) and infants (1 month to 1 year) have immature liver and kidney function, alkaline gastric juices, and an immature blood-brain barrier. Certain medication dosages are based on age due to greater risk for decreased skeletal bone growth, acute cardiorespiratory failure, or hepatic toxicity.

Δ   Additional Pharmacokinetic Factors Specific to Children

•   Reduced gastric acid production and slower gastric emptying time

•   Reduced first-pass medication metabolism

- Increased absorption of topical medications (greater body surface area and thinner skin)

- Lower blood pressure: liver and brain receive greater blood flow, kidneys less

- Higher body-water content (dilutes water-soluble medications)

- Decreased serum protein-binding sites (until age 1)

Δ Be particularly alert when administering medications to children due to the high risk for medication error.

- Adult medication forms and concentrations may require dilution, calculation, preparation, and administration of very small doses.

- Limited sites exist for IV medications.

Δ **Safe Medication Administration**

- Six Rights

    ◊ **Right client** – Verify the client's identification each time a medication is administered. Check identification band, name, and/or photograph with the medication record.

    ◊ **Right medication** – Correctly interpret medication order (verify completeness and clarity); read label three times: when container is selected, when removing dose from container, and when container is replaced. Leave unit-dose medication in its package until administration.

    ◊ **Right dose** – Calculate correct medication dose; check drug reference to ensure dose is within usual range. Have a second nurse check if unsure or if per facility policy. Use a cutting device to break a scored tablet.

    ◊ **Right time** – Give medication on time to maintain consistent therapeutic blood level. It is generally acceptable to give the medication ½ hr before or after the scheduled time. However, refer to the drug reference or facility policy for exceptions. PRN medications are given no sooner than the interval specified by the primary care provider.

    ◊ **Right route** – Select the correct preparation for the ordered route (e.g., otic vs ophthalmic topical ointment or drops). Understand how to safely and correctly administer medication. Administer injections only from preparations designed for parenteral use. If route is not designated, or if a specified route is not recommended, contact the primary care provider for clarification.

    ◊ **Right documentation** – Immediately record pertinent information, including client's response to the medication.

Key Factors

Δ   Organ system immaturity is the greatest factor that affects medication response in the pediatric client.

Δ   Pediatric clients are more sensitive to medications and show a larger individual variation than adult clients.

Δ   Psychosocial variables affecting medication response in children and adolescents include:

  • Health-illness beliefs of the child and family.

  • Previous experiences with medications.

  • Knowledge base.

  • Cultural beliefs.

  • Developmental stage.

  • Social support/financial status.

Assessment

Δ   Medication and food allergies

Δ   Medication dose appropriate for child's weight

Δ   Child's ability to cooperate with medication administration

Δ   Tissue integrity

NANDA Nursing Diagnoses

Δ   Anxiety

Δ   Fear

Δ   Deficient knowledge

Δ   Acute pain

Δ   Impaired swallowing

Δ   Impaired tissue integrity

Nursing Interventions

Δ   Administration of Oral Medications

  • Regardless of age, aspiration of oral medications is always a risk, especially if the child is crying or in a supine position.

- Do not mix medications with formula because an infant may not take all of the formula; therefore, the infant will not receive the full medication dose. This may also cause the infant to refuse formula in the future.

- The oral route is the preferred route for children. The preferred measurement is milliliters (mL): 5 mL (1 tsp), 30 mL (1 oz).

- Plastic, needleless syringes are preferred for measurement and administration of small doses of medications.

- Use of a medicine cup is appropriate once an infant is able to drink from a cup.

- If mixing medications with liquids or soft foods, administer in small amounts to ensure total dose is given.

- If tablets are used, they may need to be crushed and thoroughly dissolved in liquid to prevent aspiration.

- Do not crush enteric-coated or time-released tablets.

- Divide tablets only if scored.

- Administration of oral medications to an infant includes:

  ◊ Placing the infant in a semireclining position.

  ◊ Using a plastic needleless syringe, administering small amounts of medication into the mouth along the side of the tongue, and ensuring the infant swallows between drops.

  ◊ Placing medication into an empty nipple from which the infant can suck.

Δ Administering Oral Medications via Feeding Tube or Gastrostomy Tube

- If a nasogastric tube (NGT), orogastric tube (OGT), or gastric tube (GT) is in place, use this route for administration of oral medications.

- Flushing the tube adequately reduces the risk of occlusion and the need for replacement. Small particles can clump together and clog the tube. The volume of flush is usually 1.5 times the volume of the tube.

- Elixir or suspension is preferred.

- If tablets are the only option, they must be thoroughly crushed and dissolved in liquid.

- Rate of flow through the tube can be altered by raising the height of the administration syringe to increase flow, or lowering the height to decrease the flow.

Δ   Rectal Medication Administration

- This route is used as a substitute for oral administration (e.g., a child with nausea/vomiting or difficult oral administration).

- Acetaminophen (Tylenol), sedatives, morphine, and some antiemetics are available in suppository form.

- Cut the suppository lengthwise for partial dosing due to the irregular shaping of the suppository.

Δ   Optic, Otic, and Nasal Administration

- Procedures for these routes are similar to adult administration.

- One major difference is that the ear canal should be straightened by pulling the auricle down and back when instilling otic solutions.

- The primary problem for these routes is obtaining the child's cooperation. Strategies to gain the child's cooperation may include:

    ◊   Allowing the parent to be present. The parent may also hold the child.

    ◊   Warming otic solutions to room temperature before instilling.

    ◊   Hyperextending the child's neck for nasal medication to prevent medications from sliding down into the child's throat.

Δ   Subcutaneous (SQ) and Intradermal Medication Administration

- These administration techniques are very similar for both children and adults.

- Strategies to decrease pain with the procedure include:

    ◊   Applying a eutectic mixture of local anesthetics (lidocaine/prilocaine) (EMLA) in the form of a cream or disk 60 min prior to injection.

    ◊   Using a 3/8- to 5/8-inch, 26- to-30 gauge needle for injection.

    ◊   Changing needle if used to puncture the rubber top of a vial.

    ◊   Injecting small volumes of medication (up to 0.5 mL).

Subcutaneous (SQ)	Intradermal
• Insert needle at a 90° angle or a 45° angle for a child with minimal subcutaneous tissue. • Sites include – upper arm (lateral aspect, center third), abdomen (avoid umbilicus), anterior thigh (center third) • Common medications – insulin, allergy desensitization, hormone replacement, and some vaccines	• Insert needle at 15° angle, injecting medication to form a "bleb" or a small bubble just beneath the surface of the skin. • The intradermal site is the inside surface of the forearm, not the medial surface. • Common medications – local anesthesia, tuberculosis (TB), and allergy testing

Δ   Intramuscular (IM) Medication Administration

- Suggestions to decrease pain with this procedure may include:

  ◊ Applying a eutectic mixture of local anesthetics (lidocaine/prilocaine) (EMLA) in the form of a cream or disk a minimum of 60 min, preferably 2 to 2.5 hr, prior to injection.

  ◊ Changing needle if used to puncture the rubber top of a vial.

  ◊ Using the smallest gauge possible.

- Considerations when selecting a site include:

  ◊ The medication amount, viscosity, and type.

  ◊ The muscle mass, condition, access of site, and potential for contamination.

  ◊ Treatment course frequency and number of injections.

  ◊ The ability to obtain proper positioning of the child.

- General considerations for IM medication administration include:

  ◊ The vastus lateralis site is usually the recommended site for infants and children less than 2 years.

  ◊ After age 2, the ventral gluteal site can be used. Both of these sites can accommodate fluid up to 2 mL.

  ◊ The deltoid site has a smaller muscle mass and can only accommodate up to 1 mL of fluid.

Site	Needle size	Position	Comments
Vastus Lateralis	• 22- to 25-gauge • 0.625 to 1 inch • 0.5 mL for infants to 2.0 mL for children	• Supine • Side-lying • Sitting	• Recommended site for infants and children less than 2 years • May be used for toddlers and older children
Ventrogluteal	• 22- to 25-gauge • 0.625 to 1 inch • 0.5 mL for infants to 2.0 mL for children	• Supine • Side-lying • Prone	• Can be used for children age 2 or older; has been used for infants in actual clinical practice • Not as painful as vastus lateralis • No important nerves or blood vessels
Deltoid	• 22- to 25-gauge • 0.625 to 1 inch • 0.5 mL for infants to 1.0 mL for children	• Supine • Side-lying • Sitting	• Not as painful as vastus lateralis • Less local side effects than with vastus lateralis • Should not be used in infants/children with underdeveloped muscles • If muscle size appropriate, may use for immunization for toddlers and children

Δ   Intravenous (IV) Medication Administration

•   Peripheral venous access devices

◊   Use for continuous and intermittent IV medication administration.

◊   Children requiring short-term therapy may be discharged with a peripheral line that is maintained by a home health care nurse.

- Central venous access devices (VADs)

  ◊ Short-term or nontunneled catheters are inserted into large veins and are used in acute care, emergency situations, and intensive care units.

  ◊ Peripherally inserted central catheters (PICCs) are used for short- to moderate-length therapy. PICCs are the least costly and have the fewest incidences of complications

  ◊ Long-term central VADs may be tunneled or implanted infusion ports.

  ◊ If the child is to go home with the VAD, discharge instructions should include how to prepare and inject medication, flushing of the line, and dressing change procedures.

Primary Reference:

Hockenberry, M., Wilson, D., Winkelstein, M. (2005). *Wong's essentials of pediatric nursing care.* (7th ed.). St. Louis, MO: Mosby.

Additional Resources:

Lehne, R. A. (2007). *Pharmacology for nursing care.* (6th ed.). St. Louis, MO: Saunders.

NANDA International (2004). *NANDA nursing diagnoses: Definitions and classification 2005-2006.* Philadelphia: NANDA.

Potter, P. A., & Perry, A. G. (2005). *Fundamentals of nursing.* (6th ed.). St. Louis, MO: Mosby.

Chapter 11: Safe Administration of Medications

Application Exercises

1. A primary care provider prescribes 250 mg of cefuroxime (Ceftin) BID for a 3 year old with otitis media. The medication is available in a 200 mg/5 mL oral suspension. How many mL should the child receive with each dose?

2. A child weighs 20 lb. The primary care provider prescribes cefazolin (Ancef) 30 mg/kg in two divided doses per day. Available is cefazolin oral suspension 125 mg/5 mL. How many mL per dose should this child receive?

3. True or False: If an infant is sleeping, a nurse may ask the parents at the bedside to verify his name.

4. When administering oral medications to a child with a feeding tube, the nurse knows to

   A. flush the tubing with NS before and after administration of the medication.
   B. dissolve tablets in a premeasured amount of fluid, measure into a syringe, and give slowly into the side of the mouth to prevent clogging the feeding tube.
   C. push slowly on the plunger of the administration syringe to gently administer the medication through the feeding tube.
   D. check tube placement, administer medication by gravity flow, flush adequately, and clamp tubing.

5. Which of the following sites is the most appropriate for administering an immunization to an infant?

   A. Deltoid
   B. Ventrogluteal
   C. Vastus lateralis
   D. Dorsogluteal

6. List three interventions, with rationales, that a nurse can use to decrease the risk of medication errors when administering medications to children.

7. When instilling an otic solution into a child's ear, the nurse should pull the auricle
   _____.

8. Match the IM injection with its correct information. Each choice may be used more than once.

_____ Vastus lateralis

_____ Ventrogluteal

_____ Deltoid

A. May be used for toddlers and older children

B. Recommended site for infants < 2 years

C. Less local side effects than with vastus lateralis

D. May use the prone position

E. May use the sitting position

Chapter 11: Safe Administration of Medications

Application Exercises Answer Key

1. A primary care provider prescribes 250 mg of cefuroxime (Ceftin) BID for a 3 year old with otitis media. The medication is available in a 200 mg/5 mL oral suspension. How many mL should the child receive with each dose?

Dimensional analysis	Formula
$\dfrac{5\,mL}{200\,mg} \bullet \dfrac{250\,mg}{1} = \dfrac{1{,}250}{200} = 6.25\,mL = 6.3\,mL$	Step 1: Choose formula $\dfrac{D}{A} \bullet Q$ Step 2: Use formula $\dfrac{250mg}{200mg} \bullet 5mL = \dfrac{1{,}250}{200} = 6.25\,mL = 6.3\,mL$

2. A child weighs 20 lb. The primary care provider prescribes cefazolin (Ancef) 30 mg/kg in two divided doses per day. Available is cefazolin oral suspension 125 mg/5 mL. How many mL per dose should this child receive?

Dimensional analysis	Formula
Step 1: $\dfrac{5\,mL}{125\,mg} \bullet \dfrac{30mg}{1\,kg} \bullet \dfrac{1\,kg}{2.2\,lb} \bullet \dfrac{20\,lb}{1} = \dfrac{3{,}000}{275}$ $= 10.9\,mL\,/\,day$ Step 2: Calculate single dose $\dfrac{10.9\,mL}{2\,doses} \bullet \dfrac{1\,dose}{1} = 5.45\,mL = 5.5mL$	Step 1: Choose formula $\dfrac{D}{A} \bullet Q$ Step 2: Conversion $\dfrac{10.9\,mL}{2\,doses} \bullet \dfrac{1\,dose}{1} = 5.45\,mL$ Step 3: Calculate dose ordered for child based on weight $\dfrac{30\,mg}{1\,kg} \bullet \dfrac{9.1\,kg}{1} = 273\,mg\,/\,day$ Step 4: Use formula $\dfrac{273\,mg}{125\,mg} \bullet 5\,mL = 10.9\,mL\,/\,day$ Step 5: Calculate single dose $\dfrac{10.9\,mL}{2\,doses} \bullet \dfrac{1\,dose}{1} = 5.45\,mL = 5.5mL$

3. True or False: If an infant is sleeping, a nurse may ask the parents at the bedside to verify his name.

False: A client's identity should always be verified by the hospital identification band.

4. When administering oral medications to a child with a feeding tube, the nurse knows to

    A. flush the tubing with NS before and after administration of the medication.

    B. dissolve tablets in a premeasured amount of fluid, measure into a syringe, and give slowly into the side of the mouth to prevent clogging the feeding tube.

    C. push slowly on the plunger of the administration syringe to gently administer the medication through the feeding tube.

    D. check tube placement, administer medication by gravity flow, flush adequately, and clamp tubing.

Placement is always checked prior to giving medications through a feeding tube to prevent aspiration if the tube is not in the stomach. Flushing ensures that the tube remains patent and that the medication reaches the stomach. Medication is not given by mouth if a feeding tube is in place. NS is not used to flush feeding tubes. Medications are given by gravity flow, not forced by plunger.

5. Which of the following sites is the most appropriate for administering an immunization to an infant?

    A. Deltoid

    B. Ventrogluteal

    C. Vastus lateralis

    D. Dorsogluteal

The vastus lateralis is the most developed muscle in the infant; therefore, it is the site of choice for administering IM injections in infants.

6. List three interventions, with rationales, that a nurse can use to decrease the risk of medication errors when administering medications to children.

Intervention	Rationale
Have a second nurse verify dosage calculation.	Adult medication forms may be used requiring calculation of very small doses.
Obtain accurate weight of child.	Dosages are usually based on weight or body surface area.
Mix medications with small amounts of liquid or soft foods.	If the medication is mixed in large amounts of liquid or foods, the child may refuse to finish the dose.

7. When instilling an otic solution into a child's ear, the nurse should pull the auricle _____.

Down and back. Pulling the auricle down and back, instead of up and back as in an adult, will help open the ear canal and facilitate administration of the medication. This method straightens the child's ear canal, making it easier to instill the otic solution.

8. Match the IM injection with its correct information. Each choice may be used more than once.

  A, B, E   Vastus lateralis   A. May be used for toddlers and older children

   A, D   Ventrogluteal   B. Recommended site for infants < 2 years

  A, C, E   Deltoid   C. Less local side effects than with vastus lateralis

                                         D. May use the prone position

                                         E. May use the sitting position

Unit 1:   Basic Concepts

Chapter 12:   Pain Management
Contributor: Sally Swenson, MA, RN

 NCLEX-RN® Connections:

Learning Objective: Review and apply knowledge within "**Pain Management**" in readiness for performance of the following nursing activities as outlined by the NCLEX-RN® test plan:

Δ   Assess the child for symptoms of impaired comfort using standardized pain rating scales.

Δ   Assess the child for physiologic and behavioral responses to impaired comfort.

Δ   Plan and provide effective pain relief, and serve as a client advocate through the use of pharmacologic and nonpharmacologic interventions.

Δ   Assess and document effectiveness of pain treatment.

Δ   Evaluate the child's reaction to pain relief measures, and modify the plan of care as needed.

Δ   Reinforce client teaching regarding management of the child's health problem – acute/chronic pain.

Δ   Recognize how culture influences the child's perception of and reaction to pain.

 Key Points

Δ   Children have a right to adequate assessment and management of pain. Nurses are accountable for the assessment of pain. The nurse's role is that of an advocate and educator for proper pain management.

Δ   Pain is whatever the child says it is, and it exists whenever the child says it does. The child's report of pain is the most reliable diagnostic measurement of pain.

Δ   The type of pain children experience includes procedure-related pain, operative and trauma-associated pain, and/or acute and chronic pain from illness or injury.

Δ   Pain assessment should be done and recorded frequently by the nurse, and it may be considered the fifth vital sign.

Δ   The effectiveness of treatment should be evaluated in a timely manner (e.g., 15 min after IV pain medication administration, 30 min after IM pain medication, 30 to 60 min after oral medication administration and nonpharmacologic therapies).

- Assessment is more difficult to determine in infants and younger children because they lack the verbal skills to state how severe the pain is. Older children and adolescents are able to give self-report information about what they are experiencing.

- Behaviors in one child with pain can vary from immobility and stillness to restlessness and constant mobility.

- Physiologic changes in blood pressure, pulse, and respiratory rate are temporary changes produced by the anxiety associated with the pain. Initially, elevated vital signs will return to normal despite the persistence of pain.

- Self-report using pain scales is useful in children over 7. Children ages 3 to 7 may comprehend how to use a pain rating scale. However, their ability should be assessed. Verification with parents will validate assessment.

Δ Proper pain management includes the use of pharmacologic and nonpharmacologic pain management therapies.

Δ Children receiving opioid medication need to be monitored closely for respiratory depression.

Δ **Common Pain Scales**

Pain Assessment Tool	Form of Evaluation	Age of Child
FLACC Postoperative Pain Tool (Faces, Legs, Activity, Cry, Consolability)	• Behaviors are scored 0 to 2 • 0 = no pain; 10 = worst pain. • Behavior indicators include: ◊ Facial expressions. ◊ Position of legs. ◊ Activity. ◊ Crying. ◊ Ability to be consoled.	2 months to 7 years
Children's Hospital of Eastern Ontario Pain Scale (CHEOPS)	• 4 = no pain; 13 = worst pain. • Behavior indicators include: ◊ Cry. ◊ Facial expression. ◊ Verbalizations. ◊ Movement of torso. ◊ Movement of legs. ◊ Response to touch.	1 to 5 years
FACES	• Rating scale uses drawings of happy and sad faces to depict levels of pain.	3 years and older

Pain Assessment Tool	Form of Evaluation	Age of Child
Visual Analog Scale (VAS)	• Rating scale numbered 0 to 10. Child points to the number that best describes the pain he is experiencing.	7 years and older (may be effective with children as young as 4.5 years)

Key Factors

Δ   Age can influence how pain is perceived and how it can be communicated.

Δ   Fatigue, anxiety, and fear can increase sensitivity to pain.

Δ   Genetic sensitivity can increase or decrease the amount of pain tolerated.

Δ   Children who are cognitively impaired may not be able to report pain or report it accurately.

Δ   Prior experiences can increase or decrease sensitivity depending on whether or not adequate relief was obtained, especially in older children and adolescents.

Δ   Family and other well-known individuals can decrease sensitivity to pain by staying with the child.

Δ   Culture may influence how a child expresses pain or the meaning given to it.

Nursing Assessment

Δ   **Subjective data** can be obtained using a symptom analysis. A nurse should adapt questions to appropriate developmental level.

Location is described using anatomical terminology and landmarks.	• Ask, "Where is your pain?", "Does it hurt anywhere else?" • Ask the child to point to the location.
• Quality refers to how the pain feels. • Feelings of pain include: sharp, dull, aching, burning, stabbing, pounding, throbbing, shooting, gnawing, tender, heavy, tight, tiring, exhausting, sickening, terrifying, torturing, nagging, annoying, intense, and/or unbearable.	• Ask "What does the pain feel like?" • Give more than two choices (e.g., "Is the pain throbbing, burning, and stabbing?").
Intensity, strength, and severity are "measures" of the pain. Pain assessment tools (e.g., description scale, number rating scale) can be used to: • Measure pain. • Monitor pain. • Evaluate effectiveness of interventions.	Use a pain scale. Also, ask the following questions: • "How much pain do you have now?" • "What is the worst/best the pain has been?"

Timing – onset, duration, and frequency	This may be difficult for a child to understand. An older child or adolescent may have a better understanding of time. Ask the following questions: • "When did it start?" • "How long does it last?" • "How often does it occur?" • "Is it constant or intermittent?"
Setting	Ask the following questions: • "Where are you when you feel pain?" • "What are you doing when you feel pain?"
Associated symptoms may include fatigue, depression, nausea, and anxiety, and they should be noted.	May be difficult for a young child to answer
Aggravating/relieving factors	Ask the following questions: • "What makes the pain better?" • "What makes the pain worse?"

Δ **Objective Data**

- Behaviors complement self-report and assist in pain assessment of children unable to verbalize their feelings

  ◊ Facial expressions (e.g., grimacing, wrinkled forehead), body movements (e.g., restlessness, pacing, guarding)

  ◊ Moaning, crying

  ◊ Decreased attention span

- Physiologic measures of blood pressure, pulse, and respiratory rate will be temporarily increased by acute pain. Initially, increased vital signs will return to normal despite the persistence of pain. Therefore, physiologic indicators may not be an accurate measure of pain over time.

NANDA Nursing Diagnoses

Δ   Anxiety

Δ   Ineffective coping

Δ   Fear

Δ   Acute pain

Δ   Chronic pain

Δ   Impaired physical mobility

Δ   Disturbed sleep pattern

Δ   Impaired social interaction

Nursing Interventions

    Δ   Interventions should be determined in conjunction with the parents and child. Severity of the pain will also guide the choice of treatment.

    Δ   Pharmacologic measures include:

- Giving medications routinely versus PRN (as needed) to manage pain that is expected to last for an extended period of time.

- Using caution when administering medications to newborns less than 2 to 3 months of age because of immature liver function.

- Combining adjuvant medications (e.g., steroids, antidepressants, sedatives, antianxiety medications, muscle relaxants, and/or anticonvulsants).

- Using nonopioid and opioid medications.

    ◊ Acetaminophen (Tylenol) and nonsteroidal anti-inflammatory (NSAIDs) medications are acceptable for mild to moderate pain.

    ◊ Opioids are acceptable for moderate to severe pain. The medication of choice is morphine, but oxycodone, hydromorphone, and fentanyl may also be used.

    ◊ Combining a nonopioid and opioid medication treats pain peripherally and centrally. This offers greater analgesia with less adverse effects (e.g., respiratory depression, constipation, nausea).

    Δ   Choosing the appropriate route for medication administration should be based on what will be the most effective, the least traumatic, and appropriate to the child's developmental level.

    Δ   Appropriate routes

Route	Nursing Implications
Oral	• Oral medications are a preferred route due to their convenience, cost, and ability to maintain steady blood levels. • Oral medications take 1 to 2 hr to reach peak analgesic effect. Therefore, these medications are not suited for the child experiencing pain that requires rapid relief or pain that is fluctuating in nature.
Sublingual/buccal/transmucosal	• These medications are a very desirable form because they have a less first-pass effect than oral medications. • There are very few medications available in this form. • Fentanyl citrate (Actiq) is a transmucosal product manufactured on a stick for children to suck on. It may be used for cancer breakthrough pain and for sedation prior to surgery and/or painful procedures.
Continuous intravenous (IV)	• Continuous intravenous (IV) medication administration offers stable blood levels.

Route	Nursing Implications
Continuous subcutaneous	• A continuous subcutaneous route is used if oral/IV routes are not accessible. • This route is just as effective as continuous IV infusion.
Patient-controlled analgesia (PCA)	• PCA is used to control pain from cancer, perioperative procedures, trauma, and sickle-cell crisis. • Morphine, fentanyl, and hydromorphone are commonly used. • PCA can be controlled by the child, a family member, or the nurse.

Topical/transdermal	• One type of topical/transdermal medication is a eutectic mixture of local anesthetics (lidocaine/prilocaine [EMLA]) in the form of a cream or disk.
	  ◊ Use EMLA for any procedure in which the skin will be punctured (e.g., IV insertion, biopsy) 60 min prior to a superficial puncture, and 2.5 hr prior to a deep puncture.
	  ◊ Place a transparent dressing over the cream after application.
	  ◊ Prior to the procedure, remove the dressing or disk and wipe the skin. Indication of adequate response is reddened or blanched skin.
	  ◊ Demonstrate to the child that the skin is not sensitive by tapping or scratching lightly.
	  ◊ EMLA may be applied at home prior to coming to a health care facility/agency for the procedure.
	• Transdermal fentanyl (Duragesic)
	  ◊ Transdermal fentanyl is appropriate for children older than 12 years.
	  ◊ Transdermal fentanyl A is a patch that provides continuous pain control.
	  ◊ Onset of transdermal fentanyl is 12 to 24 hr, with a duration of 72 hr.
	  ◊ Additional medication should be ordered for breakthrough pain.
	  ◊ Respiratory depression may need to be treated with a number of doses of naloxone.

Δ   Nonpharmacologic Measures

- Positioning
- Breathing and relaxation techniques
- Splinting
- Calm environment – low noise and reduced lighting
- Ice to swollen or injured area
- Warm blankets
- Guided imagery
- Distraction – video games, cartoons, videos
- Being held or rocked
- Sucrose pacifiers for infants during procedures

Primary Reference:

Hockenberry, M., Wilson, D., Winkelstein, M. (2005). *Wong's essentials of pediatric nursing care.* (7th ed.). St. Louis, MO: Mosby.

Additional Resources:

American Academy of Pediatrics. (2001). The Assessment and Management of Acute Pain in Infants, Children, and Adolescents. *Pediatrics. 108*, 793-797. Retrieved December 27, 2006, from http://aappolicy.aappublications.org

NANDA International (2004). *NANDA nursing diagnoses: Definitions and classification 2005-2006*. Philadelphia: NANDA.

Chapter 12: Pain Management

Application Exercises

1. A 10-year-old child has just had an appendectomy following a ruptured appendix. A nurse is monitoring the child's response to antibiotics, postoperative healing, and pain control. Which of the following tools is most appropriate for assessing the child's pain?

> A. FLACC (Faces, Legs, Activity, Cry, Consolability Scale)
>
> B. FACES pain rating scale
>
> C. Children's Hospital Eastern Ontario Pain Scales (CHEOPS)
>
> D. Visual Analogue Scale (VAS)

2. A nurse suspects that a 15-year-old adolescent is experiencing pain. The nurse asks if the adolescent would like her pain medication. The adolescent tells the nurse that she will wait until the pain worsens. Which of the following statements by the nurse is most appropriate in response to the adolescent's pain?

> A. "If you let the pain get too bad, the medication will not work as well."
>
> B. "Just let me know when you are ready."
>
> C. "You need to take your pain medication now."
>
> D. "Are you sure you don't want anything now?"

3. How can prior experiences with pain influence current sensitivity to pain?

4. When should the effectiveness of nonpharmacologic pain interventions be evaluated?

5. For which of the following children should a nurse use the child's behaviors as an indication of pain versus self-report?

> A. 2 year old
>
> B. 8 year old
>
> C. 12 year old
>
> D. 16 year old

6. A 5-year-old child is scheduled for a dressing change that will produce moderate pain. What preprocedural intervention should the nurse perform?

    A. Administer pain medication prior to the procedure.

    B. Inform the child that pain medication will be available if needed during the procedure.

    C. Inform the child that pain medication will be available if needed after the procedure.

    D. Inform the child that he can play a video game if he remains still during the procedure.

7. Thirty to 60 min following the administration of an oral pain medication to a child, it is important that a nurse

    A. document the child's pain on a rating scale.

    B. evaluate the effectiveness of the pain medication.

    C. assess the child for bowel sounds.

    D. massage the child's painful area.

8. Which of the following is an appropriate nonpharmacologic pain management technique for a 5-year-old child with a fractured femur? (Select all that apply.)

    _____ Relaxation techniques

    _____ Distraction

    _____ Guided imagery

    _____ Being held or rocked

    _____ Positioning

9. An adolescent fractures his left leg. The leg is surgically repaired, and a long-leg cast is applied. During the first night in the hospital, the adolescent calls the nurse to the room and states, "My leg hurts really bad." The next action the nurse should take is to

    A. obtain more information about the characteristics of the pain.

    B. give the adolescent a dose of pain medication as prescribed.

    C. reassure the adolescent that the pain will diminish in a few days.

    D. distract the adolescent by turning on the TV.

Chapter 12: Pain Management

Application Exercises Answer Key

1. A 10-year-old child has just had an appendectomy following a ruptured appendix. A nurse is monitoring the child's response to antibiotics, postoperative healing, and pain control. Which of the following tools is most appropriate for assessing the child's pain?

   A. FLACC (Faces, Legs, Activity, Cry, Consolability Scale)

   B. FACES pain rating scale

   C. Children's Hospital Eastern Ontario Pain Scales (CHEOPS)

   D. Visual Analogue Scale (VAS)

   The VAS scale is the most appropriate for this child. The FLACC scale is used for infants and children up to 7 years. The FACES and CHEOPS scales are appropriate for early childhood.

2. A nurse suspects that a 15-year-old adolescent is experiencing pain. The nurse asks if the adolescent would like her pain medication. The adolescent tells the nurse that she will wait until the pain worsens. Which of the following statements by the nurse is most appropriate in response to the adolescent's pain?

   A. "If you let the pain get too bad, the medication will not work as well."

   B. "Just let me know when you are ready."

   C. "You need to take your pain medication now."

   D. "Are you sure you don't want anything now?"

   Giving pain medication when pain is perceived keeps the pain under control. It is easier to prevent pain than to treat it. The adolescent should be able to understand this concept.

3. How can prior experiences with pain influence current sensitivity to pain?

   Prior experience can decrease sensitivity if prior pain relief measures were effective. Prior experience can increase sensitivity if prior pain relief measures were ineffective.

4. When should the effectiveness of nonpharmacologic pain interventions be evaluated?

The effectiveness of nonpharmacologic pain interventions should be evaluated around 30 to 60 min following interventions. It usually takes about 30 to 60 min for the body to adjust to the interventions for pain reduction.

5. For which of the following children should a nurse use the child's behaviors as an indication of pain versus self-report?

    A. 2 year old
    B. 8 year old
    C. 12 year old
    D. 16 year old

A 2 year old is not able to verbalize pain. However, this child may exhibit signs of distress such as crying, irritability, and restlessness. An 8, 12, and 16 year old should be able to report the pain experienced.

6. A 5-year-old child is scheduled for a dressing change that will produce moderate pain. What preprocedural intervention should the nurse perform?

    A. Administer pain medication prior to the procedure.
    B. Inform the child that pain medication will be available if needed during the procedure.
    C. Inform the child that pain medication will be available if needed after the procedure.
    D. Inform the child that he can play a video game if he remains still during the procedure.

If the nurse knows that a procedure will produce pain for a 5 year old, it is appropriate to administer the medication prior to the start of the procedure to prevent pain. If administered during or after the procedure, the child will have already experienced pain and more medication may be needed to control it. Offering the reward of playing a video game does not address the child's potential for pain.

7. Thirty to 60 min following the administration of an oral pain medication to a child, it is important that a nurse

     A. document the child's pain on a rating scale.

     B. evaluate the effectiveness of the pain medication.

     C. assess the child for bowel sounds.

     D. massage the child's painful area.

Oral pain medications usually have an onset of 30 to 60 min; therefore, this would be the appropriate time to evaluate the effectiveness of the medication. The nurse should document the child's level of pain right after assessment and administration of the medication, not 30 to 60 min afterwards. Assessing for bowel sounds is not indicated after administration of pain medication.

8. Which of the following is an appropriate nonpharmacologic pain management technique for a 5-year-old child with a fractured femur? (Select all that apply.)

     _____ Relaxation techniques

     _**X**_ **Distraction**

     _____ Guided imagery

     _**X**_ **Being held or rocked**

     _**X**_ **Positioning**

Distraction (e.g., coloring, watching TV, playing with toys), being held or rocked, and positioning are all appropriate nonpharmacologic pain management techniques for a 5 year old. A 5 year old would not be able to practice relaxation techniques or follow guided imagery.

9. An adolescent fractures his left leg. The leg is surgically repaired, and a long-leg cast is applied. During the first night in the hospital, the adolescent calls the nurse to the room and states, "My leg hurts really bad." The next action the nurse should take is to

     A. obtain more information about the characteristics of the pain.

     B. give the adolescent a dose of pain medication as prescribed.

     C. reassure the adolescent that the pain will diminish in a few days.

     D. distract the adolescent by turning on the TV.

It is important that the nurse gather more information regarding the adolescent's report. A complete assessment of the pain should be performed before taking any action.

Unit 1:   Basic Concepts

Chapter 13:   **Hospitalization and Illness**
                 Contributor: Candyce F. Antley, RN, MN

 NCLEX-RN® Connections:

> **Learning Objective**: Review and apply knowledge within **"Hospitalization and Illness"** in readiness for performance of the following nursing activities as outlined by the NCLEX-RN® test plan:
>
> Δ   Assess the child's/family's reactions and ability to cope with hospitalization and/or illness.
>
> Δ   Identify the child's/family's ability to participate in providing effective care.
>
> Δ   Recognize the child's/family's available resources.
>
> Δ   Plan and provide age-appropriate care for the hospitalized child.
>
> Δ   Provide teaching to the child/family to assist with managing the child's change in health status.
>
> Δ   Evaluate and document care provided to the hospitalized child.

 Key Points

Δ   Hospitalization of a child is stressful for both the child and his parents.

Δ   Children are extremely vulnerable to the stress of being sick and are hospitalized due to limited coping skills.

Δ   The family is also a client when a child is ill.

Δ   Major stressors of hospitalization that affect both the child and family include separation, loss of control, bodily injury, and pain.

Δ   Separation anxiety manifests in three behavioral responses: protest, which may be expressed as crying; despair, which may be expressed as being withdrawn and quiet; and detachment/denial, which may be expressed as lack of protest when parents leave.

Δ   The child may demonstrate developmental regression to the stress of hospitalization.

Δ   The child's understanding of illness and hospitalization is dependent on the child's stage of development and cognitive ability.

Key Factors

Δ   Impact of hospitalization depends upon development.

Age	Level of Understanding	Impact of Hospitalization
Infant	• Inability to describe symptoms • Lack of understanding for the need of therapeutic procedures • Inability to follow directions	• Experiences stranger anxiety between 6 to 18 months of age • Displays physical behaviors as expression of discomfort due to inability to verbalize • May experience sleep deprivation due to strange noises, monitoring devices, and procedures
Toddler	• Limited ability to describe symptoms • Poorly developed body image and boundaries • Limited understanding for the need for therapeutic procedures • Limited ability to follow directions	• Experiences separation anxiety • May exhibit an intense reaction to any type of procedure due to the intrusion of boundaries
Preschooler	• Knows what illness feels like but does not understand the cause • Limited ability to describe symptoms • Has fears related to magical thinking • Ability to understand cause and effect inhibited by concrete thinking	• May experience separation anxiety • May harbor fears of bodily harm • May believe illness and hospitalization are a punishment
School-age child	• Beginning awareness of body functioning due to the development of cognitive abilities • Ability to describe pain symptoms • Increasing ability to understand cause and effect	• Fear of loss of control • Seeks information as a way to maintain a sense of control • May sense when not being told the truth • May experience stress related to separation from peers and regular routine

Age	Level of Understanding	Impact of Hospitalization
Adolescent	• Continues to develop ability to understand cause and effect • Severity of illness perceptions based on the degree of body-image changes	• Development of body-image disturbance • Attempt to maintain composure, embarrassed about losing control • Experiences feelings of isolation from peers • Worries about outcome and impact on school/activities • May not be compliant with treatments/medication regimen if it makes the adolescent appear different from his peer group

Δ   Family responses to the child's hospitalization may include:

- Fear and guilt regarding not bringing the child in for care earlier.

- Frustration due to their perceived inability to care for their child.

- Altered family roles.

- Worry regarding finances if the parent has to miss work.

Nursing Assessment

Δ   Child/family understanding of illness or reason for hospitalization

Δ   Stressors unique to the child/family, such as needs of other children in the family, socioeconomic situation, and/or health of other extended family members

Δ   Past experiences with hospitalization and illness

Δ   Developmental level and needs of child/family

Δ   Parenting role and parent's perception of role changes

Δ   Support available to the child/family

NANDA Nursing Diagnoses

Δ   Anxiety

Δ   Fear

Δ   Powerlessness

Δ   Altered family processes related to situational crisis

Δ   Disturbed body image

Δ   Deficient knowledge

Nursing Interventions

Δ   Teach the child and family what to expect during hospitalization.

Δ   Interventions should be based on the developmental level of the child.

Age-related interventions	
Age	Interventions
Infant	• Place the infant whose parents are not in attendance close to the nursing station so their needs can be quickly met. • Provide consistency in assigning caregivers.
Toddler	• Encourage parents to provide routine care for the child, such as changing diapers and feeding the child. • Encourage child's autonomy by giving the child appropriate choices. • Provide consistency in assigning caregivers.
Preschooler	• Explain all procedures using simple, clear language. Avoid medical jargon and terms that can be misinterpreted by the child. • Encourage the child's independence by letting the child provide self-care. • Encourage the child to express feelings. • Validate the child's fears and concerns. • Provide toys that allow for emotional expression, such as a pounding a board to release feelings of protest. • Provide consistency in assigning caregivers. • Give choices when possible, such as "Do you want your medicine in a cup or a spoon?" • Allow younger children to handle equipment if it is safe.
School-age	• Provide factual information. • Encourage the child to express feelings. • Try to maintain a "normal" routine for long hospitalizations, including time for school work. • Encourage contact with peer group.
Adolescent	• Provide factual information. • Include the adolescent in the planning of care to relieve feelings of powerlessness and lack of control. • Encourage contact with peer group.

Δ   Encourage parents or a family member to stay with the child during the hospital experience to reduce the stress.

Primary Reference:

Hockenberry, M. J., Wilson, D., & Winkelstein M. L. (2005). *Wong's essentials of pediatric nursing.* (7th ed.). St. Louis, MO: Mosby.

Additional Resources:

NANDA International (2004). *NANDA nursing diagnoses: Definitions and classification 2005-2006.* Philadelphia: NANDA.

Chapter 13: Hospitalization and Illness

Application Exercises

1. An 18-month-old child is admitted to the hospital for pneumonia. The child is in a mist tent with 24% O_2 and has an IV of D_5W 0.2 NS at 45 mL/hr infusing in his right arm. Which of the following are stressors this child and his family might experience? (Select all that apply.)

   _____ Strange environment

   _____ Lack of control

   _____ Fear of bodily harm

   _____ Concern about body image

   _____ Separation anxiety

2. Which of the following nursing interventions is most appropriate for the needs of a 7-year-old child being hospitalized for an extended time?

   A. Bring security items such as a toy and blanket.

   B. Provide play activities that foster a sense of normal routine.

   C. Limit choices whenever possible.

   D. Restrict family visiting hours.

3. Match the following behaviors to the stages of separation anxiety.

   _____ Protest   A. Withdrawal and quietness

   _____ Despair   B. Lack of protest when parents leave

   _____ Denial   C. Crying

4. Identify several measures that would help a 4 year old with the stressors of hospitalization.

5. How can a nurse assist the family of a hospitalized toddler with separation anxiety?

6. List several issues that an adolescent who is hospitalized might experience.

Chapter 13: Hospitalization and Illness

Application Exercises Answer Key

1. An 18-month-old child is admitted to the hospital for pneumonia. The child is in a mist tent with 24% O_2 and has an IV of D_5W 0.2 NS at 45 mL/hr infusing in his right arm. Which of the following are stressors this child and his family might experience? (Select all that apply.)

   __X__ **Strange environment**

   __X__ **Lack of control**

   _____ Fear of bodily harm

   _____ Concern about body image

   __X__ **Separation anxiety**

   Separation anxiety, strange environment, and lack of control are stressors toddlers experience during hospitalization. Toddlers are developing a sense of autonomy, so lack of control and a strange environment are threatening. Fear of bodily harm occurs with preschoolers, and concern about body image is associated with adolescents.

2. Which of the following nursing interventions is most appropriate for the needs of a 7-year-old child being hospitalized for an extended time?

   A. Bring security items such as a toy and blanket.

   B. Provide play activities that foster a sense of normal routine.

   C. Limit choices whenever possible.

   D. Restrict family visiting hours.

   School-age children require a sense of routine during a long hospital stay. Younger children need security. Children need to have choices that are appropriate to help them feel a sense of control. Family visiting is also important in order for the child to cope with the hospitalization.

3. Match the following behaviors to the stages of separation anxiety.

   __C__ Protest   A. Withdrawal and quietness

   __A__ Despair   B. Lack of protest when parents leave

   __B__ Denial   C. Crying

4. Identify several measures that would help a 4 year old with the stressors of hospitalization.

Allowing the child to handle equipment if it is safe

Therapeutic play

Validating the child's fears

Explaining all procedures carefully in clear simple language

5. How can a nurse assist the family of a hospitalized toddler with separation anxiety?

First, have at least one parent stay with the child as much as possible. Place the child in a room close to the nurses' desk. Finally, explain the concept of separation anxiety to the parents to help them cope with the child's behaviors.

6. List several issues that an adolescent who is hospitalized might experience.

Feelings of isolation, especially from peers

Worries regarding the outcome of the illness and how it may affect activities and school

Noncompliance with treatment regimen if it interferes with activities or makes the adolescent appear different

Concerns about body image

Unit 1:   Basic Concepts

Chapter 14:   Death and Dying

Contributor: Ann H. Johnson, MSN, RN

 NCLEX-RN® Connections:

Learning Objective: Review and apply knowledge within "**Death and Dying**" in readiness for performance of the following nursing activities as outlined by the NCLEX-RN® test plan:

Δ   Assess the child's/family's capability to deal with end-of-life interventions.

Δ   Identify and provide for end-of-life needs of the child/family.

Δ   Be responsive to the cultural practices of the child/family surrounding death and dying.

Δ   Identify the need for and offer support to the family/caregiver.

 Key Points

Δ   The death of a child may be traumatic and devastating for a family.

Δ   Parental grief may last a lifetime, may place stress on marital relations, and may impact a parent's ability to assist siblings in dealing with their grief.

Δ   Sibling grief may be reprocessed with each developmental stage the sibling goes through after the death. Sibling behaviors may include being a "perfect" child, acting out for attention, or depression.

Δ   Dysfunctional grieving characteristics include: intense and prolonged feelings of loneliness, emptiness, and yearnings; distractive thoughts; inability to sleep; and loss of interest in daily activities.

Δ   True family-centered care is required to meet the needs of each individual family member experiencing grief in his/her own way and in his/her own time.

△ Palliative Care

- Pain control, symptom management, and support of the child/family must be given top **priority** in the terminal stages of illness.

- Palliative care uses education, support, and honest communication to foster a therapeutic environment.

△ Terminal stage-of-life decisions require honest information regarding prognosis, disease progression, treatment options available, and the impact of the treatments. These decisions are made during a highly stressful time. It is important that all health care personnel are aware of the child/family's decisions.

△ Nurses may experience personal grief when caring for children with whom they have developed rapport and intimacy. In this case, the nurse may require self-reflection and perhaps a debriefing of the entire staff by professional grief/ mental health counselors.

△ Ethical issues during care of the dying child include:

- Pain control.

- Nutrition/hydration supplements.

- Chemotherapy or experimental treatments.

- Resuscitation.

- Autopsy.

Key Factors

△ **Culture and ethnicity** influence the interpretation of a loss and expression of grief.

△ Spiritual **beliefs** affect the individual's ability to cope.

△ Allow an opportunity for anticipatory grieving, which impacts the way a family will cope with the death of a child.

△ Factors that can increase the family's potential for dysfunctional grieving following the death of a child include:

- Lack of a support system.

- Presence of poor coping skills.

- Social stigma, such as suicide, associated with the child's death.

- Death of the child associated with violence.

- Sudden and unexpected death of the child.

Δ   The stage of **human development** may impact how an individual will grieve and how he will perceive death.

Infants/Toddlers (Birth to 3 years)	• Have little to no concept of death • Have egocentric thinking that prevents the them from understanding death • Mirror parental emotions (e.g., sadness, anger, depression, and/or anxiety) • React in response to the changes brought about by being in the hospital (e.g., change of routine, painful procedures, immobilization, less independence, separation from family) • May regress to an earlier stage of behavior
Preschool children (3 to 5 years)	• Egocentric thinking • Think magically, which causes them to feel guiltily, shameful, and to sense punishment • Interpret separation from parents as punishment for bad behavior • View dying as temporary, since they have no concept of time, and the dead person may still have attributes of the living (sleeping, eating, and breathing)
School-age children (5 to 12 years)	• Start to respond to logical or factual explanations • Begin to have an adult concept of death (inevitable, irreversible, and universal), which generally applies to school-age children who are older (9 to 12 years) • Experience fear of the disease process, death process, the unknown, and loss of control • May be curious about funeral services and what happens to the body after death
Adolescents (12 to 20 years)	• May have an adult-like concept of death • Discovery of who they are, establishment of identity, and dealing with issues of puberty, making the acceptance of death difficult • Rely more on their peers rather than the influence of their parent(s), which may cause the reality of a serious illness to cause an adolescent to feel isolated – inability to relate to peers and not always communicating with their parents • May become more stressed by changes in physical appearance from the medications or illness than the prospect of death • May experience guilt and shame

Nursing Assessment

Δ   Child/family knowledge and feelings regarding diagnosis, prognosis, and care

Δ   Nutritional status and growth and development patterns

Δ   Activity and energy level of the child

Δ   Parents' wishes regarding child's care and end-of-life decisions

Δ   Presence of a Do Not Resuscitate (DNR) order

Δ   Family coping and available support

Δ   The stage of grief the child/family is experiencing

Δ   Assessment for symptoms of normal grief:

- Feelings may consist of sadness, anxiety, and/or yearning.

- Feelings of guilt and/or anger toward the deceased may be experienced.

- Thoughts may consist of confusion and hopelessness, and the individual may become preoccupied with the deceased person.

- Difficulties sleeping and eating, restlessness, depression, and crying are common reactions.

- Fatigue, muscle tension, weakness, and oversensitivity to stimuli are common physical symptoms.

NANDA Nursing Diagnoses

Δ   Death anxiety

Δ   Fear

Δ   Anticipatory grieving

Δ   Risk for dysfunctional grieving

Nursing Interventions

Δ   Care Options for Terminally Ill Children

Care	Focus
Hospital care	The child cannot be managed at home (e.g., family is not able to provide necessary care, child requires intensive nursing care).
Home care	Home care agency nurse provides assessments, treatments, medications, supplies, and equipment under the direction of the primary care provider.
Hospice care	• Management of the psychological, spiritual, physical, and social needs of the child and family • Family members providing most of the care • Priority given to pain and symptom control • Family needs addressed after death occurs

Δ   Offer strategies specific to developmental level.

Age Group	Developmental Approach
Infants and toddlers	• Encourage parents to stay with the child. • Attempt to maintain a normal environment.
Preschoolers	• Encourage parents to stay with the child. • Communicate with the child in honest, simple terms. • Be aware of medical jargon that may frighten the child.
School-age children	• Encourage parents to stay with the child. • Use language that is clear regarding disease, medications, procedures, and expectations. • Encourage self-care to promote independence and self-esteem. • Allow participation in plans for funeral services.
Adolescents	• Be honest and respectful when communicating. • Encourage self-care to promote independence and self-esteem. • Allow participation in plans for funeral services. • Encourage parent(s) or other family member(s) to stay with the adolescent.

Δ   Palliative Care

- Provide comfort measures (e.g., warmth, quiet, dry linens).

- Provide adequate nutrition and hydration.

- Control pain.

  ◊   Give medications on a regular schedule.

  ◊   Treat breakthrough pain.

  ◊   Increase doses as necessary to control pain.

  ◊   Encourage use of relaxation, imagery, and distraction to help manage pain.

Δ   After death, validate the loss.

Δ   Provide and clarify information and explanations.

Δ   Encourage physical contact; address feelings; show concern, empathy, and support.

Δ   The nurse should express her own feelings of loss and sadness.

Δ   Respect the family's cultural and religious preferences and rituals.

Δ   Care for grieving families during the dying process.

- Provide information to the child/family about the disease, medications, procedures, and expected events.

- Emphasize open, honest communication among the child, family, and health care team.

- Provide opportunities for the child/family to ask questions.

- Assist parents to cope with their feelings and help them to understand their child's behaviors.

- Use books, movies, art, music, and play therapy to stimulate discussions and provide an outlet for emotions.

- Provide and encourage professional support and guidance from a trusted member of the health care team.

- Remain neutral and accepting.

- Give reassurance that the child is not in pain and that all efforts are being made to maintain comfort and support of the child's life.

- Recognize and support the individual differences of grieving. Advise families that each member may react differently on any given day.

- Give families privacy, unlimited time, and opportunities for any cultural or religious rituals. They should be given **respect** for their decisions regarding the care of their child.

- Encourage discussion of special memories and people, reading of favorite books, providing favorite toys/objects, physical contact, sibling visits, and continued verbal communication, even if the child seems unconscious.

- Issues/decisions to be addressed at the time of death include:

  ◊ Organ and/or tissue donation.

  ◊ Autopsy.

  ◊ Viewing of the body.

  ◊ Sibling's attendance at the funeral.

Primary Reference:

Hockenberry, M. J., Wilson, D., & Winkelstein M. L. (2005). *Wong's essentials of pediatric nursing.* (7th ed.). St. Louis, MO: Mosby.

Additional Resources:

NANDA International (2004). *NANDA nursing diagnoses: Definitions and classification 2005-2006.* Philadelphia: NANDA.

Chapter 14: Death and Dying

Application Exercises

1. Which of the following nursing interventions is the most appropriate when working with a school-age child who has a terminal disease?

    A. Give factual explanations of the disease, medications, and procedures.

    B. Perform all care for the child.

    C. Tell the child that everything will be okay.

    D. Reinforce that being in the hospital is not a punishment for any thoughts or actions.

2. Which of the following are ethical issues faced in the terminal stage of life? (Select all that apply.)

    _____ Nutrition/hydration supplements

    _____ Chemotherapy

    _____ Attendance of funeral by siblings

    _____ Presence of religious advisor

    _____ Resuscitation orders

3. Identify four interventions that the nurse can use when providing support to a child/family during the dying process.

4. Which of the following interventions by the nurse should have the highest priority for the family following the death of their child?

    A. Verbalizing sorrow and sadness for the loss of their child

    B. Discouraging the family from holding or touching the child

    C. Asking the family to immediately leave the room so that all medical equipment can be removed

    D. Allowing the family time to be alone with the child

Chapter 14: Death and Dying

Application Exercises Answer Key

1. Which of the following nursing interventions is the most appropriate when working with a school-age child who has a terminal disease?

   A. Give factual explanations of the disease, medications, and procedures.

   B. Perform all care for the child.

   C. Tell the child that everything will be okay.

   D. Reinforce that being in the hospital is not a punishment for any thoughts or actions.

School-age children can best be helped by giving them factual information. It is important for the school-age child to maintain some level of participation in self-care to maintain independence and self-esteem. Telling the child that everything will be okay is giving false reassurance and will not help the child develop trust in the caregiver. It is the preschool child who thinks that her actions can cause bad things to happen.

2. Which of the following are ethical issues faced in the terminal stage of life? (Select all that apply.)

   _X_ Nutrition/hydration supplements

   _X_ Chemotherapy

   _____ Attendance of funeral by siblings

   _____ Presence of religious advisor

   _X_ Resuscitation orders

Use of nutrition/hydration supplements, chemotherapy, and resuscitation are ethical concerns, as their use may prolong the life of a terminally ill child. Siblings attending a funeral, and the presence of religious advisors, are individual and personal decisions made by the family.

3. Identify four interventions that the nurse can use when providing support to a child/family during the dying process.

Establish rapport and develop a therapeutic relationship with the child/family.

Schedule time for the child/family to have uninterrupted time together.

Provide factual information and answer questions directly and honestly.

Make a referral for professional support and counseling if indicated.

Assess and monitor pain frequently. Ensure that adequate pain management is provided.

4. Which of the following interventions by the nurse should have the highest priority for the family following the death of their child?

    A. Verbalizing sorrow and sadness for the loss of their child

    B. Discouraging the family from holding or touching the child

    C. Asking the family to immediately leave the room so that all medical equipment can be removed

    D. Allowing the family time to be alone with the child

It will be most beneficial for the family to be alone with the child right after the child has died. This allows the family time to see and touch the child in privacy and express feelings they may feel uncomfortable doing in front of others. Verbalizing sorrow and sadness may be beneficial to the family; however, this is not the highest priority. The family should be encouraged to touch and hold the child. It will be important to remove all necessary medical equipment; however, if the child has just died, this again is not the highest priority.

Unit 2   Nursing Care of Children with System Disorders
Section: Nursing Care of Children with Respiratory Disorders

Chapter 15:   Oxygen and Inhalation Therapy
Contributor: Diana Rupert, MSN, RN, ABD

 NCLEX-RN® Connections:

Learning Objective: Review and apply knowledge within "**Oxygen and Inhalation Therapy**" in readiness for performance of the following nursing activities as outlined by the NCLEX-RN® test plan:

Δ   Assess the child's need for oxygen.

Δ   Assist with relevant laboratory, diagnostic, and therapeutic procedures within the nursing role, including:

- Client preparation for the procedure.
- Client teaching (before and following the procedure).
- Accurate collection of specimens.
- Evaluation of the child's response to the procedure.
- Planning and implementing body system-specific interventions as appropriate.
- Monitoring and taking actions to prevent or minimize the risk of complications.
- Accurate interpretation of procedure results.

Δ   Perform and document appropriate assessments based on the child's problem.

Δ   Apply knowledge of pathophysiology to planning care for clients with specific alterations in body systems, including recognizing associated signs and symptoms.

Δ   Interpret data that need to be reported immediately.

Δ   Monitor therapeutic devices (drainage/irrigating devices, chest tubes), if inserted, for proper functioning.

Δ   Explore resources, make referrals, collaborate with interdisciplinary team, and ensure continuity of client care.

Δ   Evaluate plans of care for multiple clients and revise plan as needed based on priorities of care and promotion of recovery.

Δ   Provide the child/family teaching regarding management of the child's health problem.

Δ   Recognize/respond to emergency situations, and evaluate/document the client's response to emergency interventions.

Key Points

Δ **Inhalation therapy** includes:

- Oxygen therapy to increase the oxygen concentration of the air that is being breathed.

- Humidification of oxygen to moisten the airways, which promotes loosening and mobilization of pulmonary secretions.

- Aerosol therapy to deliver medication droplets via a mist.

- Artificial ventilation to control or assist with respiration.

Δ Oxygen is used to maintain adequate cellular oxygenation. It is used in the treatment of many acute and chronic respiratory problems (e.g., hypoxemia, cystic fibrosis, asthma).

Δ Oxygen flow rates are varied in an attempt to maintain an SaO_2 greater than or equal to 91% by using the lowest amount of oxygen to achieve the goal without the development of complications.

Δ Supplemental oxygen may be delivered by a variety of methods depending on individual client circumstances.

Δ Humidification is an important factor for the delivery of oxygen therapy to prevent drying and injury of respiratory structures.

Δ It is also important that oxygen be warmed when administered to children to prevent hypothermia.

Δ Hypoxemia is a condition of inadequate levels of oxygen in the blood. Hypovolemia, hypoventilation, and interruption of arterial flow can lead to hypoxemia.

- Clinical signs and symptoms of hypoxemia include:

Early	Late
<ul><li>Tachypnea</li><li>Tachycardia</li><li>Restlessness</li><li>Pallor of the skin and mucous membranes</li><li>Elevated blood pressure</li><li>Symptoms of respiratory distress (use of accessory muscles, nasal flaring, tracheal tugging, adventitious lung sounds)</li></ul>	<ul><li>Confusion and stupor</li><li>Cyanosis of skin and mucous membranes</li><li>Bradypnea</li><li>Bradycardia</li><li>Hypotension</li><li>Cardiac dysrhythmias</li></ul>

Key Procedural Points

Δ   Pulse Oximetry

- A pulse oximeter is a battery- or electric-operated device with a clip-on sensor probe that is clipped securely onto the child's finger, toe, nose, earlobe, or forehead.

- A pulse oximeter measures SaO_2 (arterial oxygen saturation) via a wave of infrared light that measures light absorption by oxygenated and deoxygenated hemoglobin in arterial blood. SaO_2 and SpO_2 are used interchangeably.

- Normal values are 95 to 100%. Acceptable levels may range from 91 to 100%. Some illness states may allow for an SaO_2 of 85 to 89%.

- Results less than 91% require nursing intervention to assist the child to regain normal SaO_2 levels. Results less than 86% are considered an emergency. Life-threatening results may start at levels less than 80%. The lower the SaO_2 level, the less accurate the value.

- Do not place sensors on extremities that have arterial catheters or are being used to assess blood pressure.

- Secure the sensor with tape, and apply a self-adhering wrap to the finger or toe to prevent inaccurate readings caused by movement.

- Cover the sensor to prevent light from interfering with the readings (e.g., ceiling lights, radiant warmers).

Δ   **Oxygen Safety**

- Place "No Smoking" or "Oxygen in Use" signs to alert others of fire hazard (Oxygen is combustible.).

- Know where the closest fire extinguisher is located.

- Educate the child and others about the fire hazards of smoking with oxygen use.

- Have the child wear a cotton gown, because synthetics or wools may create sparks of static electricity.

- Ensure that all electric devices (e.g., razors, heating pads) are in working condition.

- Ensure that all electric machinery (e.g., monitors, suction machines) are grounded.

- Do not use volatile, flammable materials (e.g., alcohol, acetone) near children who are receiving oxygen.

- Frequently assess the child whose main respiratory drive is hypoxia, such as the child with cystic fibrosis, for oxygen-induced hypoventilation.

NANDA Nursing Diagnoses

Δ   Activity intolerance

Δ   Ineffective airway clearance

Δ   Anxiety

Δ   Impaired gas exchange

Nursing Interventions

Δ   **Monitor respiratory status.**

- Assess/monitor the child's respiratory rate, rhythm, and effort, observing for tachypnea, nasal flaring, retractions, and use of accessory muscles.

- Auscultate lungs for the presence or absence of breath sounds and adventitious sounds, such as crackles and wheezes.

- Assess/monitor the child's oxygenation status with an arterial blood gas (ABG) sample, which reports the status of oxygenation and acid-base balance of the blood.

- Assess/monitor the child's oxygenation status of the blood (SaO_2).

- Assess/monitor and document the child's response to oxygen therapy.

Δ   **Common interventions include:**

- Using a calm, nonthreatening approach.

- Explaining all procedures to the child/family.

- Keeping the head of the bed elevated to promote chest expansion.

- Ensuring that all equipment is working properly.

- Monitoring the child for dry mucous membranes, nose bleeding, and irritated skin.

- Monitoring for signs and symptoms of respiratory depression (e.g., decreased respiratory rate, decreased level of consciousness) and notify the primary care provider if present.

Δ   **Aerosol Therapy**

- The process of nebulization breaks up medications (e.g., bronchodilators, mucolytic agents) into minute particles that are then dispersed throughout the respiratory tract. These droplets are much finer than those created by inhalers.

- Medication can be given through a hand-held nebulizer held by the child. This is a small machine that changes a medication solution into a mist.

- A small plastic mask is held over the child's nose and mouth while she takes slow, deep breaths through her open mouth.

- The family can rent a portable device for home use.

Δ   **Metered-Dose Inhaler (MDI) or Dry Powder Inhaler (DPI)**

- These are hand-held devices that allow the child to self-administer medications on an intermittent basis.

  ◊   MDI medications should be shaken vigorously five to six times prior to use. The child may position his mouth around the device, or place the device 2 to 4 cm in front of the mouth. The child will need to depress the canister to deliver the medication. The child should wait 1 min between puffs if taking two puffs of the same medication.

  ◊   DPI medications are not to be shaken, and the child should place the mouthpiece between her lips. The medication is triggered by inhalation.

- For both types of devices, the child should exhale, inhale the medication deeply through the mouth for 3 to 5 sec, and then hold breath for 5 to 10 sec.

- A spacer can be used with an MDI to allow the medication to stay in suspension longer.

Δ   **Bronchial (Postural) Drainage**

- Use gravity and positioning to promote removal of excessive secretions from specific areas of the lungs.

- This is usually performed three times per day and at bedtime.

- Schedule treatments 1 hr before meals or 2 hr after meals to decrease the likelihood of the child vomiting or aspirating.

- Bronchial drainage is more effective if other respiratory treatments (e.g., bronchodilator medication and/or nebulizer treatment) are performed 30 min to 1 hr prior to postural drainage.

- The treatment usually lasts 20 to 30 min but will vary based on the child's condition and level of tolerance.

- The Trendelenburg position is contraindicated for infants.

Δ   Chest Physiotherapy (CPT)

- CPT involves the use of chest percussion, vibration, and postural drainage to assist the child to mobilize secretions. Chest percussion and vibration facilitate movement of secretions into the central airways. The benefits of these techniques are controversial.

- Apply manual percussion to the chest wall while the child is in a postural drainage position. The nurse uses a cupped hand or a special device over the rib cage, and the procedure should not be painful.

- Contraindications for CPT include children with decreased cardiac reserves, pulmonary embolism, or increased intracranial pressure.

Δ **Suctioning**

- Suction catheters should be one-half the size in diameter of the child's tracheostomy tube.

- Advance the suction catheter to the end of the tracheostomy tube, or no more than 0.5 cm beyond the end.

- Suction pressure for infants and child ranges from 60 to 100 mm Hg, and 40 to 60 mm Hg for infants who are premature. Use the lower range of pressure when possible.

- Suctioning should take no longer than 5 sec.

- It is no longer the standard of practice to instill sterile saline into the tracheostomy tube prior to suctioning.

Δ **Oxygen Therapy**

- Do not allow oxygen to blow directly onto the infant's face.

- Change linens and clothing frequently.

- Monitor temperature for hypothermia.

- Avoid placing toys in the tent that could induce a spark.

- Provide oxygen therapy at the lowest liter flow that will correct hypoxemia.

Δ Discontinue oxygen gradually.

Delivery System	Nursing Implications
Oxygen hood – small plastic hood that fits over the infant's head	• Use a minimum flow rate of 4 to 5 L/min to prevent carbon dioxide build-up. • Take care that the child's neck, chin, or shoulders are not rubbing against the hood. • Secure a pulse oximeter to the infant for continuous SaO_2 monitoring.

Delivery System	Nursing Implications
Oxygen tent – large plastic tent that fits over a crib or bed that can provide oxygen and humidity if prescribed	• Use for children older than 2 to 3 months. • Set tent on high flow rate to flood tent with oxygen. Then, adjust flow meter to the desired amount prior to placing the child into the tent. Repeat if the tent has been opened for an extended period of time. • An oxygen level is hard to maintain greater than 30 to 50% FiO_2 (fraction of inspired oxygen), especially if the child is restless in bed. • Keep the tent around the perimeter of the bed. • Plan care to minimize how often the tent is opened. • Monitor the temperature inside the tent to ensure appropriate level. • Use plastic or vinyl toys, avoiding soft toys and toys that are mechanical or electrical. • Keep the child warm and dry.
Nasal cannula – delivers oxygen concentrations of 24 to 40% FiO_2 at a flow rate of 1 to 6 L/min via a disposable plastic tube with two prongs for insertion into the nostrils	• This method is safe and simple, is easy to apply, and is well tolerated. • The child is able to eat, talk, and ambulate while wearing cannula. • Nasal cannula may be used by infants and older children who are cooperative. • Assess the patency of the nares. • Ensure that the prongs fit in the nares properly. • Nasal cannula may cause skin breakdown and dryness of nasal mucosa if left on for an extended amount of time. • Supply the child with water-soluble jelly if nares are dry. • Provide humidification for flow rates greater than 4 L/min. • Prongs can become easily dislodged; therefore, monitor the child frequently.
Pediatric face mask – pediatric-size mask that covers the child's nose and mouth	• Not tolerated well by children • May gain cooperation from an older child by giving explanation of need for therapy

Δ **Artificial Airways**

- Indications for artificial airways include artificial ventilation and obstruction of the upper airway.

- Artificial airways can be placed orotracheal, nasotracheal, or through a tracheostomy.

- Pediatric considerations:

  ◊ Children younger than 8 years must use an uncuffed endotracheal tube.

  ◊ Pediatric tracheostomy tubes made of plastic have a more acute angle than adult tubes. Pediatric tracheostomy tubes are softened with body temperature to shape to the contour of the child's trachea. No inner cannula is necessary, because this material resists the accumulation of dried secretions.

  ◊ Pediatric tubes made of metal have an inner cannula. These tubes have a decreased risk of causing an allergic reaction.

Complications and Nursing Implications

Δ **Oxygen Toxicity**

- Oxygen toxicity may result from high concentrations of oxygen (typically 50%), long duration of oxygen therapy (typically greater than 24 to 48 hr), and the child's degree of lung disease.

- Signs and symptoms include a nonproductive cough, substernal pain, nasal stuffiness, nausea and vomiting, fatigue, headache, sore throat, and hypoventilation.

- Interventions

  ◊ Use the lowest level of oxygen necessary to maintain adequate SaO_2.

  ◊ Monitor ABGs and notify the primary care provider if SaO_2 levels rise above expected parameters.

  ◊ Use of an oxygen mask with continuous positive airway pressure (CPAP), bilevel positive airway pressure (BiPAP), or positive end-expiratory pressure (PEEP) while a child is on a mechanical ventilator may decrease the amount of needed oxygen.

  ◊ Oxygen amount should be decreased gradually.

Primary Reference:

Hockenberry, M. J., Wilson, D., & Winkelstein M. L. (2005). *Wong's essentials of pediatric nursing.* (7th ed.). St. Louis, MO: Mosby.

Additional Resources:

NANDA International (2004). *NANDA nursing diagnoses: Definitions and classification 2005-2006.* Philadelphia: NANDA.

Potter, P. A., & Perry, A. G. (2005). *Fundamentals of nursing.* (6th ed.). St. Louis, MO: Mosby.

Timby, B. & Smith, N. (2005). *Essentials of nursing: Care of adults and children.* Philadelphia: Lippincott, Williams & Wilkins.

Chapter 15: Oxygen and Inhalation Therapy

Application Exercises

1. Match each child based on age and disorder with the most efficient oxygen administration and inhalation therapies.

_____ Oxygen provided via a nasal cannula
_____ Place in a mist/oxygen tent
_____ Place a plastic oxygen
    hood over the head
_____ Oxygen administered via a
    face mask or nasal cannula

A. An infant born with a congenital heart defect
B. An active toddler with pneumonia
C. A school-age child with asthma exacerbation
D. An adolescent who is postoperative following
    a reduction of a fractured left femur

2. Nursing interventions for a child receiving inhalation therapy in an oxygen tent include which of the following?

    A. Tuck the tent snuggly around the bottom perimeter of the bed.
    B. Keep the top of the tent closed or covered.
    C. Allow soft toys such as stuffed animals inside the tent.
    D. Maintain a prescribed temperature setting and do not readjust.

3. A nurse is caring for a child on oxygen therapy. Actions taken by the nurse to prevent or minimize the risk of complications include

    A. cooling the oxygen when administered to the child.
    B. having the child wear a cotton gown.
    C. dehumidifying the oxygen prior to administering.
    D. maintaining a fixed flow rate of oxygen administration.

4. When assessing a child removed from an oxygen tent, a nurse recognizes which of the following signs and symptoms as an early indication of hypoxemia?

    A. Nonproductive cough
    B. Hypoventilation
    C. Nasal flaring
    D. Nasal stuffiness

5. Which of the following is the most appropriate nursing intervention for a child experiencing oxygen toxicity?

        A. Immediately discontinue oxygen administration.

        B. Increase humidification of oxygen.

        C. Use lowest possible flow rate of oxygen.

        D. Monitor oxygenation with a pulse oximeter.

6. Match the following arterial oxygen saturation (SaO_2) levels with the appropriate indications associated with those values.

_____ SaO_2 saturation requiring
      nursing intervention   A. SaO_2 levels less than 91%

_____ Life-threatening SaO_2 level   B. SaO_2 levels less than 86%

_____ An emergency SaO_2 level   C. SaO_2 of 85 to 90%

_____ May be an acceptable SaO_2 D. SaO_2 levels less than 80%
      level in some illness states

7. A child with cystic fibrosis is hospitalized with an acute episode of pulmonary manifestations. Which of the following nursing interventions is contraindicated for this child?

        A. Perform chest physiotherapy three times daily.

        B. Administer oxygen at an increased flow rate.

        C. Deliver aerosolized medication to open bronchi.

        D. Teach the child to use a flutter mucus clearance device.

Chapter 15: Oxygen and Inhalation Therapy

Application Exercises Answer Key

1. Match each child based on age and disorder with the most efficient oxygen administration and inhalation therapies.

  D   Oxygen provided via a nasal cannula

  B   Place in a mist/oxygen tent

  A   Place a plastic oxygen hood over the head

  C   Oxygen administered via a face mask or nasal cannula

A. An infant born with a congenital heart defect

B. An active toddler with pneumonia

C. A school-age child with asthma exacerbation

D. An adolescent who is postoperative following a reduction of a fractured left femur

The most effective way to deliver oxygen to a neonate is by a plastic oxygen hood. The toddler should be placed in a mist/oxygen tent, allowing him to play and move around without being restricted. The school-age child may be able to tolerate a face mask and should be encouraged to do so until her condition improves. The teenager should be able to comply with directions given to maintain oxygen administration via nasal cannula.

2. Nursing interventions for a child receiving inhalation therapy in an oxygen tent include which of the following?

    A. Tuck the tent snuggly around the bottom perimeter of the bed.

    B. Keep the top of the tent closed or covered.

    C. Allow soft toys such as stuffed animals inside the tent.

    D. Maintain a prescribed temperature setting and do not readjust.

To prevent O_2 loss from the tent, it should be snuggly tucked in around the perimeter of the bed. Oxygen is not lost if the top of the tent is open, because oxygen is heavier than air and is more concentrated toward the bottom of the tent. Soft toys such as stuffed animals absorb moisture and are difficult to keep dry in the humidified tent. Also, toys that are mechanical or electronic can be a source of sparks; therefore, they are a potential fire hazard. Vinyl or plastic toys that do not absorb moisture are a better option. The temperature inside the tent will need to be frequently assessed and should be readjusted as often as needed to maintain an optimal temperature.

3. A nurse is caring for a child on oxygen therapy. Actions taken by the nurse to prevent or minimize the risk of complications include

    A. cooling the oxygen when administered to the child.

    B. having the child wear a cotton gown.

    C. dehumidifying the oxygen prior to administering.

    D. maintaining a fixed flow rate of oxygen administration.

The child should wear a cotton gown because synthetics or wools may create sparks or static electricity that can ignite the oxygen. It is important that oxygen be warmed when administered to a child to prevent hypothermia. The oxygen should be humidified to prevent drying and injury of respiratory structures. The flow rate of the oxygen should be monitored and adjusted using the lowest amount of oxygen to achieve the goal of an SaO_2 greater than or equal to 91%.

4. When assessing a child removed from an oxygen tent, a nurse recognizes which of the following signs and symptoms as an early indication of hypoxemia?

    A. Nonproductive cough

    B. Hypoventilation

    C. Nasal flaring

    D. Nasal stuffiness

Early signs of hypoxemia include tachypnea, tachycardia, restlessness, pallor of the skin and mucous membranes, elevated blood pressure, and symptoms of respiratory distress, such as nasal flaring and use of accessory muscles. Nonproductive cough, hypoventilation, and nasal stuffiness are signs and symptoms of oxygen toxicity. Other signs of oxygen toxicity include substernal pain, nausea and vomiting, fatigue, headache, and sore throat.

5. Which of the following is the most appropriate nursing intervention for a child experiencing oxygen toxicity?

    A. Immediately discontinue oxygen administration.

    B. Increase humidification of oxygen.

    C. Use lowest possible flow rate of oxygen.

    D. Monitor oxygenation with a pulse oximeter.

The appropriate intervention for a child experiencing oxygen toxicity includes using the lowest level of oxygen necessary to maintain adequate SaO_2 levels. Oxygen should be discontinued gradually. The oxygen should be humidified. Increasing humidification and monitoring oxygenation with a pulse oximeter are both appropriate interventions for a child receiving oxygen. However, neither will help resolve the oxygen toxicity.

6. Match the following arterial oxygen saturation (SaO_2) levels with the appropriate indications associated with those values.

  A SaO_2 saturation requiring
        nursing intervention   A. SaO_2 levels less than 91%

  D   Life-threatening SaO_2 level   B. SaO_2 levels less than 86%

  B   An emergency SaO_2 level   C. SaO_2 of 85 to 90%

  C   May be an acceptable SaO_2 D. SaO_2 levels less than 80%
        level in some illness states

Normal values are 95 to 100%. Acceptable levels may range from 91 to 100%. Some illness states may allow for an SaO_2 of 85 to 89%. Results less than 91% require nursing intervention to assist the child to regain normal SaO_2 levels. Results less than 86% are an emergency. Life-threatening results may start at levels less than 80%. The lower the SaO_2 level, the less accurate the value.

7. A child with cystic fibrosis is hospitalized with an acute episode of pulmonary manifestations. Which of the following nursing interventions is contraindicated for this child?

> A. Perform chest physiotherapy three times daily.
>
> **B. Administer oxygen at an increased flow rate.**
>
> C. Deliver aerosolized medication to open bronchi.
>
> D. Teach the child to use a flutter mucus clearance device.

The main respiratory drive for a child with cystic fibrosis is hypoxia. This is due to the child's respiratory center adapting to the continuously higher arterial carbon dioxide levels. Therefore, oxygen administration during an acute episode must be used cautiously. When the arterial oxygen level is elevated, the hypoxic drive is removed, causing progressive hypoventilation and chronic carbon dioxide retention. Chest physiotherapy, aerosolized medication, and the flutter mucus clearance device are all appropriate interventions for a child with cystic fibrosis.

Unit 2   Nursing Care of Children with System Disorders

Section: Nursing Care of Children with Respiratory Disorders

Chapter 16:   Asthma

                 Contributor: Diana Rupert, MSN, RN, ABD

NCLEX-RN® Connections:

Learning Objective: Review and apply knowledge within "**Asthma**" in readiness for performance of the following nursing activities as outlined by the NCLEX-RN® test plan:

Δ   Assist with relevant laboratory, diagnostic, and therapeutic procedures within the nursing role, including:

   • Client preparation for the procedure.

   • Client teaching (before and following the procedure).

   • Accurate collection of specimens.

   • Evaluation of the child's response to the procedure.

   • Planning and implementing body system-specific interventions as appropriate.

   • Monitoring and taking actions to prevent or minimize the risk of complications.

   • Accurate interpretation of procedure results.

Δ   Perform and document appropriate assessments based on the child's problem.

Δ   Apply knowledge of pathophysiology to planning care for clients with specific alterations in body systems, including recognizing associated signs and symptoms.

Δ   Interpret data that need to be reported immediately.

Δ   Monitor therapeutic devices (drainage/irrigating devices, chest tubes), if inserted, for proper functioning.

Δ   Explore resources, make referrals, collaborate with interdisciplinary team, and ensure continuity of client care.

Δ   Evaluate plans of care for multiple clients and revise plan as needed based on priorities of care and promotion of recovery.

Δ   Provide the child/family teaching regarding management of the child's health problem.

Δ   Recognize/respond to emergency situations, and evaluate/document the client's response to emergency interventions.

Key Points

Δ   Asthma is a chronic inflammatory disorder of the airways that involves mast cells, eosinophils and T lymphocytes. It is an intermittent and reversible airflow obstruction that affects the bronchioles. The child experiences frequent episodes of wheezing, breathlessness, chest tightness, and coughing.

Δ   The obstruction occurs either by inflammation or airway hyperresponsiveness.

Δ   Manifestations of Asthma

•   Mucosal edema

•   Bronchoconstriction (from bronchospasm)

•   Excessive secretion production

Δ   Asthma diagnoses are based on symptoms and classified into one of the following four categories or steps, each with increasing severity of symptoms.

Steps	Symptoms Noted
Step 1 "Mild intermittent"	• Symptoms occur less than twice a week. • No symptoms exist between exacerbations, and exacerbations are brief with frequent nighttime symptoms (less than twice a month).
Step 2 "Mild persistent"	• Symptoms occur more than two times per week, but less than daily. • Exacerbations may affect activity, and nighttime symptoms are greater than twice a month.
Step 3 "Moderate persistent"	• Symptoms occur daily. Symptoms require daily use of a short-acting beta$_2$-adrenergic agonist. • Exacerbations affect activity and occur more than twice a week and may last for several days. • Nighttime symptoms occur more than once a week
Step 4 "Severe persistent"	• Continual symptoms are associated with limited physical activity, frequent exacerbations, and frequent nighttime symptoms.

Key Factors

Δ   Asthma is a disorder that results from factors that include biochemistry, immunology, the infectious process, endocrinology, and psychosocial features.

Δ   Precipitating or Aggravating Factors

- Outdoor (e.g., grasses, pollens, spores) and indoor (e.g., mold, dust) allergens
- Emotions (e.g., fear, anxiety, anger)
- Cigarette smoke, sprays, wood smoke
- Exposure to chemicals, cold air, changes in weather or temperature, and strong odors, such as perfumes
- Foods (e.g., milk/dairy products, nuts, sulfite additives)
- Respiratory infections
- Medications (e.g., aspirin, antibiotics, nonsteroidal anti-inflammatory drugs [NSAIDs]).
- Exercise
- Animal dander (e.g., horses, cats, dogs)

Assessment

Δ   Initial diagnosis is based on nursing history, clinical findings from physical examination, and results of laboratory tests. Asthma symptoms may occur suddenly or develop over a period of time, sometimes appearing after an upper respiratory infection.

Δ   Obtain history regarding current and previous asthma exacerbations.

- Onset and duration
- Precipitating factors (stress, exercise, exposure to irritant)
- Changes in medication regimen
- Medications that relieve symptoms
- Other medications taken
- Self-care methods used to relieve symptoms

Δ   General appearance may show enlargement of chest wall/anteroposterior diameter.

Δ   During Attacks

Assessment	Clinical Manifestations
Inspection and palpation • Respiratory rate, rhythm, and effort • Use of accessory muscles • Pulse oximetry • Presence of cough • Presence of sputum – color, consistency, and amount • Skin color • Capillary refill	• Nonproductive, hacking cough • Cough becoming productive of clear, frothy sputum • Shortness of breath, agitation, and anxiety • Extended expiratory phase of respirations • Lips taking on a deep, dark red color, progressing to cyanotic nail beds and circumoral cyanosis • Poor oxygen saturation (low SaO_2) • Sluggish capillary refill • Panting, short phrases spoken
Percussion and auscultation of lungs • Chest percussion • Breath sounds	• Percussion producing hyperresonance • Inspiratory and expiratory wheezing heard throughout lung fields, becoming higher pitched • Breath sounds that are loud and coarse • Crackles

Diagnostic Procedures

Δ   Pulmonary function tests (PFTs) are the most accurate tests for diagnosing asthma and its severity.

- Forced vital capacity (FVC) is the volume of air exhaled from full inhalation to full exhalation.

- Forced expiratory volume (FEV_1) is the volume of air blown out as hard and fast as possible after the greatest full inhalation in a specified time.

- Peak expiratory flow rate (PEFR) is the fastest airflow rate reached during exhalation.

- A decrease in FEV_1 or PEFR by 15 to 20% below the expected value is common in children with asthma. An increase in these values by 12% following the administration of bronchodilators is diagnostic for asthma.

Δ   Arterial Blood Gases (ABGs)

- Decreased PaO_2

- $PaCO_2$ may be decreased in early stages of an attack due to the child's increased work of breathing. It will rise as fatigue sets in.

Δ   Chest x-ray is used to diagnose changes in chest structure over time.

Δ   Allergy skin testing is done to detect inhaled antigens.

Δ   Radioallergosorbent test (RAST) identifies allergies to specific foods.

NANDA Nursing Diagnoses

- Δ   Ineffective airway clearance

- Δ   Impaired gas exchange

- Δ   Activity intolerance

- Δ   Deficient knowledge

- Δ   Anxiety

- Δ   Disturbed sleep pattern

- Δ   Powerlessness

Nursing Interventions

- Δ   Treatment during an asthma attack includes:

  - Maintaining a calm and reassuring demeanor to decrease fear, and thus reduce respiratory effort and consumption of oxygen.

  - Administering oxygen therapy as prescribed. Monitor oxygen saturations and ABGs.

  - Placing the child in Fowler's position to facilitate air exchange.

  - Monitoring cardiac rate and rhythm for changes during an acute attack.

  - Initiating and maintaining IV access.

  - Administering medications as prescribed.

- Δ   Pharmacological Management

  - Beta$_2$-adrenergic agonists are bronchodilators that can be given orally or by inhalation. They may be used for short-term prophylaxis, relief of acute attacks, and long-term control. Beta$_2$-adrenergic agonists act by selectively activating the beta$_2$ receptors in the bronchial smooth muscle resulting in bronchodilation. As a result of this:

    - ◊   Bronchospasm is relieved.

    - ◊   Histamine release is inhibited.

    - ◊   Ciliary motility is increased.

Medication	Route	Therapeutic Uses
Albuterol (Proventil, Ventolin)	Inhaled, short-acting	• Prevention of asthma attack (exercise-induced) • Treatment for ongoing asthma attack • Minimal side effects - possible tachycardia and tremors
Salmeterol (Serevent)	Inhaled, long-acting	• Long-term control of asthma • Should only be used if also prescribed a control medication (e.g., fluticasone propionate [Flovent]) • Minimal side effects
Terbutaline (Brethine)	Oral, long-acting	• Long-term control of asthma • Possible tachycardia and tremors

- Glucocorticoids

    ◊ These medications prevent inflammation, suppress airway mucus production, and promote responsiveness of beta$_2$ receptors in the bronchial tree.

    ◊ The use of glucocorticoids does not provide immediate effects, but rather promotes decreased frequency and severity of exacerbations and acute attacks; therefore, anti-inflammatory agents are used for **long-term** prophylaxis, not for aborting ongoing asthmatic attacks.

Inhaled medications	Beclomethasone dipropionate (QVAR), budesonide (Pulmicort Turbuhaler), fluticasone propionate (Flovent, Flovent Rotadisk)	• Side effects include: ◊ Difficulty speaking. ◊ Hoarseness. ◊ Candidiasis. • Use lowest dose possible. • Use on regular, fixed schedule. • Use with spacer (except QVAR).
Oral medications	Prednisone (Deltasone)	Short-term – 3 to 10 days following acute asthma attack

- **Leukotriene antagonists**, such as montelukast (Singulair)

- **Mast cell stabilizers**, such as cromolyn sodium (Intal)

- **Monoclonal antibodies**, such as omalizumab (Xolair)

Δ   When the child is prescribed an inhaled beta$_2$-agonist and an inhaled glucocorticoid, advise the child to inhale the beta$_2$-agonist before inhaling the glucocorticoid. The beta$_2$-agonist promotes bronchodilation and enhances absorption of the glucocorticoid.

Δ   Chest physiotherapy is indicated to assist the child to strengthen respiratory muscles, promote physical and mental relaxation, and improve breathing patterns. CPT should not be used during an acute attack.

Δ   Provide teaching to the child/family about ways to avoid factors that aggravate or precipitate episodes of asthma.

Δ   Assist the child/family to eliminate allergens in the environment.

   • Avoid pets in the home.

   • Prepare meals with foods that contain no allergens.

   • Enforce no-smoking policy in house and car.

   • Keep air and heating ducts clean. Change filters monthly.

   • Keep the child's room as clutter-free as possible, eliminating unnecessary rugs, curtains, and toys.

   • Launder the child's clothing daily.

   • Encourage a daily bath/shower.

   • Promote indoor play during high-pollen season.

   • Use hot water to launder bed linens and pillows. Use nonallergenic bedding.

   • Encase bedding in allergen-protective covers.

   • Keep furniture, floors, and walls clean and dry.

Δ   Advise the child/family to avoid other aggravating factors.

   • Maintain humidity in the home between 30 to 50% with the use of a dehumidifier or air conditioner.

   • Avoid excessive temperature extremes.

Δ   Ensure adequate understanding of medication regimen.

Δ   Provide instruction in the use of equipment (e.g., hand-held nebulizer, metered-dose inhaler) to include proper use and prevention of bacterial/fungal growth.

Δ   Promote general good health practices including balanced diet, good hygiene with appropriate handwashing, appropriate exercise and rest, and maintaining follow-up care.

Δ   Limit the child's exposure to infection. An annual influenza vaccine should be obtained for the child with persistent asthma.

Δ Teach the child/family to manage asthma by measuring PEFR by using a peak expiratory flow meter (PEFM).

- The child establishes her personal best value when asthma symptoms are stable.

- This value is used to compare PEFR at any given time.

- A three-zone system is used to assist the child/family to determine how well the asthma is controlled and the need for further interventions.

Percent of Personal Best PEFR	Symptoms and Interventions
80 to 100% Green Zone	The child is asymptomatic, indicating that asthma is under good control with current treatment plan.
50 to 79% Yellow Zone	CAUTION • The child may be experiencing worsening of symptoms or an acute attack. • Increased maintenance therapy is needed. • Carefully monitor the child. • Contact the primary care provider if PEFR does not improve.
less than 50% Red Zone	ALERT • Administer a short-acting bronchodilator. • Contact the primary care provider if PEFR does not immediately improve.

Complications and Nursing Implications

Δ Status Asthmaticus

- Life-threatening episode of airway obstruction that is often unresponsive to common treatment.

- Extreme wheezing, labored breathing, use of accessory muscles, distended neck veins, and risk for cardiac and/or respiratory arrest.

- Interventions

    ◊ Establish and maintain IV access.

    ◊ As prescribed, use aerosolized bronchodilators and systemic steroid therapy to treat bronchospasm.

    ◊ Use continuous monitoring of cardiac rhythm and vital signs for side effects and response to treatment.

    ◊ Prepare for emergency intubation.

Primary Reference:

Hockenberry, M., Wilson, D., Winkelstein, M. (2005). *Wong's essentials of pediatric nursing care.* (7th ed.). St. Louis, MO: Mosby.

Additional Resources:

Lehne, R. A. (2007). *Pharmacology for nursing care.* (6th ed.). St. Louis, MO: Saunders.

NANDA International (2004). *NANDA nursing diagnoses: Definitions and classification 2005-2006.* Philadelphia: NANDA.

Timby, B. & Smith, N. (2005). *Essentials of nursing: Care of adults and children.* Philadelphia: Lippincott, Williams & Wilkins.

WebMD. (n.d.). *Find a drug.* Retrieved February 9, 2007, from http://www.webmd.com/drugs/index-drugs.aspx

Chapter 16: Asthma

Application Exercises

1. A child is exhibiting suspected clinical manifestations of asthma. The mother asks the nurse what tests will be necessary to diagnose her child. Which of the following diagnostic procedures should the nurse tell the mother is most accurate for diagnosing asthma?

    A. Arterial blood gases (ABGs)

    B. Chest x-ray

    C. Pulmonary function tests (PFTs)

    D. Allergy tests

2. A child experiencing an acute asthma attack presents to the emergency department. Which of the following medications should a nurse prepare to administer to the child as an intervention for an acute asthma attack?

    A. Terbutaline (Brethine)

    B. Beclomethasone dipropionate (QVAR)

    C. Prednisone (Deltasone)

    D. Albuterol (Proventil)

3. A nurse is providing discharge teaching for a child and family regarding management of the child's asthma. Instruction is given on monitoring the child for any adverse reactions to the prescribed medication, fluticasone propionate (Flovent). Which of the following is an adverse reaction or side effect of this medication that the child's parents should report to the primary care provider?

    A. Change in mood

    B. Difficulty speaking, hoarseness, and/or white patches in the mouth

    C. Tachycardia and tremors

    D. Fatigue and malaise

4. A nurse is providing client teaching to a child with asthma. The child is prescribed an inhaled beta$_2$-agonist, salmeterol (Serevent), and an inhaled glucocorticoid, fluticasone propionate (Flovent). The nurse evaluates that the child understands how to self-administer the medication when the child states that he will

    A. inhale the salmeterol (Serevent) medication first every time.

    B. use the fluticasone propionate (Flovent) as needed to prevent or treat an asthma attack.

    C. not use a spacer when inhaling the salmeterol (Serevent).

    D. use a PEFM before inhaling the Flovent.

5. A nurse is providing teaching to a child and his family about the use of a PEFM to measure the PEFR. The child/family is given instructions to follow based on the results of the PEFR. The child shows a PEFR of 85% of his personal best. Which of the following actions taken by the child/family indicates an understanding of the instruction?

> A. No change in treatment
>
> B. Increasing the maintenance therapy
>
> C. Administration of a short-acting bronchodilator
>
> D. Contacting the primary care provider

6. When is CPT contraindicated?

7. A nurse is assisting a child/family to eliminate allergens from the child's environment. Which of the following should be included in the client teaching to eliminate allergens? (Select all that apply.)

> _____ Avoid keeping pets in the home.
>
> _____ Prepare meals with foods that contain no allergens.
>
> _____ Enforce a no-smoking policy in the house and car.
>
> _____ Maintain humidity in the home that is between 30 and 50%.
>
> _____ Avoid excessive temperature extremes.
>
> _____ Keep air and heating ducts clean, and change filters monthly.
>
> _____ Keep furniture, floors, and walls clean and dry.
>
> _____ Dust near sleeping and personal spaces.
>
> _____ Monitor periods of exercise for exacerbations.
>
> _____ Cover mouth in cold weather.
>
> _____ Try to remain calm during periods of extreme emotions (e.g., fear, anxiety, anger).

Chapter 16: Asthma

Application Exercises Answer Key

1. A child is exhibiting suspected clinical manifestations of asthma. The mother asks the nurse what tests will be necessary to diagnose her child. Which of the following diagnostic procedures should the nurse tell the mother is most accurate for diagnosing asthma?

    A. Arterial blood gases (ABGs)

    B. Chest x-ray

    C. Pulmonary function tests (PFTs)

    D. Allergy tests

PFTs are the most accurate tests for diagnosing asthma and its severity. ABGs, allergy testing, and chest x-rays are all diagnostic procedures that will contribute to the assessment of the child with asthma, but they do not provide a diagnosis.

2. A child experiencing an acute asthma attack presents to the emergency department. Which of the following medications should a nurse prepare to administer to the child as an intervention for an acute asthma attack?

    A. Terbutaline (Brethine)

    B. Beclomethasone dipropionate (QVAR)

    C. Prednisone (Deltasone)

    D. Albuterol (Proventil)

Albuterol (Proventil) is a $beta_2$-adrenergic agonist that results in bronchodilation. It is used in acute episodes of asthma. Terbutaline (Brethine) is an oral, long-acting medication for long-term control of asthma. Beclomethasone dipropionate (QVAR) is an inhaled glucocorticoid used to prevent inflammation, suppress airway mucus production, and promote responsiveness of $beta_2$ receptors in the bronchial tree. Prednisone (Deltasone) is an oral medication used for 3 to 10 days following an acute asthma attack.

3. A nurse is providing discharge teaching for a child and family regarding management of the child's asthma. Instruction is given on monitoring the child for any adverse reactions to the prescribed medication, fluticasone propionate (Flovent). Which of the following is an adverse reaction or side effect of this medication that the child's parents should report to the primary care provider?

       A. Change in mood

       B. Difficulty speaking, hoarseness, and/or white patches in the mouth

       C. Tachycardia and tremors

       D. Fatigue and malaise

Fluticasone propionate (Flovent), an inhaled glucocorticoid, can cause the side effects of difficulty speaking, hoarseness, and candidiasis (white patches in mouth). These side effects should be reported to the primary care provider. Mood changes can be caused by prednisone (Deltasone), an oral glucocorticoid. Tachycardia and tremors can be caused by terbutaline (Brethine). Fatigue and malaise may indicate an infection but are not side effects of the medication.

4. A nurse is providing client teaching to a child with asthma. The child is prescribed an inhaled beta$_2$-agonist, salmeterol (Serevent), and an inhaled glucocorticoid, fluticasone propionate (Flovent). The nurse evaluates that the child understands how to self-administer the medication when the child states that he will

       A. inhale the salmeterol (Serevent) medication first every time.

       B. use the fluticasone propionate (Flovent) as needed to prevent or treat an asthma attack.

       C. not use a spacer when inhaling the salmeterol (Serevent).

       D. use a PEFM before inhaling the Flovent.

When the child is prescribed an inhaled beta$_2$- adrenergic agonist (salmeterol) and an inhaled glucocorticoid (fluticasone propionate), advise the child to inhale the salmeterol before inhaling the fluticasone propionate. The salmeterol promotes bronchodilation and enhances absorption of the glucocorticoids. Fluticasone propionate is a corticosteroid that should be used on a regular fixed schedule, not as needed. A spacer should always be used when inhaling fluticasone propionate, (not salmeterol) because spacers help to prevent yeast infections (candidiasis) in the mouth when inhaled corticosteroids are administered with a metered dose inhaler. A PEFM measures the peak expiratory flow rate and should be performed before or 15 min after taking medication.

5. A nurse is providing teaching to a child and his family about the use of a PEFM to measure the PEFR. The child/family is given instructions to follow based on the results of the PEFR. The child shows a PEFR of 85% of his personal best. Which of the following actions taken by the child/family indicates an understanding of the instruction?

      A. No change in treatment

      B. Increasing the maintenance therapy

      C. Administration of a short-acting bronchodilator

      D. Contacting the primary care provider

Children with a PEFR of 80 to 100% are asymptomatic, indicating that asthma is under good control with the current treatment plan. Children with a PEFR of 50 to 79% may be experiencing worsening of symptoms or an acute attack. They may need to increase maintenance therapy, continue to monitor, and contact the primary care provider if PEFR does not improve. Children with a PEFR less than 50% need to administer a short-acting bronchodilator and contact the primary care provider if the PEFR does not immediately improve.

6. When is CPT contraindicated?

Chest physiotherapy is contraindicated during an acute asthma attack. CPT is indicated to assist the child to strengthen respiratory muscles, promote physical and mental relaxation, and improve breathing patterns.

7. A nurse is assisting a child/family to eliminate allergens from the child's environment. Which of the following should be included in the client teaching to eliminate allergens? (Select all that apply.)

   X **Avoid keeping pets in the home.**

   X **Prepare meals with foods that contain no allergens.**

   X **Enforce a no-smoking policy in the house and car.**

   X **Maintain humidity in the home that is between 30 and 50%.**

   _____ Avoid excessive temperature extremes.

   X **Keep air and heating ducts clean, and change filters monthly.**

   X **Keep furniture, floors, and walls clean and dry.**

   X **Dust near sleeping and personal spaces.**

   _____ Monitor periods of exercise for exacerbations.

   _____ Cover mouth in cold weather.

   _____ Try to remain calm during periods of extreme emotions (e.g., fear, anxiety, anger).

Asthma is a disorder that results from factors that include biochemistry, immunology, the infectious process, endocrinology, and psychosocial features. All of the selections are precipitative or aggravating factors of asthma. Temperature extremes, exercise, and emotions may trigger asthma but are not classified as allergens.

Unit 2   Nursing Care of Children with System Disorders

Section: Nursing Care of Children with Respiratory Disorders

Chapter 17:   Tonsillitis and Tonsillectomy
Contributor: Diana Rupert, MSN, RN, ABD

 **NCLEX-RN® Connections:**

> **Learning Objective**: Review and apply knowledge within "**Tonsillitis and Tonsillectomy**" in readiness for performance of the following nursing activities as outlined by the NCLEX-RN® test plan:
>
> Δ   Assist with relevant laboratory, diagnostic, and therapeutic procedures within the nursing role, including:
>
>   • Client preparation for the procedure.
>
>   • Client teaching (before and following the procedure).
>
>   • Accurate collection of specimens.
>
>   • Evaluation of the child's response to the procedure.
>
>   • Planning and implementing body system-specific interventions as appropriate.
>
>   • Monitoring and taking actions to prevent or minimize the risk of complications.
>
>   • Accurate interpretation of procedure results.
>
> Δ   Perform and document appropriate assessments based on the child's problem.
>
> Δ   Apply knowledge of pathophysiology to planning care for clients with specific alterations in body systems, including recognizing associated signs and symptoms.
>
> Δ   Interpret data that need to be reported immediately.
>
> Δ   Monitor therapeutic devices (drainage/irrigating devices, chest tubes), if inserted, for proper functioning.
>
> Δ   Explore resources, make referrals, collaborate with interdisciplinary team, and ensure continuity of client care.
>
> Δ   Evaluate plans of care for multiple clients and revise plan as needed based on priorities of care and promotion of recovery.
>
> Δ   Provide the child/family teaching regarding management of the child's health problem.
>
> Δ   Recognize/respond to emergency situations, and evaluate/document the client's response to emergency interventions.

Key Points

Δ   Tonsils are masses of lymph-type tissue found in the pharyngeal area. They filter pathogenic organisms (viral and bacterial), which helps to protect the respiratory and gastrointestinal tracts. In addition, they contribute to antibody formation.

Δ   Palatine tonsils are located on both sides of the oropharynx. These are the tonsils removed during a tonsillectomy.

Δ   Other tonsils are the pharyngeal tonsils, also known as the adenoids. These are removed during an adenoidectomy.

Δ   Tonsils are highly vascular, which helps them to perform their function of protecting against infection, because foreign materials, such as viral or bacterial organisms, enter the body through the mouth.

Δ   In some instances, enlarged tonsils can block the nose and throat. This can interfere with normal breathing, nasal and sinus drainage, sleeping, swallowing, and speaking.

Δ   Enlarged tonsils can also disrupt the normal functioning of the eustachian tube, which can impede hearing.

Δ   Acute tonsillitis occurs when the tonsils become inflamed and reddened. Small patches of yellowish pus also may become visible. Acute tonsillitis may become chronic.

Δ   Contraindications to either a tonsillectomy or adenoidectomy include the presence of a cleft palate, acute infection, blood dyscrasias, and/or uncontrolled systemic illness.

Key Factors

Δ   A viral or bacterial agent may cause tonsillitis.

Δ   Tonsillitis is common in younger children due to their immature immune systems.

Assessment

Δ   Signs and symptoms include:

- History of otitis media and hearing difficulties.

- Reports of sore throat with difficulty swallowing.

- Presence of fever.

- Tonsil inflammation with redness and edema.

- Mouth odor.

- Mouth breathing.
- Snoring.
- Nasal qualities in the voice.

Diagnostic Procedures

Δ   Throat culture for group A β-hemolytic streptococci (GABHS)

Δ   Preoperative complete blood count (CBC) to assess for anemia and infection

NANDA Nursing Diagnoses

Δ   Ineffective airway clearance

Δ   Anxiety

Δ   Ineffective breathing pattern

Δ   Communication: impaired verbal

Δ   Fluid volume deficit

Δ   Infection

Δ   Imbalanced nutrition: less than body requirements

Δ   Acute pain

Nursing Interventions

Δ   Tonsillitis

- Symptomatic treatment for viral tonsillitis includes rest, fluids, warm salt-water gargles, and acetaminophen (Tylenol) or ibuprofen (Advil) for pain.
- Treat bacterial tonsillitis with appropriate antibiotic therapy.

Δ   Tonsillectomy

- Preoperative interventions
    ◊   Encourage warm salt-water gargles and the use of throat lozenges.
    ◊   Provide prescribed analgesic elixirs (e.g., acetaminophen and codeine).
    ◊   Administer antipyretics to decrease fever.
    ◊   Administer antibiotics as prescribed.
    ◊   Encourage fluid intake and monitor hydration status of the child (until required NPO status).

- Postoperative care

Positioning	• Position the child on his side to facilitate drainage. • Elevate the head of the child's bed when he is fully awake.
Assessment	• Assess the child for signs of bleeding, which include frequent swallowing, clearing the throat, restlessness, bright red emesis, tachycardia, and/or pallor. • Assess the child's airway and vital signs. • Monitor the child for any difficulty breathing related to oral secretions, edema, and/or bleeding.
Comfort measures	• Provide an ice collar and analgesics. • Keep the child's throat moist. • Administer pain medication for the first 24 hr.
Diet	• Encourage clear liquids and fluids after a return of the gag reflex, avoiding red-colored liquids and milk-based foods initially. • Advance diet with soft, bland foods.
Instruction	• Discourage coughing, throat clearing, and nose blowing in order to protect the surgical site. • Refrain from placing pointed objects in the back of the mouth. • Alert parents that there may be clots or blood-tinged mucous in vomitus.

- Discharge

    ◊ The child must be able to tolerate oral fluids and soft foods, and void prior to discharge.

- Instructions to the child and family include:

    ◊ Calling the primary care provider if the child experiences difficulty breathing, bright red bleeding, lack of oral intake, an increase in pain, and/or any signs of infection.

    ◊ Not putting anything sharp in the mouth, such as an ice-cream stick, straw, or any pointed object.

    ◊ Administering pain medications for discomfort.

    ◊ Encouraging fluid intake and diet advancement to a soft diet with no spicy foods or hard, sharp foods like corn chips.

    ◊ Limiting strenuous activity and physical play with no swimming for 2 weeks.

    ◊ Instructing the child and family that full recovery usually occurs within 10 days to 2 weeks.

Complications and Nursing Implications

- Δ Hemorrhage

  - Use a good light source and possibly a tongue depressor to directly observe the child's throat.

  - Assess the child for signs of bleeding (e.g., tachycardia, repeated swallowing and clearing of throat, hemoptysis). Hypotension is a late sign of shock.

  - Contact the primary care provider immediately if there is any indication of bleeding.

- Δ Bleeding can occur either immediately or several days after the procedure. Discharge instructions must be carefully followed.

- Δ Chronically infected tonsils may pose a potential threat to other parts of the body. Some children who have frequent bouts with severe tonsillitis may develop other diseases, such as rheumatic fever and kidney infection.

Primary Reference:

Hockenberry, M., Wilson, D., Winkelstein, M. (2005). *Wong's essentials of pediatric nursing care.* (7th ed.). St. Louis, MO: Mosby.

Additional Resources:

NANDA International (2004). *NANDA nursing diagnoses: Definitions and classification 2005-2006.* Philadelphia: NANDA.

Timby, B. & Smith, N. (2005). *Essentials of nursing: Care of adults and children.* Philadelphia: Lippincott, Williams & Wilkins.

Chapter 17: Tonsillitis and Tonsillectomy

Application Exercises

1. The primary function of the tonsils is to

    A. contribute to the functioning of the eustachian tube.

    B. filter and protect against invading pathogens.

    C. play a role in the formation of antigens.

    D. promote nasal and sinus drainage.

2. A 6-year-old child is admitted to the pediatric unit for a tonsillectomy. The child has the following vital signs: temperature 38° C (100.6° F), heart rate 104/min, respiratory rate 32/min, blood pressure 96/62 mm Hg, and pulse oximeter 97%. The child reports a sore throat. What is the next appropriate action the nurse should take?

    A. Record the vital signs on the chart and prepare the child for transport to the operating room.

    B. Ask the parents how long the child has had a sore throat, and document their report in the history and admission report.

    C. Notify the operating room and primary care provider of the child's vital signs and sore throat, and then await a response.

    D. Offer the child an analgesic and warm fluids until the primary care provider evaluates the child for surgery.

3. List several examples of diversionary activities that are appropriate for a school-age child following a tonsillectomy.

4. A nurse is caring for a child in the postoperative period following a tonsillectomy. When assessing the child, the nurse recognizes which of the following as signs and symptoms of postoperative bleeding?

    A. Hgb of 11.6 and Hct of 37%

    B. Inflamed and reddened throat

    C. Frequent swallowing and clearing of the throat

    D. Blood-tinged mucus

5. Which of the following nursing interventions should be included in the postoperative care for a child following a tonsillectomy?

      A. Encourage the child to blow nose gently to clear the sinuses.

      B. Notify the primary care provider if clots or blood-tinged mucous are observed in emesis.

      C. Avoid red-colored liquids and milk-based foods initially.

      D. Position the child supine during the initial postoperative period.

Chapter 17: Tonsillitis and Tonsillectomy

Application Exercises Answer Key

1. The primary function of the tonsils is to

 A. contribute to the functioning of the eustachian tube.

 B. filter and protect against invading pathogens.

 C. play a role in the formation of antigens.

 D. promote nasal and sinus drainage.

 Tonsils are masses of lymph-type tissue found in the pharyngeal area. The primary role of tonsils is to filter pathogenic organisms (viral and bacterial) in order to protect the respiratory and gastrointestinal tracts. They do not contribute to the functioning of the eustachian tube, nor do they promote nasal and sinus drainage. The tonsils contribute to the formation of antibodies, not antigens.

2. A 6-year-old child is admitted to the pediatric unit for a tonsillectomy. The child has the following vital signs: temperature 38° C (100.6° F), heart rate 104/min, respiratory rate 32/min, blood pressure 96/62 mm Hg, and pulse oximeter 97%. The child reports a sore throat. What is the next appropriate action the nurse should take?

 A. Record the vital signs on the chart and prepare the child for transport to the operating room.

 B. Ask the parents how long the child has had a sore throat, and document their report in the history and admission report.

 C. Notify the operating room and primary care provider of the child's vital signs and sore throat, and then await a response.

 D. Offer the child an analgesic and warm fluids until the primary care provider evaluates the child for surgery.

 Since the child has a low-grade fever and symptoms of a sore throat, the primary care provider may want to assess the child prior to surgery. The operating room needs to be notified that there may be a change in schedule. Not addressing the elevated temperature and symptoms immediately by phone is inappropriate, as the documentation may be overlooked. If a child is scheduled for surgery, the child is to have nothing by mouth. Also, no analgesia should be given to the child prior to surgery.

3. List several examples of diversionary activities that are appropriate for a school-age child following a tonsillectomy.

Watch a movie; play a board game; put a puzzle together; play cards; read a book; visit with a friend/family member; color a picture; play a video game; and/or make a craft.

4. A nurse is caring for a child in the postoperative period following a tonsillectomy. When assessing the child, the nurse recognizes which of the following as signs and symptoms of postoperative bleeding?

    A. Hgb of 11.6 and Hct of 37%

    B. Inflamed and reddened throat

    C. Frequent swallowing and clearing of the throat

    D. Blood-tinged mucus

Signs of bleeding include frequent swallowing, clearing of the throat, restlessness, bright red emesis, tachycardia, and pallor. The Hgb and Hct are within the normal values, with normal levels being Hgb of 11.5 to 15.5 g/dL and Hct of 35 to 45%. Expected findings include an inflamed and reddened throat and some blood-tinged mucus.

5. Which of the following nursing interventions should be included in the postoperative care for a child following a tonsillectomy?

    A. Encourage the child to blow nose gently to clear the sinuses.

    B. Notify the primary care provider if clots or blood-tinged mucous are observed in emesis.

    C. Avoid red-colored liquids and milk-based foods initially.

    D. Position the child supine during the initial postoperative period.

The postoperative diet following a tonsillectomy includes encouraging clear liquids and fluids after a return of the gag reflex, avoiding red-colored liquids and milk-based foods initially, and then advancing the diet with soft, bland foods. Position the child on his side to facilitate drainage, or elevate the head of the child's bed when he is fully awake. Discourage the child from coughing, throat clearing, and nose blowing in order to protect the surgical site. Alert the parents that there may be clots or blood-tinged mucous in vomitus.

Unit 2   Nursing Care of Children with System Disorders
Section: Nursing Care of Children with Respiratory Disorders

Chapter 18:   Common Respiratory Illnesses
Contributor: Diana Rupert, MSN, RN, ABD

 NCLEX-RN® Connections:

> **Learning Objective**: Review and apply knowledge within "**Common Respiratory Illnesses**" in readiness for performance of the following nursing activities as outlined by the NCLEX-RN® test plan:
>
> Δ   Assist with relevant laboratory, diagnostic, and therapeutic procedures within the nursing role, including:
>
>   • Client preparation for the procedure.
>
>   • Client teaching (before and following the procedure).
>
>   • Accurate collection of specimens.
>
>   • Evaluation of the child's response to the procedure.
>
>   • Planning and implementing body system-specific interventions as appropriate.
>
>   • Monitoring and taking actions to prevent or minimize the risk of complications.
>
>   • Accurate interpretation of procedure results.
>
> Δ   Perform and document appropriate assessments based on the child's problem.
>
> Δ   Apply knowledge of pathophysiology to planning care for clients with specific alterations in body systems, including recognizing associated signs and symptoms.
>
> Δ   Interpret data that need to be reported immediately.
>
> Δ   Monitor therapeutic devices (drainage/irrigating devices, chest tubes), if inserted, for proper functioning.
>
> Δ   Explore resources, make referrals, collaborate with interdisciplinary team, and ensure continuity of client care.
>
> Δ   Evaluate plans of care for multiple clients and revise plan as needed based on priorities of care and promotion of recovery.
>
> Δ   Provide the child/family teaching regarding management of the child's health problem.
>
> Δ   Recognize/respond to emergency situations, and evaluate/document the client's response to emergency interventions.

Key Points

Δ Disorders can affect both the upper (nasopharynx, pharynx, larynx, and upper part of the trachea) and lower (lower trachea, mainstem bronchi, segmental bronchi, subsegmental bronchioles, terminal bronchioles, and alveoli) respiratory tracts.

Δ Infections of the respiratory tract may affect more than one area.

Δ Infectious agents include Group A β-hemolytic streptococci (GABHS), respiratory syncytial virus (RSV), *Haemophilus influenzae*, *Streptococcus pneumoniae,* and *Mycoplasma pneumoniae.*

Key Factors

Δ Age

- Maternal antibodies offer protection to the infant up to around 3 months.

- Infants between 3 to 6 months are at an increased risk due to the decrease of maternal antibodies and the lack of antibody protection.

- Viral infections are more common in the toddler and preschooler. The incidence of these infections decrease by age 5.

- GABHS and *Mycoplasma pneumoniae* infection rates increase after age 5.

- Certain viral agents can cause serious illness during infancy but will only cause a mild illness in an older child.

Δ Anatomy

- A short, narrow airway can become easily obstructed with mucous or edema.

- The short respiratory tract allows infections to travel quickly to the lower airways.

- Infants and young children have a small surface area for gas exchange.

- Infectious agents have easy access to the middle ear through the short and open eustachian tube of infants and young children.

Δ Decreased resistance due to:

- Compromised immune system.

- Anemia.

- Nutritional deficiencies.

- Allergies.

- Chronic medical conditions (e.g., asthma, cystic fibrosis, congenital heart disease).

- Exposure to second-hand smoke.

Δ Seasonal Variables

- Children with asthma have a greater incidence of respiratory infections during cold weather.

- RSV and other common respiratory infections are more common during the winter and spring.

- Infections caused by *Mycoplasma pneumoniae* are more frequent during autumn and early winter.

Assessment

Δ Nursing history should include recent infections, medications taken, immunization status, and family coping.

Δ When reviewing systems, ask questions related to reports of sore throat, activity level, chest pain, fatigue, difficulty breathing, shortness of breath, and appetite.

Δ Physical Assessment

Assessment	Clinical Manifestations To Observe For
Respiratory rate, depth, rhythm, and effort	• Rate that is normal, slow, or tachypneic (rapid); irregular rate and depth • Depth that is normal, hypopneic (shallow), or hyperpneic (deep) • Irregular rate and depth • Dyspnea (labored respirations), orthopnea (difficulty breathing unless in sitting position), pulsus paradoxus (Inspiration causes a drop in blood pressure, and expiration causes a rise in blood pressure.) • Nasal flaring, inspiratory stridor, retractions, grunting, and wheezing
Pulse oximetry	• SaO_2 that decreases with activity • Inability to maintain SaO_2 greater than 91% on room air
Cough and/or sputum	• Nighttime or when arising, intermittent or continuous • Associated with activity or at rest • Quality described as croupy, wheezy, and/or barky • Moist, dry, productive • Color, consistency, odor, and amount of sputum
Skin color	• Cyanosis (e.g., peripheral, perioral) • Pallor
Breath sounds	• Wheezing heard on inspiration or expiration (may be musical or high-pitched)

Assessment	Clinical Manifestations To Observe For
Signs of infection	• Fever, lethargy, restlessness, and agitation • Tender, enlarged, cervical lymph nodes • Purulent drainage (e.g., from nose, lungs, ears) • Bad breath

Δ   Assessment Findings for Common Respiratory Infections

Respiratory Illness	Signs/Symptoms
Nasopharyngitis (common cold) • Self-limiting virus that persists for 7 to 10 days	• Nasal inflammation, rhinorrhea, cough, dry throat, sneezing, and nasal qualities heard in voice • Fever, decreased appetite, and irritability
Pharyngitis (strep throat) • Caused by the GABHS	• Inflamed throat with exudates, pain with swallowing • Headache, fever, and abdominal pain • Cervical lymphadenopathy • Truncal, axillary, and perineal rash
Croup syndromes • Bacterial epiglottitis (acute supraglottitis) ◊ Medical emergency ◊ Caused by *Haemophilus influenzae*	• Child sitting with chin pointing out, mouth opened, and tongue protruding • Dysphonia (hoarseness or difficulty speaking) • Dysphagia (difficulty swallowing) • Drooling • Anxiety with respiratory distress • Inspiratory stridor (noisy inspirations) • Sore throat, high fever, and restlessness • No cough
• Acute laryngitis ◊ Self-limiting viral infection	• Hoarseness as the only symptom
• Acute laryngotracheobronchitis ◊ Causative agents include RSV, influenza A and B, and *Mycoplasma pneumoniae*	• Low-grade fever, symptoms of upper respiratory infection (URI), restlessness, hoarseness, barky cough, inspiratory stridor, and retractions
• Acute spasmodic laryngitis ◊ Self-limiting illness that generally occurs at night	• Barky cough, restlessness, recurrences, difficulty breathing, and hoarseness
Bacterial tracheitis – an infection of the lining of the trachea	• Thick, purulent drainage from the trachea that can obstruct the airway and cause respiratory distress
Bronchitis (tracheobronchitis) – associated with an upper respiratory infection (URI) and inflammation of large airways	• Results in a persistent cough as a result of inflammation • Self-limiting and requires symptomatic relief

Respiratory Illness	Signs/Symptoms
Bronchiolitis – mostly caused by the respiratory syncytial virus (RSV); effect at the bronchiolar level	• Rhinorrhea, symptoms of URI: intermittent fever, cough, wheezing • Progression seen as an increase in coughing, wheezing, increased respiratory rate, nasal flaring, retractions, and cyanosis
Allergic rhinitis – caused by seasonal reaction to allergens most often in the autumn or spring	• Watery rhinorrhea; nasal congestion; itchiness of the nose, eyes, and pharynx; itchy and watery eyes; nasal quality of the voice; dry scratchy throat; snoring; poor sleep leading to poor performance in school; fatigue; and URI
Pneumonia (RSV, *Streptococcus pneumoniae*, *Haemophilus influenzae*, *Mycoplasma pneumoniae*)	• High fever • Cough that may be unproductive or productive of white sputum • Retractions and nasal flaring • Rapid, shallow respirations • Chest pain • Adventitious breath sounds (e.g., rhonchi, crackles) • Color may be pale progressing to cyanosis • Irritability, anxiety, agitation, and fatigue • Abdominal pain, diarrhea, lack of appetite, and vomiting • Bacterial pneumonia — sudden onset, usually following a viral infection

Diagnostic Procedures and Nursing Interventions

Δ   Throat culture for GABHS

Δ   Direct aspiration of nasal secretions are collected for immunofluorescence analysis to detect RSV. One to 3 mL of NS is instilled into one of the child's nostrils while he is lying supine. The fluid is then aspirated for evaluation. Use a sterile syringe without a needle.

Δ   Blood samples

     •   Elevated serum antistreptolysin-O (ASO) titre

     •   Elevated C-reactive protein (CRP) or sedimentation rate in response to an inflammatory reaction

Δ   Complete blood count (CBC) to assess for anemia and infection

Δ   Sputum culture and sensitivity to detect infection

Δ   Chest x-ray to identify infiltration in pneumonia

NANDA Nursing Diagnoses

Δ Activity intolerance

Δ Ineffective airway clearance

Δ Anxiety

Δ Ineffective breathing patterns

Δ Imbalanced nutrition: less than body requirements

Δ Disturbed sleep pattern

Δ Fluid volume deficit

Nursing Interventions

Δ Inpatient care includes:

- Closely monitoring progression of illness and ensuing respiratory distress. Observe for increased heart and respiratory rate, retractions, nasal flaring, and restlessness.

- Making emergency equipment for intubation readily accessible.

- Administering medications.

  ◊ Epinephrine via a nebulizer for vasoconstriction of submucosa and to decrease edema

  ◊ Corticosteroids to decrease inflammation

  ◊ Antipyretics to decrease fever

  ◊ Mild analgesic to decrease pain

  ◊ Antibiotics if bacterial infection is present

- Using oxygen and high humidity for infants and young children with hoods or tents.

- Using postural drainage and/or chest physiotherapy (CPT) to help mobilize and remove fluid from the lungs.

- Maintaining adequate hydration by offering preferred fluids at frequent intervals. If the child is unable to take oral fluids, IV therapy may be implemented.

- Allowing for the child to be held in an upright position.

Δ Home care instructions include:

- Using a warm or cool mist to decrease respiratory efforts. Instruct parents to expose the child to mist for 10 to 15 min by running a hot shower in an open shower stall. Discourage home use of steam vaporizers.

- Resting during febrile illness.

- Maintaining adequate fluid intake. Infants can be given a commercially prepared oral rehydration solution, and older children can be given a sports drink.

- Limiting use of nose drops or sprays to 3 days to prevent rebound congestion.

- Applying an ice bag or heating pad to the neck to decrease pain from enlarged cervical nodes.

- Properly administering antipyretics, antitussives, decongestants, and antibiotics, at accurate dosage and time intervals.

- Developing strategies to decrease the spread of infection. Strategies include good handwashing, covering the nose and mouth with hand or tissues when sneezing and coughing, proper disposal of tissues, no sharing of cups, eating utensils, and towels, and keeping infected children from contact with children who are well.

- Seeking further medical attention for the child if symptoms worsen or respiratory distress occurs.

Complications and Nursing Implications

Δ   Airway Obstruction

- Ensure proper body alignment. Position the child to promote lung expansion, gas exchange, and to prevent aspiration (e.g., prone, semiprone, side-lying).

- Perform suctioning of airway if indicated, limiting each attempt to 5 sec.

- Do not examine the child's throat with a tongue blade or take throat culture if suspicion of epiglottitis.

- Administer medications as prescribed to include epinephrine and corticosteroids.

- Carry out CPT.

- Assist the child to deep breathe with the use of a splint, and expectorate sputum.

- Ensure availability of emergency equipment.

Primary Reference:

Hockenberry, M., Wilson, D., & Winkelstein, M. (2005). *Wong's essentials of pediatric nursing care*. (7th ed.). St. Louis, MO: Mosby.

Additional Resources:

Klossner, N. J. & Hatfield, N. (2005). *Introductory maternity and pediatric nursing*. Philadelphia: Lippincott, Williams & Wilkins.

NANDA International (2004). *NANDA nursing diagnoses: Definitions and classification 2005-2006*. Philadelphia: NANDA.

Timby, B. & Smith, N. (2005). *Essentials of nursing: Care of adults and children*. Philadelphia: Lippincott, Williams & Wilkins.

Chapter 18: Common Respiratory Illnesses

Application Exercises

Scenario: A 2-year-old child with a history of recurrent rhinitis is brought by her parent to the primary care provider's office. The child is experiencing mild substernal retractions with nasal flaring. The child also appears very restless and is clinging to her parent.

1. List history questions that will aid in the assessment of the child.

2. List several ways in which the nurse should approach the child to obtain the needed physical assessment.

3. A pediatric respiratory disorder that is considered a medical emergency is

        A. pharyngitis.

        B. bronchitis.

        C. bacterial epiglottitis.

        D. acute spasmodic laryngitis.

4. A nurse is assessing a child who may have bacterial epiglottitis. Which of the following manifestations is likely to be present? (Select all that apply.)

      _____ Hoarseness and difficulty speaking

      _____ Difficulty swallowing

      _____ Low-grade fever

      _____ Drooling

      _____ Dry, barking cough

      _____ Stridor

5. Explain how most cases of bacterial epiglottitis are prevented.

6. A child awakens during the night with a dry, barking cough, hoarseness, anxiety, and noisy inspirations. The child's parents bring the child to the emergency department. When they arrive the child's symptoms have subsided. Which of the following home care instructions can the ED nurse provide to the family regarding future episodes the child may experience?

      A. Provide oxygen therapy using a nasal cannula.

      B. Expose the child to mist by running a hot shower.

      C. Treat the child with antipyretics.

      D. Treat the child with antibiotics.

7. Diagnosis of respiratory syncytial virus (RSV) is accomplished through

      A. collection of a sputum specimen.

      B. a throat culture.

      C. nasal aspiration.

      D. obtaining blood for a CBC.

8. Which of the following care techniques should a nurse implement for a child hospitalized for pneumonia caused by RSV? (Select all that apply.)

     _____ Antipyretics for fever reduction

     _____ Oxygen therapy with cool mist added for comfort

     _____ IV and/or oral fluid therapy

     _____ IV antimicrobial administration for bacterial infection

     _____ Postural drainage and chest physiotherapy

     _____ Routine intubation to protect the airway

Chapter 18: Common Respiratory Illnesses

Application Exercises Answer Key

Scenario: A 2-year-old child with a history of recurrent rhinitis is brought by her parent to the primary care provider's office. The child is experiencing mild substernal retractions with nasal flaring. The child also appears very restless and is clinging to her parent.

1. List history questions that will aid in the assessment of the child.

   When did the symptoms begin?

   What were the initial symptoms?

   What signs were noticed as the disease progressed?

   Is the child sleeping at night?

   How is the child's appetite?

   What is the child's fluid intake?

   Has the child typically been this restless around strangers at the provider's office?

   Is this the most restless the child has been?

2. List several ways in which the nurse should approach the child to obtain the needed physical assessment.

   Calmly talk with the child and parent. The parent's acceptance of the nurse is important in having the child accept the nurse. Smile pleasantly. Be patient. It may take some time for acceptance.

   Let the child use the stethoscope or play with a harmless piece of medical equipment. Use objects for diversional activity. Maybe the wallpaper or calendar could be a topic at the level of the toddler.

   If the child brings a toy, talk about the toy. Play with the child briefly. If the child has a doll, listen to the doll's heart.

   Let the child sit on the parent's lap or hug the parent while the nurse listens to the heart and lungs. It is difficult to hear heart and lung sounds when the child is restless or crying. If the child drifts off to sleep, this would be the best time to assess the child.

   Include the toddler in conversation whenever possible.

3. A pediatric respiratory disorder that is considered a medical emergency is

        A. pharyngitis.

        B. bronchitis.

        C. bacterial epiglottitis.

        D. acute spasmodic laryngitis.

Bacterial epiglottitis causes rapidly progressive respiratory distress, often leading to complete airway obstruction. Pharyngitis (sore throat, sometimes caused by GABHS) is painful but not an emergency situation. Bronchitis and acute spasmodic laryngitis are both self-limiting disorders.

4. A nurse is assessing a child who may have bacterial epiglottitis. Which of the following manifestations is likely to be present? (Select all that apply.)

       X   **Hoarseness and difficulty speaking**

       X   **Difficulty swallowing**

       _____ Low-grade fever

       X   **Drooling**

       _____ Dry, barking cough

       X   **Stridor**

A child ill with epiglottitis typically exhibits dysphonia (hoarseness or difficulty speaking), dysphagia (difficulty swallowing), drooling, and anxiety with respiratory distress. Inspiratory stridor (noisy inspirations) is also common. The child usually has a high fever, not a low-grade fever. A cough is not present.

5. Explain how most cases of bacterial epiglottitis are prevented.

Routine immunization with Haemophilus influenzae type B (Hib) vaccine prevents most cases of bacterial epiglottitis.

6. A child awakens during the night with a dry, barking cough, hoarseness, anxiety, and noisy inspirations. The child's parents bring the child to the emergency department. When they arrive, the child's symptoms have subsided. Which of the following home care instructions can the ED nurse provide to the family regarding future episodes the child may experience?

        A. Provide oxygen therapy using a nasal cannula.

        B. Expose the child to mist by running a hot shower.

        C. Treat the child with antipyretics.

        D. Treat the child with antibiotics.

This child has manifestations of acute spasmodic laryngitis, which often subsides when the child is placed in a warm, steamy bathroom or uses a cool mist humidifier at home. Home oxygen therapy is unnecessary, since oxygen saturation levels should be within normal limits. Antipyretic and antibiotic agents are not necessary for acute spasmodic laryngitis, since fever and infection are not present.

7. Diagnosis of respiratory syncytial virus (RSV) is accomplished through

        A. collection of a sputum specimen.

        B. a throat culture.

        C. nasal aspiration.

        D. obtaining blood for a CBC.

A positive diagnosis of RSV may be made by obtaining a direct aspiration of nasal secretions to check for immunofluorescence. A sputum specimen may be collected to test for an infection such as bacterial pneumonia. Throat cultures may be used to test for GABHS (strep throat). The CBC may be useful in testing for anemia or the presence of generalized infection.

8. Which of the following care techniques should a nurse implement for a child hospitalized for pneumonia caused by RSV? (Select all that apply.)

     __X__ **Antipyretics for fever reduction**

     __X__ **Oxygen therapy with cool mist added for comfort**

     __X__ **IV and/or oral fluid therapy**

     _____ IV antimicrobial administration for bacterial infection

     __X__ **Postural drainage and chest physiotherapy**

     _____ Routine intubation to protect the airway

Antipyretics, such as acetaminophen (Tylenol), reduce fever associated with pneumonia. Oxygen therapy is used to return oxygen saturation to normal levels and relieve dyspnea, and cool mist humidifies the airway and can provide increased comfort for the child. Fluid loss is common with pneumonia and IV and/or oral rehydration is often indicated (although caution should be used with oral fluids so that aspiration does not occur). Postural drainage and chest physiotherapy are used to mobilize and remove fluid from lungs. RSV pneumonia is caused by a virus; therefore, antimicrobial therapy would not be indicated. Intubation of the airway would never be routine for children with pneumonia and would be indicated only for respiratory failure or for a severely compromised airway.

Unit 2   Nursing Care of Children with System Disorders
Section: Nursing Care of Children with Respiratory Disorders

Chapter 19:   Cystic Fibrosis

Contributor: Diana Rupert, MSN, RN, ABD

 NCLEX-RN® Connections:

Learning Objective: Review and apply knowledge within "**Cystic Fibrosis**" in readiness for performance of the following nursing activities as outlined by the NCLEX-RN® test plan:

Δ   Assist with relevant laboratory, diagnostic, and therapeutic procedures within the nursing role, including:

- Client preparation for the procedure.
- Client teaching (before and following the procedure).
- Accurate collection of specimens.
- Evaluation of the child's response to the procedure.
- Planning and implementing body system-specific interventions as appropriate.
- Monitoring and taking actions to prevent or minimize the risk of complications.
- Accurate interpretation of procedure results.

Δ   Perform and document appropriate assessments based on the child's problem.

Δ   Apply knowledge of pathophysiology to planning care for clients with specific alterations in body systems, including recognizing associated signs and symptoms.

Δ   Interpret data that need to be reported immediately.

Δ   Monitor therapeutic devices (drainage/irrigating devices, chest tubes), if inserted, for proper functioning.

Δ   Explore resources, make referrals, collaborate with interdisciplinary team, and ensure continuity of client care.

Δ   Evaluate plans of care for multiple clients and revise plan as needed based on priorities of care and promotion of recovery.

Δ   Provide the child/family teaching regarding management of the child's health problem.

Δ   Recognize/respond to emergency situations, and evaluate/document the client's response to emergency interventions.

📖 Key Points/Key Factors

- Δ   Cystic fibrosis is hereditary and transmitted as an autosomal recessive trait; thus, both parents must be carriers of the gene.

- Δ   Cystic fibrosis is a dysfunction of the exocrine glands, causing the glands to produce thick, tenacious mucus.

- Δ   Major organs affected are the lungs, pancreas, and liver.

- Δ   Initial symptoms of cystic fibrosis may occur at varying ages during infancy, childhood, or adolescence.

- Δ   Thick mucus obstructs the respiratory passages, causing trapped air and overinflation of the lungs.

- Δ   Abnormally thick mucus leads to obstruction of the secretory ducts of the pancreas, liver, and reproductive organs, which alters the functions of those organs.

- Δ   Sweat and salivary glands excrete excessive electrolytes, specifically sodium and chloride.

- Δ   The multisystem disease results in increased viscosity of secretions, causing obstruction of small pathways in various organs (e.g., bronchioles, pancreas, small intestine, bile ducts).

- Δ   Chronic, recurrent respiratory infections are a classic sign of the disease process. Atelectasis and small lung abscess are common early complications. Bronchiectasis and emphysema may develop with pulmonary fibrosis.

Assessment

- Δ   Meconium ileus at birth manifested as distention of the abdomen, vomiting (may be bile-stained), and inability to pass stool

Δ   System-Specific Assessment

System	Assessment	Clinical Manifestations
Respiratory	• Respiratory rate, rhythm, and effort • Use of accessory muscles • Pulse oximetry • Presence of cough • Presence of sputum – color, consistency, and amount • Breath sounds	• Fatigue • Chronic cough • Thick, yellow-grey mucous • Positive sputum culture (e.g., *Pseudomonas aeruginosa, Haemophilus influenzae*) • Fever • Shortness of breath, dyspnea, and wheezing • Cyanosis • Difficulty exhaling air, resulting in hyperinflation of the lungs • Barrel-shaped chest • Clubbing of the fingers and toes
Gastrointestinal	• I&O • Weight • Stool • Bowel sounds • Palpation for tenderness	• Large, loose, fatty, sticky, foul-smelling stools • Impaired digestion • Failure to gain weight • Delayed growth patterns • Distended abdomen • Thin arms and legs • Atrophy of buttocks and thighs
Integumentary	• Color • Nails • Peripheral pulses	• Positive sweat chloride test • Sweat, tears, and saliva abnormally salty • Report of salty taste when kissing the child
Growth and Reproduction	• Height and weight • Development of secondary sex characteristics	• Delayed puberty • Viscous cervical mucous • Decreased or absent sperm count

Diagnostic Procedures

Δ   A diagnosis of cystic fibrosis includes:

• Family history.

• Sweat chloride test that measures the amount of chloride in skin sweat. Normal chloride concentration of sweat less than 40 mEq/L. Infants with values greater than 40 mEq/L are suggestive of cystic fibrosis, and children with values greater than 60 mEq/L indicate the presence of cystic fibrosis.

• Absence of pancreatic enzymes.

• Chronic respiratory problems.

Δ   A chest x-ray may indicate diffuse atelectasis and obstructive emphysema.

△ A stool analysis can indicate the presence of steatorrhea (undigested fat) and azotorrhea (foul-smelling from protein).

△ Pulmonary function tests indicate overall lung function.

△ Sputum culture and sensitivity can detect infection.

△ Abdominal x-rays can detect meconium ileus.

NANDA Nursing Diagnoses

△ Ineffective airway clearance

△ Ineffective breathing pattern

△ Imbalanced nutrition: less than body requirements

△ Activity intolerance

△ Anticipatory grieving

△ Delayed growth and development

Nursing Interventions

△ Respiratory Interventions

- Promptly treat respiratory infections with antibiotic therapy.

- Provide pulmonary hygiene with chest physiotherapy (CPT) (e.g., breathing exercises to strengthen thoracic muscles) a minimum of twice a day (in the morning and at bedtime).

- Have the child use the Flutter mucus clearance device to assist with mucus removal.

- Administer bronchodilators through metered dose inhalers (MDIs) or hand-held nebulizer to promote expectoration of excretions.

- Administer dornase alfa (Pulmozyme) through a nebulizer to decrease viscosity of mucus.

- Promote physical activity that the child enjoys to improve mental well-being, self-esteem, and mucus secretion.

△ Gastrointestinal Interventions

- Administer pancreatic enzymes with meals and snacks.

◊ The amount of enzyme replacement will vary between children based on each child's deficiency and response to the replacement.

◊ Instruct the child/family that the capsules can be swallowed whole or opened to sprinkle the contents on a small amount of food.

◊ Encourage the child to select meals and snacks if appropriate.

◊ Facilitate high-caloric, high-protein intake through meals and snacks.

◊ Multiple vitamins and water-soluble forms of vitamins A, D, E, and K are often prescribed.

Δ Hospitalization

- The child with cystic fibrosis is at an increased risk for hospitalization related to pulmonary complications (e.g., respiratory infection, acute respiratory distress).

- The child will receive respiratory treatments to include aerosol therapy, CPT, breathing exercises, and assistance with coughing/expectoration of secretions.

- Perform CPT 1 hr before meals or 2 hr after meals if possible.

- Use oxygen with caution to prevent oxygen narcosis.

- Promote adequate nutritional intake, and provide pancreatic enzymes at meals and with snacks.

- Encourage adequate fluid and salt intake.

- Provide meticulous skin care and oral hygiene.

- Provide encouragement and support to the child/family by using family-centered nursing care.

Δ Care in the Home

- Ensure parents/caregivers have information regarding access to medical equipment.

- Provide teaching about equipment prior to discharge.

- Instruct parents/caregivers in ways to provide CPT and breathing exercises. For example, a child can "stand on her head" by using a large, cushioned chair placed against a wall.

- Administer antibiotics through a venous access port. Parents/caregivers need instruction in administration techniques, side effects to observe for, and how to manage difficulties with the venous access port.

- Promote regular primary care provider visits.

- Ensure up-to-date immunizations with the addition of initial influenza vaccine at 6 months of age and then a yearly booster.

- Encourage regular physical activity.

- Encourage participation in a support group(s) and involvement in community resources.

Primary Reference:

Hockenberry, M., Wilson, D., Winkelstein, M. (2005). *Wong's essentials of pediatric nursing care*. (7th ed.). St. Louis, MO: Mosby.

Additional Resources:

NANDA International (2004). *NANDA nursing diagnoses: Definitions and classification 2005-2006*. Philadelphia: NANDA.

Timby, B. & Smith, N. (2005). *Essentials of nursing: Care of adults and children*. Philadelphia: Lippincott, Williams & Wilkins.

Chapter 19: Cystic Fibrosis

Application Exercises

1. Cystic fibrosis is hereditary and transmitted as an _____ trait; thus, both parents must be carriers of the gene.

2. Which of the following best describes the stools of a child with cystic fibrosis?

    A. Hard and dry with difficult evacuation

    B. Dark-colored tarry stools

    C. Blood-streaked stools with mucus strands

    D. Fatty and foul-smelling stools

3. Which of the following are assessment findings seen in a child with cystic fibrosis? (Select all that apply.)

    _____ Wheezy respirations

    _____ Clubbing of fingers and toes

    _____ Barrel-shaped chest

    _____ Thin watery mucus drainage

    _____ Rapid growth spurts

4. Which of the following is an appropriate nursing intervention for a child with cystic fibrosis?

    A. Administer fat-soluble forms of vitamins A, D, E, and K.

    B. Administer pancreatic enzymes with food and snacks.

    C. Place the child on a low-calorie, low-protein diet.

    D. Limit fluids.

5. A _____ test is the diagnostic procedure of choice for diagnosing cystic fibrosis.

6. A child with cystic fibrosis and his parent are receiving discharge teaching by a nurse. Which of the following statements made by the parent indicates a need for further instruction?

    A. "My child should not get an annual influenza vaccine because of increased risk."

    B. "I will have my child stand on his head for chest physiotherapy."

    C. "We will encourage our child to use the Flutter mucus clearance device."

    D. "Our child will use a metered dose inhaler to administer a bronchodilator."

Chapter 19: Cystic Fibrosis

Application Exercises Answer Key

1. Cystic fibrosis is hereditary and transmitted as an _____ trait; thus, both parents must be carriers of the gene.

> **Autosomal recessive. Autosomal recessive traits are inherited when both parents carry the defective gene.**

2. Which of the following best describes the stools of a child with cystic fibrosis?

   A. Hard and dry with difficult evacuation
   B. Dark-colored tarry stools
   C. Blood-streaked stools with mucus strands
   D. Fatty and foul-smelling stools

> **Stool analysis of a child with cystic fibrosis indicates the presence of steatorrhea (undigested fat) and azotorrhea (foul-smelling from protein). The stools are large, loose, fatty, sticky, and foul-smelling.**

3. Which of the following are assessment findings seen in a child with cystic fibrosis? (Select all that apply.)

   __X__ **Wheezy respirations**
   __X__ **Clubbing of fingers and toes**
   __X__ **Barrel-shaped chest**
   _____ Thin watery mucus drainage
   _____ Rapid growth spurts

> **Wheezy respirations are initial signs of cystic fibrosis. Continued involvement can result in clubbing of fingers and toes and a barrel-shaped chest. Cystic fibrosis results in thick, viscous mucus and delayed growth and development.**

4. Which of the following is an appropriate nursing intervention for a child with cystic fibrosis?

    A. Administer fat-soluble forms of vitamins A, D, E, and K.

    B. Administer pancreatic enzymes with food and snacks.

    C. Place the child on a low-calorie, low-protein diet.

    D. Limit fluids.

The child with cystic fibrosis must be administered pancreatic enzymes for digestion. This is because the increased viscosity of mucous gland secretions causes obstruction of the pancreatic ducts and prevents the necessary enzymes from reaching the duodenum. There is a decreased absorption of fat-soluble vitamins, so the child must be administered water-soluble forms of these vitamins. The child should be on a high-calorie, low-protein diet to promote adequate growth and development. The child should be encouraged to drink adequate fluids to prevent dehydration and decrease viscosity of secretions.

5. A _____ test is the diagnostic procedure of choice for diagnosing cystic fibrosis.

Sweat chloride. This test measures the amount of chloride in skin sweat. Abnormally high concentrations of sodium and chloride are unique to cystic fibrosis. Normal chloride concentration of sweat is less than 40 mEq/L. Cystic fibrosis is very likely to be present in infants with chloride values greater than 40 mEq/L. Children with values greater than 60 mEq/L are diagnosed with cystic fibrosis.

6. A child with cystic fibrosis and his parent are receiving discharge teaching by a nurse. Which of the following statements made by the parent indicates a need for further instruction?

    A. "My child should not get an annual influenza vaccine because of increased risk."

    B. "I will have my child stand on his head for chest physiotherapy."

    C. "We will encourage our child to use the Flutter mucus clearance device."

    D. "Our child will use a metered dose inhaler to administer a bronchodilator."

The child with cystic fibrosis should receive an influenza vaccine at 6 months of age, and then a yearly booster due to increased risk of developing influenza.

Unit 2   Nursing Care of Children with System Disorders
Section: Nursing Care of Children with Cardiovascular or Blood Disorders

Chapter 20:   **Congenital Heart Disease**
              Contributor: Pam Anthony, MSN, RN

 NCLEX-RN® Connections:

Learning Objective: Review and apply knowledge within "**Congenital Heart Disease**" in readiness for performance of the following nursing activities as outlined by the NCLEX-RN® test plan:

Δ   Assist with relevant laboratory, diagnostic, and therapeutic procedures within the nursing role, including:

   •   Client preparation for the procedure.

   •   Client teaching (before and following the procedure).

   •   Accurate collection of specimens.

   •   Evaluation of the child's response to the procedure.

   •   Planning and implementing body system-specific interventions as appropriate.

   •   Monitoring and taking actions to prevent or minimize the risk of complications.

   •   Accurate interpretation of procedure results.

Δ   Perform and document appropriate assessments based on the child's problem.

Δ   Apply knowledge of pathophysiology to planning care for clients with specific alterations in body systems, including recognizing associated signs and symptoms.

Δ   Interpret data that need to be reported immediately.

Δ   Monitor therapeutic devices (drainage/irrigating devices, chest tubes), if inserted, for proper functioning.

Δ   Explore resources, make referrals, collaborate with interdisciplinary team, and ensure continuity of client care.

Δ   Evaluate plans of care for multiple clients and revise plan as needed based on priorities of care and promotion of recovery.

Δ   Provide the child/family teaching regarding management of the child's health problem.

Δ   Recognize/respond to emergency situations, and evaluate/document the client's response to emergency interventions.

📖 Key Points

Δ   Anatomic abnormalities present at birth can lead to congenital heart disease (CHD). These abnormalities result primarily in **heart failure** and **hypoxemia**.

Δ   Anatomic defects of the heart prevent normal blood flow to the pulmonary and/or systemic system.

Δ   Any structural lesion in the heart or blood vessels that is directly proximal to the heart is described as a congenital heart defect.

Δ   Many defects will spontaneously close, but some will require surgical repair.

Δ   Most children with CHD will be diagnosed in the first year of life. Although, certain children may not exhibit manifestations until later.

Δ   Children with CHD have an increased incidence of other anatomic defects, and it is important for the nurse to assess for the presence of those defects also.

Δ   Classification of Congenital Heart Defects Based on Hemodynamic Changes

Hemodynamic Changes	Examples
Increased pulmonary blood flow (left-to-right shunt)	• Atrial septal defect (ASD) • Ventricular septal defect (VSD) • Patent ductus arteriosus (PDA) • Atrioventricular canal
Obstruction of blood flow from ventricles	• Coarctation of the aorta • Aortic stenosis (AS)
Decreased pulmonary blood flow (right-to-left shunt)	• Tetralogy of Fallot • Tricuspid atresia
Mixed blood flow	• Transposition of great arteries (TGA) • Total anomalous pulmonary venous connection • Truncus arteriosus • Hypoplastic left heart syndrome (HLHS)

Δ   Specific Cardiac Defects

Congenital Heart Defect	Manifestations
Ventricular Septal Defect (VSD) – a hole in the septum between the right and left ventricle	• Loud, harsh murmur that normally is not audible until pulmonary pressures drop at about 4 to 8 weeks of age • Heart failure (HF) • Failure to thrive • Small, possibly asymptomatic defects

Congenital Heart Defect	Manifestations
Atrial Septal Defect (ASD) – a hole in the septum between the right and left atria	• Loud, harsh murmur • Many children asymptomatic • Mild HF • May have enlarged right atrium • Increased oxygen saturations in the right atrium
Patent ductus arteriosus (PDA) – the normal fetal circulation conduit between the pulmonary artery and the aorta that fails to close	• Murmur (machine-hum) • Wide pulse pressure • Bounding pulses • May be asymptomatic
Pulmonary stenosis – a narrowing of the pulmonary valve or pulmonary artery	• Systolic ejection murmur • Right ventricular enlargement • Exercise intolerance • Cyanosis with severe narrowing
Aortic stenosis – a narrowing at, above, or below the aortic valve	• Murmur • Left ventricular enlargement • Chest pain; exercise intolerance; weak, thready pulses; hypotension; dizziness; syncope
Coarctation of the aorta – a narrowing of the lumen of the aorta, usually at or near the ductus arteriosus	• Increased blood pressure and oxygen saturation in the upper extremities compared to the lower extremities • Nosebleeds • Headaches, vertigo, leg pain, weak or absent lower extremity pulses (indicate decreased cardiac output)
Transposition of the Great Arteries • The aorta is connected to the right ventricle instead of the left. • The pulmonary artery is connected to the left ventricle instead of the right.	• Murmur • Severe cyanosis appearing hours to days after birth (as the PDA closes) • Cardiomegaly • HF
Tricuspid Atresia • Complete closure of the tricuspid valve	• No blood flow from the right atrium to the right ventricle • Severe cyanosis within hours after birth (increased as the PDA closes) • HF • Chronic hypoxemia • Failure to thrive and growth retardation

Congenital Heart Defect	Manifestations
Tetralogy of Fallot • Pulmonary stenosis • Ventricular septal defect • Overriding aorta • Right ventricular hypertrophy	• Murmur • Cyanosis, severe dyspnea, clubbing of the fingers, hypercyanotic spells, and acidosis • Polycythemia, clot formation • Child frequently assuming a squatting position (decreases venous return) • Failure to thrive and growth retardation

Key Factors

Δ Risk Factors

- Cardiac development occurs very early in fetal life, making it difficult to identify cause of defects.

- Maternal factors

  ◊ Rubella in early pregnancy

  ◊ Alcohol and/or other substance abuse intake during pregnancy

  ◊ Diabetes mellitus

- Genetic factors

  ◊ History of congenital heart disease in other family members

  ◊ Trisomy 21 (Down syndrome)

  ◊ Presence of other congenital anomalies or syndromes

Assessment

Δ Mother's health status, history of pregnancy and birth

Δ Other family history of congenital heart disease

Δ Review of systems – Ask questions related to activity tolerance, difficulty breathing, shortness of breath, appetite, and developmental milestones.

Δ Family coping and support

Δ Physical exam

- Check vital signs including blood pressure in upper and lower extremities and oxygen saturation. Observe for hypotension and hypoxemia.

- Inspect the child's general appearance, nutritional status, skin color, presence/absence of clubbing of fingers, deformities of the chest, visible pulsations, respiratory rate, and rhythm and effort.

- Palpate the child's chest for thrills or abnormal pulsations.

- Palpate peripheral pulses, noting rhythm irregularities and decreased strength or inequality.

- Palpate the extremities for slow capillary refill.

- Auscultate the heart rate and rhythm, assessing for bradycardia, tachycardia, or dysrhythmias.

- Auscultate for abnormal heart sounds, murmurs, and/or extra sounds (S_3, S_4).

- Palpate and percuss the abdomen for an enlarged liver and/or spleen.

Δ Signs and Symptoms of Heart Failure (HF)

- Impaired myocardial function

◊ Tachycardia, diaphoresis, decreased urinary output, fatigue, pale and cool extremities, weak peripheral pulses, cardiomegaly, failure to thrive, anorexia

- Pulmonary congestion

◊ Tachypnea, dyspnea, retractions, nasal flaring, exercise intolerance, stridor, grunting, recurrent respiratory infections

- Systemic venous congestion

◊ Hepatomegaly, peripheral edema, ascites, neck vein distention (not seen in infants)

Δ Signs and symptoms of hypoxemia

- Cyanosis, clubbing, polycythemia, squatting (rarely seen), chest deformities

- Hypercyanotic spells (blue, or "Tet," spells) are manifested as acute cyanosis and hyperpnea.

Diagnostic Procedures and Nursing Interventions

Δ Radiography (Chest X-ray)

- Demonstrates cardiomegaly, increased or decreased pulmonary vascularity associated with congenital anomalies

Δ Echocardiography

- Confirms cardiac dysfunction in children without resorting to cardiac catheterization

Δ Cardiac catheterization

- Invasive test used for diagnosing, repairing some defects, and evaluating dysrhythmias. A radiopaque catheter is peripherally inserted and threaded into the heart with the use of fluoroscopy. A contrast medium (may be iodine-based) will be injected, and images of the blood vessels and heart will be taken as the medium is diluted and circulated throughout the body.

- Preprocedure nursing care

  ◊ Perform a nursing history and physical exam. Signs and symptoms of infections, such as a severe diaper rash, may necessitate canceling the procedure if femoral access is required.

  ◊ Check for allergies to iodine and shellfish.

  ◊ Provide age-appropriate teaching (e.g., school-age children can understand simple explanations; adolescents may benefit from watching a video of the procedure), being sure to include parents.

  ◊ Describe how long the procedure will take, how the child will feel, and what care will be required after the procedure.

  ◊ Provide for NPO status 4 to 6 hr prior to the procedure. (If the procedure is performed as outpatient, be sure the child/family is given instructions in advance.)

  ◊ Obtain baseline vital signs including oxygen saturation.

  ◊ Locate and mark both the dorsalis pedis and posterior tibial pulses.

  ◊ Determine the amount of sedation based on the child's age, condition, and type of procedure being performed.

- Postprocedure nursing care

  ◊ Continuously monitor cardiac and pulse oximetry to assess for bradycardia, dysrhythmias, hypotension, and hypoxemia.

  ◊ Assess pulses for equality and symmetry.

  ◊ Assess temperature and color. A cool extremity with skin that blanches may indicate arterial obstruction.

  ◊ Assess insertion site (femoral or antecubital area) for bleeding and/or hematoma.

  ◊ Maintain clean dressing.

  ◊ Monitor I&O to assess for adequate urine output, hypovolemia, or dehydration.

  ◊ Monitor for hypoglycemia. Intravenous fluids with dextrose may be necessary.

  ◊ Prevent bleeding by maintaining affected extremity in a straight position for 4 to 8 hr.

  ◊ Encourage oral intake, starting with clear liquids.

  ◊ Encourage the child to void to promote excretion of contrast medium.

- Potential cardiac catheterization complications and interventions

  ◊ Nausea, vomiting

  ◊ Low-grade fevers

◊ Loss of pulse in the catheterized extremity

◊ Transient dysrhythmias

◊ Acute hemorrhage from entry site

° Apply direct continuous pressure at 2.5 cm (1 in) above the catheter entry site to localize pressure over the location of the vessel puncture.

° Position the child flat to reduce the gravitational effect on the rate of bleeding.

° Notify the surgeon or the primary care provider immediately.

° Prepare for the possible administration of replacement fluids and/or medication to control emesis.

NANDA Nursing Diagnoses

∆ Decreased cardiac output

∆ Ineffective tissue perfusion

∆ Activity intolerance

∆ Delayed growth and development

∆ Imbalanced nutrition: less than body requirements

∆ Readiness for enhanced coping

Nursing Interventions

∆ General Interventions

• Remain calm when providing care.

• Keep the child well-hydrated.

• Interventions to conserve energy should include frequent rest periods; clustering of care; small, frequent feedings; bathing PRN; and keeping crying to a minimum in cyanotic children.

• Perform daily weight and I&O to monitor fluid status.

• Monitor heart rate, blood pressure, serum electrolytes, and renal function to assess for complications.

• Monitor the child's nutritional status using a calorie count.

• Monitor laboratory work including hemoglobin (Hgb), hematocrit (Hct), and serum electrolytes.

• Provide support and resources for parents to promote developmental growth in the infant/child (ongoing evaluation of growth and development).

Δ   Management of Heart Failure

- Improve cardiac function.

  ◊   Digoxin (Lanoxin) to improve myocardial contractility

  ◊   Angiotensin-converting (ACE) enzyme inhibitors (e.g., captopril [Capoten], enalapril [Vasotec]) to reduce afterload by causing vasodilation, resulting in decreased pulmonary and systemic vascular resistance

- Rid body of excess fluid and sodium.

  ◊   Potassium-wasting diuretics (e.g., furosemide [Lasix], chlorothiazide [Diuril])

  ◊   Potassium supplements

  ◊   Possible sodium and fluid restriction

- Decrease workload of the heart.

  ◊   Strategies include bedrest, maintaining body temperature, decreasing effort of breathing by encouraging semi-Fowler's position (e.g., head of bed elevated 30°; sitting up in infant seat), and possibly sedation for the irritable child.

- Increase tissue oxygenation.

  ◊   Provide cool, humidified oxygen.

Δ   Management of Hypoxemia

- Hypercyanotic spells can result in severe hypoxemia leading to cerebral hypoxemia and should be treated as an emergency. The nurse should immediately place the child in the knee-chest position, attempt to calm the child, and call for help.

- Teach the child/family about endocarditis prophylaxis.

Δ   Provide child/family discharge teaching regarding:

- Cardiac catheterization.

  ◊   Teach the family how to monitor for possible complications: bleeding, infection, and thrombosis.

  ◊   Limit activity for 24 hr.

  ◊   Encourage fluids.

- Digoxin administration.

  ◊   Administer digoxin at regularly scheduled intervals at 1 hr before or 2 hr after feedings.

  ◊   Direct oral elixir toward the side and back of mouth when administering.

◊ Give water following administration to prevent tooth decay if the child has teeth.

◊ If a dose is missed by more than 4 hr, withhold the dose and do not double the next dose.

◊ If the child vomits, do not re-administer the dose.

◊ Observe for signs of digoxin toxicity (e.g., Monitor pulse prior to medication administration for a slow pulse rate and/or irregular heartbeat. Observe for decreased appetite, nausea, and/or vomiting.).

- Diuretic administration.

◊ Mix the oral elixir with juice in order to disguise the bitter taste and prevent intestinal irritation.

◊ Observe for side effects of diuretics, which may include nausea, vomiting, and diarrhea.

◊ Observe for signs and symptoms of serum potassium level imbalances resulting from potassium-wasting diuretics (e.g., muscle weakness, irritability, excessive drowsiness, increased or decreased heart rate).

◊ Ensure adequate potassium intake to counteract potassium lost from diuretic administration.

- Observing for signs and symptoms of worsening heart failure.

◊ Increased sweating

◊ Decreased urinary output (fewer wet diapers or less frequent toileting)

Complications and Nursing Implications

Δ Bacterial Endocarditis

- The child should follow the American Heart Association recommendations for bacterial endocarditis prophylaxis. This includes receiving prophylactic antibiotic therapy prior to dental and surgical procedures (e.g., dental extractions, endodontic surgery, surgical procedures that involve the respiratory or gastrointestinal mucosa).

Δ Stroke

- Maintain adequate hydration to decrease blood viscosity.

- Monitor for polycythemia: Hgb/Hct and hyperbilirubinemia.

Δ Heart Failure Requiring Transplant

- Maintain pharmacologic support as ordered (oxygen, diuretics, digoxin, afterload reducers such as ACE inhibitors).

- Provide family and child support.

Primary Reference:

Hockenberry, M., Wilson, D., Winkelstein, M. (2005). *Wong's essentials of pediatric nursing care*. (7th ed.). St. Louis, MO: Mosby.

Additional Resources:

American Heart Association (2006). Bacterial Endocarditis Wallet Card. Retrieved December 6, 2006, from http://www.americanheart.org/downloadable/heart/1023826501754walletcard.pdf

Hogan, M. H., & White, J. (2002). *Child health nursing reviews and rationales*. Upper Saddle River, NJ: Prentice Hall.

NANDA International (2004). *NANDA nursing diagnoses: Definitions and classification 2005-2006*. Philadelphia: NANDA.

Chapter 20: Congenital Heart Disease

Application Exercises

1. Match the description of the structural defect to the correct specific cardiac defect nomenclature.

_____ Ventricular septal defect	A. A narrowing at, above, or below the aortic valve
_____ Atrial septal defect	B. A hole in the septum between the right and left ventricle
_____ Patent ductus arteriosus	C. Complete closure of the tricuspid valve
_____ Pulmonary stenosis	D. A hole in the septum between the right and left atria
_____ Aortic stenosis	E. Consists of four anomalies: pulmonary stenosis, ventricular septal defect, overriding aorta, and right ventricular hypertrophy
_____ Coarctation of the aorta	F. Normal fetal circulation conduit between the pulmonary artery and the aorta that fails to close
_____ Transposition of the great arteries	G. A narrowing of the pulmonary valve or pulmonary artery
_____ Tricuspid atresia	H. Aorta connected to the right ventricle instead of the left; pulmonary artery connected to the left ventricle instead of the right
_____ Tetralogy of Fallot	I. A narrowing of the lumen of the aorta usually at or near the ductus arteriosus

Scenario: A nurse is preparing for the discharge of a 7-month-old infant with Tetralogy of Fallot. The infant will be discharged with a prescription for digoxin. The infant's mother tells the nurse that she is uncertain about what exactly is wrong with her infant's heart and that she is concerned about giving the infant the digoxin.

2. What methods of instruction should the nurse use to help the mother understand her infant's cardiac defect? List several examples.

3. What information should the nurse include in an explanation to the infant's mother about this medication?

   A. "Do not allow your baby to drink anything after the digoxin is administered."

   B. "Digoxin speeds the heart rate up to allow the heart to pump out more fluid."

   C. "Digoxin can have serious side effects; therefore, you must be certain to give the correct amount at regularly scheduled times."

   D. "If your baby vomits a dose, you should repeat the dose to assure that he gets the correct amount."

4. For what manifestations should the nurse instruct the mother to call the cardiologist?

_____

Scenario: A 2-year-old child who is cyanotic is in the hospital for a cardiac catheterization to repair cardiac defects. The child will be transferred to the pediatric ICU following the procedure.

_____

5. Which of the following is an appropriate nursing action when providing care to this child?

      A. Place on NPO status for 12 hr prior to the procedure.

      B. Check for iodine or shellfish allergies prior to the procedure.

      C. Elevate the affected extremity following the procedure.

      D. Restrict fluids following the procedure until gag reflex is intact.

6. If bleeding occurs at the insertion site after the cardiac catheterization, the first action the nurse should implement is to

      A. apply pressure.

      B. administer vitamin K.

      C. call the surgeon.

      D. apply a tighter pressure dressing.

_____

7. Match the medication with the intended effect.

_____ Digoxin (Lanoxin)	A. Rids body of excess fluid and sodium
_____ Furosemide (Lasix)	B. Increases tissue oxygenation
_____ Captopril (Capoten)	C. Improves myocardial contractility
_____ Oxygen	D. Reduces afterload

Chapter 20: Congenital Heart Disease

Application Exercises Answer Key

1. Match the description of the structural defect to the correct specific cardiac defect nomenclature.

B	Ventricular septal defect	A. A narrowing at, above, or below the aortic valve
D	Atrial septal defect	B. A hole in the septum between the right and left ventricle
F	Patent ductus arteriosus	C. Complete closure of the tricuspid valve
G	Pulmonary stenosis	D. A hole in the septum between the right and left atria
A	Aortic stenosis	E. Consists of four anomalies: pulmonary stenosis, ventricular septal defect, overriding aorta, and right ventricular hypertrophy
I	Coarctation of the aorta	F. Normal fetal circulation conduit between the pulmonary artery and the aorta that fails to close
H	Transposition of the great arteries	G. A narrowing of the pulmonary valve or pulmonary artery
C	Tricuspid atresia	H. Aorta connected to the right ventricle instead of the left; pulmonary artery connected to the left ventricle instead of the right
E	Tetralogy of Fallot	I. A narrowing of the lumen of the aorta usually at or near the ductus arteriosus

Scenario: A nurse is preparing for the discharge of a 7-month-old infant with Tetralogy of Fallot. The infant will be discharged with a prescription for digoxin. The infant's mother tells the nurse that she is uncertain about what exactly is wrong with her infant's heart and that she is concerned about giving the infant the digoxin.

2. What methods of instruction should the nurse use to help the mother understand her infant's cardiac defect? List several examples.

The nurse should use diagrams, verbal explanation, and/or written materials. The nurse should make use of instructional software that will visually and verbally describe the defect and also provide information about the care of the infant. In addition, the nurse can provide the mother with Internet resources that could augment the information given (e.g., www.americanheart.org, www.pediheart.org).

3. What information should the nurse include in an explanation to the infant's mother about this medication?

    A. "Do not allow your baby to drink anything after the digoxin is administered."

    B. "Digoxin speeds the heart rate up to allow the heart to pump out more fluid."

    C. "Digoxin can have serious side effects; therefore, you must be certain to give the correct amount at regularly scheduled times."

    D. "If your baby vomits a dose, you should repeat the dose to assure the he gets the correct amount."

The correct amount of digoxin should be administered at regularly scheduled times to maintain therapeutic blood levels. If the child has teeth, the dose should be followed by water to prevent tooth decay. Digoxin slows the heart rate. If the infant vomits after the dose it should not be re-administered because there is no way to know if the infant received any of the medication.

4. For what manifestations should the nurse instruct the mother to call the cardiologist?

The mother should be instructed to call the cardiologist if the infant experiences decreased appetite, nausea, vomiting, increased sweating, and/or decreased urine output (fewer wet diapers).

Scenario: A 2-year-old child who is cyanotic is in the hospital for a cardiac catheterization to repair cardiac defects. The child will be transferred to the pediatric ICU following the procedure.

---

5. Which of the following is an appropriate nursing action when providing care to this child?

    A. Place on NPO status for 12 hr prior to the procedure.

    B. Check for iodine or shellfish allergies prior to the procedure.

    C. Elevate the affected extremity following the procedure.

    D. Restrict fluids following the procedure until gag reflex is intact.

Iodine-based dyes may be used in this procedure. If the child is allergic to iodine or shellfish, use of such a dye could lead to anaphylaxis. The child only needs to be NPO 4 to 6 hr prior to the procedure. The affected extremity should be maintained in a straight position. Fluids should be encouraged after the procedure to maintain adequate urine output and prevent dehydration and hypovolemia.

6. If bleeding occurs at the insertion site after the cardiac catheterization, the first action the nurse should implement is to

    A. apply pressure.

    B. administer vitamin K.

    C. call the surgeon.

    D. apply a tighter pressure dressing.

The first action the nurse should take if bleeding occurs at the insertion site is to apply direct continuous pressure at 2.5 cm (1 in) above the catheter entry site to localize pressure over the location of the vessel puncture. Vitamin K is necessary for the manufacture of blood clotting factors but will not immediately stop bleeding. The surgeon should be called, but only after the nurse has applied pressure to the site. A tighter pressure dressing may be indicated, but first the nurse must stop the bleeding with direct pressure.

7. Match the medication with the intended effect.

__C__	Digoxin (Lanoxin)	A. Rids body of excess fluid and sodium
__A__	Furosemide (Lasix)	B. Increases tissue oxygenation
__D__	Captopril (Capoten)	C. Improves myocardial contractility
__B__	Oxygen	D. Reduces afterload

Unit 2   Nursing Care of Children with System Disorders
Section: Nursing Care of Children with Cardiovascular or Blood Disorders

Chapter 21:   Epistaxis
              Contributors: Pam Anthony, MSN, RN
              Michele Hinds, PhD, RN

 NCLEX-RN® Connections:

Learning Objective: Review and apply knowledge within "**Epistaxis**" in readiness for performance of the following nursing activities as outlined by the NCLEX-RN® test plan:

Δ   Assist with relevant laboratory, diagnostic, and therapeutic procedures within the nursing role, including:

  •   Client preparation for the procedure.

  •   Client teaching (before and following the procedure).

  •   Accurate collection of specimens.

  •   Evaluation of the child's response to the procedure.

  •   Planning and implementing body system-specific interventions as appropriate.

  •   Monitoring and taking actions to prevent or minimize the risk of complications.

  •   Accurate interpretation of procedure results.

Δ   Perform and document appropriate assessments based on the child's problem.

Δ   Apply knowledge of pathophysiology to planning care for clients with specific alterations in body systems, including recognizing associated signs and symptoms.

Δ   Interpret data that need to be reported immediately.

Δ   Monitor therapeutic devices (drainage/irrigating devices, chest tubes), if inserted, for proper functioning.

Δ   Explore resources, make referrals, collaborate with interdisciplinary team, and ensure continuity of client care.

Δ   Evaluate plans of care for multiple clients and revise plan as needed based on priorities of care and promotion of recovery.

Δ   Provide the child/family teaching regarding management of the child's health problem.

Δ   Recognize/respond to emergency situations, and evaluate/document the client's response to emergency interventions.

Key Points

- Δ   Epistaxis
  - •   Common in childhood
  - •   May be spontaneous or induced by trauma to the nose
  - •   May produce anxiety for the child/parent
  - •   Is rarely an emergency

Key Factors

- Δ   Mucous membranes in the nose are vascular and fragile.

- Δ   Trauma, such as picking or rubbing the nose, may cause mucous membrane to tear and bleed.

- Δ   Low humidity, allergic rhinitis, upper respiratory virus, blunt injury, or foreign body in the nose may all precipitate a nosebleed.

- Δ   Medications, such as antihistamines that dry mucous membranes, may increase the number of nosebleeds.

- Δ   Medications that affect clotting factors, such as warfarin (Coumadin), may increase bleeding.

- Δ   Epistaxis may be the result of underlying diseases, such as von Willebrand's disease, hemophilia, idiopathic thrombocytopenia purpura (ITP), or leukemia.

- Δ   The child should sit up and slightly forward so blood does not flow down the throat and cause the child to cough.

- Δ   Bleeding may last up to 20 min.

- Δ   Medical treatment should be considered if bleeding lasts longer than 30 min.

Assessment

- Δ   History of bleeding gums or blood in body fluids and/or stool

- Δ   Amount and force of bleeding

- Δ   Length of time the nose has been bleeding

- Δ   History of trauma, illness, allergies, or placing foreign bodies in the nose

- Δ   Physical assessment for other areas of bruising

- Δ   The child's/parents' level of anxiety

NANDA Nursing Diagnoses

Δ   Anxiety

Δ   Fear

Δ   Impaired tissue integrity

Nursing Interventions

Δ   Maintain calm demeanor with the child/family.

Δ   Have the child sit up with the head tilted slightly forward to promote draining of blood out of the nose instead of down the back of the throat. Swallowing of blood can promote coughing and lead to nausea, vomiting, and diarrhea.

Δ   Apply pressure to the lower nose, or instruct the child to use her thumb and forefinger to press the nares together for 5 to 10 min.

Δ   If needed, cotton or tissue can be packed into the side of the nose that is bleeding.

Δ   Encourage the child to breathe through her mouth while her nose is bleeding.

Δ   Apply ice across the bridge of the nose if possible.

Δ   Keep the child from rubbing or picking her nose after bleeding is stopped.

Δ   Instruct the child and family on home care.

- Keep fingernails short.

- Use a humidifier during the dry winter months.

- Have the child open her mouth when sneezing.

Complications and Nursing Interventions

Δ   Excessive Bleeding

- Instruct the child/family to seek medical care if bleeding lasts longer than 30 min or is caused by an injury/trauma.

- Cauterization or packing may be indicated.

Primary Reference:

Hockenberry, M., Wilson, D., Winkelstein, M. (2005). *Wong's essentials of pediatric nursing care.* (7th ed.). St. Louis, MO: Mosby.

Additional Resources:

American Academy of Family Physicians. (2006, December). *Nosebleeds: What to do when your nose bleeds.* Retrieved December 8, 2006, from http://familydoctor.org/132.xml

NANDA International (2004). *NANDA nursing diagnoses: Definitions and classification 2005-2006.* Philadelphia: NANDA.

Chapter 21: Epistaxis

Application Exercises

1. A nurse is providing teaching to a child and his family about the management of epistaxis. Which of the following positions should the nurse instruct the child to take when experiencing a nosebleed?

    A. Sit up and lean forward.

    B. Tilt the head back.

    C. Lie down supine.

    D. Lie in prone position.

2. A nurse is providing client education on management of epistaxis. Which of the following are appropriate interventions during an episode of epistaxis? (Select all that apply.)

    _____ Press nares together for 5 to 10 min.

    _____ Breathe through the nose until bleeding stops.

    _____ Pack cotton or tissue into the side of the nose that is bleeding.

    _____ Use a humidifier in the winter.

    _____ Apply ice across the bridge of the nose.

3. A nurse is providing child/family teaching about epistaxis. Which of the following statements by a child's parent indicates the need for further teaching regarding epistaxis?

    A. "If my child has a nosebleed, I should bring him to the emergency department to prevent excessive blood loss."

    B. "It is common for children to develop nosebleeds because the skin inside the nose is fragile."

    C. "If my child's nosebleed lasts longer than 30 min, he may need to have nasal packing placed inside his nose."

    D. "I know that my child may develop a nosebleed from allergies or injuries."

4. Which of the following nursing interventions has the highest priority when caring for a young child with a nosebleed?

    A. Tell the child's parent to leave the room.

    B. Maintain a calm demeanor.

    C. Determine the cause.

    D. Prepare the child for cauterization.

Chapter 21: Epistaxis

Application Exercises Answer Key

1. A nurse is providing teaching to a child and his family about the management of epistaxis. Which of the following positions should the nurse instruct the child to take when experiencing a nosebleed?

   A. Sit up and lean forward.
   B. Tilt the head back.
   C. Lie down supine.
   D. Lie in prone position.

   Sitting up with the head tilted slightly forward promotes draining of blood out of the nose instead of down the back of the throat. Swallowing of blood can promote coughing and lead to nausea, vomiting, and diarrhea.

2. A nurse is providing client education on management of epistaxis. Which of the following are appropriate interventions during an episode of epistaxis? (Select all that apply.)

   __X__ **Press nares together for 5 to 10 min.**
   _____ Breathe through the nose until bleeding stops.
   __X__ **Pack cotton or tissue into the side of the nose that is bleeding.**
   _____ Use a humidifier in the winter.
   __X__ **Apply ice across the bridge of the nose.**

   Pressing the nares together, packing the nose with cotton or tissue, and applying ice across the bridge of the nose are all appropriate interventions during an episode of epistaxis. The child should be instructed to breathe through her mouth while her nose is bleeding. Use of a humidifier in the winter may help decrease the incidence of epistaxis but will not treat an acute nosebleed.

3. A nurse is providing child/family teaching about epistaxis. Which of the following statements by a child's parent indicates the need for further teaching regarding epistaxis?

    A. "If my child has a nosebleed, I should bring him to the emergency department to prevent excessive blood loss."

    B. "It is common for children to develop nosebleeds because the skin inside the nose is fragile."

    C. "If my child's nosebleed lasts longer than 30 min, he may need to have nasal packing placed inside his nose."

    D. "I know that my child may develop a nosebleed from allergies or injuries."

Nosebleeds are not an emergency and usually can be managed at home with proper instruction to the child and family.

4. Which of the following nursing interventions has the highest priority when caring for a young child with a nosebleed?

    A. Tell the child's parent to leave the room.

    B. Maintain a calm demeanor.

    C. Determine the cause.

    D. Prepare the child for cauterization.

The highest priority nursing intervention is for the nurse to maintain a calm demeanor to alleviate the child's fear and anxiety. There is no reason for the child's parent to leave the room. Reassuring the child and remaining calm have a higher priority than determining the cause. The majority of nosebleeds are not emergencies, are self-limiting, and do not require cauterization.

Unit 2 Nursing Care of Children with System Disorders

Section: Nursing Care of Children with Cardiovascular or Blood Disorders

Chapter 22: Leukemia

Contributor: Pam Anthony, MSN, RN

 NCLEX-RN® Connections:

Learning Objective: Review and apply knowledge within "**Leukemia**" in readiness for performance of the following nursing activities as outlined by the NCLEX-RN® test plan:

Δ Assist with relevant laboratory, diagnostic, and therapeutic procedures within the nursing role, including:

- Client preparation for the procedure.

- Client teaching (before and following the procedure).

- Accurate collection of specimens.

- Evaluation of the child's response to the procedure.

- Planning and implementing body system-specific interventions as appropriate.

- Monitoring and taking actions to prevent or minimize the risk of complications.

- Accurate interpretation of procedure results.

Δ Perform and document appropriate assessments based on the child's problem.

Δ Apply knowledge of pathophysiology to planning care for clients with specific alterations in body systems, including recognizing associated signs and symptoms.

Δ Interpret data that need to be reported immediately.

Δ Monitor therapeutic devices (drainage/irrigating devices, chest tubes), if inserted, for proper functioning.

Δ Explore resources, make referrals, collaborate with interdisciplinary team, and ensure continuity of client care.

Δ Evaluate plans of care for multiple clients and revise plan as needed based on priorities of care and promotion of recovery.

Δ Provide the child/family teaching regarding management of the child's health problem.

Δ Recognize/respond to emergency situations, and evaluate/document the client's response to emergency interventions.

Key Points

Δ   Leukemia is the term for a group of malignancies that affect the bone marrow and lymphatic system.

Δ   Leukemia is classified by the type of WBC that becomes neoplastic and is commonly divided into two groups: acute lymphoid leukemia (ALL) and acute myelogenous or nonlymphoid leukemia (AML/ANLL).

Δ   Leukemia causes bone marrow dysfunction that leads to anemia and neutropenia.

Δ   Leukemia causes an increase in the production of immature WBCs, which leads to infiltration of organs and tissues.

•   Bone marrow infiltration causes crowding of cells that would normally produce RBCs, platelets, and mature WBCs.

◊   Deficient RBCs cause anemia.

◊   Deficient mature WBCs (neutropenia) increase the risk for infection.

◊   Deficient platelets (thrombocytopenia) cause bruising.

•   Infiltration of spleen, liver, and lymph nodes leads to tissue fibrosis.

•   Infiltration of the CNS causes increased intracranial pressure.

•   Other tissues may also be infiltrated, including testes, prostate, ovaries, and gastrointestinal tract.

Δ   Clinical manifestations are related to area of involvement (e.g., bone pain, abdominal pain, and neurosensory changes).

Key Factors

Δ   Leukemia is the most common cancer of childhood.

Δ   ALL is the most common form of leukemia in children. There is an increased incidence in boys older than 1 year, with peak onset being between 2 and 6 years.

Δ   ALL has a survival rate of approximately 80%. AML has a survival rate of approximately 45 to 50%.

Δ   Children with trisomy 21 (Down syndrome) have a greater risk of developing ALL.

Assessment

Δ   History and physical assessment findings may reveal vague reports (e.g., anorexia, headache, fatigue).

Δ   Early manifestations include:

- Low-grade fever.

- Pallor.

- Increased bruising and petechiae.

- Listlessness.

- Enlarged liver, lymph nodes, and joints.

- Abdominal, leg, and joint pain.

- Constipation.

- Headache.

- Vomiting and anorexia.

- Unsteady gait.

- Low platelet and RBC count.

- Increased immature WBC.

Δ   Late manifestations include:

- Hematuria.

- Ulcerations in the mouth.

- Enlarged kidneys and testicles.

- Signs of increased intracranial pressure.

Diagnostic Procedures and Nursing Interventions

Δ   Blood Studies

- CBC normal values

Age	Hgb	Hct
2 months	9.0 to 14.0 g/dL	28 to 42%
6 to 12 years	11.5 to 15.5 g/dL	35 to 45%
12 to 18 years	13.0 to 16.0 g/dL (male) 12.0 to 16.0 g/dL (female)	37 to 49% (male) 36 to 46% (female)

- WBC normal values

◊   1 month – 5,000 to 19,500/mm³

◊   1 to 3 years – 6,000 to 17,500/mm³

◊   4 to 7 years – 5,000 to 15,500/mm³

◊   8 to 13 years – 4,500 to 13,500/mm³

◊   Adult – 4,500 to 11,000/mm³

- Platelets – normal value: 150,000 to 400,000/mm^3
- Peripheral blood smear will reveal:
  ◊ Anemia (low blood counts).
  ◊ Thrombocytopenia (low platelets).
  ◊ Neutropenia (low neutrophils).
  ◊ Leukemic blasts (immature WBCs).

Δ Bone marrow aspiration or biopsy analysis is the most definitive diagnostic procedure. If leukemia is present, the specimen will show prolific quantities of immature leukemic blast cells and protein markers indicating a specific type of leukemia.

- Bone marrow aspiration or biopsy is performed by a primary care provider.
  ◊ Apply topical anesthetic, such as a eutectic mixture of local anesthetics (lidocaine/prilocaine [EMLA]), over the biopsy area 1 hr prior to procedure.
  ◊ Induce unconscious sedation with general anesthetic, such as propofol (Diprivan).
  ◊ Obtain a specimen from the posterior or anterior iliac crest or tibia.
  ◊ If the child awakens during the procedure, two people may be required to hold the child down.
  ◊ Interventions after the procedure include:
    ° Applying pressure to the site for 5 to 10 min.
    ° Assessing vital signs frequently.
    ° Applying a pressure dressing.
    ° Monitoring for signs of bleeding and infection for 24 hr.

Δ Cerebrospinal fluid (CSF) is taken to determine central nervous system involvement, such as increased intracranial pressure.

- Collect CSF with a lumbar puncture (performed by a primary care provider).
  ◊ Have the child empty his bladder.
  ◊ Place the child in the fetal position and assist in maintaining position. Distraction may need to be used.
  ◊ Sedate the child if necessary with fentanyl (Sublimaze) and midazolam (Versed).
  ◊ Clean the skin and inject local anesthetic. If time allows, apply EMLA cream over L3 and L5 1 hr prior to the procedure.
  ◊ Insert needle into the subarachnoid space.
  ◊ Take pressure readings. Readings may be difficult to obtain if the child is crying.

◊ Collect three to five test tubes of CSF.

◊ Remove the needle, apply pressure, and cover the injection site with a dressing.

◊ Label specimens appropriately and deliver them to the laboratory.

• The child should remain in bed for 4 to 8 hr in a flat position to prevent leakage and a resulting spinal headache. This may not be possible for an infant, toddler, or preschooler.

• Monitor the site for hematoma or infection.

Δ Sonograms are used to detect liver and spleen infiltration, enlargement, and fibrosis.

Δ Liver and kidney function studies are used for baseline functioning before chemotherapy.

NANDA Nursing Diagnoses

Δ Activity intolerance

Δ Anticipatory grieving

Δ Anxiety

Δ Disturbed body image

Δ Interrupted family processes

Δ Delayed growth and development

Δ Anticipatory grieving

Δ Risk of infection

Δ Acute pain

Nursing Interventions

Δ Management of the child before, during, and after diagnostic procedures includes:

• Providing anticipatory guidance for the child/family about what to expect during diagnostic procedures.

• Administering prescribed anesthesia, such as conscious sedation, analgesia, and topical anesthetics for procedures.

• Using nonpharmacological interventions to provide comfort.

• Assessing for bleeding and infection during and after diagnostic procedures.

Δ   Assess pain using age-appropriate pain scale.

     •   Use pharmacologic and nonpharmacologic interventions to provide around-the-clock pain management.

Δ   Administer chemotherapy as ordered, following facility policy.

Δ   Manage side effects of treatment.

Side Effect	Nursing Intervention
Mucosal ulceration	• Provide frequent oral care. • Inspect the child's mouth for ulceration and hemorrhage. • Use soft-bristled toothbrush or soft disposable toothbrushes for oral care. • Lubricate lips to prevent cracking. • Offer foods that are soft and bland. • Assist the child to use mouthwashes frequently (e.g., 1 tsp salt mixed with 1 pint of water or 1 tsp baking soda mixed with 1 qt of water).
Skin breakdown	• Inspect skin daily. • Assess rectal mucosa for fissures. • Avoid rectal temperatures. • Provide sitz baths as needed. • Reposition frequently. • Use a pressure reduction system.
Neuropathy	Constipation • Encourage a diet high in fiber. • Administer stool softeners and laxatives as needed. • Encourage fluids. Footdrop • Use footboard in bed. • Assist with ambulation. Jaw pain • Provide for a soft diet.
Loss of appetite	• Monitor fluid intake and hydration status.. • Provide small, frequent, well-balanced meals. • Involve the child in meal planning. • Administer enteral nutrition if needed. • Weigh the child daily. • Monitor electrolyte values. • Administer chemotherapy early in day.
Hemorrhage cystitis	• Encourage fluids. • Encourage frequent voiding.
Alopecia	• Prepare the child/family in advance of hair loss. • Encourage use of a hat, scarf, or wig if the child is self-conscious about hair loss.

Δ   Provide anticipatory guidance to the child/family about effects of chemotherapy.

- The use of steroid treatment may cause moon face.

- The child may experience mood changes.

- Control vomiting with anticipatory treatment with antiemetics (i.e. before the child experiences nausea).

Δ   Provide emotional support to the child/family.

- Prepare the child/family for diagnostic and therapeutic procedures.

- Encourage peer contact for age-appropriate children.

- Provide information regarding support services for the child/family.

Δ   Provide instruction to the family for home care.

- Teach the family to recognize signs of infection, skin breakdown, and nutritional deficiency.

- Encourage the child/family to maintain good hygiene.

- Teach the child/family to avoid individuals with colds/infection/viruses.

- Instruct the child/family to administer medications and nutritional support at home.

- Instruct the family in the proper use of vascular access devices.

- Instruct the child/family about bleeding precautions and management of active bleeding.

Therapeutic Interventions and Nursing Interventions

Δ   Chemotherapy is used to treat leukemia. Treatment may include radiation of the brain and spinal cord.

Phase	Goal	Procedure	Length of Time
Induction therapy (places client at high risk for infection and hemorrhage following this phase)	To induce remission (defined as absence of all signs of leukemia including less than 5% blasts in bone marrow)	CNS prophylaxis administered as chemotherapy to the CSF (intrathecal) or as radiation to the brain and spinal cord	Lasts 4 to 6 weeks
Consolidation or intensification therapy	To eradicate any residual leukemic cells	High doses of chemotherapy frequently administered	Lasts about 6 months

Phase	Goal	Procedure	Length of Time
Maintenance therapy	Prevention of relapse	Use of oral chemotherapy	Lasts 2 to 3 years; boys remaining on maintenance therapy longer due to the possibility of testicular involvement
Reinduction therapy (for the child that relapses)	Primary purpose is to place the child back in remission	Combinations of chemotherapy used to achieve remission	Probability of relapse occurring decreasing over time

Δ   Some children may undergo a hematopoietic stem cell transplant (HCST).

- HCST is not indicated for all children with ALL until after a second relapse. Positive results appear in children with AML during first remission.

- HCST involves high-dose chemotherapy and radiation to destroy tumor cells.

- After tumor cells are destroyed, the child is given donor bone marrow or other stem cells, such as those cells from cord blood.

- Implantation of new cells may take 2 to 6 weeks.

- The child is at an increased risk for infection and bleeding until the transfused stem cells grow.

Complications and Nursing Implications

Δ   Prevent complications of myelosuppression.

- Infection

  ◊   Provide the child with a private room. The room should be designed to allow for adequate air flow in order to reduce airborne pathogens.

  ◊   Restrict visitors and health personnel with active illness.

  ◊   Adhere to strict handwashing.

  ◊   Assess potential sites of infections (e.g., oral ulcer, open cut) and monitor temperature.

  ◊   Administer antibiotics as prescribed.

  ◊   Monitor the child's absolute neutrophil count (ANC).

  ◊   Encourage adequate protein intake.

- Bleeding

  ◊   Monitor for signs of bleeding (e.g., petechiae, ecchymosis, hematuria, bleeding gums, hematemesis, tarry stools).

  ◊   Encourage/provide meticulous oral care to prevent gingival bleeding. Use a soft toothbrush and avoid astringent mouthwash.

◊ Avoid unnecessary skin punctures and use surgical aseptic technique when performed. Apply pressure for 5 min to stop bleeding.

◊ Treat a nosebleed with cold and pressure.

◊ Administer platelets as ordered.

◊ Avoid taking rectal temperatures.

◊ Teach the parent measures for controlling epistaxis.

• Anemia

◊ Administer blood transfusion as ordered.

◊ Allow for frequent rest periods.

◊ Administer oxygen therapy.

◊ Administer IV fluid replacement.

Δ Long-term effects of treatment include cardiotoxicity and delayed growth and development.

Primary Reference:

Hockenberry, M., Wilson, D., & Winkelstein, M. (2005). *Wong's essentials of pediatric nursing care.* (7th ed.). St. Louis, MO: Mosby.

Additional Resources:

NANDA International (2004). *NANDA nursing diagnoses: Definitions and classification 2005-2006.* Philadelphia: NANDA.

Chapter 22: Leukemia

Application Exercises

1. Match the following conditions with possible manifestations/complications of bone marrow suppression.

_____ Anemia   A. Bruising, nosebleed

_____ Neutropenia   B. Fever, pneumonia

_____ Thrombocytopenia   C. Fatigue, shortness of breath

2. A child with leukemia is experiencing severe thrombocytopenia. Which of the following nursing interventions will avoid the risk for injury based on this diagnosis? (Select all that apply.)

_____ Avoid injections and skin punctures.

_____ Wash hands frequently.

_____ Limit visitors.

_____ Monitor platelet count.

_____ Avoid rectal temperatures.

_____ Monitor for fever.

3. A child with leukemia is hospitalized with lethargy, headache, vomiting, and blurred vision. Which of the following complications of leukemia do these manifestations suggest?

    A. Anemia

    B. Hypermetabolism

    C. Increased intracranial pressure

    D. Infiltration of leukemic cells into bone marrow

4. A nurse is assessing a child with leukemia undergoing chemotherapy. The child is losing weight, experiencing nausea, and has no appetite. Identify at least three nursing interventions the nurse can use to promote adequate nutritional intake.

5. A child with leukemia has mucosal ulceration in his mouth and throat due to neutropenia. An intervention to ease discomfort from these ulcers is

    A. allowing the child to suck on lemon glycerin swabs for comfort.

    B. applying milk of magnesia to ulcers with a soft applicator.

    C. rinsing the child's mouth with NS frequently.

    D. having the child gargle with hydrogen peroxide every 2 hr.

6. A child with leukemia who has been in remission for 8 months is experiencing a relapse. The child is admitted to the hospital for treatment and prescribed a new chemotherapy regimen. Which of the following terms is used to describe the child's new regimen?

        A. Maintenance therapy

        B. Induction therapy

        C. Intensification therapy

        D. Reinduction therapy

Chapter 22: Leukemia

Application Exercises Answer Key

1. Match the following conditions with possible manifestations/complications of bone marrow suppression.

   __C__ Anemia   A. Bruising, nosebleed

   __B__ Neutropenia   B. Fever, pneumonia

   __A__ Thrombocytopenia   C. Fatigue, shortness of breath

   With anemia, a decreased number of circulating RBCs causes decreased oxygenation, which manifests itself as fatigue and shortness of breath. Neutropenia, which is a decreased neutrophil count, causes secondary infections, such as pneumonia, and can also result in manifestations such as fever. Thrombocytopenia, which is a decreased platelet count, results in complications such as bleeding and bruising.

2. A child with leukemia is experiencing severe thrombocytopenia. Which of the following nursing interventions will avoid the risk for injury based on this diagnosis? (Select all that apply.)

   __X__ **Avoid injections and skin punctures.**

   _____ Wash hands frequently.

   _____ Limit visitors.

   __X__ **Monitor platelet count.**

   __X__ **Avoid rectal temperatures.**

   _____ Monitor for fever.

   The child with thrombocytopenia is at risk for injury due to the high risk for bleeding. The nurse should avoid punctures to the skin whenever possible, monitor the thrombocyte (platelet) count, and avoid rectal temperatures, which could cause intestinal bleeding. Washing hands frequently, limiting visitors, and monitoring for fever are interventions for the nursing diagnosis, "risk for injury," which is related to neutropenia.

3. A child with leukemia is hospitalized with lethargy, headache, vomiting, and blurred vision. Which of the following complications of leukemia do these manifestations suggest?

    A. Anemia

    B. Hypermetabolism

    C. Increased intracranial pressure

    D. Infiltration of leukemic cells into bone marrow

The manifestations listed suggest CNS involvement with increased intracranial pressure caused by infiltration of the CNS by leukemic cells and blockage of the ventricles. Anemia could cause lethargy and drowsiness, but not vomiting, blurred vision, or headaches. Manifestations of hypermetabolism include anorexia, fatigue, and weight loss. Invasion of leukemic cells into bone marrow causes severe bone pain and fractures.

4. A nurse is assessing a child with leukemia undergoing chemotherapy. The child is losing weight, experiencing nausea, and has no appetite. Identify at least three nursing interventions the nurse can use to promote adequate nutritional intake.

Involve the child in food selection.

Do not give the child favorite foods when nauseated.

Medicate the child for nausea before meals.

Encourage small, frequent meals.

Encourage high-protein, high-calorie food choices.

Give the child high-protein, high-calorie shakes.

Weigh the child daily to monitor weight loss or gain.

Make food attractive and unusual, such as cutting a sandwich into a star shape with a cookie cutter.

Allow the parents to bring the child's favorite food from home.

Involve parents in order to learn about the child's usual preferences.

5. A child with leukemia has mucosal ulceration in his mouth and throat due to neutropenia. An intervention to ease discomfort from these ulcers is

  A. allowing the child to suck on lemon glycerin swabs for comfort.

  B. applying milk of magnesia to ulcers with a soft applicator.

  C. rinsing the child's mouth with NS frequently.

  D. having the child gargle with hydrogen peroxide every 2 hr.

NS or sodium bicarbonate mouth rinses are gentle, will not damage or dry tissue, and provide comfort when a child has mouth ulcers. Lemon glycerin swabs further irritate tissue and can erode teeth. Milk of magnesia can dry mucosa. Using hydrogen peroxide can delay healing by irritating mucosa.

6. A child with leukemia who has been in remission for 8 months is experiencing a relapse. The child is admitted to the hospital for treatment and prescribed a new chemotherapy regimen. Which of the following terms is used to describe the child's new regimen?

  A. Maintenance therapy

  B. Induction therapy

  C. Intensification therapy

  D. Reinduction therapy

Reinduction therapy places the child back into remission after relapse. Maintenance therapy is the maintenance dose used after a remission is achieved. Induction therapy is the term used for initial high-dose chemotherapy. Intensification therapy is a period of intensified chemotherapy that attempts to kill all residual leukemic cells after induction therapy.

Unit 2   Nursing Care of Children with System Disorders

Section: Nursing Care of Children with Cardiovascular or Blood Disorders

Chapter 23:   Iron Deficiency Anemia

Contributor: Pam Anthony, MSN, RN

 NCLEX-RN® Connections:

Learning Objective: Review and apply knowledge within **"Iron Deficiency Anemia"** in readiness for performance of the following nursing activities as outlined by the NCLEX-RN® test plan:

Δ   Assist with relevant laboratory, diagnostic, and therapeutic procedures within the nursing role, including:

- Client preparation for the procedure.

- Client teaching (before and following the procedure).

- Accurate collection of specimens.

- Evaluation of the child's response to the procedure.

- Planning and implementing body system-specific interventions as appropriate.

- Monitoring and taking actions to prevent or minimize the risk of complications.

- Accurate interpretation of procedure results.

Δ   Perform and document appropriate assessments based on the child's problem.

Δ   Apply knowledge of pathophysiology to planning care for clients with specific alterations in body systems, including recognizing associated signs and symptoms.

Δ   Interpret data that need to be reported immediately.

Δ   Monitor therapeutic devices (drainage/irrigating devices, chest tubes), if inserted, for proper functioning.

Δ   Explore resources, make referrals, collaborate with interdisciplinary team, and ensure continuity of client care.

Δ   Evaluate plans of care for multiple clients and revise plan as needed based on priorities of care and promotion of recovery.

Δ   Provide the child/family teaching regarding management of the child's health problem.

Δ   Recognize/respond to emergency situations, and evaluate/document the client's response to emergency interventions.

Key Points

Δ   Iron deficiency anemia is the most prevalent nutritional and mineral deficiency in the United States.

Δ   Iron deficiency anemia is the most common anemia in children ages 6 months to 2 years. It is also commonly diagnosed in adolescents 12 to 20 years of age.

Δ   RBCs with decreased Hgb levels will have a decreased capacity to carry oxygen to tissues.

Δ   Manifestations are related to the degree of anemia and the result of decreased oxygen to the tissues.

Δ   Prolonged anemia can lead to:

- Growth retardation.

- Developmental delays.

Key Factors

Δ   Production of Hgb requires iron. Iron deficiency will result in decreased Hgb levels in RBCs. Iron deficiency anemia usually results from an inadequate dietary supply of iron.

Δ   Risk factors for iron deficiency anemia include:

- Premature birth resulting in decreased iron stores.

- Excessive intake of cow's milk in toddlers.

   ◊   Whole milk is not a good source of iron.

   ◊   Substance in the milk binds with iron and interferes with absorption.

- Malabsorption disorders due to prolonged diarrhea.

- Poor dietary intake of iron.

- Periods of rapid growth, such as adolescence.

- Increased iron requirements (blood loss).

- Infection.

- Chronic disorders such as folate deficiency, sickle cell anemia, and hemophilia.

Assessment

Δ   Obtain nursing history, which includes:

- Birth history.

- Chronic illnesses such as sickle cell anemia, folate deficiency, or thalassemia.

- Sources of blood loss such as GI bleeding.

- Dietary intake (e.g., intake of iron-fortified foods or foods high in iron).

- Excessive milk or milk product intake.

Δ   Obtain baseline height and weight. Identify variations from norms.

Δ   Perform a developmental assessment and determine if the child is meeting milestones.

Δ   Physical assessment findings may include:

- Shortness of breath/fatigue.

- Tachycardia.

- Dizziness or fainting with exertion.

- Pallor.

- Nail bed deformities.

- Lethargy, irritability, and muscle weakness

- Impaired healing, loss of skin elasticity, and thinning of hair.

- Abdominal pain, nausea, vomiting, and loss of appetite.

- Low-grade fever

- Systolic heart murmur and/or heart failure

Diagnostic Procedures

Δ   Blood Studies

- Normal values

Age	Hgb	Hct
2 months	9.0 to 14.0 g/dL	28 to 42%
6 to 12 years	11.5 to 15.5 g/dL	35 to 45%
12 to 18 years	13.0 to 16.0 g/dL (male) 12.0 to 16.0 g/dL (female)	37 to 49% (male) 36 to 46% (female)

- CBC – decreased RBC count, decreased Hgb, and decreased Hct

- RBC indices – decreased indicating microcytic/hypochromic RBCs

  ◊ Mean corpuscular volume (MVC) – average size of RBC

  ◊ Mean corpuscular Hgb (MCH) – average weight of RBC

  ◊ Mean corpuscular hemoglobin concentration (MCHC) – amount of Hgb relative to size of cell

- Reticulocyte count – indication of bone marrow production of RBCs (may be decreased)

NANDA Nursing Diagnoses

Δ Imbalanced nutrition: less than required

Δ Ineffective tissue perfusion

Δ Activity intolerance

Δ Delayed growth and development

Nursing Interventions

Δ Preterm or low birth weight infants that are breastfed require iron supplements.

Δ Encourage breastfeeding for infants younger than 4 to 6 months of age.

Δ Recommend iron-fortified formula for infants not being breastfed.

Δ Modify diet to include high iron, vitamin C, and protein.

Δ Restrict milk intake in toddlers.

  - Give only 1 qt per day.

  - Avoid giving milk until after a meal.

  - Do not allow toddlers to carry bottles or cups of milk.

Δ Allow for frequent rest periods.

Δ Iron Administration

  - Give 1 hr before or 2 hr after milk or antacid to prevent decreased absorption.

  - Gastrointestinal side effects (e.g., diarrhea, constipation, nausea) are common at start of therapy. These will decrease over time.

  - Administer iron on an empty stomach. However, administration may not be tolerated during initial treatment.

  - Give vitamin C to help increase absorption.

  - Use a straw with liquid preparation to prevent staining of teeth. After administration, the child should rinse his mouth with water.

- Evenly distribute doses throughout the day. RBC production is maximized because bone marrow is provided a continuous supply of iron.

- Use Z-track into deep muscle for parenteral injections. Do not massage after injection.

- Stools may be tarry. Administration may cause constipation.

Δ If packed RBCs are required, follow protocols for administration.

Δ Family and Child Education

- Appropriate iron administration

  ◊ Avoid milk and antacids 1 hr before and 2 hr after administration to prevent decreased absorption.

  ◊ Avoid herbal supplements to prevent interference with absorption.

  ◊ Iron may need to be given with food until gastrointestinal disturbances subside.

  ◊ Use a straw and rinse the mouth after liquid preparation.

- Increase fiber and fluids to prevent constipation.

- Dietary sources of iron

  ◊ Infants – iron-fortified formula and cereal

  ◊ Older children – dried legumes; nuts; green, leafy vegetables; iron-fortified breads; iron-fortified flour; and red meat

- Include sources of vitamin C.

- Store iron in a child-proof bottle out of the reach of children. This will prevent accidental overdose.

- Encourage parents to allow the child to rest.

- Inform the parents that length of treatment will be determined by the child's response to the treatment. Hgb levels can take up to 3 months to increase.

Complications and Nursing Implications

Δ Heart Failure

- Heart failure can develop due to the increased demand on the heart to increase oxygen to tissues.

- Treat anemia.

- Monitor cardiac rhythm.

- Give cardiac medications as ordered.

Δ   Developmental Delay

- • Accurately assess level of functioning.

- • Improve nutritional intake.

- • Refer to appropriate developmental services.

Primary Reference:

Hockenberry, M., Wilson, D., & Winkelstein, M. (2005). *Wong's essentials of pediatric nursing care*. (7ᵗʰ ed.). St. Louis, MO: Mosby.

Additional Resources:

Lehne, R. A. (2007). *Pharmacology for nursing care*. (6ᵗʰ ed.). St. Louis, MO: Saunders.

NANDA International (2004). *NANDA nursing diagnoses: Definitions and classification 2005-2006*. Philadelphia: NANDA.

Chapter 23: Iron Deficiency Anemia

Application Exercises

Scenario: A nurse is assessing a 15-month-old child with iron deficiency anemia. The child's mother tells the nurse that she breastfed for the first year and then weaned the child to cow's milk. She also states that her child loves milk, drinks it at least four times a day, and is a "picky" eater. She stopped giving the child his prescribed iron supplements when he stopped consuming breast milk.

1. What teaching should the nurse provide to the mother regarding the child's nutritional intake?

2. List at least four foods that are rich in iron.

3. The child is discharged home with a prescription for liquid iron. The mother tells the nurse she hopes she can give this iron with her child's milk. Explain why the nurse needs to further educate the mother.

4. List several signs and/or symptoms a nurse may observe when assessing a child with iron deficiency anemia.

5. Which of following are considered normal Hgb and Hct levels for a 7-year-old child?

    A. Hgb 6 g/dL, Hct 18%
    B. Hgb 10 g/dL, Hct 30%
    C. Hgb 14 g/dL, Hct 42%
    D. Hgb 20 g/dL, Hct 60%

6. Which of the following statements by the parents of a child with iron deficiency anemia indicates that the parents understand the effects of oral iron therapy?

    A. "My child may develop diarrhea while on iron."
    B. "I should call the doctor if my child has tarry stools."
    C. "I will give the iron with milk to help prevent an upset stomach."
    D. "My child should rinse his mouth after taking the liquid iron."

7. A nurse is administering parenteral iron dextran to a child by the Z-track method. Which of the following strategies is correct when using the Z-track method to administer iron?

    A. Watch the child carefully for an allergic reaction after administration.

    B. Use the deltoid muscle for administration in school-age children.

    C. Massage the injection site for comfort after administration.

    D. Administer no more than 3 mL of iron into one site at a time.

Chapter 23: Iron Deficiency Anemia

Application Exercises Answer Key

Scenario: A nurse is assessing a 15-month-old child with iron deficiency anemia. The child's mother tells the nurse that she breastfed for the first year and then weaned the child to cow's milk. She also states that her child loves milk, drinks it at least four times a day, and is a "picky" eater. She stopped giving the child his prescribed iron supplements when he stopped consuming breast milk.

1. What teaching should the nurse provide to the mother regarding the child's nutritional intake?

   Cow's milk is not high in iron, and consuming milk to the exclusion of most other foods does result in anemia, as well as deficiencies of other nutrients. The mother needs to be instructed about which foods are high in iron and how to provide a healthy, well-balanced diet for her child. In addition, the nurse should tell the mother to continue administering iron supplements.

2. List at least four foods that are rich in iron.

   Red meats

   Legumes (dried beans and peas)

   Green leafy vegetables (spinach, chard, beet greens)

   Iron-fortified breads and cereals and whole grain breads/cereals

   Nuts and seeds

   Dried fruits

3. The child is discharged home with a prescription for liquid iron. The mother tells the nurse she hopes she can give this iron with her child's milk. Explain why the nurse needs to further educate the mother.

   Taking supplemental iron with milk decreases the absorption of iron. The mother should be instructed to give the iron with foods high in vitamin C, such as orange juice, which facilitates iron absorption. The child should not drink milk for 1 hr before or 2 hr after taking the iron supplement.

4. List several signs and/or symptoms a nurse may observe when assessing a child with iron deficiency anemia.

Fatigue, lethargy, irritability, and muscle weakness

Shortness of breath

Tachycardia, tachypnea, possible low-grade fever

Dizziness or fainting with exertion

Pallor

Nail bed deformities

Impaired healing, loss of skin elasticity, and thinning of hair

Systolic heart murmur, heart failure

5. Which of following are considered normal Hgb and Hct levels for a 7-year-old child?

    A. Hgb 6 g/dL, Hct 18%
    B. Hgb 10 g/dL, Hct 30%
    C. Hgb 14 g/dL, Hct 42%
    D. Hgb 20 g/dL, Hct 60%

Normal Hgb levels range from 11.5 to 15.5 g/dL of whole blood for children 6 to 12 years old. Normal Hct is approximately three times the Hgb level or 35 to 45%.

6. Which of the following statements by the parents of a child with iron deficiency anemia indicates that the parents understand the effects of oral iron therapy?

    A. "My child may develop diarrhea while on iron."
    B. "I should call the doctor if my child has tarry stools."
    C. "I will give the iron with milk to help prevent an upset stomach."
    D. "My child should rinse his mouth after taking the liquid iron."

Liquid iron supplements can stain teeth, so they should be taken with a straw or dropper, and the child should rinse his mouth after swallowing the medication. Development of constipation and tarry-colored stools are expected in the child taking iron supplements. Taking iron with milk decreases absorption and should be discouraged.

7. A nurse is administering parenteral iron dextran to a child by the Z-track method. Which of the following strategies is correct when using the Z-track method to administer iron?

A. Watch the child carefully for an allergic reaction after administration.

B. Use the deltoid muscle for administration in school-age children.

C. Massage the injection site for comfort after administration.

D. Administer no more than 3 mL of iron into one site at a time.

Iron dextran may also be prescribed via IV to prevent painful IM injections and skin staining. However, with both methods, the child should be observed carefully for allergic reaction. A large muscle mass must be used for IM injection of irritating medications, such as iron dextran; therefore, the deltoid muscle should be avoided. Massaging the injection site is avoided to prevent permanent skin staining with the dark-colored iron product. No more than 2 mL should be injected by the IM method in one site, except the deltoid, which should not have more than 1 mL injected.

Unit 2   **Nursing Care of Children with System Disorders**

Section: Nursing Care of Children with Cardiovascular or Blood Disorders

Chapter 24:	Sickle Cell Anemia
	Contributor: Pam Anthony, MSN, RN

 NCLEX-RN® Connections:

Learning Objective: Review and apply knowledge within "**Sickle Cell Anemia**" in readiness for performance of the following nursing activities as outlined by the NCLEX-RN® test plan:

Δ   Assist with relevant laboratory, diagnostic, and therapeutic procedures within the nursing role, including:

- Client preparation for the procedure.

- Client teaching (before and following the procedure).

- Accurate collection of specimens.

- Evaluation of the child's response to the procedure.

- Planning and implementing body system-specific interventions as appropriate.

- Monitoring and taking actions to prevent or minimize the risk of complications.

- Accurate interpretation of procedure results.

Δ   Perform and document appropriate assessments based on the child's problem.

Δ   Apply knowledge of pathophysiology to planning care for clients with specific alterations in body systems, including recognizing associated signs and symptoms.

Δ   Interpret data that need to be reported immediately.

Δ   Monitor therapeutic devices (drainage/irrigating devices, chest tubes), if inserted, for proper functioning.

Δ   Explore resources, make referrals, collaborate with interdisciplinary team, and ensure continuity of client care.

Δ   Evaluate plans of care for multiple clients and revise plan as needed based on priorities of care and promotion of recovery.

Δ   Provide the child/family teaching regarding management of the child's health problem.

Δ   Recognize/respond to emergency situations, and evaluate/document the client's response to emergency interventions.

Key Points

Δ   Sickle cell disease (SCD) is a group of diseases in which there is abnormal sickle hemoglobin S (HbS).

Δ   Manifestations and complications of sickle cell anemia are the result of RBC sickling, leading to increased blood viscosity, obstruction of blood flow, and tissue ischemia.

Δ   Manifestations of sickle cell anemia are not usually apparent before 4 to 6 months of life, due to the presence of fetal Hgb in the infant.

Δ   The RBCs have the ability to develop a sickled shape. This is usually precipitated by increased oxygen demands (e.g., infection, emotional stress, pain) or decreased levels of oxygen (e.g., pulmonary infections, high altitude).

Δ   The sickle-shaped RBC is rigid, leading to obstruction of capillary blood flow and tissue hypoxia. Tissue hypoxia causes tissue ischemia, which results in pain.

Δ   Increased destruction of RBCs also occurs.

Δ   Sickle cell crisis is the exacerbation of sickle cell anemia.

Key Factors

Δ   Sickle cell anemia (SCA) is the most common type of this group and is found primarily in African-Americans. Other forms of SCD may affect individuals of Mediterranean, Indian, or Middle Eastern descent.

Δ   SCA is an autosomal recessive genetic disorder in which normal hemoglobin A (HbA) is partially or completely replaced with HbS.

Δ   Sickle cell trait may be present in a heterozygous individual with HbA and HbS, whereas sickle cell anemia is present in a homozygous individual largely with HbS.

Δ   Children with sickle cell trait do not manifest the disease but can pass the trait to their offspring.

Assessment

Δ   Obtain nursing history, which includes:

•   Family history of sickle cell anemia or sickle cell trait.

•   Reports of pain, crisis, and management.

Δ   Obtain baseline height and weight. Identify variations from norms.

Δ   Perform a developmental assessment and determine if the child is meeting milestones.

Δ   Physical assessment findings may include:

- Shortness of breath/fatigue.

- Tachycardia.

- Pallor, jaundice.

- Nail bed deformities.

- Lethargy, irritability, and muscle weakness.

- Impaired healing, loss of skin elasticity, and thinning of hair.

- Abdominal pain, nausea, vomiting, and loss of appetite.

- Low-grade fever.

- Systolic heart murmur and heart failure.

Δ   Assessment Findings in Sickle Cell Crisis

Crisis	Manifestations
Vaso-occlusive (painful episode), usually lasting 4 to 6 days	Acute • Severe pain usually in bones, joints, and abdomen • Swollen joints, hands, and feet • Anorexia, vomiting, and fever • Hematuria • Obstructive jaundice • Visual disturbances Chronic • Increased risk of respiratory infections and/or osteomyelitis • Retinal detachment and blindness • Systolic murmurs • Renal failure and enuresis • Liver failure • Seizures • Deformities of the skeleton
Sequestration	• Excessive pooling of blood in the liver (hepatomegaly) and spleen (splenomegaly) • Tachycardia, dyspnea, weakness, pallor, and shock
Aplastic	• Extreme anemia as a result of decreased RBC production
Hyperhemolytic	• Increased rate of RBC destruction leading to anemia, jaundice, and/or reticulocytosis

Diagnostic Procedures

Δ   Laboratory Tests

- A prenatal diagnosis can be done as early as 8 to 10 weeks of gestation.

- Sickledex (sickle solubility test) is a screening tool that will detect the presence of HbS but will not differentiate the trait from the disease.

- Hgb electrophoresis separates the various forms of Hgb and is the definitive diagnosis of sickle cell anemia.

Δ Transcranial Doppler (TCD) test is used to assess intracranial vascular flow and detect the risk for cerebrovascular accident (CVA). Children with SCA ages 2 to 16 should have this test annually.

Δ Blood studies are used to identify anemia and infection.

- CBC normal values

Age	Hgb	Hct
2 months	9.0 to 14.0 g/dL	28 to 42%
6 to 12 years	11.5 to 15.5 g/dL	35 to 45%
12 to 18 years	13.0 to 16.0 g/dL (male) 12.0 to 16.0 g/dL (female)	37 to 49% (male) 36 to 46% (female)

- WBC normal values
  - ◊ 1 month – 5,000 to 19,500/mm^3
  - ◊ 1 to 3 years – 6,000 to 17,500/mm^3
  - ◊ 4 to 7 years – 5,000 to 15,500/mm^3
  - ◊ 8 to 13 years – 4,500 to 13,500/mm^3
  - ◊ Adult – 4,500 to 11,000/mm^3
- Platelets – normal value: 150,000 to 400,000/mm^3

NANDA Nursing Diagnoses

Δ Acute pain

Δ Altered tissue perfusion

Δ Fluid volume deficit

Δ Risk for injury

Δ Risk for infection

Δ Delayed growth and development

Δ Interrupted family processes

Nursing Interventions

Δ Promote rest to decrease oxygen consumption of the tissues.

Δ Administer oxygen as prescribed if hypoxia is present.

Δ   Pain Management

  •   Use an interdisciplinary approach.

  •   Treat mild to moderate pain with acetaminophen (Tylenol) or ibuprofen (Advil).

  •   Treat severe pain around the clock with opioids (e.g., codeine, morphine sulfate, oxycodone) by the oral or IV route. High-dose IV methylprednisolone (Solu-Medrol) may also be used.

  •   Use patient-controlled analgesia if appropriate.

  •   Apply comfort measures such as warm packs to painful joints.

Δ   Maintain fluid and electrolyte balance.

  •   Monitor I&O.

  •   Give oral fluids.

  •   Administer IV fluids with electrolyte replacement.

Δ   Monitor and report laboratory results: RBCs, Hgb, Hct, and liver function.

Δ   Administer blood products and exchange transfusions per facility protocols. Observe for signs of hypervolemia and transfusion reaction.

Δ   Encourage passive range-of-motion exercises to prevent venous stasis.

Δ   Prevent infection, which includes:

  •   Frequent handwashing.

  •   Giving oral prophylactic penicillin.

  •   Administering immunizations to include: pneumococcal vaccine (PCV), meningococcal vaccine (MCV4), and yearly influenza vaccine.

Δ   Family Support

  •   Provide emotional support, and refer to social services if appropriate.

  •   Instruct in signs and symptoms of crisis and infection.

  •   Advise the family of the importance of promoting rest and adequate nutrition for their child.

  •   Encourage the child/family to maintain good hand hygiene and avoid individuals with colds/infection/viruses.

  •   Give specific directions regarding fluid intake requirements, such as how many bottles or glasses of fluid should be consumed daily.

  •   Provide information about genetic counseling.

Complications and Nursing Implications

Δ CVA

- Assess and report signs and symptoms, which include:
  ◊ Seizures.
  ◊ Abnormal behavior.
  ◊ Weak extremity and/or inability to move an extremity.
  ◊ Slurred speech.
  ◊ Changes in vision.
  ◊ Vomiting.
  ◊ Severe headache.
- Blood transfusions every 3 to 4 weeks following a CVA

Δ Acute Chest Syndrome

- Can be life threatening
- Assess and report signs and symptoms, which include:
  ◊ Chest pain.
  ◊ Fever of 38.8° C (102° F) or higher.
  ◊ Congested cough.
  ◊ Tachycardia.
  ◊ Dyspnea.
  ◊ Retractions.
  ◊ Decreased oxygen saturations.

Primary Reference:

Hockenberry, M., Wilson, D., & Winkelstein, M. (2005). *Wong's essentials of pediatric nursing care*. (7th ed.). St. Louis, MO: Mosby.

Additional Resources:

Daniels, R. (2003). *Delmar's manual of laboratory and diagnostic tests*. (1st ed.). Clifton Park, NY.: Thomson Delmar Learning.

NANDA International (2004). *NANDA nursing diagnoses: Definitions and classification 2005-2006*. Philadelphia: NANDA.

Chapter 24: Sickle Cell Anemia

Application Exercises

Scenario: A 7-year-old child has been admitted to the emergency department with the diagnosis of vaso-occlusive crisis.

1. List several pieces of information specific to the child's diagnosis that are important for the nurse to obtain during the admission assessment.

2. What should be the priority nursing diagnosis for this child?

3. What medical interventions might the nurse anticipate for this child?

4. The nurse is planning interventions for this child. Based on knowledge of sickle cell anemia and vaso-occlusive crisis, the nurse should include what interventions in the care of this child?

5. A screening test reveals that an infant possibly has sickle cell disease. Which of the following tests is a definitive diagnosis for sickle cell anemia?

   A. Sickle solubility test (Sickledex)
   B. Hgb electrophoresis
   C. CBC
   D. Transcranial Doppler

6. A 9-year-old child with frequent sickle cell crises is jaundiced. What are possible causes of jaundice in the child with SCA? (Select all that apply.)

   _____ Liver failure caused by chronic vaso-occlusive crises
   _____ Cardiomegaly
   _____ Obstruction of bile ducts
   _____ Rapid destruction of sickled red blood cells
   _____ An aplastic crisis

7. Nursing interventions to prevent infection in a child hospitalized with sickle cell crisis include administering

        A. IV fluids with electrolyte replacement.

        B. IV narcotics for pain relief.

        C. pneumococcal vaccine.

        D. exchange transfusions.

Chapter 24: Sickle Cell Anemia

Application Exercises Answer Key

Scenario: A 7-year-old child has been admitted to the emergency department with the diagnosis of vaso-occlusive crisis.

1. List several pieces of information specific to the child's diagnosis that are important for the nurse to obtain during the admission assessment.

    What activities may have precipitated this crisis?

    What have the parents already done at home (e.g., pain medication)?

    How many episodes of vaso-occlusive crisis has the child had this year?

    What has worked well in the past for pain management?

    Has the child had any recent illnesses?

2. What should be the priority nursing diagnosis for this child?

    Acute pain is usually the priority in vaso-occlusive crisis. Other important diagnoses for this child include risk for fluid volume deficit and altered tissue perfusion.

3. What medical interventions might the nurse anticipate for this child?

    IV pain medications

    IV fluids

    Exchange transfusion if child has had repeated frequent episodes of vaso-occlusive crisis

4. The nurse is planning interventions for this child. Based on knowledge of sickle cell anemia and vaso-occlusive crisis, the nurse should include what interventions in the care of this child?

Bedrest

Around-the-clock pain management or patient-controlled analgesia

Frequent assessment of pain rating

Fluids at 125 to 150% of 24 hr maintenance requirements

Application of warm pack(s) to painful joints

5. A screening test reveals that an infant possibly has sickle cell disease. Which of the following tests is a definitive diagnosis for sickle cell anemia?

        A. Sickle solubility test (Sickledex)
        B. Hgb electrophoresis
        C. CBC
        D. Transcranial Doppler

Hgb electrophoresis diagnoses sickle cell anemia and differentiates it from sickle cell trait. The Sickledex test is a screening test for SCA and trait. The CBC tests for a variety of general problems, such as anemia and infection. Transcranial Doppler is used to diagnose the presence of CVA.

6. A 9-year-old child with frequent sickle cell crises is jaundiced. What are possible causes of jaundice in the child with SCA? (Select all that apply.)

        __X__ **Liver failure caused by chronic vaso-occlusive crises**
        _____ Cardiomegaly
        __X__ **Obstruction of bile ducts**
        __X__ **Rapid destruction of sickled red blood cells**
        _____ An aplastic crisis

Several phenomena could cause jaundice in the child with SCA including liver failure, obstruction of bile ducts by clumps of sickle-shaped cells, and increased destruction of the abnormal sickled cells. Cardiomegaly does not lead to jaundice. Aplastic crisis and sudden stoppage of red blood cell production would cause severe anemia but not jaundice.

7. Nursing interventions to prevent infection in a child hospitalized with sickle cell crisis include administering

>   A. IV fluids with electrolyte replacement.
>
>   B. IV narcotics for pain relief.
>
>   **C. pneumococcal vaccine.**
>
>   D. exchange transfusions.

Administration of vaccines for pneumococcal pneumonia, meningococcal disease, and influenza can help prevent infection. The other interventions are used for fluid volume deficits (IV fluid administration), extreme pain (IV narcotics), and to decrease the number of circulating sickled cells (exchange transfusions).

Unit 2   Nursing Care of Children with System Disorders
Section: Nursing Care of Children with Cardiovascular or Blood Disorders

Chapter 25:   Hemophilia
               Contributor: Pam Anthony, MSN, RN

 NCLEX-RN® Connections:

> **Learning Objective**: Review and apply knowledge within "**Hemophilia**" in readiness for performance of the following nursing activities as outlined by the NCLEX-RN® test plan:
>
> Δ Assist with relevant laboratory, diagnostic, and therapeutic procedures within the nursing role, including:
>
>   • Client preparation for the procedure.
>
>   • Client teaching (before and following the procedure).
>
>   • Accurate collection of specimens.
>
>   • Evaluation of the child's response to the procedure.
>
>   • Planning and implementing body system-specific interventions as appropriate.
>
>   • Monitoring and taking actions to prevent or minimize the risk of complications.
>
>   • Accurate interpretation of procedure results.
>
> Δ Perform and document appropriate assessments based on the child's problem.
>
> Δ Apply knowledge of pathophysiology to planning care for clients with specific alterations in body systems, including recognizing associated signs and symptoms.
>
> Δ Interpret data that need to be reported immediately.
>
> Δ Monitor therapeutic devices (drainage/irrigating devices, chest tubes), if inserted, for proper functioning.
>
> Δ Explore resources, make referrals, collaborate with interdisciplinary team, and ensure continuity of client care.
>
> Δ Evaluate plans of care for multiple clients and revise plan as needed based on priorities of care and promotion of recovery.
>
> Δ Provide the child/family teaching regarding management of the child's health problem.
>
> Δ Recognize/respond to emergency situations, and evaluate/document the client's response to emergency interventions.

📖 Key Points

Δ   Hemophilia is a disorder that results in impaired ability to control bleeding.

Δ   Bleeding time is extended due to lack of clotting factors. Bleeding may be internal or external.

Δ   Manifestations may be present early in infancy but may not be evident until the infant begins teething, sitting up, or crawling.

Δ   Parents may observe excessive bruising with minor falls or contact.

Δ   Hemarthrosis, which is bleeding into joint spaces, leads to impaired range of motion, pain, tenderness, and swelling, and can develop into joint deformities. Hemarthrosis most frequently affects the knees, elbows, and ankles.

Δ   Hemophilia has different levels of severity depending on the percentage of clotting factor a child's body contains. For example, a child with mild hemophilia. A may have up to 49% of the normal factor VIII in his body, while a person with severe hemophilia has very little factor VIII.

Key Factors

Δ   Types of Hemophilia

Hemophilia A	Hemophilia B
• Deficiency of factor VIII • Also referred to as classic hemophilia • Accounts for 80% of cases	• Deficiency of factor IX • Also referred to as Christmas disease

Δ   Both hemophilia A and B are X-linked recessive disorders.

Assessment

Δ   Nursing history should include episodes of bleeding, excessive bleeding, reports of joint pain and stiffness, impaired mobility, activity intolerance, and previous treatment.

Δ   Assess pain quality, location, and severity.

Δ   Assess for evidence of active bleeding, which includes bleeding gums, epistaxis, hematuria, and/or tarry stools.

Δ   Assess for hematomas and/or bruising.

Δ   Assess joints for decreased range of motion and deformities.

Δ   Assess joints for hemarthrosis.

- Manifestations include joint pain and stiffness.

- Other manifestations include pain, warmth, swelling, redness, and loss of range of motion. Repeated episodes of bleeding lead to deformities.

Δ   Assess neurologic status for headache, slurred speech, and a decreased level of consciousness.

Diagnostic Procedures

Δ   Use DNA testing to detect for classic hemophilia trait in females.

Δ   Laboratory Testing

- Prolonged activated partial thromboplastin time (aPTT)

- Factor-specific assays to determine deficiency

NANDA Nursing Diagnoses

Δ   Activity intolerance

Δ   Risk for injury

Δ   Acute pain

Δ   Impaired physical mobility

Nursing Interventions

Δ   Management of Bleeding in Hospital

- Avoid taking temperature rectally.

- Avoid unnecessary skin punctures and use surgical aseptic technique.

- Apply pressure for 5 min after injections, venipuncture, or needlesticks.

- Monitor urine, stool, and nasogastric fluid for occult blood.

- Control localized bleeding.

  ◊ Administer factor replacement to deep tissue, organs, and joint spaces.

  ◊ Observe for side effects, which include headache, flushing, low sodium, and alterations in heart rate and blood pressure.

  ◊ Encourage the child to rest and immobilize the affected joints.

  ◊ Elevate and apply ice to the affected joints.

Δ   Administer corticosteroids to treat hematuria, acute episodes of hemiarthrosis, and chronic synovitis.

Δ   Use nonsteroidal anti-inflammatory agents with caution, as they can lead to decreased platelet aggregation.

Δ   Family and Child Support

- Prevent bleeding at home.

    ◊   Place the child in a padded crib.

    ◊   Provide for a safe home and play environment that is free of clutter. Place padding on corners of furniture.

    ◊   Dress toddlers in extra layers of clothing to provide additional padding.

    ◊   Set activity restrictions to avoid injury. Acceptable activities include low-contact sports such as tennis, swimming, and golf. While participating in these activities, children should wear protective equipment.

    ◊   Use soft-bristled toothbrushes

- Encourage regular exercise and physical therapy after active bleeding is controlled.

- Teach how and when to administer factor at home.

- Teach importance of wearing a Medic Alert bracelet or necklace.

- Teach signs and symptoms of internal bleeding and hemarthrosis.

Therapeutic Procedures

Δ   Administer recombinant factor VIII concentrate during bleeding episodes. It is used to treat excessive bleeding or hemarthrosis. Dosage is based on the severity of bleeding.

Δ   Treatment with prophylaxis will vary. Regimens include:

- Infusion of factor VIII concentrate prior to joint bleed.

- Three times a week after the first joint bleed.

- High dose after joint bleed followed for 2 days with lower dose and then continued every other day for 1 week.

Δ   DDAVP (1-deamino-8-d-arginine vasopressin)

- Effective for mild hemophilia

- May be given prior to dental or surgical procedures

Δ   Antifibrinolytic agents inhibit the breakdown of fibrin, including epsilon-aminocaproic acid (Amicar). These agents are only effective for mouth or trauma surgery. They must be preceded by a dose of factor concentrate.

Δ   Blood transfusions are indicated for severe bleeding.

Complications and Nursing Implications

Δ   Uncontrolled bleeding (e.g., intracranial hemorrhage, airway obstruction from bleeding in mouth, neck, or chest)

- Monitor vital signs for evidence of impending shock.

- Take measures to control bleeding.

- Administer replacement factor.

- Administer blood transfusion as prescribed.

- Conduct neurologic assessment for evidence of intracranial bleed.

Δ   Joint deformity and crippling from repeated episodes of hemarthrosis

- Take appropriate measures to rest, immobilize, elevate, and apply ice to the affected joints during active bleeding.

- Encourage active range of motion after active bleeding is controlled.

- Maintain ideal weight to minimize stress on joints.

- Maintain regular exercise and physical therapy.

Primary Reference:

Hockenberry, M., Wilson, D., & Winkelstein, M. (2005). *Wong's essentials of pediatric nursing care.* (7th ed.). St. Louis, MO: Mosby.

Additional Resources:

For information about hemophilia, go to the National Hemophilia Foundation Web site, www.hemophilia.org.

NANDA International (2004). *NANDA nursing diagnoses: Definitions and classification 2005-2006.* Philadelphia: NANDA.

Chapter 25: Hemophilia

Application Exercises

Scenario: A nurse is planning educational intervention for the family of a toddler who has recently been diagnosed with hemophilia. The specific information regarding factor administration was covered in another session. For this session the nurse is planning to discuss safety measures with the family.

1. List at least two interventions the nurse should teach the family in order to keep the toddler safe by preventing bleeding episodes. Include a rationale for each intervention.

2. The mother tells the nurse she is upset that her child will never be able to take part in any sporting activities. Which of the following statements by the nurse is appropriate regarding the mother's statement?

    A. "Your child will be able to take part in the same contact sports as any other child."
    B. "You should prepare your child for a quiet life with no outside activities."
    C. "Your child will be able to participate in swimming, fishing, walking, or golfing."
    D. "You should restrain your child from taking part in play activities with other children."

3. A child with hemophilia cuts his arm while playing outside. Which of the following emergency measures will help stop the bleeding? (Select all that apply.)

    _____ Apply warm, wet soaks.
    _____ Apply ice to the area.
    _____ Apply direct compression.
    _____ Elevate extremity above heart level.
    _____ Administer replacement factor VIII concentrate.
    _____ Encourage slow movement of the extremity.

4. True or False: Encouraging appropriate physical activity in children with hemophilia strengthens muscles and joints and may actually prevent frequent bleeding episodes.

5. True or False: Sudden onset of slurred speech and headache in a child with hemophilia may indicate the onset of an episode of hemarthrosis.

6. True or False: Aspirin and ibuprofen are the best choices for pain relief in a child with hemophilia.

Chapter 25: Hemophilia

Application Exercises Answer Key

Scenario: A nurse is planning educational intervention for the family of a toddler who has recently been diagnosed with hemophilia. The specific information regarding factor administration was covered in another session. For this session the nurse is planning to discuss safety measures with the family.

1. List at least two interventions the nurse should teach the family in order to keep the toddler safe by preventing bleeding episodes. Include a rationale for each intervention.

Intervention	Rationale
Pad corners of furniture and dress the child in extra clothing.	The toddler is acquiring new motor skills and is more likely to fall into furniture. Padding will decrease the possibility of injury and subsequent bleeding.
Use child safety gates.	Safety gates will prevent the toddler from accessing stairs and other dangerous areas.
Decrease clutter in the home.	The toddler is more likely to fall and experience bleeding if there is additional clutter in the home.
Use soft toothbrushes and/or water irrigating devices for oral care.	Soft toothbrushes, tooth cleaning appliances, and/or water irrigating devices will help prevent bleeding gums in the toddler.
Obtain Medic-Alert bracelet or necklace for the child.	A Medic-Alert bracelet/necklace informs others of the child's condition if parents are not present.

2. The mother tells the nurse she is upset that her child will never be able to take part in any sporting activities. Which of the following statements by the nurse is appropriate regarding the mother's statement?

   A. "Your child will be able to take part in the same contact sports as any other child."

   B. "You should prepare your child for a quiet life with no outside activities."

   C. **"Your child will be able to participate in swimming, fishing, walking, or golfing."**

   D. "You should restrain your child from taking part in play activities with other children."

The parents should encourage noncontact activities for their child such as those described above. The child should take part in safe play activities with other children in order to live a normal life that allows for social, psychological, and physical growth. Contact sports should be discouraged, but the overall prognosis for children with hemophilia is that they can live a normal life by managing their disease.

3. A child with hemophilia cuts his arm while playing outside. Which of the following emergency measures will help stop the bleeding? (Select all that apply.)

_____ Apply warm, wet soaks.

__X__ **Apply ice to the area.**

__X__ **Apply direct compression.**

__X__ **Elevate extremity above heart level.**

__X__ **Administer replacement factor VIII concentrate.**

_____ Encourage slow movement of the extremity.

Emergency treatment should include immobilization of the extremity, elevation, ice, compression, and factor replacement. Warm, wet soaks and movement of the extremity would encourage further bleeding.

4. True or False: Encouraging appropriate physical activity in children with hemophilia strengthens muscles and joints and may actually prevent frequent bleeding episodes.

True. Appropriate physical activity will strengthen muscles and joints and may play a role in preventing a bleeding episode.

5. True or False: Sudden onset of slurred speech and headache in a child with hemophilia may indicate the onset of an episode of hemarthrosis.

False. Hemarthrosis is bleeding into a joint cavity such as the knee or elbow. Slurred speech, headache, and decreased level of consciousness may mean that the child has a cranial bleed.

6. True or False: Aspirin and ibuprofen are the best choices for pain relief in a child with hemophilia.

False. Aspirin and other NSAIDs inhibit platelet function, which causes further risk for bleeding.

Unit 2   Nursing Care of Children with System Disorders

Section: Nursing Care of Children with Cardiovascular or Blood Disorders

Chapter 26:   Rheumatic Fever
Contributor: Michele Woodbeck, MS, RN

 NCLEX-RN® Connections:

Learning Objective: Review and apply knowledge within "**Rheumatic Fever**" in readiness for performance of the following nursing activities as outlined by the NCLEX-RN® test plan:

Δ   Provide and instruct the child/family regarding appropriate infection control interventions.

Δ   Assist with relevant laboratory, diagnostic, and therapeutic procedures within the nursing role, including:

- Client preparation for the procedure.

- Client teaching (before and following the procedure).

- Accurate collection of specimens.

- Evaluation of the child's response to the procedure.

- Planning and implementing body system-specific interventions as appropriate.

- Monitoring and taking actions to prevent or minimize the risk of complications.

- Accurate interpretation of procedure results.

Δ   Perform and document appropriate assessments based on the child's problem.

Δ   Apply knowledge of pathophysiology to planning care for clients with specific alterations in body systems, including recognizing associated signs and symptoms.

Δ   Interpret data that need to be reported immediately.

Δ   Monitor therapeutic devices (drainage/irrigating devices, chest tubes), if inserted, for proper functioning.

Δ   Explore resources, make referrals, collaborate with interdisciplinary team, and ensure continuity of client care.

Δ   Evaluate plans of care for multiple clients and revise plan as needed based on priorities of care and promotion of recovery.

Δ   Provide the child/family teaching regarding management of the child's health problem.

Δ   Recognize/respond to emergency situations, and evaluate/document the client's response to emergency interventions.

Key Points

Δ   Rheumatic fever is a self-limiting inflammatory disease of the connective tissue. System involvement includes the connective tissue of the heart, joints, central nervous system, skin, and subcutaneous tissue.

Δ   This disease has a low incidence in the United States but is common in developing nations.

Δ   Rheumatic heart disease is the major complication of rheumatic fever, resulting in cardiac valve damage.

Key Factors

Δ   Rheumatic fever is an inflammatory disease occurring as a reaction to Group A β-hemolytic streptococcus (GABHS) infection of the throat.

Δ   Rheumatic fever usually occurs within 2 to 6 weeks following an untreated or partially treated upper respiratory infection (e.g., strep throat) with GABHS.

Assessment

Δ   Nursing history should include recent infections, medications taken, immunization status, and family coping.

Δ   Review of systems – Ask questions related to reports of sore throat, activity level, chest pain, fatigue, joint pains, and rash.

Δ   Physical exam should include:

   •   Checking vital signs, which include oxygen saturation. Observe for hypotension, fever, and hypoxemia.

   •   Assessing for symptoms of carditis, such as low-grade fever, pallor, listlessness, poor appetite, and dyspnea on exertion. Auscultate the heart, noting tachycardia, new murmurs, and muffled heart sounds.

   •   Performing ECG as ordered, observing for prolonged PR interval.

   •   Assessing the joints for painful swelling (polyarthritis); paying specific attention to large joints such as the knees, elbows, ankles, wrists, and shoulders. Symptoms last a few days and then disappear without treatment, frequently returning in another joint.

   •   Palpating the skin near the joints for nontender, subcutaneous nodules.

   •   Assessing the skin for eruptions referred to as erythema marginatum, a pink macular rash on the trunk and abdomen (not seen on the face). These eruptions are usually nonpruritic, appear and disappear rapidly, and are significant in diagnosing the disease.

- Assessing for signs of chorea. Chorea is a disorder of the CNS characterized by involuntary, purposeless, muscle movements; muscle weakness; involuntary facial movements; difficulty performing fine motor activities; labile emotions; and random, uncoordinated movements of the extremities. Tension, irritability, poor concentration, and behavioral problems may be present. The child may laugh and cry inappropriately.

- Noting abdominal pain.

Diagnostic Procedures

Δ Throat Culture for GABHS

Δ Blood Samples

- Elevated or rising serum antistreptolysin-O (ASO) titre – most reliable
- Elevated C-reactive protein (CRP) or sedimentation rate in response to an inflammatory reaction

Δ Cardiac Function

- ECG to reveal the presence of conduction disturbances
- Echocardiogram to evaluate function of the heart and valves

Δ The diagnosis of rheumatic fever is made on the basis of modified Jones criteria. The child should demonstrate the presence of two major criteria or the presence of one major and two minor criteria following an acute infection with GABHS infection.

- Major criteria
    ◊ Carditis
    ◊ Polyarthritis
    ◊ Chorea
    ◊ Subcutaneous nodules
    ◊ Rash (erythema marginatum)
- Minor criteria
    ◊ Fever
    ◊ Arthralgia

NANDA Nursing Diagnoses

Δ Acute pain

Δ Impaired physical mobility

Δ Decreased cardiac output

Δ Activity intolerance

Nursing Interventions

Δ   Interventions to prevent permanent damage to the heart and to provide palliation of other symptoms include:

- Administering antibiotics such as penicillin – or erythromycin if the child is allergic to penicillin – as prescribed to eliminate the streptococcal infection. Assess the child for an allergic response (e.g., anaphylaxis, hives, rashes). Assess for nausea, vomiting, or diarrhea.

- Administering aspirin as prescribed for anti-inflammatory effect.

    ◊   Parents may want to avoid aspirin in children. (Reye syndrome is associated with the use of aspirin for a viral illness.)

    ◊   Reassure parents and explain the reason for aspirin therapy. (Rheumatic fever is bacterial, not viral.)

- Maintaining bedrest as prescribed. This is usually until tachycardia and fever subside.

- Assisting with activities of daily living (ADLs) if chorea prevents the child from bathing, feeding.

- Adjusting care to promote independence.

- Handling painful joints carefully.

- Providing for quiet diversional activities such as games, puzzles, and/or art activities.

- Arranging for the child to keep up with school work if appropriate.

Δ   Discharge Instructions

- Reinforce with the child/family the importance of completing the entire 10-day course of antibiotics as prescribed, even if the child starts to feel better after a few doses.

- Promote rest and adequate nutrition.

- Provide information and reassurance related to development of chorea and its self-limiting nature.

- Follow the primary care provider's prescribed prophylactic treatment regimen, which may include one of the following: two daily oral doses of 200,000 units of penicillin, a monthly intramuscular injection of 1.2 million units of penicillin, or a daily oral dose of 1 g of sulfadiazine. The length of prophylaxis treatment may vary.

- Seek medical care if suspicion of infection recurrence.

- Obtain antibiotic prophylaxis therapy for all dental work and invasive procedures.

- Arrange for medical follow-up every 5 years.

Complications and Nursing Implications

Δ   Bacterial Endocarditis and Damage to the Mitral or Aortic Valve

- Initial treatment with 10-day course of penicillin
- Careful monitoring of cardiac rate, rhythm, and presence of murmurs
- Activity restriction if carditis is present
- Strict compliance with the prophylactic antibiotic regimen
- Medical follow-up care for at least 5 years following an acute infection

Primary Reference:

Hockenberry, M., Wilson, D., & Winkelstein, M. (2005). *Wong's essentials of pediatric nursing care.* (7th ed.). St. Louis, MO: Mosby.

Additional Resources:

Ball, J. W., & Bindler, R. C. (2005). *Child health nursing: Partnering with children and families.* (1st ed.). Upper Saddle River, NJ: Prentice-Hall.

Chin, T., & Worley, C. (2006). Rheumatic fever. Retrieved January 30, 2007, from http://www.emedicine.com/ped/topic2006.htm

NANDA International (2004). *NANDA nursing diagnoses: Definitions and classification 2005-2006.* Philadelphia: NANDA.

Chapter 26: Rheumatic Fever

Application Exercises

1. Which of the following are manifestations of rheumatic fever? (Select all that apply.)

     _____ Erythema marginatum (rash)
     _____ Continuous joint pain of the digits
     _____ Tender, subcutaneous nodules
     _____ Decreased erythrocyte sedimentation rate
     _____ Elevated C-reactive protein
     _____ Uncoordinated movements of the extremities

2. Rheumatic fever can be avoided by identification of _____ infections and treatment with _____.

3. Which of the following diagnostic tests is most definitive for diagnosing rheumatic fever?

     A. Throat swab and culture
     B. Electrocardiogram (ECG) and echocardiogram
     C. Elevated CRP or erythrocyte sedimentation
     D. Elevated or rising serum antistreptolysin-O (ASO) titer

4. A 6-year-old child is admitted to the pediatric unit with a diagnosis of rheumatic fever. Which of the following medications should the nurse administer to meet the child's need for comfort?

     A. Aspirin
     B. Ibuprofen
     C. Penicillin
     D. Erythromycin

5. True or False: Chorea leads to permanent nerve damage and seizures.

6. True or False: Antibiotics may need to be continued for an extended period of time for prophylaxis.

Chapter 26: Rheumatic Fever

Application Exercises Answer Key

1. Which of the following are manifestations of rheumatic fever? (Select all that apply.)

   _X_ Erythema marginatum (rash)
   ____ Continuous joint pain of the digits
   ____ Tender, subcutaneous nodules
   ____ Decreased erythrocyte sedimentation rate
   _X_ Elevated C-reactive protein
   _X_ Uncoordinated movements of the extremities

   Erythema marginatum, positive C-reactive protein, and uncoordinated movements of the extremities are all manifestations of rheumatic fever. Migratory joint pain of the large joints, nontender subcutaneous nodules beneath the skin, and increased erythrocyte sedimentation rate are also manifestations.

2. Rheumatic fever can be avoided by identification of _____ infections and treatment with _____.

   GABHS

   Antibiotics (penicillin [erythromycin if the child is allergic to penicillin])

   Early identification of GABHS and subsequent appropriate antimicrobial treatment can help prevent the development of rheumatic fever.

3. Which of the following diagnostic tests is most definitive for diagnosing rheumatic fever?

   A. Throat swab and culture

   B. Electrocardiogram (ECG) and echocardiogram

   C. CRP or erythrocyte sedimentation

   D. Elevated or rising serum antistreptolysin-O (ASO) titer

   The most definitive diagnostic test for rheumatic fever is an elevated or rising serum antistreptolysin-O (ASO) titer. This indicates the presence of streptococcal antibodies.

4. A 6-year-old child is admitted to the pediatric unit with a diagnosis of rheumatic fever. Which of the following medications should the nurse administer to meet the child's need for comfort?

    A. Aspirin
    B. Ibuprofen
    C. Penicillin
    D. Erythromycin

Aspirin is the medication of choice for inflammatory pain, fever, and general discomfort. Rheumatic fever is bacterial in origin; therefore, use of aspirin is not contraindicated. Ibuprofen does not have anti-inflammatory effects. Penicillin and erythromycin are used to treat infection.

5. True or False: Chorea leads to permanent nerve damage and seizures.

False. Chorea, which is characterized by involuntary, purposeless, muscle movements; muscle weakness; involuntary facial movements; difficulty performing fine motor activities; labile emotions; and random, uncoordinated movements of the extremities, is transitory and will eventually resolve.

6. True or False: Antibiotics may need to be continued for an extended period of time for prophylaxis.

True. Antibiotics may need to be continued for prophylaxis. The length of treatment has not been determined.

Unit 2 — Nursing Care of Children with System Disorders
Section: Nursing Care of Children with Lymphatic/Infectious/Immune Disorders

Chapter 27: Immunizations

Contributor: Michele Woodbeck, MS, RN

 NCLEX-RN® Connections:

Learning Objective: Review and apply knowledge within "**Immunizations**" in readiness for performance of the following nursing activities as outlined by the NCLEX-RN® test plan:

Δ Assess the immunization needs and status of the child/family/significant others.

Δ Identify precautions and contraindications for immunizations.

Δ Recognize side effects and allergic/adverse reactions to immunizations.

Δ Provide appropriate treatment and comfort measures to children with side effects and adverse/allergic reactions to immunizations.

Δ Provide teaching regarding immunization schedules and the importance of maintaining their currency.

Δ Provide teaching to manage common adverse effects of immunizations (e.g., fever, inflammation).

 Key Points

Δ Immunization has been credited with the elimination and control of many serious infectious illnesses.

Δ **Acquired immunity** can be natural or artificial and be obtained actively or passively.

• **Active immunity** includes:

◊ Natural immunity, which is obtained when the child gets a disease and develops antibodies against that disease.

◊ Artificial immunity, which is obtained with immunization. An antigen, introduced into the body as a vaccine, stimulates the body to produce antibodies against that specific disease without causing clinical disease. Some immunizations require repeat stimulation with the antigen to confer acceptable protection.

- **Passive immunity** includes:

  ◊ Natural immunity that is obtained by the neonate from the mother.

  ◊ Artificial immunity, which is obtained when antibodies, in the form of immunoglobins, are administered when an individual is exposed to a disease and requires protection more quickly than the body could respond to the agent.

Key Factors

Δ **Current immunization recommendations** for childhood vaccinations can be found by going to the 2007 Centers for Disease Control and Prevention (CDC) Web site, *www.cdc.gov/nip/*.

- Recommendations for healthy infants **less than 12 months** include:

  ◊ **Birth** – Hepatitis B (Hep B).

  ◊ **2 months** – Hep B; rotavirus vaccine (Rota); diphtheria and tetanus toxoids and pertussis (DTaP); *Haemophilus influenzae* type B (Hib); pneumococcal vaccine PCV; and inactivated poliovirus (IPV).

  ◊ **4 months** – Rota, DTaP, Hib, PCV, and IPV.

  ◊ **6 months** – Hep B (6 to 12 months), Rota, DTaP, PCV, and IPV (6 to 18 months).

  ◊ Infants 6 to 12 months should receive a yearly influenza vaccination. The trivalent inactivated influenza vaccine (TIV) is available as an intramuscular injection, or the live, attenuated influenza vaccine (LAIV) is available as an intranasal spray.

- Recommendations for healthy toddlers **12 months to 3 years** of age include:

  ◊ **12 to 15 months** – *Haemophilus influenzae* type B (Hib); pneumococcal vaccine (PCV), IPV (6 to 18 months); measles, mumps, and rubella (MMR); and varicella.

  ◊ **12 to 23 months** – Hepatitis A (Hep A), given in two doses, at least 6 months apart.

  ◊ **15 to 18 months** – Diphtheria and tetanus toxoids and pertussis (DTaP).

  ◊ **12 to 36 months** – Yearly trivalent inactivated influenza vaccine (TIV).

- Recommendations for healthy preschool children **3 to 5 years and children to 6 years of age** include:

  ◊ 4 to 6 years – Diphtheria and tetanus toxoids and pertussis (DTaP); inactivated poliovirus (IPV); measles, mumps, and rubella (MMR); and varicella.

  ◊ Yearly trivalent inactivated influenza vaccine (TIV) for preschoolers **36 to 59 months**.

- Recommendations for healthy school-age children **5 to 12 years** of age include:

  ◊ If not given between ages **4 to 5**, then by age 6: diphtheria and tetanus toxoids and pertussis (DTaP); inactivated poliovirus (IPV); measles, mumps, and rubella (MMR); and varicella.

  ◊ **11 to 12 years** – Tetanus and diphtheria toxoids and pertussis vaccine (Tdap); measles, mumps, and rubella (MMR); human papillomavirus vaccine (HPV) in 3 doses; and meningococcal vaccine (MCV4).

Δ Recommendations for the healthy adolescent **12 to 20** years of age include:

  ◊ If not given at age 11 to 12: tetanus and diphtheria toxoids and pertussis vaccine (Tdap); human papillomavirus vaccine (HPV) series; hepatitis B (Hep B) series; inactivated poliovirus (IPV) series; measles, mumps, and rubella (MMR) series; varicella series; and meningococcal (MCV4).

- Immunocompromised individuals are defined by the CDC as those with hematologic or solid tumors, congenital immunodeficiency, or on long-term immunosuppressive therapy, including corticosteroids.

Δ Contraindications to vaccinations require the primary care provider to analyze data and weigh the risks that come with vaccinating or not vaccinating.

Δ Contraindications to all immunizations include a severe allergy to any component (anaphylaxis).

Δ Contraindications to specific vaccinations include:

Immunizations	Side Effects	Contraindications
MMR	<ul><li>Local reactions (e.g., rash; fever; swollen glands in cheeks, neck; pain under the jaw)</li><li>Anaphylaxis such as difficulty breathing, urticaria, thrombocytopenia, and low platelet count with bruising</li></ul>	<ul><li>During pregnancy, and children who are allergic to eggs, gelatin, and neomycin</li><li>In children who have a history of thrombocytopenia or thrombocytopenic purpura</li><li>Immunocompromised children</li><li>Children with advanced HIV</li><li>Children who recently received blood products or immunoglobulins</li></ul>

Immunizations	Side Effects	Contraindications
DTaP	Encephalopathy (e.g., fever, irritability, persistent crying that cannot be consoled), seizures, and/or local reaction at the site of injection (e.g., pain, swelling, redness)	• Severe febrile illness • A history of prior anaphylactic reaction to the DTaP vaccination • An occurrence of encephalopathy 7 days after the administration of the DTaP immunization • An occurrence of seizures within 3 days of the vaccination • Uncontrollable crying that cannot be consoled by parents/caregiver; can usually last more than 3 hr and occurs within 48 hr of vaccination
IPV	Vaccine-associated paralytic poliomyelitis, and/or local reaction (e.g., pain, redness, swelling)	Allergy to neomycin (Mycifradin) and/or streptomycin Pregnancy usually a contraindication and must be decided on an individual basis
Hepatitis A and B vaccines	• Local reaction (e.g., anorexia, soreness, fatigue) • Anaphylaxis	Hep B: • A prior history of anaphylactic reaction • An allergy to Baker's yeast Hep A: • Allergy to aluminum • Pregnancy may be a contraindication
Varicella vaccine	Varicella-like rash, local or generalized (e.g., vesicles on the body)	• During pregnancy • Children with cancer, such as leukemia or lymphomas • Children with a history of allergy to neomycin and/or gelatin • Immunocompromised children, such as children with HIV • Children with congenital immunodeficiency • Children taking immunosuppressive medications
Pneumococcal vaccine (PCV)	Mild local reaction, fever, and no serious adverse effects	Hypersensitivity to diphtheria toxoid

Immunizations	Side Effects	Contraindications
Influenza vaccine	Guillain-Barré syndrome (e.g., ascending paralysis, weakness of lower extremities, difficulty breathing), local reaction, and fever	• During pregnancy • Acute febrile illness – Vaccination is deferred until symptoms resolve. • Hypersensitivity to eggs (vaccine is grown in eggs and may contain small amounts of egg proteins) – Conduct a skin test prior to administration. • Immunocompromised children, such as children with HIV • Children on antimicrobial therapy
Meningococcal vaccine (MCV4)	Mild local reaction and rare risk of allergic response	• Hypersensitivity to components of the vaccine (e.g., diphtheria toxoid, latex); moderate to severe illness

Assessment

Δ   Obtain accurate history of previous immunizations.

Δ   Assess the child for contraindications to scheduled vaccines.

•   Moderate to severe illness

•   Allergies (e.g., specific medications, eggs, gelatin, or any vaccine)

•   Serious reaction following vaccine administration in the past

•   History of seizures or other neurological condition

•   Immunosuppression (e.g., cancer, HIV, chronic steroid use)

•   Blood transfusion, immuneglobulin, or recent tuberculosis test

•   Pregnancy

NANDA Nursing Diagnoses

Δ   Health-seeking behaviors

Δ   Deficient knowledge

Δ   Fear

Δ   Anxiety

Δ   Risk for injury

Nursing Interventions

Δ   Provide written vaccine information sheets and review the content with parents.

Δ   Obtain parental consent.

Δ   Follow storage and reconstitution directions. If reconstituted, use within 30 min.

Δ   Intramuscular vaccinations are given in the vastus lateralis muscle in infants and young children, and into the deltoid muscle for older children, adolescents, and adults.

Δ   Note the date, route, and site of vaccination on the child's immunization record at the time of immunization.

Δ   Use strategies to minimize discomfort.

- Instruct in application of topical anesthetic.
- Use a needle of sufficient length to reach the muscle.
- Provide for distraction.
- Do not allow the child to delay the procedure.
- Encourage parent to use comforting measures (cuddling, pacifiers).
- Provide praise afterward.
- Apply colorful bandage, if appropriate.

Δ   Discuss with the parent measures to maintain comfort after immunization, which include:

- Use of nonopioid analgesics (e.g., acetaminophen [Tylenol], ibuprofen [Advil]). Instruct parent(s) to avoid administering aspirin to children to treat fever following varicella immunization due to the risk of the development of Reye syndrome.
- Application of cool compresses to injection site.
- Gentle movement of the involved extremity.

Δ   Instruct the parent(s) to observe for complications and to notify the primary care provider if side effects occur.

Δ   Encourage the parent(s) to maintain up-to-date immunizations for the child.

Δ   There is a small risk of the varicella vaccine virus being transmitted. If a child develops a rash following the vaccination, measures should be taken to protect any pregnant woman and others at risk from exposure, such as those who are immunocompromised.

Complications and Nursing Implications

Δ   Anaphylaxis

- Review symptoms with parents.

- Instruct parents to call 911 or other emergency number, and to keep the child quiet until help arrives.

Δ   Encephalitis, Seizures, and/or Neuritis

- Review symptoms with parents. Instruct parents when to seek medical care.

- Teach parents to prevent injury during a seizure.

Δ   Thrombocytopenia

- Thrombocytopenia is usually associated with the measles vaccination.

- Teach parents to observe for bleeding.

- Instruct the parents to call the primary care provider if bleeding, bruising, or red dot-like rash occurs.

Primary Reference:

Hockenberry, M., Wilson, D., & Winkelstein, M. (2005). *Wong's essentials of pediatric nursing care.* (7th ed.). St. Louis, MO: Mosby.

Additional Resources:

Centers for Disease Control and Prevention. (2007). *2007 childhood & adolescent immunization schedules: Are your child's vaccinations up to date?*. Retrieved February 28, 2007, from http://www.cdc.gov/nip/recs/child-schedule.htm

Centers for Disease Control and Prevention. (2007). Guide to contraindications to vaccinations. Retrieved February 28, 2007, from http://www.cdc.gov/nip/recs/contraindications.htm

Centers for Disease Control and Prevention. (2007). Parents' guide to childhood immunizations. Retrieved February 22, 2007, from http://www.cdc.gov/nip/publications/Parents-Guide/default.htm#pguide

Mayo Foundation for Medical Education and Research. (2005, August). How vaccines work. Retrieved February 22, 2007, from http://www.mayoclinic.com/health/vaccines/ID00023

NANDA International (2004). *NANDA nursing diagnoses: Definitions and classification 2005-2006.* Philadelphia: NANDA.

Chapter 27: Immunizations

Application Exercises

Scenario: A nurse in a well-infant clinic is examining a 2-month-old infant who has not been examined since he was 2 days old. The infant weighs 5 kg (11 lb). His birth weight was 8 lb 2 oz. The mother states that he has a yellow discharge from his nose and a cough. She lives in a rural area and usually has no transportation.

1. What data should the nurse gather at this point concerning the infant's immunization status?

2. The infant's axillary temperature is 38° C (100.4° F). What should the nurse do?

3. What immunizations (if any) should the child receive at this visit?

4. What should the nurse do to assure that the mother is willing and able to obtain future immunizations for her child?

5. What teaching should the nurse provide to the mother about the immunizations the infant receives today?

6. A mother of a 2-month-old child asks a nurse about the Hib vaccine before the child is immunized. The nurse tells her that Hib protects the child from a variety of serious early childhood diseases caused by *Haemophilus influenzae* type B, including

        A. respiratory syncytial virus (RSV).

        B. bacterial meningitis.

        C. polio.

        D. acute laryngitis.

7. Which of the following sets of injections is typically given at the 4-month check-up?

        A. Hep B, Rota, DTaP, Hib, PCV, and IPV

        B. Hep B, Rota, DTaP, PCV, and IPV

        C. Rota, DTaP, Hib, PCV, and IPV

        D. DTaP, Hep A, MMR, PVC, and varicella

8. A nurse is preparing to administer a second DTaP immunization to a child. To screen for a contraindication for this DTaP dose, which of the following questions should the nurse ask the child's parent?

> A. "Did the child spit up?"
>
> B. "Did the child seem more fussy than usual?"
>
> C. "Did you notice any seizure activity?"
>
> D. "Was your child's leg red and swollen?"

9. A nurse is instructing a mother about strategies to promote comfort after her child receives an immunization. Which of the following strategies is recommended? (Select all that apply.)

> _____ Administer aspirin.
>
> _____ Apply cool compresses to the site.
>
> _____ Administer a safe dose of children's acetaminophen or ibuprofen.
>
> _____ Encourage the child to use the affected extremity gently.
>
> _____ Apply a heating pad to the site.

Chapter 27: Immunizations

Application Exercises Answer Key

Scenario: A nurse in a well-infant clinic is examining a 2-month-old infant who has not been examined since he was 2 days old. The infant weighs 5 kg (11 lb). His birth weight was 8 lb 2 oz. The mother states that he has a yellow discharge from his nose and a cough. She lives in a rural area and usually has no transportation.

1. What data should the nurse gather at this point concerning the infant's immunization status?

Determine if the child had a Hep B injection at the hospital prior to discharge.

Verify that the child has had no immunizations prior to this point in his life.

Ask the mother about any allergies.

2. The infant's axillary temperature is 38° C (100.4° F). What should the nurse do?

The nurse may take a rectal temperature to verify that the child has a low-grade temperature elevation. The nurse needs to auscultate the lungs and examine the child to confirm that the child is not seriously ill. If the infant has only mild to moderate illness, the nurse should proceed with the scheduled immunizations. Because of the child's infrequent contact with health care, it would be important not to miss an opportunity to immunize if possible.

3. What immunizations (if any) should the child receive at this visit?

The child should receive: Hep B, Rota, DTaP, Hib, IPV, and PCV.

4. What should the nurse do to assure that the mother is willing and able to obtain future immunizations for her child?

Provide information regarding implications for the child if immunizations are not received.

Provide a list of clinics in the area that will provide free or inexpensive immunizations. Assist the mother to call and set up appointments.

Discuss transportation options and assist the mother to develop a plan to implement.

Assist the mother to identify support people who will be able to assist her.

5. What teaching should the nurse provide to the mother about the immunizations the infant receives today?

The mother should be given vaccine information sheets from the CDC.

The nurse should inform the mother of possible side effects to expect, such as fever and discomfort at the injection, and ways to manage these side effects (e.g., administration of acetaminophen).

In addition, the nurse should listen to any concerns the mother has about immunizing her child and answer her questions.

6. A mother of a 2-month-old child asks a nurse about the Hib vaccine before the child is immunized. The nurse tells her that Hib protects the child from a variety of serious early childhood diseases caused by *Haemophilus influenzae* type B, including

    A. respiratory syncytial virus (RSV).
    B. bacterial meningitis.
    C. polio.
    D. acute laryngitis.

Hib protects against bacterial meningitis, epiglottitis, bacterial pneumonia, and acute otitis media. It does not protect against polio or the viruses that cause RSV or acute laryngitis.

7. Which of the following sets of injections is typically given at the 4-month check-up?

> A. Hep B, Rota, DTaP, Hib, PCV, and IPV
> B. Hep B, Rota, DTaP, PCV, and IPV
> **C. Rota, DTaP, Hib, PCV, and IPV**
> D. DTaP, Hep A, MMR, PVC, and varicella

The set of immunizations in A is given at 2 months of age.

The set of immunizations in B is given at 6 months of age. In addition to these immunizations, infants 6 to 12 months should also receive a yearly influenza vaccination.

The set of immunizations in D is given to toddlers 12 months to 3 years of age. In addition, toddlers should receive the Hep A vaccine, given in two doses, at least 6 months apart, and a yearly trivalent inactivated influenza vaccine (TIV).

8. A nurse is preparing to administer a second DTaP immunization to a child. To screen for a contraindication for this DTaP dose, which of the following questions should the nurse ask the child's parent?

> A. "Did the child spit up?"
> B. "Did the child seem more fussy than usual?"
> **C. "Did you notice any seizure activity?"**
> D. "Was your child's leg red and swollen?"

Seizures are a serious contraindication to this immunization. Reports of seizure activity would need to be referred to the primary care provider for further detailed screening. Vomiting or fussiness is not contraindicated for these (or any other) immunizations. A red and swollen injection site may occur after an injection, but it is not a contraindication to a vaccination.

9. A nurse is instructing a mother about strategies to promote comfort after her child receives an immunization. Which of the following strategies is recommended? (Select all that apply.)

    _____ Administer aspirin.

    _X_ Apply cool compresses to the site.

    _X_ Administer a safe dose of children's acetaminophen or ibuprofen.

    _X_ Encourage the child to use the affected extremity gently.

    _____ Apply a heating pad to the site.

Cool compresses, administration of safe doses of acetaminophen or ibuprofen, and encouraging gentle use of the extremity are all comfort strategies useful for discomfort in an injection site. Aspirin should not be used because of the risk for Reye syndrome. Use of heat will not provide comfort for a sore injection site.

Unit 2   Nursing Care of Children with System Disorders
Section: Nursing Care of Children with Lymphatic/Infectious/Immune Disorders

Chapter 28:   Communicable Diseases
Contributor: Michele Woodbeck, MS, RN

⟳ NCLEX-RN® Connections:

Learning Objective: Review and apply knowledge within **"Communicable Diseases"** in readiness for performance of the following nursing activities as outlined by the NCLEX-RN® test plan:

Δ   Inform the child/family of appropriate immunization schedules.

Δ   Provide and instruct family regarding appropriate infection control interventions.

Δ   Assist with relevant laboratory, diagnostic, and therapeutic procedures within the nursing role, including:

- Client preparation for the procedure.

- Client teaching (before and following the procedure).

- Accurate collection of specimens.

- Evaluation of the child's response to the procedure.

- Planning and implementing body system-specific interventions as appropriate.

- Monitoring and taking actions to prevent or minimize the risk of complications.

- Accurate interpretation of procedure results.

Δ   Perform and document appropriate assessments based on the child's problem.

Δ   Apply knowledge of pathophysiology to planning care for clients with specific alterations in body systems, including recognizing associated signs and symptoms.

Δ   Interpret data that need to be reported immediately.

Δ   Monitor therapeutic devices (drainage/irrigating devices, chest tubes), if inserted, for proper functioning.

Δ   Explore resources, make referrals, collaborate with interdisciplinary team, and ensure continuity of client care.

Δ   Evaluate plans of care for multiple clients and revise plan as needed based on priorities of care and promotion of recovery.

Δ   Provide the child/family teaching regarding management of the child's health problem.

Δ   Recognize/respond to emergency situations, and evaluate/document the client's response to emergency interventions.

Key Points

Δ Communicable diseases are easily spread through airborne, droplet, or direct contact transmission.

Δ Most communicable disease can be prevented with immunizations.

Δ The child who is immunocompromised is most susceptible to complications of communicable diseases.

Key Factors

Δ Risks for communicable diseases in children include:

- Immunocompromised status.

- Crowded living conditions.

- Poor sanitation.

- Poor nutrition.

- Poor oxygenation and impaired circulation.

- Chronic illness.

Δ Communicable Diseases

Disease/Spread	Spread	Incubation	Communicability
Varicella (chickenpox)/ varicella-zoster virus	• Direct contact • Droplet • Contaminated objects	10 to 21 days	One day before lesions to 6 days after first lesions appear
Rubella (German measles)/rubella virus	• Direct contact • Droplet	14 to 21 days	7 days before to 5 days after rash
Rubeola (measles)/rubeola virus	• Direct contact • Droplet	10 to 21 days	4 days before to 5 days after rash
Pertussis (whooping cough)/Bordetella pertussis	Droplet	6 to 20 days	Catarrhal stage before paroxysms
Mumps/ paramyxovirus	• Direct contact • Droplet	14 to 21 days	Immediately before and after swelling
Epstein-Barr (EBV) virus (infectious mononucleosis)	Direct contact	4 to 6 weeks	Unknown

Assessment and Nursing Interventions

Varicella (chickenpox)	
Assessment	**Nursing Interventions**
• Fever, malaise, headache, and irritability • Abdominal discomfort • Lesions first appearing as macules, progressing to papules, then to clear fluid-filled vesicles that become crusted over • Lesions possible in mouth and throat; can interfere with intake • Intense pruritus possible from lesions • No longer contagious once all lesions have crusted over	• Varicella immune globulin to prevent and/or minimize severity of the illness in an unvaccinated child exposed to varicella • Acyclovir administered IV to children who are immunocompromised • Symptomatic treatment

Rubella (German measles)	
Assessment	**Nursing Interventions**
• Low-grade fever and mild rash lasting 2 to 3 days • Headache and malaise • Rash usually beginning on face, spreading down the trunk, and fading in a few days	• Exposure prevention for women who are pregnant • Symptomatic treatment

Measles (rubeola)	
Assessment	**Nursing Interventions**
• High fever, malaise • Enlarged lymph nodes, sore throat, cough, and conjunctivitis • Koplik spots on buccal mucosa (small, bright red spots with a blue-white center that usually appear 2 days before rash) • Rash of red maculopapular lesions that begin at hairline and usually spread down the body, eventually turning brown • Runny nose • Symptoms worsening and then decreasing about 2 days after the appearance of the rash	• Postexposure prophylaxis available either by giving the immunization within 72 hr or immunoglobulin within 6 days of exposure • Symptomatic treatment

Pertussis (whooping cough)

Assessment	Nursing Interventions
• Nighttime cough with sudden inspirations and a high-pitched sound • Paroxysm coughing with eyes bulging and tongue protruding • Thick mucous plug that may dislodge with coughing	• Antimicrobial therapy • Pertussis immune globulin administration. • Hospitalization for infants to provide high humidity and monitor for airway obstruction • Symptomatic treatment

Mumps

Assessment	Nursing Interventions
• Fever, headache, malaise • Anorexia for 24 hr • Earache increasing with chewing • Parotid glands becoming swollen, tender, and painful	• IV fluid if vomiting or unable to eat and drink • Soft foods for difficulty swallowing

Infectious mononucleosis

Assessment	Nursing Interventions
• Headache, malaise, and fatigue • Loss of appetite • Puffy eyes • Fever, sore throat • Cervical adenopathy • Splenomegaly, tender upper abdomen • Palatine petechiae • Pharyngitis/tonsillitis exudate • Diagnostic blood tests to include: mono spot blood smear for heterophile antibodies, which are specific for disease; antibodies present within 1 week of symptoms, will peak in 2 to 5 weeks, and may be present for 1 year. • WBC often elevated, atypical lymphocytes detected • Possible liver enzymes elevation (AST, ALT)	• May need to restrict activities for 2 to 3 months • Symptomatic treatment

Conjunctivitis

Assessment	Nursing Interventions
• Redness and inflammation of conjunctiva • Purulent drainage, crusted eyelids (bacterial) • Watery drainage (viral or allergic) • Pain, tearing (foreign body) • Recurrent conjunctivitis in infants possibly indicating an obstruction of the nasolacrimal duct; not contagious	• Viral self-limiting • Bacterial – topical antibacterial agents specific to infectious agent (e.g., *Chlamydia trachomatis*, *Neisseria gonorrhoeae*) • Removal of foreign body

Δ   Symptomatic Treatment

- Follow airborne, droplet, and contact precautions for a child who is hospitalized.

- Administer an antipyretic for fever. To prevent risk of Reye syndrome, do not administer aspirin.

- Administer analgesics for pain.

- Provide fluids and nutritious foods the child prefers.

- Skin care

  ◊   Administer diphenhydramine hydrochloride (Benadryl) to control itching.

  ◊   Provide calamine lotion for topical relief.

  ◊   Keep the child's skin clean and dry to prevent secondary infection.

  ◊   Keep the child cool, but prevent chilling.

  ◊   Give baths in tepid water, possibly with oatmeal.

  ◊   Keep the child's fingernails clean and short.

  ◊   Teach good oral hygiene. The child may gargle with warm water for a sore throat.

- Provide quiet, diversional activities.

- Promote adequate rest with naps, if necessary.

- Notify the child's school or day care center of the child's infection. Obtain a plan from the school so that the child can continue working on school work at home.

- Notify the health department of infection if necessary (pertussis, mumps, and measles).

- Instruct parents to teach the child to cover nose and mouth when coughing/sneezing. Parents should also wash the child's bed linens in mild detergent.

- Keep lights dim if the child develops photophobia.

- Teach parents of children who are immunocompromised to seek prompt medical care if symptoms develop.

Δ   Encourage adolescent to participate in decision making.

Δ   Most communicable diseases can have serious complications.

- Varicella (chickenpox) – secondary bacterial infections, including pneumonia and sepsis encephalitis, and chronic or transient thrombocytopenia.

- Rubella (German measles) – few complications, but there is a teratogenic effect on the fetus of exposed pregnant women.

- Rubeola (measles) – possible complications include otitis media, pneumonia, bronchiolitis, laryngitis and laryngotracheitis, and encephalitis.

- Pertussis (whooping cough) – pneumonia, otitis media, seizures, hemorrhage (caused by forceful coughing), hernia, prolapsed rectum, weight loss, and dehydration.

- Mumps – epididymo-orchitis in males, hearing loss, encephalitis, meningitis, myocarditis, arthritis, and hepatitis.

- Infectious mononucleosis – few complications, but ruptured spleen may result from blow to upper abdomen if splenomegaly is present.

NANDA Nursing Diagnoses

Δ   Activity intolerance

Δ   Disturbed body image

Δ   Hyperthermia

Δ   Imbalanced nutrition: less than body requirements

Δ   Impaired oral mucous membranes

Δ   Acute pain

Δ   Impaired swallowing

Complications and Nursing Interventions

Δ   Reye Syndrome

- Reye Syndrome frequently follows an episode of viral illness (e.g., influenza, varicella).

- Reye syndrome may be associated with use of aspirin or nonaspirin salicylates during a viral illness.

- The best prognosis for Reye syndrome is achieved with prompt diagnosis and aggressive treatment.

- Nursing care is provided in the ICU and includes maintaining vital functions, assisting with lumbar puncture, obtaining blood samples, administering IV fluids, performing nasogastric intubation, and inserting a Foley catheter.

Primary References:

Hockenberry, M., Wilson, D., & Winkelstein, M. (2005). *Wong's essentials of pediatric nursing care.* (7th ed.). St. Louis, MO: Mosby.

Additional Resources:

For information about communicable diseases, go to the Centers for Disease Control and Prevention Web site, *http://www.cdc.gov/*.

NANDA International (2004). *NANDA nursing diagnoses: Definitions and classification 2005-2006.* Philadelphia: NANDA.

Chapter 28: Communicable Diseases

Application Exercises

1. A mother tells a nurse that she is afraid to vaccinate her 15-month-old child against MMR. What information should the nurse give this mother?

Scenario: A nurse is caring for a 5-year-old child who recently immigrated to the United States. The child is recovering from appendicitis when he develops a high fever. During morning care, the nurse notices unusual bluish spots inside his mouth near his molars.

2. What should the nurse do regarding this assessment information?

3. Given the assessment information, why might the nurse suspect this child has rubeola?

4. If this child does have rubeola, when should the nurse expect him to break out in a rash? Describe the appearance of the rash.

5. In which of the following communicable diseases would pneumonia occur? (Select all that apply.)

_____ Conjunctivitis

_____ German measles (rubella)

_____ Measles (rubeola)

_____ Whooping cough (pertussis)

_____ Chickenpox

_____ Mumps

6. A woman who is pregnant should avoid exposure to which of the following communicable diseases?

A. Whooping cough

B. Mumps

C. Measles (rubeola)

D. German measles (rubella)

7. An adolescent has been diagnosed with mononucleosis. She has symptoms of fever, fatigue, swollen lymph nodes, sore throat, and a sore upper abdomen. Which of the following interventions should the nurse discuss with this adolescent and her parents? (Select all that apply.)

_____ Take antibiotics until symptoms subside.

_____ Drink plenty of liquids.

_____ Avoid participating in strenuous activities.

_____ Allow for periods of rest.

_____ Take aspirin as needed for fever and discomfort.

_____ Gargle with salt water every 2 to 3 hr.

8. What assessment data is consistent with a primary varicella infection?

A. High fever, malaise, Koplik spots, and maculopapular lesions

B. Fever, malaise, and rash with clear vesicles

C. Low-grade fever, mild rash beginning on face and spreading down trunk

D. Sore throat, painful enlarged lymph nodes, and tender abdomen

9. Which of the following interventions is helpful for a child who is scratching varicella lesions?

A. Warm baths and antifungal powder

B. Tepid sponge baths and lubricating creams

C. Oatmeal baths and short fingernails

D. Baths with baby soap and antibiotic ointment

Chapter 28: Communicable Diseases

Application Exercises Answer Key

1. A mother tells a nurse that she is afraid to vaccinate her 15-month-old child against MMR. What information should the nurse give this mother?

   The nurse should relate the seriousness of these diseases. The mother may consider them mild childhood illnesses and not realize that children can develop encephalitis or other complications from measles. There is information specifically addressing this information that can be printed out for her from the CDC Web site.

Scenario: A nurse is caring for a 5-year-old child who recently immigrated to the United States. The child is recovering from appendicitis when he develops a high fever. During morning care, the nurse notices unusual bluish spots inside his mouth near his molars.

---

2. What should the nurse do regarding this assessment information?

   The nurse should notify the primary care provider and the infection control officer of the facility. The child may need to be isolated until a diagnosis has been made.

3. Given the assessment information, why might the nurse suspect this child has rubeola?

   Recent immigrants are at risk for rubeola because they may not have been immunized. The child has a fever and may have Koplik's spots in his mouth, which are symptomatic of the early stage of rubeola.

4. If this child does have rubeola, when should the nurse expect him to break out in a rash? Describe the appearance of the rash.

   The rash does not appear until the third or fourth day after early symptoms of fever, malaise, and the presence of Koplik's spots. It starts as a red maculopapular rash on the face and spreads downward on the body. It begins to fade to a brown color in 3 to 4 more days.

---

5. In which of the following communicable diseases would pneumonia occur? (Select all that apply.)

     _____ Conjunctivitis

     _____ German measles (rubella)

     __X__ **Measles (rubeola)**

     __X__ **Whooping cough (pertussis)**

     __X__ **Chickenpox**

     _____ Mumps

Rubeola, pertussis, and chickenpox may cause pneumonia. The other communicable diseases do not result in pneumonia.

6. A woman who is pregnant should avoid exposure to which of the following communicable diseases?

     A. Whooping cough

     B. Mumps

     C. Measles (rubeola)

     D. German measles (rubella)

German measles (rubella) is teratogenic to the fetus if the pregnant woman develops the disease. The other disorders could cause illness in a woman who develops them, but they are not teratogenic.

7. An adolescent has been diagnosed with mononucleosis. She has symptoms of fever, fatigue, swollen lymph nodes, sore throat, and a sore upper abdomen. Which of the following interventions should the nurse discuss with this adolescent and her parents? (Select all that apply.)

     _____ Take antibiotics until symptoms subside.

     __X__ **Drink plenty of liquids.**

     __X__ **Avoid participating in strenuous activities.**

     __X__ **Allow for periods of rest.**

     _____ Take aspirin as needed for fever and discomfort.

     __X__ **Gargle with salt water every 2 to 3 hr.**

Interventions for mononucleosis include drinking liquids to stay hydrated, avoiding strenuous activities, resting, and gargling salt water to relieve a sore throat. Antibiotics should not be administered for this viral illness unless there is a presence of strep throat. Aspirin is not indicated due to the possibility of Reye syndrome. Acetaminophen (Tylenol) is usually recommended for discomfort and fever.

8. What assessment data is consistent with a primary varicella infection?

    A. High fever, malaise, Koplik spots, and maculopapular lesions

    B. Fever, malaise, and rash with clear vesicles

    C. Low-grade fever, mild rash beginning on face and spreading down trunk

    D. Sore throat, painful enlarged lymph nodes, and tender abdomen

Primary varicella (chickenpox) usually begins with malaise, fever, and a vesicular rash, which eventually forms crusts and scabs. Option A is consistent with rubeola; C is consistent with rubella; and D is consistent with infectious mononucleosis.

9. Which of the following interventions is helpful for a child who is scratching varicella lesions?

    A. Warm baths and antifungal powder

    B. Tepid sponge baths and lubricating creams

    C. Oatmeal baths and short fingernails

    D. Baths with baby soap and antibiotic ointment

Oatmeal baths are the most soothing for a rash that is intensely itching. Short fingernails will prevent skin tears. A very warm bath could increase itching, and antifungal powder is not useful, since varicella is not caused by a fungus. Lubricating creams could increase itching. Soap of any kind can increase itching, and antibiotic ointment is not indicated.

Unit 2   Nursing Care of Children with System Disorders

Section: Nursing Care of Children with Lymphatic/Infectious/Immune Disorders

Chapter 29:   Acute Otitis Media
              Contributor: Michele Woodbeck, MS, RN

 NCLEX-RN® Connections:

> **Learning Objective**: Review and apply knowledge within "**Acute Otitis Media**" in readiness for performance of the following nursing activities as outlined by the NCLEX-RN® test plan:
>
> Δ Assist with relevant laboratory, diagnostic, and therapeutic procedures within the nursing role, including:
>
>   • Client preparation for the procedure.
>
>   • Client teaching (before and following the procedure).
>
>   • Accurate collection of specimens.
>
>   • Evaluation of the child's response to the procedure.
>
>   • Planning and implementing body system-specific interventions as appropriate.
>
>   • Monitoring and taking actions to prevent or minimize the risk of complications.
>
>   • Accurate interpretation of procedure results.
>
> Δ Perform and document appropriate assessments based on the child's problem.
>
> Δ Apply knowledge of pathophysiology to planning care for clients with specific alterations in body systems, including recognizing associated signs and symptoms.
>
> Δ Interpret data that need to be reported immediately.
>
> Δ Monitor therapeutic devices (drainage/irrigating devices, chest tubes), if inserted, for proper functioning.
>
> Δ Explore resources, make referrals, collaborate with interdisciplinary team, and ensure continuity of client care.
>
> Δ Evaluate plans of care for multiple clients and revise plan as needed based on priorities of care and promotion of recovery.
>
> Δ Provide the child/family teaching regarding management of the child's health problem.
>
> Δ Recognize/respond to emergency situations, and evaluate/document the client's response to emergency interventions.

📖 **Key Points**

Δ   Acute otitis media (AOM) is an infection of the structures of the middle ear.

Δ   Otitis media with effusion (OME) is present when there is a collection of fluid in the middle ear but no infection.

Δ   Repeated infections may cause impaired hearing and speech delays.

Δ   Many infections clear spontaneously in a few days.

Key Factors

Δ   The eustachian tubes in children are shorter and more horizontal than those of adults. Therefore, children have an increased risk for developing otitis media.

Δ   Otitis media is most common in the first 24 months of life, with an increase again when children enter school (ages 5 to 6). Otitis media infrequently occurs after age 7.

Δ   Otitis media is usually triggered by a bacterial (e.g., *Streptococcus pneumoniae*, *Haemophilus influenzae*, *Moraxella catarrhalis*) or viral infection, allergies, or enlarged tonsils.

Δ   There is a lower incidence of otitis media in breastfed infants (possibly due to the presence of immunoglobulin [Ig] A in breast milk, which protects against infection.

Δ   Risk Factors

   •   Male gender, preschool age

   •   Recent respiratory infection with respiratory syncytial virus or influenza

   •   Exposure to large numbers of children (day care)

   •   Exposure to second-hand smoke

   •   Cleft lip and/or cleft palate

   •   Down syndrome

Assessment

Δ   Nursing history may include history of upper respiratory infection, changes in the child's behavior, frequent crying, irritability, fussiness, inability to console the child, tugging at ear, reports of ear pain, anorexia, nausea, and vomiting.

Δ   Physical Assessment Findings of AOM

   •   Rubbing or pulling on ear

- Crying

- Lethargy

- Purulent material in middle ear or drainage from external canal if tympanic membrane has ruptured

- Decreased or no tympanic movement with pneumatic otoscopy

- Lymphadenopathy of the neck and head

- Temperature (may be as high as 40° C [104° F])

- Hearing difficulties and speech delays if otitis media becomes a chronic condition

Δ   Physical Assessment Findings of OME

- Feeling of fullness in the ear

- Dull gray or yellowish coloration of the tympanic membrane with decreased movement

- Transient hearing loss and balance disturbances

Diagnostic Procedures and Nursing Interventions

Δ   A pneumatic otoscope is used to visualize the tympanic membrane and middle ear structures. The otoscope also assesses tympanic membrane movement.

- Assessment technique includes gently pulling the pinna down and back to visualize the tympanic membrane of a child younger than 3 years old. For a child older than 3 years, gently pull the pinna up and back.

- AOM findings include:

◊   Red or yellow membrane.

◊   Purulent exudates.

◊   Bulging or nonbulging membranes.

- OME findings include diminished membrane mobility as a result of fluid in the middle ear (effusion).

NANDA Nursing Diagnoses

Δ   Risk for delayed development

Δ   Hyperthermia

Δ   Acute pain

Δ   Disturbed sleep pattern

Nursing Interventions

Δ   Provide comfort measures.

- Position ice compress over the affected ear.

- Provide diversional activities.

- Administer analgesics/antipyretics as ordered.

  ◊   Acetaminophen (Tylenol) 10 to 15 mg/kg may be given every 4 hr.

  ◊   Ibuprofen (Advil) 10 mg/kg may be given every 6 hr.

Δ   Administer antibiotic therapy as prescribed (usually at home).

- Amoxicillin is the antibiotic of first choice. It is usually given in high doses (80 to 90 mg/kg/day). Amoxicillin-clavulanate (Augmentin) and azithromycin (Zithromax) are second-line antibiotics that may be used.

- Usual course of treatment is 10 to 14 days in children younger than 6 years old. The course may be shorter for older children.

Δ   Instruct parents in home care.

- Instruct in comfort measures.

- Provide direction for proper medication administration.

  ◊   Ear drops should be administered using appropriate technique.

  ◊   The entire dosage should be completed.

  ◊   Observe for signs of allergy to antibiotic (e.g., rash, difficulty breathing).

  ◊   Discourage use of decongestants or antihistamines.

- Encourage the parents to feed child in an upright position when bottle or breastfeeding.

- Clean external ear if draining with sterile cotton swabs. Apply antibiotic ointment.

- Teach the parents to avoid risk factors if possible (e.g., second-hand smoke, exposure to individuals with viral/bacterial respiratory infections).

- Stress the importance of seeking medical care at initial signs and symptoms of infections (e.g., change in child's behavior, tugging on ear).

- Encourage the parents to keep the child's immunizations up to date.

Therapeutic Procedures and Nursing Interventions

Δ   Myringotomy and placement of tympanoplasty tubes may be indicated for the child with multiple episodes of otitis media. This procedure may now be performed by laser treatment.

- This procedure is performed in an outpatient setting with administration of general anesthesia. It usually can be completed in 15 min.

- A small incision is made in the tympanic membrane, and tiny plastic or metal tubes are placed into the eardrum to equalize pressure and minimize effusion.

- Recovery takes place in a PACU, and discharge usually occurs within 1 hr.

- Postoperative pain is not common and, if present, will be mild.

- Antibiotic ear drops may be prescribed for a few days.

- Limit the child's activities for a few days following surgery.

- The child should avoid getting water into the ears while the tubes are in place. The effectiveness of earplugs is not conclusive. Advise the parents to follow the primary care provider's instructions.

- Tubes come out by themselves (usually in 6 to 12 months). Instruct parents to notify the primary care provider when this occurs. This usually does not require replacement of tubes.

Complications and Nursing Implications

Δ   Hearing Loss and/or Speech Delays

- The child should be assessed and monitored for deficits.

- Refer the child for audiology testing if needed.

- Speech therapy may be necessary.

Primary Reference:

Hockenberry, M., Wilson, D., & Winkelstein, M. (2005). *Wong's essentials of pediatric nursing care*. (7th ed.). St. Louis, MO: Mosby.

Additional Resources:

American Academy of Otolaryngology-Head and Neck Surgery. (2007). *Doctor, please explain ear tubes*. Retrieved February 2, 2007, from http://www.entnet.org/healthinfo/ears/Ear-Tubes.cfm

Ball, J. W., & Bindler, R. C. (2005). *Child health nursing: Partnering with children and families*. (1st ed.). Upper Saddle River, NJ: Prentice-Hall.

NANDA International (2004). *NANDA nursing diagnoses: Definitions and classification 2005-2006*. Philadelphia: NANDA.

Chapter 29: Acute Otitis Media

Application Exercises

1. A mother brings her 14-month-old child into the clinic for a well-child check. She tells the nurse that three children in her daughter's day care have developed an ear infection, and she wants to know how she can determine if her daughter has developed one. How should the nurse respond?

2. How should a nurse explain myringotomy and placement of tympanoplasty tubes to a parent?

3. Develop a plan to teach a parent how to administer acetaminophen (Tylenol) every 4 to 6 hr as needed and amoxicillin suspension three times a day to an 18-month-old child.

4. A 2-year-old child has had three ear infections in the past 5 months. For which of the following long-term complications of otitis media with effusion should the nurse screen the child?

    A. Balance difficulties

    B. Tinnitus

    C. Speech delays

    D. Pneumonia

5. Which of the following health practices should a nurse emphasize to a parent of a child with multiple ear infections?

    A. Avoid exposing the child to second-hand smoke.

    B. Keep the child indoors at all times.

    C. Keep a hat on the child when going outside.

    D. Avoid exposing the child to extremely loud noises.

6. An 8-month-old infant with signs and symptoms of acute otitis media is brought to the outpatient facility by his parent. Which of the following factors, if present, place the infant at risk for otitis media? (Select all that apply.)

    _____ The infant is breastfed.

    _____ The infant attends day care.

    _____ The infant has all of his immunizations.

    _____ The infant was born with a cleft palate.

    _____ The infant's father smokes cigarettes.

Chapter 29: Acute Otitis Media

Application Exercises Answer Key

1. A mother brings her 14-month-old child into the clinic for a well-child check. She tells the nurse that three children in her daughter's day care have developed an ear infection, and she wants to know how she can determine if her daughter has developed one. How should the nurse respond?

The nurse should tell the mother that her child will likely become irritable and difficult to console. The child may then experience disturbed sleeping routines, may pull, tug, or rub on one or both ears, and may develop a temperature, diarrhea, vomiting, and/or loss of appetite. These symptoms may accompany an upper respiratory infection.

2. How should a nurse explain myringotomy and placement of tympanoplasty tubes to a parent?

A myringotomy tube involves making a small incision into the tympanic membrane. Tubes are placed to help equalize pressure and relieve the fluid when there is chronic effusion. The procedure is usually done on an outpatient basis, and the child goes home the same day.

3. Develop a plan to teach a parent how to administer acetaminophen (Tylenol) every 4 to 6 hr as needed and amoxicillin suspension three times a day to an 18-month-old child.

It is important for the parent to understand how to measure the correct dosage. Acetaminophen (Tylenol) can be toxic to the child's liver; therefore, it is important that the parent understand the importance of not exceeding the recommended dosage. The nurse needs to ascertain what type of measuring device the parent has available and discourage the use of household teaspoons for measurement. The nurse should observe the parent measuring both medications. Children at this age may resist taking medications; therefore, suggestions include using a plastic, needleless syringe to administer small amounts of the medication into the child's mouth along the side of the tongue, or mixing the medication in a small amount of applesauce or pudding.

4. A 2-year-old child has had three ear infections in the past 5 months. For which of the following long-term complications of otitis media with effusion should the nurse screen the child?

   A. Balance difficulties

   B. Tinnitus

   C. Speech delays

   D. Pneumonia

Speech delay is a common and serious complication. Balance difficulties and tinnitus may be present with otitis media, but are not long-term complications. Pneumonia is not a complication of otitis media.

5. Which of the following health practices should a nurse emphasize to a parent of a child with multiple ear infections?

   A. Avoid exposing the child to second-hand smoke.

   B. Keep the child indoors at all times.

   C. Keep a hat on the child when going outside.

   D. Avoid exposing the child to extremely loud noises.

Second-hand (passive) smoke increases congestion and respiratory secretions. Therefore, children often exposed to smoke experience frequent bouts of otitis media. Keeping the child indoors has nothing to do with otitis media. Keeping a hat on the child and avoiding loud noises do not prevent otitis, although they can prevent ear pain if infection is present.

6. An 8-month-old infant with signs and symptoms of acute otitis media is brought to the outpatient facility by his parent. Which of the following factors, if present, places the infant at risk for otitis media? (Select all that apply.)

   _____ The infant is breastfed.

   __X__ **The infant attends day care**.

   _____ The infant has all of his immunizations.

   __X__ **The infant was born with a cleft palate.**

   __X__ **The infant's father smokes cigarettes.**

Infants who attend day care have an increased risk of exposure. Infants born with cleft lip and/or palate are more prone to AOM because micro-organisms can more easily move up the eustachian tubes due to reflux of milk. Exposure to second-hand smoke is also a risk factor for AOM. Breastfeeding is protective for AOM because breast milk contains secretory IgA. Being up to date with immunizations can help prevent AOM since it is a complication of some communicable diseases, such as measles.

Unit 2   Nursing Care of Children with System Disorders

Section: Nursing Care of Children with Lymphatic/Infectious/Immune Disorders

Chapter 30:   Cancer (Neuroblastoma and Wilms' Tumor)
Contributor: Michele Woodbeck, MS, RN

 NCLEX-RN® Connections:

> **Learning Objective**: Review and apply knowledge within "**Cancer (Neuroblastoma and Wilms' Tumor)**" in readiness for performance of the following nursing activities as outlined by the NCLEX-RN® test plan:
>
> Δ   Assist with relevant laboratory, diagnostic, and therapeutic procedures within the nursing role, including:
>
> •   Client preparation for the procedure.
>
> •   Client teaching (before and following the procedure).
>
> •   Accurate collection of specimens.
>
> •   Evaluation of the child's response to the procedure.
>
> •   Planning and implementing body system-specific interventions as appropriate.
>
> •   Monitoring and taking actions to prevent or minimize the risk of complications.
>
> •   Accurate interpretation of procedure results.
>
> Δ   Perform and document appropriate assessments based on the child's problem.
>
> Δ   Apply knowledge of pathophysiology to planning care for clients with specific alterations in body systems, including recognizing associated signs and symptoms.
>
> Δ   Interpret data that need to be reported immediately.
>
> Δ   Monitor therapeutic devices (drainage/irrigating devices, chest tubes), if inserted, for proper functioning.
>
> Δ   Explore resources, make referrals, collaborate with interdisciplinary team, and ensure continuity of client care.
>
> Δ   Evaluate plans of care for multiple clients and revise plan as needed based on priorities of care and promotion of recovery.
>
> Δ   Provide the child/family teaching regarding management of the child's health problem.
>
> Δ   Recognize/respond to emergency situations, and evaluate/document the client's response to emergency interventions.

Key Points/Key Factors

Δ **Wilms' tumor (nephroblastoma)** is a malignancy that occurs in the kidneys or abdomen.

- This cancer occurs more often in girls, and age 3 is the peak age of occurrence.

- A genetic link may play a role in the development of this tumor.

- Metastasis is rare.

Δ **Neuroblastoma** is a malignancy that occurs in the adrenal gland, the sympathetic chain of the retroperitoneal area, head, neck, pelvis, or chest.

- This cancer occurs more often in boys, and most are diagnosed before age 10.

- Most tumors have spread by metastasis at the time of diagnosis.

Δ Presenting signs and symptoms will vary with the type of cancer.

Assessment

Δ Obtain a history of congenital anomalies and family history of malignancies.

Δ Wilms' tumor presents as an abdominal swelling or mass that is usually firm, nontender, and unilateral.

Δ Neuroblastoma presents as an asymmetrical, firm, nontender mass in the abdomen. This mass crosses the midline.

Δ Wilms' tumor and neuroblastoma can cause urinary symptoms (e.g., frequency, urgency) with compression on renal structures.

Δ Signs and symptoms of metastasis include:

- Edema (periorbital) with ecchymosis around eyes.

- Lymphadenopathy (predominantly cervical and supraclavicular in neuroblastoma).

- Weight loss, anemia, and fatigue.

- Hepatomegaly, splenomegaly.

- Possible bone pain.

- Respiratory involvement leading to shortness of breath, decreased breath sounds, cough, and respiratory distress.

- Paralysis that will have varying degrees (neuroblastoma).

Diagnostic Procedures and Nursing Interventions

Δ Chest x-ray, computed tomography (CT) scan, magnetic resonance imaging (MRI), positron emission tomography (PET) scan, and single photon emission computed tomography (SPECT) scans are used to visualize tumors and metastasis and determine the stage of the cancer.

- Educate the child/family about the procedure.
  - ◊ Assess the child for allergies to dye or shellfish.
  - ◊ Tell the child to remain still during the procedure.
  - ◊ Instruct the child to drink oral contrast if prescribed.
  - ◊ Sedate the child if prescribed.
  - ◊ For MRI, assess for the presence of metal objects (e.g., surgical clip, pacemaker, jewelry).
  - ◊ Provide emotional support.

Δ Blood studies are used to identify anemia and infection.

- CBC normal values

Age	Hgb	Hct
2 months	9.0 to 14.0 g/dL	28 to 42%
6 to 12 years	11.5 to 15.5 g/dL	35 to 45%
12 to 18 years	13.0 to 16.0 g/dL (male) 12.0 to 16.0 g/dL (female)	37 to 49% (male) 36 to 46% (female)

- WBC normal values
  - ◊ 1 month – 5,000 to 19,500/mm^3
  - ◊ 1 to 3 years – 6,000 to 17,500/mm^3
  - ◊ 4 to 7 years – 5,000 to 15,500/mm^3
  - ◊ 8 to 13 years – 4,500 to 13,500/mm^3
  - ◊ Adult – 4,500 to 11,000/mm^3
- Platelets – normal value: 150,000 to 400,000/mm^3
- WBC is often elevated: 20,000 to 100,000/mm^3.
- CBC: Hgb, Hct, and platelets are decreased.
- Bleeding times increase.

Δ Serum BUN and creatinine levels are used to assess renal function.

△ Urine may be evaluated for the presence of breakdown products of catecholamines (vanillylmandelic acid, homovanillic acid, dopamine, and norepinephrine) to diagnose adrenal or sympathetic tumors.

△ Use liver function tests to assess liver function.

△ Biopsy may be a local procedure to obtain a sample of tissue for diagnosis. A biopsy can also be obtained during surgery under general anesthesia, possibly in conjunction with excision or resection of the tumor at the same time. During the procedure, provide emotional support.

△ Following the biopsy:

- Assess the site for bleeding.

- Prevent infection at the biopsy site.

- Provide pain relief.

△ Following bone marrow aspiration and biopsy:

- Apply pressure to the site for 5 to 10 min.

- Assess vital signs frequently.

- Apply pressure dressing.

- Monitor for signs of bleeding and infection for 24 hr.

NANDA Nursing Diagnoses

△ Disturbed body image

△ Fatigue

△ Fluid volume deficit

△ Risk for infection

△ Imbalanced nutrition: less than body requirements

△ Impaired oral mucous membranes

△ Acute pain/chronic pain

Nursing Interventions

△ Assess child/family coping and support.

△ Assess for developmental delays related to illness.

△ Assess physical growth (height and weight).

Δ   Monitor I&O and nutritional status.

Δ   Assess and monitor bowel status.

Δ   Provide education and support to the child/family regarding diagnostic testing, treatment plan, ongoing therapy, and prognosis.

Δ   Provide preoperative teaching to the child/family that includes length of surgery, where the child will recover, and what equipment will be in place (e.g., nasogastric tube, IV line, Foley catheter).

Δ   Avoid preoperative palpation of Wilms' tumor.

Δ   Immunosuppression necessitates ongoing assessments, which include:

- Monitoring vital signs. Low-grade temperature may be a sign of infection.

- Monitoring blood counts for anemia, granulocytopenia, and thrombocytopenia.

- Monitoring for signs of infection that can include lung congestion, redness, swelling, pain around IV sites, lesions in mouth, wound sites, and immunization status.

- Following special immunization guidelines for immunosuppressed children.

Δ   Administer chemotherapy agents according to established protocols.

Δ   Administer antibiotics as prescribed for infection.

Δ   Keep the child's skin clean, dry, and lubricated.

Δ   Provide oral hygiene and keep the child's lips lubricated.

Δ   Engage in age-appropriate diversional activities.

Δ   Provide support to the child/family/siblings.

- Avoid false reassurance.

- Listen to the child's concerns.

- Allow time for the child/family to discuss feelings regarding loss and to grieve.

Therapeutic Procedures and Nursing Interventions

Δ   Treatment may be a combination of surgery, chemotherapy, and radiation or any combination of these modalities.

Δ   Chemotherapy is administered according to a protocol that uses multiple agents to have the greatest therapeutic effect while minimizing side effects.

Δ   The chemotherapy may be administered orally, intravenously, or locally (such as intrathecally for a CNS tumor).

Δ   The child undergoing chemotherapy may have a long-term venous access device in place, such as an implanted port or a Hickman catheter.

Δ   Radiation therapy is dose-calculated and usually delivered in divided treatments over several weeks.

Δ   Both chemotherapy and radiation affect rapidly growing cells in the body; therefore, cells that normally have a fast turnover may be affected as well as cancer cells.

Δ   Postoperative chemotherapy agents include vincristine (Oncovin), doxorubicin (Adriamycin), cyclophosphamide (Cytoxan), actinomycin D (Dactinomycin) for Wilms' tumor, and cisplatin (Abiplatin) for neuroblastoma.

Δ   Treatment for Wilms' tumor includes:

•   Preoperative chemotherapy or radiation to decrease the size of the tumor.

•   Surgical removal of the tumor and affected organs.

•   Chemotherapy treatment that can last anywhere from 6 to 15 months.

•   Radiation for children with recurrent disease, large tumors, and/or metastasis.

Δ   Treatment for neuroblastoma includes:

•   Surgical removal of the tumor.

•   Radiation in an emergency to decrease the size of a tumor that is compressing the spinal cord.

•   Radiation to decrease the size of tumors and palliation for metastasis.

Δ   Side Effects and Nursing Interventions

Side Effect – Bone marrow depression resulting in anemia, neutropenia, and/or thrombocytopenia

Nursing Interventions
- Monitor blood counts for anemia, neutropenia, and thrombocytopenia.
- Monitor vital signs and report increased temperature. Low-grade temperature may be a sign of infection.
- Monitor for signs of infection, which include lung congestion, redness, swelling, and pain around IV sites, lesions in mouth, wound sites, and immunization status.
- Protect the child from sources of possible infection.
  ◊ Use good handwashing
  ◊ Encourage the child and family to use good handwashing.
  ◊ Encourage the child to avoid crowds while undergoing chemotherapy.
  ◊ Instruct the child to avoid fresh fruits and vegetables.
- Avoid invasive procedures (e.g., injections, rectal temps, catheters). Apply pressure to puncture sites for 5 min.
- Avoid ASA/NSAIDs.
- Administer filgrastim (Neupogen), a granulocyte colony-stimulating factor that stimulates WBC production.
  ◊ Administer filgrastim subcutaneously daily.
  ◊ Monitor the child for headache, fever, and mild to moderate bone pain.
- Administer epoetin alfa (Procrit) to stimulate RBC formation.
  ◊ Administer epoetin alfa subcutaneously two to three times a week.
  ◊ Monitor blood pressure.
- Administer interleukin-11 to stimulate platelet formation.
- Encourage use of a soft toothbrush.
- Use gentle handling and positioning to protect from injury.
- Organize care to provide for rest. Schedule rest periods.

Side Effect – Anorexia, nausea, vomiting

- Avoid strong odors. Provide a pleasant atmosphere for meals.
- Suggest and assist in selecting foods/fluids.
- Provide smaller, more frequent meals.
- Administer antiemetics as ordered, which is usually before meals.

Side Effect – Diarrhea will occur if abdominal area is radiated. Some chemotherapeutic agents may cause constipation. If mobility and nutrition decrease, the child is more likely to develop constipation.

- Provide meticulous skin care.
- Provide a nutritious diet.
- Determine if certain foods worsen the condition of the child (high-fiber, lactose-rich foods/drinks).
- Monitor I&O and daily weight.

Side Effect – Stomatitis, dry mouth

- Visit the dentist before therapy.
- Provide soft toothbrush and/or swabs.
- Use NS or sodium bicarbonate (e.g., 1 tsp salt mixed with 1 pint of water, 1 tsp baking soda mixed with 1 qt water) mouth washes.
- Lubricate the child's lips.
- Give soft, nonacidic foods. A puréed or liquid diet may be required.
- Administer prescribed oral preparations.
- Provide analgesics.

Side Effect – Alopecia with chemotherapy and radiation of head and/or neck

- Assess feelings.
- Discuss cutting long hair.
- Use gentle shampoos. Gently brush the child's hair.
- Avoid blow dryers and curling irons.
- Suggest wearing a hat or scarf.
- Discuss purchasing a wig.

Side Effect – Impaired skin integrity from radiation

- Avoid the use of soaps, creams, and/or lotions over the area being radiated.
- Avoid using hot or cold water.
- Wear loose clothing.
- Avoid tape over the area.
- Avoid sunlight to the radiated area.
- Seek medical care for blisters, weeping, and red/tender skin.

Complications and Nursing Implications

Δ Pancytopenia

- Neutropenia secondary to disease and/or treatment (increases the risk of infection)

   ◊ Maintain a hygienic environment and encourage the child to do the same.

   ◊ Closely monitor the child for signs of infection (cough, alterations in breath sounds, urine, or feces). Report temperature greater than 37.8° C (100° F).

   ◊ Administer antimicrobial, antiviral, and antifungal medications as prescribed.

   ◊ Monitor absolute neutrophil count (ANC). ANC less than 2,000/mm³ suggests an increased risk of infection. ANC of less than 500/mm³ indicates a severe risk of infection.

   ◊ Administer blood products (e.g., granulocytes) as needed.

- Thrombocytopenia secondary to disease and/or treatment (increases the risk for bleeding)

  ◊ Minimize the risk of trauma (safe environment).

  ◊ Monitor platelet counts. Platelet counts less than 50,000/mm^3 suggest an increased risk of bleeding, and spontaneous bleeds can occur at less than 20,000/mm^3.

  ◊ Administer blood products (e.g., platelets) as needed.

- Anemia secondary to disease and/or treatment (increases the risk of hypoxemia)

  ◊ Maintain an environment that does not overly tax the child's energy resources/capability.

  ◊ Monitor RBC counts.

  ◊ Provide a diet high in protein and carbohydrates.

  ◊ Administer colony-stimulating factors, such as epoetin alfa, as prescribed.

  ◊ Administer blood products (e.g., packed RBCs) as needed.

Primary Reference:

Hockenberry, M., Wilson, D., & Winkelstein, M. (2005). *Wong's essentials of pediatric nursing care*. (7th ed.). St. Louis, MO: Mosby.

Additional Resources:

NANDA International (2004). *NANDA nursing diagnoses: Definitions and classification 2005-2006*. Philadelphia: NANDA.

WebMD. (n.d.). Find a drug. Retrieved February 9, 2007, from http://www.webmd.com/drugs/index-drugs.aspx

Wong, D. L., Wilson, D., & Kline, N. E. (2003). *Wong's nursing care of infants and children*. (7th ed.). St. Louis, MO: Mosby.

Chapter 30: Cancer (Neuroblastoma and Wilms' Tumor)

Application Exercises

Scenario: A 3-year-old child with Wilms' tumor of the right kidney is admitted to the pediatric oncology unit. He is to undergo a course of chemotherapy that will begin during admission. Radiation treatments are scheduled following initial chemotherapy to shrink the tumor before surgically removing it, the kidney, and adjacent adrenal gland.

1. Explain what baseline assessments the nurse should obtain.

2. When completing the child's admission assessment, which of the following components of the abdominal assessment is unacceptable for the nurse to perform?

    A. Auscultation

    B. Palpation

    C. Percussion

    D. Inspection

3. What should the nurse tell the parent(s) regarding the frequent blood draws that are prescribed for the child?

4. Which of the following interventions is a priority when, after several weeks of outpatient chemotherapy, the child's laboratory results indicate a Hgb of 12.7 g/dL, a Hct of 36%, a WBC of 1,000/mm^3, and a platelet count of 210,000/mm^3?

    A. Provide the child with extra nap time.

    B. Hold all venipuncture sites for 10 full minutes.

    C. Prepare to treat with epoetin alpha (Procrit).

    D. Wash the child's and caregiver's hands before meals and snacks.

5. The child is now ready to begin outpatient radiation treatments. What should the nurse teach his parents about this therapy?

6. A child has undergone surgical removal of a Wilms' tumor. Which of the following nursing diagnoses should receive priority in the immediate postoperative period?

     A. Activity intolerance

     B. Risk for infection

     C. Risk for injury

     D. Imbalanced nutrition: less than body requirements

7. A primary care provider has ordered a clear liquid diet for a child who is postoperative surgical removal of a Wilms' tumor. Which of the following assessment findings requires that the nurse clarify this order?

     A. Abdominal girth 1 cm larger than yesterday

     B. Report of pain at the operative site

     C. Absence of bowel sounds on second postoperative day

     D. Passing flatus every 30 min

8. A child who is 2 days postoperative surgical removal of a Wilms' tumor is sobbing and reporting abdominal pain. The child was medicated 30 min ago, and the nurse observes that the child's abdominal girth has increased by 6 cm from 2 hr previously. The child's skin is cool and moist. Which of the following actions should the nurse take first?

     A. Assess vital signs and dressing.

     B. Provide diversion for 30 more minutes to allow medication to take effect.

     C. Reposition the child into the semi-Fowler's position.

     D. Provide the child with a quiet environment.

9. When assessing a child with a neuroblastoma of the adrenal gland, which of the following findings indicate to the nurse that the child has developed metastasis from the primary site? (Select all that apply.)

     _____ Weight gain

     _____ Bone pain

     _____ Varying degrees of paralysis

     _____ Dependent edema

     _____ Hepatomegaly

Chapter 30: Cancer (Neuroblastoma and Wilms' Tumor)

Application Exercises Answer Key

Scenario: A 3-year-old child with Wilms' tumor of the right kidney is admitted to the pediatric oncology unit. He is to undergo a course of chemotherapy that will begin during admission. Radiation treatments are scheduled following initial chemotherapy to shrink the tumor before surgically removing it, the kidney, and adjacent adrenal gland.

1. Explain what baseline assessments the nurse should obtain.

Vital signs including temperature

Skin to assess for reddened and/or broken areas

Mucous membranes

Last dental visit

Height and weight

Nutritional preferences and normal meal patterns

Activity and mobility levels

Fears and knowledge level of the child/family.

2. When completing the child's admission assessment, which of the following components of the abdominal assessment is unacceptable for the nurse to perform?

    A. Auscultation
    B. Palpation
    C. Percussion
    D. Inspection

Palpation of the abdomen could rupture the encapsulated tumor. None of the other components of abdominal assessment puts pressure on the tumor.

3. What should the nurse tell the parent(s) regarding the frequent blood draws that are prescribed for the child?

The nurse should reinforce instructions that were provided by the primary care provider. The nurse must determine what the parent(s) understand about the side effects of chemotherapy. The nurse needs to discuss with the parent(s) that frequent assessments, particularly of WBC, RBC, and platelets, will help detect early signs of impairment so that proper corrective treatments can begin early.

4. Which of the following interventions is a priority when, after several weeks of outpatient chemotherapy, the child's laboratory results indicate a Hgb of 12.7 g/dL, a Hct of 36%, a WBC of 1,000/mm^3, and a platelet count of 210,000/mm^3?

    A. Provide the child with extra nap time.

    B. Hold all venipuncture sites for 10 full minutes.

    C. Prepare to treat with epoetin alpha (Procrit).

    D. Wash the child's and caregiver's hands before meals and snacks.

Scrupulous attention to handwashing for both the child and his caregivers is important due to the high risk for infection (the child has a very low WBC). Extra nap time might be required if the child experiences fatigue. Epoetin alpha might be prescribed due to low Hgb and Hct; however, these levels are normal. Holding venipuncture sites much longer than normal might be indicated if thrombocyte (platelet) count is low; however, it is within normal limits.

5. The child is now ready to begin outpatient radiation treatments. What should the nurse teach his parents about this therapy?

The nurse should explain to the parent(s) that the child will probably have marks on his skin to outline the targeted area(s). These should be left in place. The nurse reinforces information about side effects discussed by the primary care provider. The nurse should also teach the parent(s) to wash the marked area(s) with lukewarm water, pat dry, and take care not to remove the markings. Avoid the use of creams, lotions, and/or powders unless they are prescribed. The area(s) should also be protected from the sun.

6. A child has undergone surgical removal of a Wilms' tumor. Which of the following nursing diagnoses should receive priority in the immediate postoperative period?

      A. Activity intolerance

      B. Risk for infection

      C. Risk for injury

      D. Imbalanced nutrition: less than body requirements

In the immediate postoperative period, the risk for injury (hemorrhage) is high due to the high vascularity of the surgery. Activity intolerance is not as high a priority as postoperative hemorrhage. Risk for infection is present, but it is also not the priority. Nutrition is a concern, but this child will be NPO for several hours to days.

7. A primary care provider has ordered a clear liquid diet for a child who is postoperative surgical removal of a Wilms' tumor. Which of the following assessment findings requires that the nurse clarify this order?

      A. Abdominal girth 1 cm larger than yesterday

      B. Report of pain at the operative site

      C. Absence of bowel sounds on second postoperative day

      D. Passing flatus every 30 min

The absence of bowel sounds is an indication that GI motility is absent. This is an indication that the child should not eat. The increase in girth is probably secondary to edema (it is not significant enough to indicate distention); pain is normal on the second postoperative day; and the child should be medicated with pain medication. Passing gas is a positive sign, indicating good bowel motility.

8. A child who is 2 days postoperative surgical removal of a Wilms' tumor is sobbing and reporting abdominal pain. The child was medicated 30 min ago, and the nurse observes that the child's abdominal girth has increased by 6 cm from 2 hr previously. The child's skin is cool and moist. Which of the following actions should the nurse take first?

> **A. Assess vital signs and dressing.**
>
> B. Provide diversion for 30 more minutes to allow medication to take effect.
>
> C. Reposition the child into the semi-Fowler's position.
>
> D. Provide the child with a quiet environment.

> The priority nursing action is to assess the child for blood loss/shock due to the sudden increase in abdominal girth. Vital signs can indicate possible blood loss if pulse and respirations are increased and blood pressure has decreased. Checking the dressing is another way to assess for bleeding. Waiting 30 more minutes for pain medication to take effect is not acceptable for this child. If blood loss is occurring, repositioning the child into a semi-Fowler's position would further decrease blood pressure. Providing a quiet environment is not a priority and serves little purpose at this time.

9. When assessing a child with a neuroblastoma of the adrenal gland, which of the following findings indicate to the nurse that the child has developed metastasis from the primary site? (Select all that apply.)

> _____ Weight gain
>
> __X__ **Bone pain**
>
> __X__ **Varying degrees of paralysis**
>
> _____ Dependent edema
>
> __X__ **Hepatomegaly**

> Bone pain, varying degrees of paralysis, and hepatomegaly are signs and symptoms of metastasis. Weight loss, rather than weight gain, and periorbital edema, rather than dependent edema, will be identified.

HIV/AIDS **CHAPTER** 31

Unit 2   Nursing Care of Children with System Disorders

Section: Nursing Care of Children with Lymphatic/Infectious/Immune Disorders

Chapter 31:   HIV/AIDS

Contributor: Michele Woodbeck, MS, RN

NCLEX-RN® Connections:

Learning Objective: Review and apply knowledge within "**HIV/AIDS**" in readiness for performance of the following nursing activities as outlined by the NCLEX-RN® test plan:

Δ   Identify communicable diseases and the methods of organism transmission, and report as appropriate.

Δ   Provide and instruct the child/family regarding appropriate infection control interventions.

Δ   Assist with relevant laboratory, diagnostic, and therapeutic procedures within the nursing role, including:

•   Client preparation and teaching for the procedure.

•   Accurate collection of specimens.

•   Evaluation of the child's response to the procedure.

•   Planning and implementing body system-specific interventions as appropriate.

•   Monitoring and taking actions to prevent or minimize the risk of complications.

•   Accurate interpretation of procedure results.

Δ   Perform and document appropriate assessments based on the child's problem.

Δ   Apply knowledge of pathophysiology to planning care for clients with specific alterations in body systems, including recognizing associated signs and symptoms.

Δ   Interpret data that need to be reported immediately.

Δ   Monitor therapeutic devices, if inserted, for proper functioning.

Δ   Explore resources, make referrals, collaborate with interdisciplinary team, and ensure continuity of client care.

Δ   Evaluate plans of care for multiple clients and revise plan as needed based on priorities of care and promotion of recovery.

Δ   Provide the child/family teaching regarding management of the child's health problem.

Δ   Recognize/respond to emergency situations, and evaluate/document the client's response to emergency interventions.

Key Points

Δ   HIV infection is a viral infection in which the virus infects the T-lymphocytes, causing immune dysfunction. This leads to organ dysfunction and a variety of opportunistic infections in a weakened host. In addition, HIV infection that progresses to AIDS places the child at risk for developing a variety of malignancies (e.g., Kaposi's sarcoma, cranial or Burkitt's lymphoma).

Δ   Children diagnosed with HIV have varied prognosis. Some children will become acutely ill and others will only experience mild symptoms of the disease.

Key Factors

Δ   Sexual contact or exposure to blood and body fluids results in horizontal transmission.

Δ   Vertical transmission occurs when a woman with HIV passes the infection to her fetus. A woman can also vertically transmit the virus when breastfeeding her infant.

Δ   All women who are pregnant should be screened for HIV.

  •   Pregnant women with HIV are usually given antiviral medications during pregnancy.

  •   Cesarean birth may be performed to limit the possibility of exposure from the birth canal.

Δ   Casual contact is not a proven mode of transmission (e.g., visiting the home of a child with HIV, being in the same classroom as a child with HIV).

Assessment

Δ   Nursing history should include prior treatment of infections, level of pain, frequent episodes of diarrhea, reports of behavior changes, fatigue, impaired mobility, and activity intolerance.

Δ   Obtain baseline height and weight. Identify variations from norms.

Δ   Perform a developmental assessment and determine if the child is meeting milestones. Frequently, children with HIV demonstrate delays in growth and development.

Δ Physical assessment findings help determine the severity of the illness.

Mild	Moderate	Severe
• Lymphadenopathy • Liver and spleen enlargement • Oral candidiasis • Recurrent upper respiratory infections, otitis media • Dermatitis • Parotitis	• Anemia • Episode of meningitis, pneumonia, and/or sepsis of bacterial origin • Oropharyngeal candidiasis • Cardiomyopathy • Viral infections (e.g., cytomegalovirus, herpes simplex virus, complicated varicella) • Lymphoid interstitial pneumonitis (LLP) • Liver and kidney dysfunction • Persistent fever	• Multiple or recurrent bacterial infections (e.g., meningitis, septicemia, pneumonia) • Pulmonary candidiasis • *Pneumocystis carinii* pneumonia (PCP) • HIV encephalopathy • Motor deficits • Tuberculosis • Kaposi's sarcoma • Cranial lymphoma

Δ Children with HIV may be below norms for height and weight, and have impaired motor skills and communication deficits.

Diagnostic Procedures

Δ Screen infants/toddlers up to 18 months using HIV polymerase chain reaction (PCR) to determine presence of proviral DNA. Identifying HIV antibodies will not provide accurate diagnosis because passive immunoglobins from the mother will persist in the infant's blood for up to 18 months.

Δ For children older than 18 months use:

• Antibody assays: positive

◊ Enzyme-linked immunosorbent assay (ELISA)

◊ Western blot

Δ Use CD4+ T-lymphocyte count and percentages to determine the level of the child's immunosuppression. Classification of illness is made after numbers are adjusted for age.

• The CD4+ T-lymphocyte counts for infants will be 750 to 1499/mm^3 when moderate suppression is evident and less than 750/mm^3 when severe suppression is evident.

• The CD4+ T-lymphocyte counts for children 1 to 5 years will be 500 to 999/mm^3 when moderate suppression is evident and less than 500/mm^3 when severe suppression is evident.

• The CD4+ T-lymphocyte counts for children 6 to 13 years will be 200 to 499/mm^3 when moderate suppression is evident and less than 200/mm^3 when severe suppression is evident.

• When an HIV-infected child has a CD4+ T-cell count less than 200/mm^3, a diagnosis of AIDS will be given.

NANDA Nursing Diagnoses

- Δ   Ineffective airway clearance
- Δ   Interrupted family processes
- Δ   Fatigue
- Δ   Delayed growth and development
- Δ   Risk for infection
- Δ   Imbalanced nutrition: less than body requirements
- Δ   Social isolation

Nursing Interventions

- Δ   Encourage a balanced diet that is high in calories and protein. Obtain the child's preferred food and beverages. A more aggressive treatment may be required such as total parenteral nutrition (TPN).

- Δ   Provide for good oral care and report abnormalities for treatment.

- Δ   Keep the child's skin clean and dry.

- Δ   Assess the child for pain and provide adequate pain management. Use of medications may include nonsteroidal anti-inflammatory drugs (NSAIDs), acetaminophen (Tylenol), opioids, muscle relaxants, and/or a eutectic mixture of local anesthetics (EMLA [lidocaine/prilocaine]) for numerous diagnostic procedures.

- Δ   Protect/prevent infection using standard precautions.

  - •   Encourage deep breathing and coughing.

  - •   Maintain good hand hygiene.

  - •   Teach the child/parent to avoid individuals with colds/infection/viruses.

  - •   Encourage proper immunizations to include pneumococcal vaccine (PCV) and influenza vaccine.

  - •   Monitor for signs of opportunistic infections.

- Δ   Prophylaxis treatment for newborns of HIV-infected mothers includes trimethoprim-sulfamethoxazole (TMP-SMZ) for PCP.

Δ   Administer antiretroviral medications as prescribed. They may be used in combination to delay medication resistance.

- Entry/infusion inhibitors (enfuvirtide [Fuzeon]) help to decrease the amount of virus in the body as well as limit its spread.

- Nucleoside reverse transcriptase inhibitors (e.g., medication combination of abacavir and Lamivudine zidovudine [Trizivir], each of which may be used alone) interfere with the virus's ability to convert RNA into DNA.

- Non-nucleoside reverse transcriptase inhibitors (e.g., delavirdine [Rescriptor], efavirenz [Sustiva]) inhibit viral replication in cells.

- Protease inhibitors (e.g., amprenavir [Agenerase], nelfinavir [Viracept]) inhibit an enzyme needed for the virus to replicate.

- Monitor laboratory results such as CBC, WBC, and liver function tests. Antiretroviral medications may increase serum glutamic oxaloacetic transaminase (SGPT), alanine aminotransferase (ALT), serum glutamic oxaloacetic transaminase (SGOT), aspartate aminotransferase (AST), bilirubin, mean corpuscular volume (MCV), high-density lipoproteins (HDLs), total cholesterol, and triglycerides.

Δ   Administer medications as prescribed for opportunistic infections (e.g., acyclovir [Zovirax] for herpes simplex virus, amphotericin B [Amphocin] for serious fungal infections).

Δ   Child/family support

- Educate the child/family on the chronicity of the illness and the need for life-long medication administration.

- Instruct the family when to notify the primary care provider. Signs and symptoms requiring medical care include headache, fever, lethargy, warmth, tenderness, redness at joints, and neck stiffness.

- Educate the child/family about transmission of virus (e.g., mode of transmission, high-risk behaviors).

- Identify stressors that may be affecting the family and make appropriate referrals (e.g., school/community response to child, finances, access to health care).

- Practice safety precautions when using needles/syringes and administering medications.

Complications and Nursing Implications

Δ   Failure to Thrive

- Obtain baseline height and weight and continue to monitor.

- Promote optimal nutrition. May require administration of TPN.

- Assess growth and development. Monitor for delays.

- Provide opportunities for normal development (e.g., age-appropriate toys, playing with children of own age).

Δ PCP

- Assess and monitor respiratory status, which includes respiratory rate and effort, oxygen saturation, and breath sounds.

- Administer appropriate antibiotics.

- Administer antipyretic and/or analgesics, if prescribed.

- Provide adequate hydration and maintain fluid and electrolyte balance.

- Use postural drainage and chest physiotherapy to mobilize and remove fluid from lungs.

- Promote adequate rest.

Primary Reference:

Hockenberry, M., Wilson, D., & Winkelstein, M. (2005). *Wong's essentials of pediatric nursing care.* (7th ed.). St. Louis, MO: Mosby.

Additional Resources:

Centers for Disease Control and Prevention. (2006, October). *HIV and its transmission.* Retrieved February 11, 2007, from http://www.cdc.gov/hiv/resources/factsheets/transmission.htm

Centers for Disease Control and Prevention. (1998, October). *Revised classification system for human immunodeficiency virus infection in children less than 13 years of age.* Retrieved February 1, 2007, from http://wonder.cdc.gov/wonder/prevguid/m0032890/m0032890.asp#Table_1

Kee, J. L., Hayes, E. R., & McCuistion, L. E. (2005). *Pharmacology: A nursing process approach.* (5th ed.). St. Louis, MO: Saunders.

NANDA International (2004). *NANDA nursing diagnoses: Definitions and classification 2005-2006.* Philadelphia: NANDA.

National Institute of Allergy and Infectious Diseases. (2003, February, 27). *The evidence that HIV Causes AIDS.* Retrieved February 1, 2007, from http://www.niaid.nih.gov/factsheets/evidhiv.htm

U. S. Department of Health and Human Services. (2007). *AIDSinfo drug database.* Retrieved February 2, 2007, from http://aidsinfo.nih.gov/DrugsNew/Default.aspx?MenuItem=Drugs

Chapter 31: HIV/AIDS

Application Exercises

1. How should a nurse explain to an expectant mother who is HIV positive the steps that will be taken to interrupt transmission to her unborn fetus? Explain what will be done after birth.

Scenario: A child who is HIV positive is admitted to the emergency department. The child has a high fever, rapid, shallow respirations, productive cough of white sputum, and crackles heard in the lower lung fields bilaterally. Following assessment by the primary care provider, the child is diagnosed with pneumonia and is admitted to the hospital.

2. A priority nursing diagnosis is identified as ineffective airway clearance related to increased sputum. What nursing interventions should be implemented at this time?

3. What information regarding medication administration and preventing infection should be provided to the parent?

4. A parent of a child with HIV is at risk for disease transmission in which of the following situations? (Select all that apply.)

_____ Hugging the child

_____ Being kissed by the child

_____ Sharing finger food with the child from a central plate

_____ Cleaning up after the child has a nose bleed

_____ Wiping the child's tears with a handkerchief when she is crying

_____ Assisting the child to wash after she has been sweating

_____ Sharing the same toothbrush

5. What should a nurse do to promote nutrition in a child who is HIV positive?

6. A child with AIDS reports a headache and sore throat. What should be the primary concern of the nurse at this time?

7. Which of the following infections indicates that a child with AIDS is severely ill?

    A. Oral-pharyngeal candidiasis

    B. Otitis media

    C. PCP

    D. Herpes simplex virus

Chapter 31: HIV/AIDS

Application Exercises Answer Key

1. How should a nurse explain to an expectant mother who is HIV positive the steps that will be taken to interrupt transmission to her unborn fetus? Explain what will be done after birth.

> The mother will be prescribed AZT or other antiviral medications throughout her pregnancy. CD4+ T-lymphocyte counts may be done to determine the severity of her illness. Management for labor and delivery may include IV antiviral agents administered just prior to the fetus being delivered by cesarean birth. The infant may need blood work prior to discharge from the hospital and will need to be brought to the primary care provider for blood tests over the first few months of life. The infant will be started on AZT within a few hours of birth, and the mother should be instructed on how to administer an oral medication to her infant. Prenatal teaching should include the reason for avoiding breastfeeding and ways to successfully bottle feed her infant.

Scenario: A child who is HIV positive is admitted to the emergency department. The child has a high fever, rapid, shallow respirations, productive cough of white sputum, and crackles heard in the lower lung fields bilaterally. Following assessment by the primary care provider, the child is diagnosed with pneumonia and is admitted to the hospital.

2. A priority nursing diagnosis is identified as ineffective airway clearance related to increased sputum. What nursing interventions should be implemented at this time?

> Monitor the child's vital signs and report an increase in temperature.
>
> Anticipate that a chest x-ray and sputum culture may be ordered.
>
> Administer oxygen as ordered to maintain O_2 saturation at appropriate level.
>
> Assess the child's lungs and compare to previous findings to determine effectiveness of treatment.
>
> Administer antipyretics as prescribed.
>
> Encourage oral fluids, as tolerated, and provide IV fluids as prescribed.
>
> Administer antibiotics in a timely manner.
>
> Monitor I&O and GI function.

3. What information regarding medication administration and preventing infection should be provided to the parent?

> The parent will require written instructions about the name and frequency of the medication dosage. She needs to understand side effects to observe for with specific medications; that the child will require periodic blood work monitoring for side effects; and that antiviral medications do not make it impossible for the child to infect others. The parent should be instructed on how to monitor the child's temperature and protect the child from others who are ill.

4. A parent of a child with HIV is at risk for disease transmission in which of the following situations? (Select all that apply.)

_____ Hugging the child

_____ Being kissed by the child

_____ Sharing finger food with the child from a central plate

__X__ **Cleaning up after the child has a nose bleed**

_____ Wiping the child's tears with a handkerchief when she is crying

_____ Assisting the child to wash after she has been sweating

__X__ **Sharing the same toothbrush**

> The only situations posing any risks are cleaning up after the child has a nose bleed and sharing the same toothbrush. HIV is transmitted by direct contact with blood and body fluids (e.g., semen, vaginal secretions). It is important not to share personal hygiene items such as razors or toothbrushes, which could contain blood. None of the other activities should place a person at risk. Even though the virus has been found in small amounts in tears, mucous, and sweat, there is no evidence that transmission has ever occurred unless blood is present.

5. What should a nurse do to promote nutrition in a child who is HIV positive?

> The nurse should first assess the child's nutritional status. Weight and height should be obtained and plotted on a growth chart. Laboratory values such as serum protein and electrolyte levels should be monitored. The nurse should assess the child's likes and dislikes and assist with menu selection. If possible, group the child with other children of the same age during meals. The nurse should offer fluids frequently, preferably drinks that are high in calories and protein.

6. A child with AIDS reports a headache and sore throat. What should be the primary concern of the nurse at this time?

The nurse should be concerned about CNS complications such as meningitis and encephalopathy. These symptoms should be reported. Even if meningitis or encephalopathy is not present, any infection is a risk if the child is immunocompromised.

7. Which of the following infections indicates that a child with AIDS is severely ill?

    A. Oral-pharyngeal candidiasis

    B. Otitis media

    C. PCP

    D. Herpes simplex virus

The presence of PCP indicates that the child is severely ill with AIDS. Otitis media is a sign of mild illness, and oral-pharyngeal candidiasis and the presence of herpes simplex virus are symptoms of moderate illness.

Nursing Care of Children with System Disorders
Nursing Care of Children with Integumentary Disorders

Chapter 32: **Burns**

Contributor: Glenda J. Bondurant, MSN, RN

 NCLEX-RN® Connections:

Learning Objective: Review and apply knowledge within "**Burns**" in readiness for performance of the following nursing activities as outlined by the NCLEX-RN® test plan:

Δ   Assist with relevant laboratory, diagnostic, and therapeutic procedures within the nursing role, including:

- Client preparation for the procedure.

- Client teaching (before and following the procedure).

- Accurate collection of specimens.

- Evaluation of the child's response to the procedure.

- Planning and implementing body system-specific interventions as appropriate.

- Monitoring and taking actions to prevent or minimize the risk of complications.

- Accurate interpretation of procedure results.

Δ   Perform and document appropriate assessments based on the child's problem.

Δ   Apply knowledge of pathophysiology to planning care for clients with specific alterations in body systems, including recognizing associated signs and symptoms.

Δ   Interpret data that need to be reported immediately.

Δ   Monitor therapeutic devices (drainage/irrigating devices, chest tubes), if inserted, for proper functioning.

Δ   Explore resources, make referrals, collaborate with interdisciplinary team, and ensure continuity of client care.

Δ   Evaluate plans of care for multiple clients and revise plan as needed based on priorities of care and promotion of recovery.

Δ   Provide the child/family teaching regarding management of the child's health problem.

Δ   Recognize/respond to emergency situations, and evaluate/document the client's response to emergency interventions.

Key Points

Δ   Burn injuries (**type** of injury) may be caused by exposure to heat, cold, electrical current, and chemicals.

Δ   Tissue destruction is related to the strength of the heat source, the length of time of exposure, the tissue involved, and how rapidly the heat is dissipated from the skin.

Δ   How much tissue is destroyed will impact the body's response, where the child will be treated, what management will be used, and the prognosis.

Δ   The **extent** of the injury is identified as a percentage of the TBSA. Standardized charts for age groups are used to identify the extent of the injury.

Δ   The **depth** of injury refers to the layers of skin and tissue burned.

Δ   The **severity** of the burn is based on the percentage of total body surface area (**TBSA**). Severity is also influenced by how deep the burn is, body location of the burn, age of the child, what caused the burn, presence of other injuries, involvement of the respiratory system, and overall health of the child.

- Superficial (First degree)
- Partial thickness (Second degree)
  - ◊   Minor burn – less than 10% TBSA, usually outpatient treatment
  - ◊   Moderate – greater than 10 to 20% TBSA, inpatient care
  - ◊   Major – greater than 20% TBSA, requires burn center treatment
- Full-thickness (Third degree)
  - ◊   All are major and require burn center treatment.

Δ   Three phases of burn care include:

- Emergent (also called the acute or resuscitative phase).
  - ◊   First 24 to 48 hr after the burn occurs
- Management.
  - ◊   Begins when resuscitation is finished
  - ◊   Ends when the wound is covered by tissue
- Rehabilitative.
  - ◊   Begins when most of the burn area is healed
  - ◊   Ends when reconstructive and corrective procedures are complete (may last for years)

Key Factors

Δ   Preventing burns in children is best done by educating them based on their developmental level.

Δ   Thermal causes

• Water heater set above 120° F

• Hot liquids (coffee)

• Burners on stove

• Hot pots and pans on top of stove

• Space heaters

• Faucets (hot water) in bathroom

• Matches and lighters

• Irons and curling irons

Δ   Chemical causes

• Lye-based chemicals, such as drain cleaner

• Household cleansers that are caustic in nature

Δ   Electrical causes

• Uncovered electric outlets

• Access to drop cords/surge protectors

• Exposed electrical cords

Δ   Burns are initially considered clean due to lack of pathogens. However, they may become contaminated by dirt or unclean water.

Δ   Risk for infection occurs after 3 to 5 days.

Assessment

Δ   Obtain history of injury including causative agent, chronic or acute illnesses, and last tetanus shot.

Δ   Physical assessment includes noting airway patency, oxygenation status, respiratory effort, observing for respiratory distress, blood pressure, heart rate, fluid status, and observing for signs of shock.

• Signs of inhalation injury may include mouth (burn injury on lips and face), nose (singed hairs), and pharynx (edema of the larynx). Clinical manifestations may not be evident for 24 to 48 hr and are seen as wheezing, hoarseness, and increased respiratory secretions.

- Signs of carbon monoxide inhalation (suspected if the injury took place in an enclosed area) include erythema and edema, followed by sloughing of the respiratory tract mucosa.

- Estimate severity of burn by using charts intended for specific ages.

Δ Altered level of consciousness, spiking fever, and hypoactive bowel signs may be signs of impending sepsis.

Δ Observe for irritability, crying, and restlessness.

Δ Determine location and extent of injury.

Δ Assess depth of injury.

Δ Estimate severity of burn by using charts intended for specific age groups.

Depth	Area Involved/Appearance	Sensation/Healing
Superficial (First degree)	• Epidermis is red, tender, possibly swollen, and without blisters. • Mild edema present.	• Painful • Heals within 5 to 10 days • No scarring
Partial thickness (Second degree)	• Epidermis and dermis are damaged with blisters formed. • If blisters rupture, skin is moist, but discolored.	• Painful, sensitive to changes in temperature, air exposure, and light touch • Heals spontaneously in about 14 days • Scarring likely
Full thickness (Third degree)	• May have partial thickness areas around the full thickness areas. • Damage extends into the subcutaneous tissue. • Nerve endings, sweat glands, and hair follicles are involved. • Skin is tough without moisture. • Color may be red to tan, black, brown, or white.	• Pain from surrounding injured skin • Full thickness area is not painful due to destruction of nerve endings. • As burn heals, painful sensations return and severity of pain increases.
Full thickness (Fourth degree)	• Damage extends to the muscle, fascia, and possibly the bone. Skin is black.	• No pain at full thickness area • Surrounding area may become painful during healing.

Δ Burns may have systemic effects depending on depth and degree of burns.

- Superficial burns have minimal systemic effect.

- Partial thickness burns cause edema due to damaged capillaries.

- Major burns of greater than 30% TBSA can result in increased capillary permeability, leading to shifting of fluids, electrolytes, and plasma proteins from the intracellular to extracellular areas (third space shift). This reduces the circulating fluid volume, producing hypovolemia.

- RBC destruction creates anemia.

- Metabolism increases to maintain body heat.

Diagnostic Procedures

Δ Laboratory values that should be evaluated include: CBC, serum electrolytes, BUN, ABGs, fasting blood glucose, random blood glucose, liver enzymes, urinalysis, and clotting studies.

- Initial fluid shift (first 24 hr after injury)

  ◊ Hgb and Hct become elevated due to loss of fluid volume and fluid shifts into interstitial (third spacing) fluid.

  ◊ Sodium decreases due to third spacing.

  ◊ Potassium increases due to cell destruction.

- Fluid mobilization (48 to 72 hr after injury)

  ◊ Hgb and Hct decrease due to fluid shift from interstitial back into vascular fluid.

  ◊ Sodium decreases due to renal and wound loss.

  ◊ Potassium decreases due to renal loss and movement back into cells.

  ◊ WBC initially increases and then decreases with left shift.

  ◊ Glucose levels elevate due to stress response.

  ◊ ABGs show slight hypoxemia, metabolic acidosis.

  ◊ Total protein and albumin are low due to fluid loss.

Δ Monitor for infection using wound culture and sensitivity.

NANDA Nursing Diagnoses

Δ Deficient fluid volume

Δ Acute pain

Δ Impaired tissue integrity

Δ Ineffective breathing pattern

Δ Imbalanced nutrition: less than body requirements

Δ Risk for infection

Δ Disturbed body image

Nursing Interventions

Δ Emergent Care

- Stop the burning process.

  ◊ Remove clothing or jewelry that might conduct heat.

  ◊ Position the child horizontally to prevent flames from rising to head.

  ◊ Flush chemical burns with large amounts of water.

- Assess and maintain airway, breathing, and circulation.

- Cover the burn with clean cloth to prevent contamination and hypothermia.

- Provide warmth.

- If necessary, bring the child to a health care facility for medical care.

Δ Superficial Burns (sunburn)

- Primary intervention is prevention.

  ◊ Avoid sun exposure between 10 a.m. and 4 p.m.

  ◊ Wear protective clothing, such as cotton.

  ◊ Apply sunscreen or sunblock liberally.

- Treatment includes eliminating the burning source, cool water soaks, or immersion in a tepid bath to decrease the inflammatory response, and application of moisturizing lotion to rehydrate the skin.

Δ Minor Burns

- Apply cold to area by immersion or ice packs (avoid hypothermia).

- Provide analgesia.

- Cleanse with soap and water (avoid excess friction).

- Cover the wound to keep clean.

- Obtain a tetanus prophylaxis if last prophylaxis was given more than 5 years prior to burn.

- Use antimicrobial ointment.

- Apply a dressing if the burn area is irritated by clothing.

- Educate the family to avoid using greasy lotions or butter on burn.

Δ   Moderate and Severe Burns

- Maintain airway and ventilation.

- Provide humidified supplemental oxygen as ordered.

- Monitor vital signs.

- Maintain cardiac output.

    ◊   Initiate intravenous access.

    ◊   Fluid replacement is important during the first 24 hr.

    - Fluid replacement needed for tissue perfusion is 20 mL/kg.

    - Crystalloid solutions, such as 0.9% NS or lactated Ringer's solution, are used during the early stage of burn recovery.

    - Colloid solutions, such as albumin or plasmalyte, may be used after the first 24 hr of burn recovery.

    - Maintain urine output of 1 to 2 mL/kg/hr if the child weighs less than 30 kg (66 lb).

    - Maintain urine output of 30 mL/hr if the child weighs more than 30 kg (66 lb).

    - Be prepared to administer blood products as needed.

    ◊   Monitor for manifestations of shock.

    - Alterations in sensorium (confusion)

    - Increased capillary refill time

    - Urine output less than 1 to 2 mL/kg/hr in a child weighing less than 30 kg (66 lb); less than 30 mL/hr for a child weighing 30 kg (66 lb) or greater

    - Blood pressure may remain normotensive even in hypovolemia

    ◊   Notify the primary care provider of findings.

Δ   Pain Management

- Establish ongoing monitoring of pain and effectiveness of pain treatment.

- Avoid IM or subcutaneous injections.

- Administer analgesia and sedation right before procedural pain.

- Morphine sulfate is the medication of choice for analgesia.

- Provide sedation and analgesia with midazolam (Versed) and fentanyl (Sublimaze).

Δ   Wound Care

- Premedicate with analgesic as prescribed prior to all wound care.

- Remove all previous dressings.

- Monitor for odors, drainage, and discharge.

- Cleanse the wound as ordered, removing all previous ointments (it is important to cleanse the wound thoroughly).

- Support the child during hydrotherapy/debridement.

- Apply a thin layer of topical antibiotic ointment as ordered. This protects the wound from being exposed to the air.

- Apply dressing as necessary to cover the area using surgical aseptic technique.

- Systemic antibiotic therapy is only used if actual infection with causative organism is identified.

Δ   Skin and Musculoskeletal Care

- Maintain correct body alignment, splint extremities, and facilitate position changes to prevent contractures.

- Maintain active and passive range of motion.

- Closely monitor areas at high risk for pressure sores (e.g., heels, sacrum, back of head).

Δ   Nutritional Support

- Increase caloric intake to meet increased metabolic demands and prevent hypoglycemia.

- Increase protein intake to prevent tissue breakdown and promote healing.

- Enteral therapy or parenteral hyperalimentation may be necessary due to decreased gastrointestinal motility and increased caloric needs.

Δ   Maintain gastric decompression using nasogastric tube as ordered.

Δ   Insert urinary catheter as ordered (close monitoring of I&O).

Δ   Provide developmentally appropriate support for the child.

Δ   Provide emotional support for family members.

Antimicrobial Cream	Uses and Advantages	Disadvantages
Silver nitrate 0.5%	• May be used on wound exposed to air, or with modified or occlusive dressing • May affect joint movement • Reduces fluid evaporation • Bacteriostatic against pseudomonas and staphylococcus • Inexpensive	• Does not penetrate eschar • Stains clothing and linen • Discolors wound, making assessment difficult
Silver sulfadiazine 1%	• May be used with occlusive dressings • Contraindicated in children with allergies • Joint mobility maintained • Effective against gram-negative bacteria	• May cause transient neutropenia • Does not penetrate eschar • Painful to remove from wound • Decreases granulocyte formation
Mafenide acetate 10%	• My be used on wounds exposed to air • May be used as a solution for occlusive dressings to keep the dressing moist • Penetrates eschar and goes into underlying tissues • Effective with electrical and infected wounds • Biostatic against gram-positive and gram-negative organisms	• Cream is painful to apply and remove • May cause metabolic acidosis, hypercapnia • Inhibits wound healing • Hypersensitivity may develop
Bacitracin	• May be used on wounds exposed to air or with modified dressings • Joint motion maintained • Bacteriostatic against gram-positive organisms • Painless and easy application	• Limited effectiveness on gram-negative organisms

Therapeutic Procedures and Nursing Interventions

Δ Debridement by hydrotherapy cleans the wound, removes eschar, and promotes wound healing (painful procedure).

- Perform preprocedure assessment.

- Medicate for pain prior to start of procedure.

- Hydrotherapy is used once or twice a day for up to 20 min.

- At the end of the hydrotherapy session, loose tissue around the wound is carefully removed and the wound is redressed.

- Provide reassurance during the procedure.

- When redressing the wound, maintain careful use of surgical aseptic technique.

Δ Biologic skin coverings may be used to promote healing of large burns.

- Allograft (homograft) – human cadavers donate skin that is used for partial and full thickness burn wounds

- Xenograft – obtained from animals, such as pigs, for partial thickness burn wounds

- Synthetic skin coverings – used for partial thickness burn wounds

- Nursing care includes pain management, wound care, and emotional support.

Δ Permanent skin coverings may be the treatment of choice for burns covering large areas of the body.

- Sheet graft – sheet of skin used to cover wound

- Mesh graft – sheet of skin placed in mesher so skin graft has small slits in it; allows graft to cover larger areas of burn wound

- Artificial skin – synthetic product that is used for partial and full-thickness burn wounds (healing is faster)

- Cultured epithelium – epithelia cells cultured for use when grafting sites are limited

- Nursing care includes pain management, wound care, and emotional support.

Δ Monitor for signs of infection before and after skin coverings or grafts are applied.

- Discoloration of unburned skin surrounding burn wound

- Green color to subcutaneous fat

- Degeneration of granulation tissue

- Development of subeschar hemorrhage

- Hyperventilation indicating systemic involvement of infection

- Vasomotor fluctuation

- Unstable body temperature

Complications and Nursing Implications

Δ **Airway Injury**

- Thermal injuries to the airway can result from steam or chemical inhalation, aspiration of scalding liquid, and explosion while breathing. If the injury took place in an enclosed space, carbon monoxide poisoning should be suspected.

- Indication of direct thermal injury to the upper respiratory tract is evidenced by edema of the larynx, face and lip burns, and scorched nasal hairs.

- Clinical manifestations may be delayed for 24 to 48 hr.

- Signs and symptoms include progressive hoarseness, brassy cough, difficulty swallowing, drooling, increased secretions, adventitious breath sounds, and expiratory sounds that include audible wheezes, crowing, and stridor.

- Maintain airway and ventilation, and provide oxygen as prescribed.

Δ **Fluid and Electrolyte Imbalances**

- Assess fluid volume status.

  ◊ Daily weights

  ◊ Meticulous I&O

- Monitor laboratory results and compare to previous data.

  ◊ Glucose – Monitor for hypoglycemia secondary to stress.

  ◊ Potassium – Monitor for hyperkalemia with cellular destruction.

  ◊ BUN – Monitor for dehydration and a potential renal problem if creatinine is elevated.

  ◊ Creatinine – Monitor because increases are indicative of nephron damage.

  ◊ Serum protein – Monitor because albumin is necessary for healing and maintaining serum osmolarity.

  ◊ Anticipate administration of IV fluids.

Δ **Wound Infections**

- Assess for discoloration, edema, odor, and drainage.

- Assess for fluctuations in temperature and heart rate.

- Conduct a wound culture for *Pseudomonas aeruginosa*.

- Monitor laboratory results, observing for anemia and infection.

- Maintain surgical aseptic technique with dressing changes.

- Therapeutic interventions include early excision of the wound and use of biological skin coverings.

Primary Reference:

Hockenberry, M., Wilson, D., & Winkelstein, M. (2005). *Wong's essentials of pediatric nursing care.* (7th ed.). St. Louis, MO: Mosby.

Additional Resources:

NANDA International (2004). *NANDA nursing diagnoses: Definitions and classification 2005-2006.* Philadelphia: NANDA.

Chapter 32: Burns

Application Exercises

Scenario: An emergency department nurse is preparing for the admission of two children burned in a house fire. The first child is a 9-month-old infant with burns to her feet and legs. The second child is 3 years old with burns to her hands, arms, and anterior thorax. The cause of the house fire was due to the 3-year-old child playing with matches.

1. Why should the nurse be concerned about respiratory complications in the children?

2. What developmental considerations are most important for these two children?

3. What will be the focus of discharge teaching for these parents?

4. A child is brought by his parent to the emergency department with first-degree burns to his shoulders from sun exposure. Which of the following interventions are indicated for this type of burn?

   A. Start an IV of D_5LR.

   B. Apply cool, wet compresses.

   C. Scrub the area with a soft-bristle brush.

   D. Administer morphine sulfate for pain relief.

5. A child experiences third-degree burns to both his legs after they were immersed in boiling water. Which of the following nursing diagnoses should receive priority during the first 24 hr?

   A. Deficient fluid volume

   B. Imbalanced nutrition: less than body requirements

   C. Impaired breathing pattern

   D. Disturbed body image

6. A child is scheduled for debridement of leg wounds. In what order should the nurse perform the following procedures?

_____ Remove the dressing.

_____ Medicate the child for pain.

_____ Pour water on the dressing to loosen it.

_____ Assess the need for dressing supplies.

Chapter 32: Burns

Application Exercises Answer Key

Scenario: An emergency department nurse is preparing for the admission of two children burned in a house fire. The first child is a 9-month-old infant with burns to her feet and legs. The second child is 3 years old with burns to her hands, arms, and anterior thorax. The cause of the house fire was due to the 3-year-old child playing with matches.

1. Why should the nurse be concerned about respiratory complications in the children?

Carbon monoxide poisoning is a risk for both children because the fire was contained in an enclosed room where carbon monoxide can easily build up. In addition, due to the 3-year-old child's burns, both immediate and ongoing assessment for thermal burns to the upper airway should be carried out. Symptoms of respiratory tract involvement, such as wheezing, increasing secretions, and adventitious breath sounds, may not be present during the initial assessment, but may be delayed for up to 48 hr after a burn injury.

2. What developmental considerations are most important for these two children?

The infant is at risk for separation anxiety, which affects children from age 6 to 30 months of age. The 3-year-old child may be at risk for separation anxiety, but is at the age where fear of bodily injury is an important consideration. From 3 to 5 years of age the child must deal with the psychosocial needs of initiative versus development of guilt. The interactions between this child and her parents will be important as they deal with the problem of blame for the fire.

3. What will be the focus of discharge teaching for these parents?

Discharge teaching will be focused on preventing further injuries and safe guarding the home. In addition, teaching related to wound care, identifying signs and symptoms of infection, and nutrition support with high-protein, high-calorie diet should be carried out.

4. A child is brought by his parent to the emergency department with first-degree burns to his shoulders from sun exposure. Which of the following interventions are indicated for this type of burn?

> A. Start an IV of D$_5$LR.
>
> **B. Apply cool, wet compresses.**
>
> C. Scrub the area with a soft-bristle brush.
>
> D. Administer morphine sulfate for pain relief.

The child has sustained first-degree burns, which require the application of cool compresses to minimize the burning sensation. IV fluid is not necessary in a superficial burn injury. Scrubbing a first-degree burn is unnecessary unless debris is imbedded; however, gentle cleansing with tepid water may be indicated. Morphine sulfate is indicated for major burns; in this case, cool compresses should ease initial pain.

5. A child experiences third-degree burns to both his legs after they were immersed in boiling water. Which of the following nursing diagnoses will receive priority during the first 24 hr?

> **A. Deficient fluid volume**
>
> B. Imbalanced nutrition: less than body requirements
>
> C. Impaired breathing pattern
>
> D. Disturbed body image

A child with third-degree burns loses fluid secondary to fluid shifts and fluid volume deficit. Imbalanced nutrition may become a problem, but is not the highest priority. This child is not at risk for airway involvement since his burns were sustained to the lower extremities. Disturbed body image may be a high priority problem in later stages, but other physical needs take precedence immediately after the injury.

6. A child is scheduled for debridement of leg wounds. In what order should the nurse perform the following procedures?

> **4** Remove the dressing.
>
> **1** Medicate the child for pain.
>
> **3** Pour water on the dressing to loosen it.
>
> **2** Assess the need for dressing supplies.

The child must first be premedicated for pain. While waiting for the pain medication to take effect, the nurse should assess what supplies are needed. Pouring water on the dressing to loosen it will decrease pain. Lastly, the dressing should be removed.

Unit 2   Nursing Care of Children with System Disorders
Section: Nursing Care of Children with Integumentary Disorders

Chapter 33:   Skin Infections and Infestations
Contributors: Michele Hinds, PhD, RN
Glenda J. Bondurant, MSN, RN

 NCLEX-RN® Connections:

Learning Objective: Review and apply knowledge within "**Skin Infections and Infestations**" in readiness for performance of the following nursing activities as outlined by the NCLEX-RN® test plan:

Δ   Assist with relevant laboratory, diagnostic, and therapeutic procedures within the nursing role, including:

- Client preparation for the procedure.

- Client teaching (before and following the procedure).

- Accurate collection of specimens.

- Evaluation of the child's response to the procedure.

- Planning and implementing body system-specific interventions as appropriate.

- Monitoring and taking actions to prevent or minimize the risk of complications.

- Accurate interpretation of procedure results.

Δ   Perform and document appropriate assessments based on the child's problem.

Δ   Apply knowledge of pathophysiology to planning care for clients with specific alterations in body systems, including recognizing associated signs and symptoms.

Δ   Interpret data that need to be reported immediately.

Δ   Monitor therapeutic devices (drainage/irrigating devices, chest tubes), if inserted, for proper functioning.

Δ   Explore resources, make referrals, collaborate with interdisciplinary team, and ensure continuity of client care.

Δ   Evaluate plans of care for multiple clients and revise plan as needed based on priorities of care and promotion of recovery.

Δ   Provide the child/family teaching regarding management of the child's health problem.

Δ   Recognize/respond to emergency situations, and evaluate/document the client's response to emergency interventions.

Key Points

Δ   Certain skin disorders are common in different age groups (e.g., birthmarks in newborns, acne in adolescents)

Δ   More than 50 percent of skin disorders in children are inflammatory. The inflammatory response is usually similar, but the causative agent and course of the dermatitis have wide variations.

Δ   Most changes caused by dermatitis are reversible unless complicated by ulceration, infection, and/or scratching.

Δ   Streptococcal and staphylococcal bacteria are normally found on the skin.

Δ   Viruses cause epidermal inflammation and formation of vesicles or warts.

Δ   Characteristic rashes are present with communicable viral diseases (*Refer to chapter 28, Communicable Diseases.*).

Δ   Dermatophytoses cause fungal infections, which affect the stratum corneum, hair, and nails. The lesions are superficial and not in the skin.

Δ   Pediculosis (head lice) is a contagious parasitic infestation.

   •   Pediculosis is transmitted through sharing of personal items (e.g., hair brushes, combs, hats) or when personal items such as coats and hats are kept close together.

   •   Female lice lays eggs (nits) that attach to the hair follicles and hatch within 7 to 10 days.

   •   Lice can live up to 1 month on the host but only 48 hr without the host.

   •   Movement and saliva of the lice cause pruritus.

Δ   Scabies is a contagious skin infestation caused by a microscopic mite.

Δ   Lyme disease is caused by a spirochete, which is contained within the saliva and feces of ticks (mainly the deer tick). The spirochete is transferred to a human when the tick attaches to the person's skin.

Key Factors

Δ   Causes of skin lesions in children include genetic factors and systemic illnesses (e.g., rheumatic fever, cancer).

Δ   Causative agents include bacteria, viruses, fungi, mites, and infected insects.

Δ   General health status affects a child's resistance to skin infections.

Δ   Risks for developing bacterial skin infections include:

- Immunodeficiency disorders (AIDS, leukemia or solid tumors [e.g., lymphoma]).

- Long-term immunosuppressive therapy (corticosteroids).

Δ   Lice infestation can occur during periods of time when children are in close contact (e.g., day care, school, summer camp) and sharing personal care items (e.g., comb/hair brush, hats).

Δ   Scabies spreads quickly under crowded conditions. Infestation may also occur with the sharing of infested clothing, towels, and bedding. Individuals with weakened immune systems are at the greatest risk for infestation.

Assessment

Δ   Identify parasite.

Δ   Nursing history information should include:

- Exposure to a causative agent.

- Allergies.

- History of prior skin disorder.

- Onset of skin disorder and whether or not it might be related to any medications, food, soaps, or contact with animals.

- Reports of itching, pain, (e.g., head, genital area, back).

Δ   Assess for fever, fatigue, and/or malaise.

Δ   Assess the general condition of the skin, hair, and nails, including color (e.g., redness, pallor, cyanosis), cleanliness, warmth, swelling, and bleeding of mucous membranes.

Δ   Assess for presence, pattern, and location of vesicles, warts, rash, hives, or open wounds.

Δ   Assess for signs of a wound infection, which may include:

- Swelling.

- Purulent drainage.

- Pain.

- Increased temperature.

- Redness extending beyond the wound margin.

Infection/Causative Agents	Manifestations
Impetigo contagiosa (bacteria) • Staphylococcus	• Red macule that becomes vesicle and ruptures • Thick, crusted, amber-colored exudate • Spreads easily • Pruritus
Verruca (warts) • Human papillomavirus	• Well-circumscribed papule with rough texture
Cold sores, fever blisters • Herpes simplex virus 1 (HSV1) Genital herpes • Herpes simplex 2 (HSV2)	• Vesicles grouped on inflamed skin usually around lips or genitalia; burning painful sensation • Vesicles dry, skin exfoliates and heals within 8 to 10 days
Tinea capitis (ringworm, head) Fungus • *Trichophyton tonsurans* • *Microsporum canis*	• Circular patches • Lesions beginning in scalp and possibly progressing to neck or hairline • Alopecia around lesions
Tinea corporis (ringworm, body) Fungus • *Trichophyton rubrum* • *Trichophyton mentagrophytes* • *Microsporum canis*	• Circular red patches • Clearing beginning in the middle of the patches, then proceeding to the edges • Usually not bilateral
Candidiasis (thrush) Fungus • *Candida albicans*	• Inflamed areas with white exudates • Bleeds easily • Pruritic
Pediculosis (head lice) - Parasite • *Pediculosis capitis* (head lice) • *Pediculosis humanus corporis* (body lice) • *Pediculosis pubis* (pubic lice)	• Generalized itching on head or genital area • Rash • Scratching can cause sores to become infected with bacteria or fungi • Visible nits in hair, behind ears, and at base of scalp (hatch in about a week), and in seams of clothing (may take 30 days to hatch)

Infection/Causative Agents	Manifestations
Scabies (mite) • *Sarcoptes scabiei*	• Grayish-brown, threadlike burrows with a black dot at the end (mite) • Eczematous eruption in infants • Intense itching can cause sores to become infected • Pattern of lesions including interdigital, antecubital, popliteal, and inguinal areas • Pruritic • May take 30 to 60 days to develop
Lyme disease • *Borrelia burgdorferi*	• Stage 1: red-ringed rash about 3 to 31 days after possible tick bite • Stage 2: neurologic, cardiac, and musculoskeletal involvement • Stage 3: musculoskeletal pain in joints and supporting structures

Diagnostic Procedures

Δ   Identify parasite.

Δ   Lice are wingless, free-moving, grayish tan in color, and found behind the ears and at the base of the scalp.

Δ   Nits (small white oval eggs) attach to hair follicles about ¼ inch from the scalp.

Δ   Translucent (empty) nits may be found farther down the hair shaft.

Δ   Take a wound culture for bacterial infections.

Δ   Conduct a microscopic exam of tissue or lesions for ringworm.

Δ   Use serologic testing for late stages of Lyme disease.

NANDA Nursing Diagnoses

Δ   Impaired skin integrity

Δ   Risk for infection

Δ   Disturbed body image

Δ   Social isolation

Δ   Acute pain

Nursing Interventions

Δ   Assess and document general skin condition.

Δ   Assess and document lesions for color, shape, distribution, texture, moisture, and presence of exudate.

Δ   Gently clean affected areas.

Δ   Apply topical antibiotics or antifungal creams as prescribed.

Δ   Trim and clean child's fingernails.

Δ   Encourage the child to wear gloves at night to prevent scratching.

Δ   Teach the family how to avoid the spread of infections.

- Use good handwashing technique.

- Avoid sharing clothing, hats, combs, brushes, and/or towels.

- Keep the child from touching the affected area by using distraction.

- Do not squeeze vesicles.

- Apply topical medication.

- Administer oral medications as prescribed.

- Clean surfaces that might be harboring causative agents, including bed linens, clothing, and furniture.

Δ   Teach family how to prevent arthropod bites.

- Avoid tick-infested areas. If bitten, carefully remove ticks and observe skin for development of any reactions.

- Wear light-colored clothing when going into areas that may have ticks so that ticks can be identified and removed.

- Apply insect repellants cautiously to avoid neurologic complications.

Δ   Interventions Specific to Causative Agent

Infection/Causative Agents	Management
Impetigo contagiosa • Staphylococcus	• Use 1:20 Burow's solution compresses to remove crusted exudate. • Use topical antibacterial or oral antibiotics.
Verruca (warts) • Human papillomavirus	• Usually resolve without treatment. Invasive treatments usually leave scars.

Infection/Causative Agents	Management
Cold sores, fever blisters • (HSV1)	• Sores usually heal without scarring. • A secondary infection may develop. This infection can be fatal to an immunocompromised child.
Genital herpes • (HSV2)	
Tinea capitis (ringworm, head) • *Trichophyton tonsurans* • *Microsporum canis*	• The child may need to take oral griseofulvin for several months. • May use topical antifungal medications that are appropriate for affected areas (e.g., clotrimazole, miconazole). • Use a selenium sulfide shampoo.
Tinea corporis (ringworm, body) • *Trichophyton rubrum* • *Trichophyton mentagrophytes* • *Microsporum canis*	• The child may need to take oral griseofulvin for several months. • May use topical antifungal medications that are appropriate for affected areas (e.g., clotrimazole, miconazole). Apply 1 inch past the edge of the lesion and continue treatment 1 to 2 weeks after resolution of the lesion.
Candidiasis (thrush) • *Candida albicans*	• Apply nystatin ointment or solution to affected areas.
Pediculosis	• Apply an OTC or prescribed pediculicide shampoo to the infected child and family according to product instructions. • Do not use hair product with conditioner prior to treatment. Hair should not be rewashed for 1 to 2 days following treatment. • Use a comb designed to remove nits. Inspect hair every 2 to 3 days for 2 to 3 weeks. • Treat the child again at specific intervals based on inspection results and the pediculicide product used. • Wear clean clothing after treatment. • Wash clothing, linens, combs, and hairbrushes worn or used 2 days prior to treatment in hot water (130° F). Place clothing and linens in dryer on high heat until dry. • Dry clean clothes that are nonwashable. • Nonwashable items should be sealed in a plastic bag for 2 weeks. • Vacuum the area most occupied by the infected child.

Infection/Causative Agents	Management
Scabies • *Sarcoptes scabiei*	• Apply topical medication on the child's neck down to his toes. • Give the child clean clothes, towels, and bedding. • Leave on skin for 8 to 12 hr. • Bathe the child to remove medication.
Lyme disease • *Borrelia burgdorferi*	• Administer oral antibiotics (amoxicillin to children younger than 8 years, doxycycline to children older than 8 years). • Use erythromycin or cefuroxime in the child allergic to penicillin.

Complications and Nursing Implications

Δ   Cellulitis secondary to infection (e.g., staphylococcus, streptococcus, *Haemophilus influenzae)*

• Clinical manifestations include:

◊ Red inflammation of skin with swelling.

◊ Possible lymphangitis (red streaking).

◊ Possible lymph node involvement.

◊ Possible development of abscess, fever, and malaise.

• Nursing interventions include:

◊ Administering antibiotics, antipyretics, and antipruritics as prescribed.

◊ Keeping lesions clean and dry.

◊ Applying dressings as prescribed.

Primary Reference:

Hockenberry, M., Wilson, D., & Winkelstein, M. (2005). *Wong's essentials of pediatric nursing care.* (7th ed.). St. Louis, MO: Mosby.

Additional Resources:

Centers for Disease Control and Prevention. (2005, August). *Treating head lice infestation.* Retrieved January 30, 2007, from http://www.cdc.gov/ncidod/dpd/parasites/lice/factsht_head_lice_treating.htm

NANDA International (2004). *NANDA nursing diagnoses: Definitions and classification 2005-2006.* Philadelphia: NANDA.

Chapter 33: Skin Infections and Infestations

Application Exercises

Scenario: A 5-year-old child is hospitalized with Lyme disease. His symptoms include heart failure, confusion, and decreased level of consciousness.

1. This child exhibits manifestations of Stage _____ Lyme disease.

2. The child's mother asks the nurse how her son could have gotten such a serious disease. What is an appropriate response by the nurse?

3. The mother tells the nurse that her family recently moved to a new home and the back yard has a lot of trees and grassy areas. List several suggestions the nurse might offer the mother to help prevent tick infestation in her child (other than staying inside).

4. List the manifestations of Stage 1 Lyme disease for which children should be instructed to observe in order to prevent Stage 2 disease.

5. A small, superficial, elevated lesion containing serous fluid is called a

   A. macule.

   B. pustule.

   C. vesicle.

   D. papule.

6. Which of the following are the manifestations of scabies? (Select all that apply.)

   _____ Nits present

   _____ Threadlike rash between fingers and other moist areas

   _____ Circular rash on extremities

   _____ Pruritus

   _____ Eczematous eruption in infants

Scenario: A mother contacts the clinic to report possible head lice on her child. She tells the nurse that her child has just had a sleepover with four other children. During the sleepover, the mother remembers some of the children wearing and exchanging hats and sleeping on the same pillows and sheets.

7. Explain how the nurse can instruct the mother in properly identifying head lice.

8. The mother asks the nurse if she can use an OTC remedy instead of a prescription. What is an appropriate response by the nurse?

9. The mother questions the nurse about what else she should do to rid her child of the lice. What is an appropriate response by the nurse?

10. Match the following skin disorders with their cause.

_____ Impetigo contagiosa   A. Fungal infection

_____ Scabies   B. Bacterial infection

_____ Lyme disease   C. Viral infection

_____ Cold sore, fever blister   D. Caused by a spirochete

_____ Ringworm   E. Caused by a burrowing mite

Chapter 33: Skin Infections and Infestations

Application Exercises Answer Key

Scenario: A 5-year-old child is hospitalized with Lyme disease. His symptoms include heart failure, confusion, and decreased level of consciousness.

1. This child exhibits manifestations of Stage _____ Lyme disease.

> **Stage 2 Lyme disease. Stage 2 includes systemic neurologic, cardiac, and musculoskeletal manifestations that occur several weeks after Stage 1 symptoms have disappeared (unless early treatment occurs).**

2. The child's mother asks the nurse how her son could have gotten such a serious disease. What is an appropriate response by the nurse?

> **Lyme disease is caused by the spirochete Borrelia burgdorferi, which enters the system through ticks (mainly the deer tick). The spirochete is contained within the saliva and feces of the tick and is transferred to a human when the tick attaches to the person's skin. The longer the tick is attached to a human, the greater the chance of the Lyme disease spirochete being transferred from tick to human.**

3. The mother tells the nurse that her family recently moved to a new home and the back yard has a lot of trees and grassy areas. List several suggestions the nurse might offer the mother to help prevent tick infestation in her child (other than staying inside).

> **Tuck the child's pant legs into boots when outside.**
>
> **Instruct the child to wear shoes and long-sleeved shirts in wooded areas.**
>
> **Remove the child's clothes after being outside and inspect closely for ticks, including in the child's scalp.**
>
> **Ticks should be removed with tweezers. Attach tweezers to the head of the tick and pull steadily upward. Clean the area with disinfectant after making sure that all parts of the tick are removed.**

4. List the manifestations of Stage 1 Lyme disease for which children should be instructed to observe in order to prevent Stage 2 disease.

A raised, macular (reddened) area at the site where the tick was imbedded (usually occurs 3 to 31 days later)

Flu-like symptoms

The symptoms listed usually disappear with or without treatment. However, without treatment, the person may develop systemic complications of Stage 2 Lyme disease.

5. A small, superficial, elevated lesion containing serous fluid is called a

        A. macule.

        B. pustule.

        C. vesicle.

        D. papule.

A vesicle is an elevated, superficial lesion less than 1 cm in diameter that contains serous fluid. An example of a vesicle is the lesion of herpes simplex. A macule is a flat, nonpalpable lesion, such as a freckle or the rash of rubella. A pustule is similar to a vesicle except it contains purulent fluid. A papule is a firm, palpable lesion, such as a wart, which does not contain fluid.

6. Which of the following are the manifestations of scabies? (Select all that apply.)

      _____ Nits present

      __X__ **Threadlike rash between fingers and other moist areas**

      _____ Circular rash on extremities

      _X_ **Pruritus**

      _X_ **Eczematous eruption in infants**

Scabies is caused by the scabies mite, which burrows into the skin. This mite is often found between the fingers or in other moist areas, such as antecubital, popliteal, or inguinal areas. The burrows seen on the skin often appear grayish-brown and threadlike with a black dot at the end (the mite). Skin lesions are extremely pruritic in nature. In infants the skin lesions may look like eczema. The presence of nits indicates pediculosis. Circular rash on extremities may indicate Lyme disease or possibly ringworm.

Scenario: A mother contacts the clinic to report possible head lice on her child. She tells the nurse that her child has just had a sleepover with four other children. During the sleepover, the mother remembers some of the children wearing and exchanging hats and sleeping on the same pillows and sheets.

7. Explain how the nurse can instruct the mother in properly identifying head lice.

   Instruct the mother to inspect behind the child's ears and at the base of the skull for reddened areas that are caused by scratching. She may also be able to visualize the louse, which is wingless, small, grayish-tan in color, and usually moving around the scalp. Finally, she should look to see if nits (eggs) are attached to the hair shaft about one-quarter inch from the scalp. The nits are small, whitish, oval specks which, unlike dandruff, adhere to the hair.

8. The mother asks the nurse if she can use an OTC remedy instead of a prescription. What is an appropriate response by the nurse?

   The nurse should tell the mother that OTC remedies are available. The mother should be advised to follow the package directions exactly as written.

9. The mother questions the nurse about what else she should do to rid her child of the lice. What is an appropriate response by the nurse?

   The nurse should tell the mother to use a nit comb to inspect the child's hair every 2 to 3 days for 2 to 3 weeks, since the life cycle of the egg is 14 days. The nurse should also tell the mother to wash all clothing, linens, pillows, hair items, stuffed animals, and other items that may be contaminated in hot water (130° F) and dry on a hot cycle in the dryer. If items are nonwashable, the mother should seal them in a plastic container for 14 days.

10. Match the following skin disorders with their cause.

   B Impetigo contagiosa   A. Fungal infection
   E Scabies   B. Bacterial infection
   D Lyme disease   C. Viral infection
   C Cold sore, fever blister   D. Caused by a spirochete
   A Ringworm   E. Caused by a burrowing mite

Unit 2

Nursing Care of Children with System Disorders

Section:

Nursing Care of Children with Integumentary Disorders

Chapter 34:   Dermatitis and Acne

Contributor: Michele Hinds, PhD, RN

 NCLEX-RN® Connections:

Learning Objective: Review and apply knowledge within "**Dermatitis and Acne**" in readiness for performance of the following nursing activities as outlined by the NCLEX-RN® test plan:

Δ   Assist with relevant laboratory, diagnostic, and therapeutic procedures within the nursing role, including:

- Client preparation for the procedure.
- Client teaching (before and following the procedure).
- Accurate collection of specimens.
- Evaluation of the child's response to the procedure.
- Planning and implementing body system-specific interventions as appropriate.
- Monitoring and taking actions to prevent or minimize the risk of complications.
- Accurate interpretation of procedure results.

Δ   Perform and document appropriate assessments based on the child's problem.

Δ   Apply knowledge of pathophysiology to planning care for clients with specific alterations in body systems, including recognizing associated signs and symptoms.

Δ   Interpret data that need to be reported immediately.

Δ   Monitor therapeutic devices (drainage/irrigating devices, chest tubes), if inserted, for proper functioning.

Δ   Explore resources, make referrals, collaborate with interdisciplinary team, and ensure continuity of client care.

Δ   Evaluate plans of care for multiple clients and revise plan as needed based on priorities of care and promotion of recovery.

Δ   Provide the child/family teaching regarding management of the child's health problem.

Δ   Recognize/respond to emergency situations, and evaluate/document the client's response to emergency interventions.

Contact Dermatitis

 Key Points/Key Factors

Δ   Contact dermatitis is an inflammatory reaction of the skin. It is caused when the skin comes into contact with chemicals or other irritants (e.g., feces, urine, soaps, poison ivy, animals, metal, dyes, medications).

- Diaper dermatitis may be caused by detergents, soaps, and/or chemicals that come in contact with the genital area. It may also be a result of *Candida albicans*.

- Urushiol is the offending agent in contact dermatitis resulting from exposure to poisonous plants.

- Seborrheic dermatitis (cradle cap) has an unknown etiology but is most common in infancy and then again at puberty

Assessment

Δ   Obtain history of exposure to irritant and/or allergies.

Δ   Note presence of pruritus and/or pain.

Δ   Note pattern and areas of redness, inflammation, and/or blistering.

- Diaper dermatitis

  ◊   Red, inflamed skin on areas in most contact with urine, feces, and/or chemical irritants

  ◊   Lesions manifested are varied in type and pattern.

  ◊   Most involved areas include folds of the buttocks, inner thighs, and scrotum

- Poison dermatitis

  ◊   Reaction may be mild to severe and include rash, redness, swelling, blisters, and/or pruritus

- Medication reactions

  ◊   Reactions can occur immediately after administration of the medication, or they may be delayed. It may take up to 7 days for a child who has never been exposed to a particular medication to have an adverse response.

  ◊   Reactions can range from a simple rash to a full body response, and be mild or severe. These reactions may look similar to other skin disorders.

◊ Most often a medication response is seen as a sudden onset of a generalized inflammatory response with itching and GI discomfort. However, this response can progress to anemia, kidney, and/or liver dysfunction.

- Seborrheic dermatitis

   ◊ Thick, yellow adhesions on scalp, eyelids, and external ear canals

Atopic Dermatitis

 Key Points/Key Factors

Δ Atopic dermatitis (AD) is a type of eczema (describes a category of integumentary disorders and not specific disorders with a determined etiology) that is characterized by pruritus and associated with a history of allergies and a tendency to be inherited (atopy).

Δ New lesions develop with continued scratching and increase the risk of secondary infection.

Δ Classifications of atopic dermatitis are based on the child's age, how the lesions are distributed, and appearance of the lesions.

Assessment

Δ Nursing history information should include :

- Exposure to causative agent.

- Presence of allergic condition and family history of atopy.

- Previous skin disorder(s) and exacerbation of present skin disorder.

- Onset of skin disorder and whether or not it might be related to any medications, food, soaps or contact with animals.

- Presence of itching and/or pain.

- Questions related to behavior – for younger children (e.g., sleeping patterns, appetite, irritability).

Δ   Assess for presence, pattern, and location of lesions.

Classification	Distribution	Lesions
Infant – onset at 2 to 6 months with spontaneous remission by age 3	• Redness on cheeks, scalp, trunk, hands and feet	• Usually symmetric • Weeping, oozing, or may be crusty and scaly • Erythematous vesicles and papules
Childhood –progression of infant form or starts at age 2 with full symptoms evident by age 5	• Redness or irritation in antecubital and popliteal fossae, on wrists, ankles, and feet	• Red or tan-colored patches or clusters of papules • Hyperpigmented • Dry • Thickened skin • Keratosis pilaris
Preadolescent and adolescent – onset at age 12 and may continue into adulthood	• Face, neck, hands and feet, less antecubital and popliteal fossae involvement than childhood	• Same as childhood • Papules that appear blended together • Larger, dry, thickened patches

Δ   Assess general condition of the skin, hair, and nails including color (e.g., redness, pallor, cyanosis), cleanliness, warmth, swelling, and bleeding of mucous membranes.

•   Unaffected skin may appear dry and rough.

•   Hypopigmentation of skin may occur in small, diffuse areas.

•   Pallor surrounds nose, mouth, and ears.

•   There is a bluish discoloration on the face and underneath the eyes.

•   Numerous infections of the nails may be present.

Δ   Assess for lymphadenopathy, especially around affected areas.

Δ   Assess for signs of a wound infection, which can include swelling, purulent drainage, pain, increased temperature, and redness extending beyond the wound margin.

NANDA Nursing Diagnoses

Δ   Disturbed body image

Δ   Risk for infection

Δ   Impaired skin integrity

Δ   Social isolation

Nursing Interventions

Δ   Diaper Dermatitis

- Promptly remove wet diaper.

- Clean urine off infant with nonsoap cleanser. Clean feces off with warm water and mild soap.

- Expose affected area to air.

- Use superabsorbent disposable diapers to reduce skin exposure.

- Apply a skin barrier such as zinc oxide. Do not wash off with each diaper change.

- Use of cornstarch may reduce friction between diaper and skin.

Δ   Contact Dermatitis

- Rinse areas exposed to poisonous plants with cold water. If outdoors, the child can go into a body of water with his clothes still on.

- Remove all clothing that has come into contact with the plant and wash in hot water and detergent.

- Encourage the child not to scratch skin to prevent secondary infection from developing.

Δ   Medication Reactions

- Discontinue medication.

- Administer antihistamines and corticosteroids as prescribed.

- Anaphylaxis is a medical emergency and requires immediate medical attention. (*Refer to chapter 54, Pediatric Emergencies.*)

Δ   Treat seborrheic dermatitis by gently scrubbing the scalp with mild pressure and shampooing daily with mild soap or antiseborrheic shampoo.

Δ   Treat secondary infection with antibiotics.

Δ   Teach the family how to prevent future episodes.

- Identify causative agent.

- Educate the child to recognize poisonous plants and to avoid contact. Remove the agent from the child's environment if possible.

- Use mild detergents to wash clothing and linens.

- Change diapers when wet or soiled.

Δ   Keep skin hydrated with tepid bath (with/without soap, or emulsifying oil) and then apply an emollient within 3 min of bathing. Two or 3 baths may be given daily with one prior to bedtime.

Δ   Wash skin folds and genital area frequently with plain water.

Δ   Provide relief of itching.

  • Colloidal bath made with cornstarch

  • Nonsedating oral antihistamines (e.g., loratadine [Claritin]) for daytime and sedating oral antihistamines (e.g., hydroxyzine [Atarax] or diphenhydramine [Benadryl]) for bedtime

  • Cool compresses

  • Topical lotions such as calamine

  • Burrow's solution

Δ   Provide parental instructions to minimize itching and scratching, as well as to prevent infection.

  • Keep nails short and trimmed.

  • Place gloves or cotton socks over hands for sleeping.

  • Dress young child in soft cotton, one-piece, long-sleeve, long-pant outfits.

  • Remove items that may promote itching (e.g., woolen blankets, scratchy fabrics). Soft, synthetic fabrics should be used for cold weather outdoor clothing.

  • Use mild detergents to wash clothing and linens. Wash cycle may be repeated without soap.

  • Avoid latex products, second-hand smoke, furry pets, dust, and molds.

  • Follow specific directions regarding topical medications, soaks, baths. It is important for the parent to understand the sequence of treatments to maximize the benefit of therapy and prevent complications.

  • Do not overheat the bedroom during winter months.

Δ   Treat dermatitis exacerbations of inflammation.

  • Use topical steroids to decrease inflammation and oral steroids for severe reactions.

  • Obtain a prescription for an immunomodulator (e.g., tacrolimus [Protopic] and pimecrolimus [Elidel]) at the start of exacerbation of AD when skin turns red and starts to itch.

Acne

 Key Points/Key Factors

Δ   Acne is the most common skin problem during adolescence.

Δ   Acne is self-limiting and non life-threatening. However, it poses a threat to self-image for adolescents.

Δ   Acne involves the hair follicles and sebaceous glands of the face, neck, chest, and back.

Δ   *Propionibacterium acnes* may be a causative agent leading to infection.

Δ   Acne may be genetically inherited.

Δ   Acne is more common in males than in females.

Δ   Research does not support an association between stress and acne.

Δ   Although there is no dietary intake link with acne, adolescents working at fast food restaurants may have an increased incidence of acne due to exposure to cooking grease.

Assessment

Δ   Nursing history information should include:

• Onset of lesions.

• Exacerbations and remissions.

• History of treatment for acne and effectiveness including home treatments.

• Impact on self-concept and body image.

• Nutritional status and sleep/rest patterns.

• Hygiene, especially areas affected.

• Activities, especially outdoor sports or activities.

• Behavioral changes such as unexpected violent outbursts, suicidal ideation and/or depression if prescribed isotretinoin (Accutane).

Δ   Lesions (comedones) are either open (blackheads) or closed (whiteheads). Both are most often found on the face, neck, back, and chest.

Δ   *Propionibacterium acnes* may lead to inflammation manifesting as papules, pustules, nodules, or cysts.

NANDA Nursing Diagnoses

Δ   Impaired skin integrity

Δ   Disturbed body image

Δ   Social isolation

Δ   Risk for infection

Nursing Interventions

Δ   Discuss the process of acne with the child/family.

Δ   Encourage the child to eat a balanced, healthy diet.

Δ   Encourage sleep, rest, and daily exercise.

Δ   Teach the child to wash the affected area gently with a mild cleanser once or twice daily and not to pick or squeeze comedones.

Δ   Encourage frequent shampooing.

Δ   Encourage family support of the child and encourage the family members to assist the child in coping with body-image changes.

Δ   Instruct the child to wear protective clothing and sunscreen when outside.

Δ   Teach the child to avoid the use of tanning beds.

Δ   Teach the child and family about medications prescribed, especially side effects.

Medication	Action	Nursing Considerations
Tretinoin (Retin-A)	Interrupts abnormal keratinization that causes comedones	• Tretinoin may irritate skin. • Avoid sun exposure. • Use sunscreen (SPF 15 or greater) to avoid sunburn.
Benzoyl peroxide	• Antibacterial agent • Inhibits growth of *P. acnes*	Benzoyl peroxide may bleach bed linens, but not skin.
Topical antibacterial agents	Inhibits growth of *P. acnes*	• Various antibacterial agents may be used; however, be alert to allergic reactions. • Avoid overexposure to sun. • Use sunscreen with SPF of 15 or greater when exposure to sun is unavoidable.

Medication	Action	Nursing Considerations
Isotretinoin (Accutane)	Affects factors involved in the development of acne	• Isotretinoin is only prescribed by a dermatologist. • Side effects include dry skin and mucous membranes, dry eyes, decreased night vision, headaches, photosensitivity, elevated cholesterol and triglycerides, depression, suicidal ideation, and/or violent behaviors. • Monitor for behavioral changes. • Isotretinoin is contraindicated in pregnant women.

Complications and Nursing Implications

Δ Lesions of dermatitis and/or acne can develop into a secondary infection and cellulitis.

• Assess for signs of redness, swelling, and pain that may indicate cellulitis.

• Teach the family signs and symptoms of cellulitis and to notify the primary care provider.

Primary Reference:

Hockenberry, M., Wilson, D., & Winkelstein, M. (2005). *Wong's essentials of pediatric nursing care.* (7th ed.). St. Louis, MO: Mosby.

Additional Resources:

NANDA International (2004). *NANDA nursing diagnoses: Definitions and classification 2005-2006.* Philadelphia: NANDA.

Chapter 34: Dermatitis and Acne

Application Exercises

Scenario: A 2-month-old infant is brought to the public health clinic by his mother for immunizations. The mother shows the nurse the infant's scalp, which is half-covered by thick, crusty, yellowish, solid patches. The mother asks the nurse, "Is this something he caught from other children at day care?"

1. What are these patches and how should the nurse respond to the mother's statement?

2. How is cradle cap treated?

3. Match each type of dermatitis with its description.

_____ Diaper dermatitis   A. Weeping, red vesicles and papules

_____ Infantile eczema   B. Comedones or pustules

_____ Acne   C. Red, inflamed skin

_____ Seborrheic dermatitis   D. Thick, yellow scaly areas

4. Which of the following medications can be used for children with eczema? (Select all that apply.)

_____ Corticosteroids

_____ Accutane

_____ Peroxide

_____ Antihistamines

_____ Calamine lotion

5. True or False: Diaper dermatitis can be largely prevented by changing an infant's diapers frequently and keeping the diaper area clean and dry.

6. True or False: Eczema usually appears on the cheeks of a 4-year-old child.

7. True or False: A complication that may occur with acne and most types of dermatitis is cellulitis.

Chapter 34: Dermatitis and Acne

Application Exercises Answer Key

Scenario: A 2-month-old infant is brought to the public health clinic by his mother for immunizations. The mother shows the nurse the infant's scalp, which is half-covered by thick, crusty, yellowish, solid patches. The mother asks the nurse, "Is this something he caught from other children at day care?"

1. What are these patches and how should the nurse respond to the mother's statement?

   The patches are most likely cradle cap or seborrheic dermatitis, which has an unknown cause. However, cradle cap is not contagious and may be caused by increased secretion of sebum, an oily substance secreted by sebaceous glands on the skin.

2. How is cradle cap treated?

   Cradle cap is treated by shampooing the scalp regularly with mild shampoo. The shampoo is left on the infant's head for a few minutes until the crusts are softened and then the scalp is rinsed. A fine-tooth comb or a soft brush can help to remove the loosened crusts from the hair after it is shampooed.

3. Match each type of dermatitis with its description.

   C Diaper dermatitis   A. Weeping, red vesicles and papules

   A Infantile eczema   B. Comedones or pustules

   B Acne   C. Red, inflamed skin

   D Seborrheic dermatitis   D. Thick, yellow scaly areas

4. Which of the following medications can be used for children with eczema? (Select all that apply.)

   X **Corticosteroids**

_____ Accutane

_____ Peroxide

   X **Antihistamines**

   X **Calamine lotion**

Corticosteroids can be used topically or orally to treat inflammation of eczema. Antihistamines are used to prevent scratching. Lotions, such as Calamine, may be soothing when applied to the skin. Accutane and peroxide are medications that may be used for acne.

5. True or False: Diaper dermatitis can be largely prevented by changing an infant's diapers frequently and keeping the diaper area clean and dry.

True. Although some infants are more susceptible to diaper dermatitis than others; many problems can be prevented by frequent diaper changes and keeping the area dry and clean.

6. True or False: Eczema usually appears on the cheeks of a 4-year-old child.

False. Eczema is most likely to be seen on the antecubital and popliteal fossae of children ages 2 to 5. In infants, the cheeks are a common area for eczema.

7. True or False: A complication that may occur with acne and most types of dermatitis is cellulitis.

True. Cellulitis, which is an inflammation of the connective tissue underlying the skin, is usually caused by a secondary bacteria infection.

Unit 2   Nursing Care of Children with System Disorders
Section: Nursing Care of Children with Gastrointestinal Disorders

Chapter 35:   Acute Gastrointestinal Disorders
                Contributor: Diana Rupert, MSN, RN, ABD

 NCLEX-RN® Connections:

> **Learning Objective**: Review and apply knowledge within "**Acute Gastrointestinal Disorders**" in readiness for performance of the following nursing activities as outlined by the NCLEX-RN® test plan:
>
> Δ   Assist with relevant laboratory, diagnostic, and therapeutic procedures within the nursing role, including:
>
>   • Client preparation for the procedure.
>
>   • Client teaching (before and following the procedure).
>
>   • Accurate collection of specimens.
>
>   • Evaluation of the child's response to the procedure.
>
>   • Planning and implementing body system-specific interventions as appropriate.
>
>   • Monitoring and taking actions to prevent or minimize the risk of complications.
>
>   • Accurate interpretation of procedure results.
>
> Δ   Perform and document appropriate assessments based on the child's problem.
>
> Δ   Apply knowledge of pathophysiology to planning care for clients with specific alterations in body systems, including recognizing associated signs and symptoms.
>
> Δ   Interpret data that need to be reported immediately.
>
> Δ   Monitor therapeutic devices (drainage/irrigating devices, chest tubes), if inserted, for proper functioning.
>
> Δ   Explore resources, make referrals, collaborate with interdisciplinary team, and ensure continuity of client care.
>
> Δ   Evaluate plans of care for multiple clients and revise plan as needed based on priorities of care and promotion of recovery.
>
> Δ   Provide the child/family teaching regarding management of the child's health problem.
>
> Δ   Recognize/respond to emergency situations, and evaluate/document the client's response to emergency interventions.

Key Points/Key Factors

Δ   Childhood gastrointestinal disorders may result from infection, infestation (parasitic worms), structural anomalies, an inflammatory response, or difficulty with motility within the gastrointestinal tract.

Δ   Gastroenteritis is the inflammation of the stomach and intestines. It usually accompanies numerous gastrointestinal disorders including anorexia, nausea, vomiting, abdominal distention, and diarrhea.

  •   Fluid and electrolyte imbalances (e.g., hypokalemia, hyponatremia) and/or acid base imbalances (e.g., metabolic acidosis or alkalosis) may develop during the acute phase of gastroenteritis.

Δ   Vomiting is common during childhood. It may be self-limiting or indicate an obstruction or other problem with the gastrointestinal tract.

Δ   Diarrhea may be mild to severe, acute or chronic, and may result in mild to severe dehydration.

  •   Acute diarrhea may follow secondary to an upper respiratory or urinary tract infection or antibiotic use.

  •   Acute infectious diarrhea (infectious gastroenteritis) is a result of various bacterial, viral, and/or parasitic infections. The onset of gastroenteritis is often abrupt with rapid loss of fluids and electrolytes from persistent vomiting and diarrhea.

  •   Chronic diarrhea is related to chronic conditions (e.g., malabsorption syndrome, lactose intolerance, food allergies, inflammatory bowel disease).

Δ   Risk factors for *Enterobius vermicularis* (pinworm) include crowded places (e.g., school, day care) or crowded living spaces (e.g., family living together).

Assessment

Δ   Nursing history should include:

  •   Exposure to causative agent, recent travel.

  •   Eating pattern (usual pattern and recent pattern).

  •   Onset and description of symptoms, including duration of symptoms.

  •   Recent weight loss.

  •   Stool pattern (usual/recent pattern).

  •   Reports of fatigue, malaise, change in behavior, poor appetite, and pain.

Δ   Obtain baseline height and weight.

Δ   Perform nutritional assessment including fluid intake. Monitor I&O.

△   Signs and Symptoms of Specific Pathogens

Pathogen	Manifestations	Transmission/Incubation
Rotavirus	• Common cause of diarrhea in young children • Fever and vomiting for 2 days • Watery diarrhea for 5 to 7 days	• Fecal-oral transmission • Incubation period – 48 hr
Escherichia coli (E. coli)	• Watery diarrhea for 1 to 2 days, followed by severe abdominal cramping • Could lead to hemolytic uremic syndrome (HUS)	• Transmission depends on strain of *E. coli* • Incubation period – 3 to 4 days
Salmonella nontyphoidal groups	• Nausea • Vomiting • Abdominal cramping • Bloody diarrhea • Fever (may be afebrile in infants) • Headache, confusion, drowsiness, and seizures • May lead to meningitis or septicemia	• Transmitted through undercooked meats and poultry • Incubation period – 6 to 72 hr
Clostridium difficile (*C. difficile*)	• Mild, watery diarrhea for a few days • Children may experience less severe symptoms than adults • May cause leukocytosis, hypoalbuminemia, and high fever in certain children • May lead to pseudomembranous colitis	• Transmission through contact with colonized spores, commonly transmitted in health care settings • Nonspecified incubation period
Clostridium botulinum (*C. botulinum*)	• Abdominal pain, cramping, and diarrhea • May cause respiratory compromise or CNS symptoms	• Transmitted through contaminated food products • Incubation period – 12 to 26 hr
Staphylococcus	• Food poisoning resulting in severe diarrhea, nausea, and vomiting	• Transmitted through food that is inadequately cooked or refrigerated • Incubation period – 1 to 8 hr
Enterobius vermicularis (pinworm) is a parasitic worm that is white, threadlike, and approximately ⅓ to ½ inch long.	• Perianal itching • Enuresis • Sleeplessness, restlessness, and irritability due to itching	• Infestation beginning when eggs are inhaled or swallowed (fecal-oral transmission)

Δ   Assess for signs and symptoms of dehydration.

- Dry and pale skin

- Cool lips

- Dry mucous membranes

- Decreased skin turgor

- Diminished urinary output

- Concentrated urine

- Thirst

- Rapid pulse

- Sunken fontanels

- Decreased blood pressure

Diagnostic Procedures and Nursing Interventions

Δ   Infectious Gastroenteritis

- Rotavirus – enzyme immunoassay (stool sample)

- *E. coli* – Sorbitol-MacConkey agar (stool sample)

- *Salmonella* – gram-stained stool culture

- *C. difficile* – stool culture

- *C. botulinum* – blood and stool culture

- *Staphylococcus* – identification of organism in stool, blood, food, or aspirate

Δ   Provide instructions to the parent/caregiver regarding the tape test for *Enterobius vermicularis*.

- Place transparent tape over the child's anus at night. Remove the tape the following morning prior to the child toileting or bathing. If possible, have the parent apply tape after the child has gone to sleep and remove before the child awakens.

- Bring specimen to the laboratory for microscopic evaluation.

- Use good handwashing during this procedure.

Δ   Diagnostic laboratory work for a child who is hospitalized might include:

- CBC with differential to determine anemia and/or infection.

- Serum electrolytes, BUN, creatinine, and urine-specific gravity to determine hydration. Hct, Hgb, BUN, creatinine, and urine-specific gravity levels are usually elevated with dehydration.

- Test stool for occult blood.

- Conduct urinalysis.

NANDA Nursing Diagnoses

- Δ   Anxiety

- Δ   Diarrhea

- Δ   Deficient fluid volume

- Δ   Hyperthermia

- Δ   Imbalanced nutrition: less than body requirements

- Δ   Acute pain

- Δ   Impaired skin integrity

Nursing Interventions

- Δ   Obtain daily weights, at same time of day.

- Δ   Avoid taking rectal temperature.

- Δ   Assess and monitor I&O (urine and stool).

- Δ   Initiate IV fluids as ordered.

- Δ   Administer antibiotic as ordered. Metronidazole (Flagyl) is used for the child who is symptomatic of *C. difficile.*

- Δ   Oral rehydration therapy (ORT) guidelines include:

  - Starting replacement with an oral replacement solution (ORS) of 75 to 90 mEq of Na+/L at 40 to 50 mL/kg over 4 hr.

  - Determining further rehydration after initial replacement. Maintenance therapy should limit ORS to 150 mL/kg/day.

  - Giving ORS of 40 to 60 mEq of Na+/L for children with diarrhea but no significant dehydration.

  - Giving water, breast milk, or lactose-free formula if supplementary fluid is needed.

  - Advancing infants and older children to their regular diet while on maintenance ORT.

  - Replacing each diarrheal stool with 10mL/kg of ORS for ongoing diarrhea.

- Δ   Inform or have parent inform school or day care center of the child's infection/infestation. The child should stay home during the incubation period.

Δ   Teach the family to use commercially prepared ORS when the child experiences diarrhea. Foods and fluids to avoid include:

• Fruit juices, carbonated sodas, and gelatin, which are all high in carbohydrates, low in electrolyte content, and have a high osmolality.

• Caffeine, due to its mild diuretic effect.

• Chicken or beef broth, which has too much sodium and not enough carbohydrates.

• Bananas, rice, applesauce, and toast (BRAT diet). This diet carries low nutritional value, high carbohydrate content, and low electrolytes.

Δ   Teach the parent/caregiver to administer medications as prescribed.

• Pyrantel pamoate (Antiminth) and mebendazole (Vermox) are the medications of choice. Both are administered in a single dose that may need to be repeated in 2 weeks.

• All members of the family should be treated.

Δ   Instruct the family about home treatment for *Enterobius vermicularis*.

• Wash bed linens and underwear in hot water and dry in a hot clothes dryer daily for several days.

• Cleanse toys and child care areas thoroughly to prevent further spread or re-infestation.

• Keep toys separate and avoid shaking linen to prevent spread of disease.

Δ   Teach the family how to avoid the spread of infectious diseases.

• Avoid undercooked or under-refrigerated food.

• Promote and instruct on proper handwashing.

• Clip nails and discourage nail biting and thumb sucking.

• Clean toilet area.

Complications and Nursing Implications

Δ   Dehydration

• Classification of dehydration

Type of Dehydration	Manifestations
Isotonic	• Water and sodium lost in nearly equal amounts • Major loss of fluid from extracellular fluid; therefore, circulating fluid volume reduced • May lead to hypovolemic shock • Serum sodium within normal limits (130 to 150 mEq/L)

Type of Dehydration	Manifestations
Hypotonic	• Electrolyte loss greater than water loss • Water moving from extracellular fluid to intracellular fluid • Physical manifestations more severe with smaller fluid loss • Serum sodium less than 130 mEq/L
Hypertonic	• Water loss greater than electrolyte loss • Fluid shifting from intracellular to extracellular • Less likely to result in shock • Possible occurrence of neurologic changes such as decreased focusing or muscular hyperreflexia • Serum sodium concentration greater than 150 mEq/L

Δ Levels of Dehydration

Level	Weight Loss	Manifestations
Mild	5% in infants 3 to 4% in children	• Behavior, mucous membranes, anterior fontanel, pulse, and BP all within normal limits • Capillary refill greater than 2 sec • May experience slight thirst • Urine-specific gravity greater than 1.020
Moderate	10% in infants 6 to 8% in children	• Capillary refill between 2 to 4 sec • May have thirst, irritability • Slightly increased pulse with normal to orthostatic BP • Dry mucous membranes, decreased tears and skin turgor • Urine-specific gravity greater than 1.020, oliguria
Severe	15% in infants 10% in children	• Capillary refill greater than 4 sec • Tachycardia, orthostatic BP that may progress to shock • Extreme thirst • Very dry mucous membranes, tenting of skin • Sunken anterior fontanel • Oliguria or anuria

- Nursing interventions

  ◊ Administer IV fluids as prescribed; usually D_5NS.

  ◊ Fluid replacement takes place rapidly for isotonic and hypotonic dehydration but should take 24 to 48 hr for hypertonic dehydration to prevent cerebral edema.

  ◊ Antiemetics are not recommended because vomiting usually resolves with treatment of dehydration.

  ◊ Determine the cause of diarrhea. Antibiotics are usually reserved for children who are immunocompromised.

Primary Reference:

Hockenberry, M., Wilson, D., & Winkelstein, M. (2005). *Wong's essentials of pediatric nursing care.* (7th ed.). St. Louis, MO: Mosby.

Additional Resources:

NANDA International (2004). *NANDA nursing diagnoses: Definitions and classification 2005-2006.* Philadelphia: NANDA.

Timby, B. K. & Smith, N. E. (2004). *Essentials of nursing: Care of adults and children.* Philadelphia: Lippincott, Williams & Wilkins.

Chapter 35: Acute Gastrointestinal Disorders

Application Exercises

Scenario: A 5-month-old infant who is lethargic is brought to the emergency department by his parents. The parents tell the nurse that the infant has experienced fever, vomiting, and diarrhea for the past 2 days. They also state that the child is unable to tolerate clear liquids. The nurse suspects gastroenteritis.

1. When preparing for the admission assessment, what findings should the nurse anticipate when completing the infant's head-to-toe admission assessment?

Level of consciousness	
Head	
Lung fields	
Cardiovascular system	
Abdomen	
Urinary status	
Bowel status	
Activity level	
Nutrition/fluid intake	
Skin turgor	

2. The infant weighed 9.1 kg (20 lb) before the onset of symptoms. During the assessment, his weight is recorded as 8.2 kg (18 lb). His capillary refill takes about 3 sec, and his skin turgor is decreased. Based on this information, the nurse should assess his level of dehydration as

   A. none.
   B. mild.
   C. moderate.
   D. severe.

3. The infant's stool cultures are returned with a diagnosis of rotavirus. The parents state that they also have a 2-year-old child at home and are afraid of spreading the disease. What suggestions should the nurse give to the parents that will be most beneficial to them?

4. The priority nursing diagnosis for the above infant should be _____.

5. A child has lost electrolytes and some water through vomiting. The child's serum sodium is 115 mEq/L. The nurse determines that the child is _____.

6. Which of the following fluids is an appropriate choice to rehydrate a child who has experienced diarrhea due to *E. coli* for the past 3 days?

      A. Oral rehydration therapy

      B. IV isotonic saline with glucose

      C. Gelatin

      D. Chicken broth

7. Which of the following symptoms demonstrated by a child might indicate the presence of *Enterobius vermicularis* (pinworm)?

      A. Bloody diarrhea

      B. Perianal itching

      C. Moderate dehydration

      D. Abdominal pain

Chapter 35: Acute Gastrointestinal Disorders

Application Exercises Answer Key

Scenario: A 5-month-old infant who is lethargic is brought to the emergency department by his parents. The parents tell the nurse that the infant has experienced fever, vomiting, and diarrhea for the past 2 days. They also state that the child is unable to tolerate clear liquids. The nurse suspects gastroenteritis.

1. When preparing for the admission assessment, what findings should the nurse anticipate when completing the infant's head-to-toe admission assessment?

Level of consciousness	Irritable and lethargic
Head	Sunken fontanel, pale, sunken eyes
Lung fields	Clear, no retractions or nasal flaring, and good air exchange
Cardiovascular system	Blood pressure low, increased pulse that is thready in nature
Abdomen	Distended, hyperactive bowel sounds, cries when palpated, verbalizes cramping or displays discomfort by crying and being hunched over
Urinary status	Diminished urine output, concentrated urine when wet, and elevated specific gravity
Bowel status	Frequent stools, stool consistency watery, greenish appearance, possibly blood tinged, and foul smelling
Activity level	Lethargic, wants to be held by parents, and not interested in surroundings
Nutrition/fluid intake	Disinterested and unable to tolerate formula/breast milk and/or clear liquids
Skin turgor	Tented, poor turgor, and excoriated in diaper area

2. The infant weighed 9.1 kg (20 lb) before the onset of symptoms. During the assessment, his weight is recorded as 8.2 kg (18 lb). His capillary refill takes about 3 sec, and his skin turgor is decreased. Based on this information, the nurse should assess his level of dehydration as

      A. none.

      B. mild.

      C. moderate.

      D. severe.

The infant with moderate dehydration has lost about 10% of his body weight; capillary refill takes 3 sec or slightly longer; and decreased skin turgor is present. With mild dehydration, weight loss is around 5%, and other parameters may be slightly higher than the child's normal, but still within normal limits. In severe dehydration, 15% of body weight is lost; capillary refill takes more than 4 sec; and tenting of the skin is seen when turgor is assessed.

3. The infant's stool cultures are returned with a diagnosis of rotavirus. The parents state that they also have a 2-year-old child at home and are afraid of spreading the disease. What suggestions should the nurse give to the parents that will be most beneficial to them?

Use good handwashing. Wash hands after each diaper change and when coming into close contact with other children.

Disinfect the area around the child and/or keep the sick child in one area when sleeping and/or playing.

Take dirty diapers outside the home.

Wash any soiled sheets immediately.

Do not share cups or utensils among family members. Wash utensils in hot, soapy water or place in dishwasher.

4. The priority nursing diagnosis for the above infant should be _____.

Deficient fluid volume. This infant is exhibiting signs and symptoms of fluid volume deficit related to vomiting, diarrhea, and fever of 48 hr duration. Other nursing diagnoses such as imbalanced nutrition: less than body requirements, anxiety, and/or impaired skin integrity are important. However, rehydration therapy is vital to replace electrolytes and fluid lost by disease.

5. A child has lost electrolytes and some water through vomiting. The child's serum sodium is 115 mEq/L. The nurse determines that the child is _____.

Hypotonic. The child has hypotonic dehydration with net loss of more electrolytes than water (hyponatremia). In hypertonic dehydration, water loss is much more than electrolyte loss, and hypernatremia results. In isotonic dehydration, electrolytes and sodium are lost in equal amounts and serum sodium levels are normal.

6. Which of the following fluids is an appropriate choice to rehydrate a child who has experienced diarrhea due to *E. coli* for the past 3 days?

    A. Oral rehydration therapy

    B. IV isotonic saline with glucose

    C. Gelatin

    D. Chicken broth

Oral rehydration solution is made specifically for replacing water and electrolytes lost during diarrhea. It is less expensive and will be less painful than IV therapy. Gelatin is high in carbohydrates, low in electrolytes, and has a high osmolality; therefore, this makes it ineffective for rehydration. Broth is high in sodium and has no carbohydrates.

7. Which of the following symptoms demonstrated by a child might indicate the presence of *Enterobius vermicularis* (pinworm)?

    A. Bloody diarrhea

    B. Perianal itching

    C. Moderate dehydration

    D. Abdominal pain

Severe perianal itching is a common symptom of pinworm infestation. Other symptoms include enuresis, irritability, restlessness, and difficulty sleeping. None of the other symptoms mentioned is present with pinworm infestation.

Unit 2   Nursing Care of Children with System Disorders
Section: Nursing Care of Children with Gastrointestinal Disorders

Chapter 36:   Gastrointestinal Structural Disorders
                Contributor: Diana Rupert, MSN, RN, ABD

 NCLEX-RN® Connections:

> **Learning Objective**: Review and apply knowledge within "**Gastrointestinal Structural Disorders**" in readiness for performance of the following nursing activities as outlined by the NCLEX-RN® test plan:
>
> Δ Assist with relevant laboratory, diagnostic, and therapeutic procedures within the nursing role, including:
>   • Client preparation for the procedure.
>   • Client teaching (before and following the procedure).
>   • Accurate collection of specimens.
>   • Evaluation of the child's response to the procedure.
>   • Planning and implementing body system-specific interventions as appropriate.
>   • Monitoring and taking actions to prevent or minimize the risk of complications.
>   • Accurate interpretation of procedure results.
>
> Δ Perform and document appropriate assessments based on the child's problem.
>
> Δ Apply knowledge of pathophysiology to planning care for clients with specific alterations in body systems, including recognizing associated signs and symptoms.
>
> Δ Interpret data that need to be reported immediately.
>
> Δ Monitor therapeutic devices (drainage/irrigating devices, chest tubes), if inserted, for proper functioning.
>
> Δ Explore resources, make referrals, collaborate with interdisciplinary team, and ensure continuity of client care.
>
> Δ Evaluate plans of care for multiple clients and revise plan as needed based on priorities of care and promotion of recovery.
>
> Δ Provide the child/family teaching regarding management of the child's health problem.
>
> Δ Recognize/respond to emergency situations, and evaluate/document the client's response to emergency interventions.

 Key Points/Key Factors

Δ **Gastroesophageal reflux disease** (GERD) occurs when the gastric contents reflux back up into the esophagus, making esophageal mucosa vulnerable to injury from gastric acid.

- GERD may lead to failure to thrive if the child is unable to gain adequate nutrition.

- GERD may lead to respiratory difficulties if the child aspirates gastric content that has moved into the esophageal area.

- GERD is caused by the relaxation of the lower esophageal sphincter due to:

  ◊ Gastric distention.

  ◊ High abdominal pressure caused by CNS disease or coughing.

  ◊ Slowed gastric emptying.

  ◊ Hiatal hernia.

  ◊ Presence of a gastrostomy tube.

- GERD is more likely to occur in premature infants and others born with congenital defects such as neurologic disorders, esophageal disorders, cystic fibrosis, and cerebral palsy.

Δ **Hypertropic pyloric stenosis** is the thickening and tightening of the pyloric sphincter, creating an obstruction.

- Hypertrophic pyloric stenosis has a genetic component and is more common in first-born children who are male.

Δ **Hirschsprung's disease**, or congenital aganglionic megacolon, is a structural anomaly of the gastrointestinal (GI) tract caused by lack of ganglionic cells in segments of the colon, causing mechanical obstruction.

- Stool accumulates due to lack of peristalsis in the non-enervated area of the bowel (usually rectosigmoid) causing the bowel to dilate.

- Hirschsprung's disease is usually diagnosed in infants, but chronic milder symptoms may occur in late childhood.

- Hirschsprung's disease is more common in boys than girls and may be either an acute or chronic disorder.

Δ **Appendicitis** is inflammation of the appendix caused by an obstruction of the opening of the appendix possibly due to fecal matter, swollen lymphoid tissue, or a parasite.

  ◊ Appendicitis, the most common cause of emergency abdominal surgery in children, occurs at an average age of 10 years.

◊   Delayed diagnosis of appendicitis due to nonspecific symptoms causes perforated appendix in one-third of cases.

◊   Death can occur from peritonitis.

Δ   **Meckel's diverticulum** is the remnant of a fetal duct, which in most newborns has resolved completely.

- The diverticulum may be up to 4 inches in length and is found in the small intestine.

- The remnant is more common in boys and complications are also more common in boys.

- Most symptoms occur in children less than 2 years of age but may occur in children up to 10 years.

Δ   **Intussusception** is the telescoping of the intestine over itself. This usually occurs in infants and young children up to age 3, but is most common between 5 and 9 months of age.

- Intussusception is more common in boys and in children with cystic fibrosis.

- The etiology of intussusception is usually unknown; however, it sometimes occurs after a viral infection.

NANDA Nursing Diagnoses

Δ   Risk for constipation

Δ   Diarrhea

Δ   Risk for disproportionate growth

Δ   Risk for deficient fluid volume

Δ   Ineffective infant feeding pattern

Δ   Imbalanced nutrition: less than body requirements

Δ   Acute pain

Assessment

Δ   Obtaining family history is important for some structural GI disorders (e.g., pyloric stenosis, Hirschsprung's disease).

Δ   For all GI disorders, nursing history should include:

- Onset, frequency, duration, and description of symptoms.

- Pain using the appropriate pain scale.

- Fatigue.

- Eating pattern (usual pattern and recent pattern).

- Stool pattern (usual pattern and recent pattern).

- Nutritional assessment, including fluid intake.

Δ Physical assessment should include:

- General physical appearance.

- Presence of diarrhea and/or constipation and duration of either/both.

- Assessment for dehydration, including skin that is dry and/or pale, cool lips, dry mucous membranes, decreased skin turgor, diminished urinary output, concentrated urine, thirst, rapid pulse, sunken eyes, and decreased blood pressure.

Δ Assessments for Specific GI Structural Problems

Structural Problem	Assessments
GERD	<ul><li>History of premature birth, bronchopulmonary dysplasia, cerebral palsy, tracheoesophageal or esophageal atresia repair, cystic fibrosis</li><li>Excessive spitting up or forceful vomiting</li><li>Irritability, heartburn</li><li>Hematemesis, blood in stool</li><li>Apnea or apparent life-threatening event</li></ul>
Hypertropic pyloric stenosis	<ul><li>Vomiting that often occurs 30 to 60 min after a meal and becomes projectile as obstruction worsens</li><li>Constant hungry</li><li>Olive-shaped mass in right upper quadrant of abdomen and possible observation of peristalsis when lying supine</li><li>Weight loss, signs of dehydration</li></ul>
Hirschsprung's disease	<ul><li>Newborn – failure to pass meconium, refusal to eat, vomits bile, and a distended abdomen</li><li>Infant – failure to thrive, constipation, abdominal distention, episodes of vomiting and diarrhea, fever, explosive diarrhea</li><li>Older child – constipation, abdominal distention, visible peristalsis, ribbon-like stool, obvious fecal mass, malnourished appearance</li></ul>

Structural Problem	Assessments
Appendicitis	• Abdominal pain (right lower quadrant, called McBurney point) that increases with movement • Eliciting rebound tenderness is not recommended because it causes extreme pain and is not a reliable medicator • Fever, possible vomiting, constipation and/or diarrhea, anorexia, pallor, lethargy, and/or irritability
Meckel's diverticulum	Abdominal pain, bloody stools without pain, bright red mucus in infant stools
Intussusception	• Periods of sudden and acute pain • Palpable, sausage-shaped mass in abdomen and/or distended abdomen • Currant jelly consistency of stool

Diagnostic Procedures

Δ   Radiologic studies of abdomen, sonograms of specific areas, and barium studies are used to assist with the diagnosis of GI structural disorders.

Δ   Hypertrophic Pyloric Stenosis

- Hypertrophic pyloric stenosis can be diagnosed by ultrasound of the abdomen.

- Serum electrolytes will show decreased chloride levels.

- Elevated BUN indicates dehydration.

- ABGs show increased pH and bicarbonate caused by metabolic alkalosis.

Δ   Hirschsprung's Disease

- A rectal biopsy is taken to determine the presence or absence of ganglionic cells.

Δ   Appendicitis

- Appendicitis may be diagnosed by ultrasound or CT scan of the abdomen.

- CBC usually shows WBC count greater than 10,000/mm^3 with shift to left (increased immature neutrophils referred to as bands).

Δ   Meckel's diverticulum is diagnosed using a radionucleotide scan.

Δ   Intussusception

- An x-ray is performed first to rule out perforation of the bowel.

- Intussusception may obstruct flow of barium from barium enema.

Nursing Interventions

Δ Nursing interventions for the child who is vomiting include:

- Positioning the child on side or with head elevated to prevent aspiration.

- Monitoring fluid and electrolyte balance to assess for deficits.

- Providing oral care after vomiting to prevent damage to teeth from hydrochloric acid contact.

- Documenting amount and characteristics of vomitus, as well as describing vomiting behavior to aid in diagnosis of etiology.

Δ When abdominal distention is a problem, monitor abdominal circumference.

- Measure abdominal girth with a paper tape measure at the level of the umbilicus or at the widest point of the abdomen.

- Mark the area with a pen to assure continuity of future measurements.

Δ Treatment for infants/children with GERD is based on severity and includes:

- Offering small frequent feedings of thickened formula.

- Positioning the child with the head elevated after eating.

- Placing the infant in prone position for sleep, which can prevent aspiration of stomach contents. This is only recommended for the child with severe GERD.

- Placing the child older than 1 year in the side-lying position with the head of the bed elevated for sleep.

Therapeutic Procedures and Nursing Interventions

Δ Procedures for Structural Disorders

Structural Disorder	Procedure
GERD	May require fundoplication or manipulative surgery, which wraps fundus of stomach around distal esophagus to decrease chance of reflux
Hypertropic pyloric stenosis	Surgical incision into pyloric sphincter (pylorotomy)
Hirschsprung's disease	Surgical removal of aganglionic section; may require temporary colostomy
Appendicitis	Surgical removal of appendix via laparoscopic or open method
Meckel's diverticulum	Surgical removal of diverticulum

Structural Disorder	Procedure
Intussusception	Attempt to resolve the intussusception by inflating bowel with air or administering a barium enema; if not successful, surgical reduction necessary

Δ   Nursing interventions include:

- Preparing the child for surgical or therapeutic procedure.

- Observing for brown-formed stool after radiologic reduction of intussusception.

- Teaching the parents of a child with a temporary colostomy for Hirschsprung's disease how to perform colostomy care before discharge.

- Care after surgical pylorotomy for hypertrophic pyloric stenosis includes:

  ◊   Instituting feedings beginning with a solution of clear liquid/glucose/ electrolytes and assessing for readiness to progress back to breast milk or formula.

  ◊   Positioning the infant with head slightly elevated to prevent reflux. The infant usually progresses well and is discharged on second or third postoperative day.

Complications and Nursing Interventions

Δ   Complications of severe GERD include aspiration pneumonia, failure to thrive, and erosive esophagitis.

Δ   Peritonitis occurs when the intestinal lining and/or peritoneum is perforated, allowing intestinal contents to enter the peritoneal cavity. Peritonitis may be a result of a ruptured appendix. Peritonitis often occurs within 48 hr of onset of appendicitis.

- Assessment for peritonitis

  ◊   Rigid, board-like abdomen

  ◊   Absent bowel sounds

  ◊   Severe pain

  ◊   High fever

  ◊   Greatly increased WBCs

  ◊   Possible shock and death

- Nursing care includes:

  ◊   Giving pain management.

  ◊   Managing IV fluid therapy.

◊   Managing nasogastric tube suction.

◊   Administering IV antibiotics for infection.

◊   Providing pre- and postsurgical nursing care.

◊   Providing surgical wound care with wound irrigation and/or dressings if delayed wound closure is necessary.

◊   Educating and providing psychosocial support for the child/family.

Δ   **Enterocolitis**, which is inflammation of the bowel, is a serious complication of Hirschsprung's disease.

- Manifestations include fever and lethargy, increasing abdominal girth, nausea, vomiting, explosive diarrhea, and rectal bleeding.

- Treatment includes forceful rectal washouts to decompress colon, IV antibiotics, and possibly colostomy (surgery).

- Nursing care includes:

    ◊   Monitoring for peritonitis or shock caused by enterocolitis.

    ◊   Monitoring and managing fluid, electrolyte, and blood product replacement.

    ◊   Administering antibiotics.

Δ   **GI hemorrhage** may occur with ruptured Meckel's diverticulum.

Primary Reference:

Hockenberry, M., Wilson, D., & Winkelstein, M. (2005). *Wong's essentials of pediatric nursing care.* (7th ed.). St. Louis, MO: Mosby

Additional Resources:

Kass, D. A., & Sinert, R. (2006, February). *Pediatrics, pyloric stenosis.* Retrieved February 10, 2007, from http://www.emedicine.com/emerg/topic397.htm.

NANDA International (2004). *NANDA nursing diagnoses: Definitions and classification 2005-2006.* Philadelphia: NANDA.

The American Pediatric Surgical Association. (2003). *Hirschsprung's disease.* Retrieved February 10, 2007, from http://www.eapsa.org/parents/hirschsprungs3.htm

Chapter 36: Gastrointestinal Structural Disorders

Application Exercises

Scenario: A 6-year-old child is brought to the outpatient facility by his mother. The mother tells the nurse that her child has been experiencing abdominal pain that has lasted almost 2 days without relief. The child is nauseous, has slight constipation, a low-grade fever, and no appetite. He is admitted to an acute pediatric care facility. Soon after admission his pain begins to worsen.

1. If this child has appendicitis, where should his abdominal pain most likely be located?

2. Which of the following diagnostic test results is used for a child suspected of having appendicitis? (Select all that apply.)

    _____ Increased BUN levels

    _____ Increased WBCs

    _____ Increased band (immature neutrophil) count

    _____ Urinalysis containing large numbers of bacteria

    _____ Barium enema testing positive for structural defect

    _____ Rectal biopsy showing aganglionic cells

3. The child is diagnosed with acute appendicitis and is sent to surgery. During surgery a ruptured appendix is found, which has also caused peritonitis. List the nursing interventions the nurse should plan for when the child returns to the pediatric unit.

4. Match the following structural defects with the correct assessment data.

    _____ Hirschsprung's disease   A. Olive-shaped mass in right upper quadrant

    _____ Intussusception   B. Painless, bloody stools

    _____ Hypertrophic pyloric stenosis   C. Severe constipation with bouts of diarrhea; failure to pass meconium in newborns

    _____ GERD   D. Stool of currant jelly consistency

    _____ Meckel's diverticulum   E. Excess spitting up or forceful vomiting

5. True or False: A barium enema can diagnose, as well as medically treat, intussusception.

6. True or False: Nursing care for a child with chronic Hirschsprung's disease focuses on relieving persistent diarrhea.

7. True or False: An infant with severe GERD may have orders to be placed on his stomach to sleep, rather than the usual back to sleep position.

Chapter 36: Gastrointestinal Structural Disorders

Application Exercises Answer Key

Scenario: A 6-year-old child is brought to the outpatient facility by his mother. The mother tells the nurse that her child has been experiencing abdominal pain that has lasted almost 2 days without relief. The child is nauseous, has slight constipation, a low-grade fever, and no appetite. He is admitted to an acute pediatric care facility. Soon after admission his pain begins to worsen.

1. If this child has appendicitis, where should his abdominal pain most likely be located?

   Pain is usually most intense in the right lower quadrant over McBurney point, which is halfway between the anterior superior iliac crest and the umbilicus.

2. Which of the following diagnostic test results is used for a child suspected of having appendicitis? (Select all that apply.)

   _____ Increased BUN levels

   __X__ **Increased WBCs**

   __X__ **Increased band (immature neutrophil) count**

   _____ Urinalysis containing large numbers of bacteria

   _____ Barium enema testing positive for structural defect

   _____ Rectal biopsy showing aganglionic cells

   Increased WBCs with an increased neutrophil count may indicate appendicitis. An increased BUN level may indicate dehydration with hypertrophic pyloric stenosis. Large numbers of bacteria in urinalysis may indicate a urinary tract infection. A barium enema indicating structural defect may be diagnostic of intussusception. Rectal biopsy demonstrating aganglionic cells indicates Hirschsprung's disease.

3. The child is diagnosed with acute appendicitis and is sent to surgery. During surgery a ruptured appendix is found, which has also caused peritonitis. List the nursing interventions the nurse should plan for when the child returns to the pediatric unit.

Administer IV pain medications and antibiotics.

Monitor vital signs per facility protocol.

Monitor for infection (presence of fever, WBC levels).

Provide NG tube maintenance until bowel motility returns.

Provide postoperative activity such as turning, initiating deep breathing, moving extremities, and ambulating, as ordered.

Support coping mechanisms of the child/family.

Provide teaching for the child/family.

Change dressings, irrigate wound if necessary, maintain wound drains, and perform wet-to-dry dressing changes if wound is left open to drain.

4. Match the following structural defects with the correct assessment data.

C	Hirschsprung's disease	A. Olive-shaped mass in right upper quadrant
D	Intussusception	B. Painless, bloody stools
A	Hypertrophic pyloric stenosis	C. Severe constipation with bouts of diarrhea; failure to pass meconium in newborns
E	GERD	D. Stool of currant jelly consistency
B	Meckel's diverticulum	E. Excess spitting up or forceful vomiting

5. True or False: A barium enema can diagnose, as well as medically treat, intussusception.

True. Intussusception is a telescoping of one piece of bowel into another portion. The use of a barium enema can show what the problem is as well as force the telescoped portion of bowel into a normal position. Surgery may need to be done in certain cases.

6. True or False: Nursing care for a child with chronic Hirschsprung's disease focuses on relieving persistent diarrhea.

   False. The child with Hirschsprung's disease does not experience persistent diarrhea. Instead, stool accumulates due to lack of peristalsis on the non-enervated segment of the bowel. Surgery is the treatment of choice to remove the affected part of the bowel. The child will have a temporary colostomy for a period of time. When the temporary colostomy is closed the child should have normal bowel function.

7. True or False: An infant with severe GERD may have orders to be placed on his stomach to sleep, rather than the usual back to sleep position.

   True. Although lying supine has been found to prevent sudden infant death syndrome (SIDS), ordered treatment for an infant with severe GERD may include placing him on his stomach to prevent aspiration of stomach contents.

Unit 2   Nursing Care of Children with System Disorders
Section: Nursing Care of Children with Gastrointestinal Disorders

Chapter 37:   **Cleft Lip and Palate**
           Contributor: Diana Rupert, MSN, RN, ABD

 NCLEX-RN® Connections:

> **Learning Objective**: Review and apply knowledge within "**Cleft Lip and Palate**" in readiness for performance of the following nursing activities as outlined by the NCLEX-RN® test plan:
>
> Δ   Assist with relevant laboratory, diagnostic, and therapeutic procedures within the nursing role, including:
>
> - Client preparation for the procedure.
> - Client teaching (before and following the procedure).
> - Accurate collection of specimens.
> - Evaluation of the child's response to the procedure.
> - Planning and implementing body system-specific interventions as appropriate.
> - Monitoring and taking actions to prevent or minimize the risk of complications.
> - Accurate interpretation of procedure results.
> - Perform and document appropriate assessments based on the child's problem.
> - Apply knowledge of pathophysiology to planning care for clients with specific alterations in body systems, including recognizing associated signs and symptoms.
> - Interpret data that need to be reported immediately.
> - Monitor therapeutic devices (drainage/irrigating devices, chest tubes), if inserted, for proper functioning.
> - Explore resources, make referrals, collaborate with interdisciplinary team, and ensure continuity of client care.
> - Evaluate plans of care for multiple clients and revise plan as needed based on priorities of care and promotion of recovery.
> - Provide the child/family teaching regarding management of the child's health problem.
> - Recognize/respond to emergency situations, and evaluate/document the client's response to emergency interventions.

📖 Key Points

Δ   Cleft lip, which is the failure of the lip to grow together, develops between gestation weeks 7 and 11 and may be unilateral or bilateral.

Δ   Cleft palate, which is failure of the palates to close, develops between 7 and 12 weeks gestation.

Δ   Cleft palate may be accompanied by a nasal deformity and dental disorders such as deformed, missing, or supernumerary teeth.

Δ   Although a cleft lip and palate normally occur together, either defect may appear alone. Unilateral clefts of the left side are more common.

Key Factors

Δ   Cleft lip and palate result from the failure of the maxillary and premaxillary processes to fuse during the fifth to eighth week of intrauterine life.

Δ   Inheritance of cleft lip and/or palate is multifactorial.

  •   Heredity factors play a role, as the incidence of cleft palate is higher in relatives of people with the defect.

  •   Environmental factors, such as lack of folic acid during pregnancy, seem to play a role, but are not yet fully understood.

  •   Risk factors include exposure to teratogens (especially maternal intake of phenytoin [Dilantin]), maternal smoking, and family tendency.

  •   Cleft lip and palate occurs more often then just cleft palate. Cleft lip and palate occur most often in boys (approximately 60 to 80% of cases).

  •   Cleft palate alone is more common in girls.

Assessment

  •   Assess the extent of the defect and the infant's ability to suck and eat.

  •   Assess family and infant interactions.

  •   Monitor for aspiration and respiratory complications.

Δ   Preoperative

  •   Inspect the infant's lip and palate using a gloved finger to palpate the infant's palate.

  •   Assess the infant's ability to suck.

  •   Obtain the baseline weight.

  •   Observe interaction between the family and infant.

- Determine family coping and support.

NANDA Nursing Diagnoses

Δ   Risk for aspiration

Δ   Risk for impaired parent/infant attachment

Δ   Ineffective breastfeeding

Δ   Caregiver role strain

Δ   Imbalanced nutrition: less than body requirements

Δ   Acute pain

Δ   Impaired skin integrity

Nursing Interventions

Δ   Support and encourage parents in the general care of their child pre- and postoperatively.

Δ   Preoperative Interventions

- Encourage the parents as they provide care. Parents should foster a bond with their infant.

- Help parents focus on the infant rather than on the infant's cleft lip/palate.

- Support the mother's decision to continue breastfeeding her infant. Assist her to be open to alternatives, such as using breast milk placed in special feeding devices, if necessary.

- Provide instruction to promote feeding. Teach the parents to use an enlarged nipple, which will stimulate the infant's suck reflex and ensure that the infant swallows appropriately. After feeding, the infant should be allowed to rest.

- Identify alternate feeding devices, such as a special nipple for a bottle.

- Teach parents to feed the infant in an upright position.

- Teach parents to burp the infant more frequently due to the amount of air swallowed. This will help prevent aspiration and abdominal distention.

- Prepare parents for impending surgery.

Δ   Postoperative Interventions

- Keep the infant/child pain free postoperatively to decrease crying and stress on repair.

- Keep repair sites clean.

- Assess operative sites for signs of infection.

- Assess infant/child's ability to eat. Monitor I&O and weigh daily.

- Observe family's interaction with the infant/child.

- Assess family coping and support.

- Cleft lip repair

  ◊ Monitor integrity of postoperative protective device to ensure proper positioning.

  ◊ Position infant upright (infant car seat position), back, or side in the immediate postoperative period to maintain integrity of repair.

  ◊ Apply elbow restraints to keep the infant from pulling at the repair site. The cuff of the restraints may be pinned to the infant's clothing. A jacket restraint may be necessary to prevent an older infant from rolling over.

  ◊ Restraints should be removed periodically to assess skin, allow limb movement, and provide for comfort.

  ◊ Use saline on a sterile swab to clean the incision site. Apply antibiotic ointment if prescribed.

  ◊ Gently aspirate secretions of mouth and nasopharynx to prevent respiratory complications.

- For cleft palate

  ◊ A child with a cleft palate is allowed to be positioned on the abdomen in the immediate postoperative period.

  ◊ Maintain intravenous fluids until the child is able to eat and drink.

  ◊ Monitor packing, which is usually removed in 2 to 3 days.

  ◊ Assist the child to breathe by facilitating upright position.

  ◊ Avoid using objects for feeding that could harm cleft palate repair, such as forks.

  ◊ Avoid placing objects such as a tongue depressor or pacifier in the child's mouth after cleft palate repair.

  ◊ The child may be discharged on a soft diet.

- Teach parents how to provide home care following surgical repair.

  ◊ The child may require elbow restraints for 4 to 6 weeks. Instruct the child's parents in the proper use of the restraints and to periodically remove them one at a time.

  ◊ Assist parents with proper feeding techniques.

  ◊ Instruct parents in proper care of operative site.

Therapeutic Procedures and Nursing Intervention

Δ   Surgical repair of the cleft(s) is necessary.

- Cleft lip repair (cheiloplasty) takes place early in infancy.

- Cleft palate repair (palatoplasty) traditionally takes place after the palate has developed, but new surgical techniques may allow repair to take place earlier.

- Surgery may be done in stages throughout several years.

- Nursing interventions include preoperative teaching, postoperative care, and family support.

Complications and Nursing Implications

Δ   Risk for Aspiration

- Feed infant in upright position.

- Burp often.

- Use a bulb syringe to suction oral and nasopharyngeal secretions.

Δ   Ear Infections and Hearing Loss Related to Recurrent Infections

- Teach parents signs/symptoms of ear infections and encourage early intervention.

Δ   Speech and Language Delay – More Common with Cleft Palate

- Parents will be referred to a speech therapist for care.

Δ   Dental problems – Teeth may not erupt normally and orthodontia is usually necessary later in life.

- Encourage parents to seek early dental care.

Primary Reference:

Hockenberry, M., Wilson, D., & Winkelstein, M. (2005). *Wong's essentials of pediatric nursing care*. (7th ed.). St. Louis, MO: Mosby.

Additional Resources:

American Academy of Family Physicians. (2006, July). *Cleft lip and cleft palate*. Retrieved February 14, 2007, from http://familydoctor.org/034.xml?printxml

NANDA International (2004). *NANDA nursing diagnoses: Definitions and classification 2005-2006*. Philadelphia: NANDA.

University of Virginia Health System. (2004, February). *High-risk newborn: Cleft lip/ cleft palate*. Retrieved February 14, 2007, from http://www.healthsystem.virginia.edu/uvahealth/peds_hrnewborn/cleft.cfm

Chapter 37: Cleft Lip and Palate

Application Exercises

Scenario: A mother has given birth to a newborn who has a unilateral cleft lip and palate. She gave birth to her first child 2 years ago. This child was born without a cleft lip/palate.

1. What initial therapeutic nursing intervention(s) is most appropriate following delivery?

2. How might the nursing care for this newborn/family differ from the nursing care provided to a newborn/family without a cleft lip/palate?

3. What discharge instructions are essential for the newborn's home care prior to discharge?

4. The newborn's cleft lip is surgically repaired. List several teaching points that the nurse can provide the family when they are observing the newborn for possible signs of infection.

5. An infant has received surgery for a cleft palate. Which of the following nursing interventions should the nurse provide for the infant's family regarding prevention of damage to the surgical site? (Select all that apply.)

   _____ Maintain pain management.
   _____ Remove any packing from inside the infant's mouth whenever it becomes soiled.
   _____ Use a cotton-tipped swab to clean the inside of the infant's mouth.
   _____ Use elbow restraints.
   _____ Give the infant soft finger foods.

6. A mother of a child with cleft lip and palate asks the nurse why she has specifically been told to observe for signs of ear infection. Which of the following responses by the nurse is appropriate?

   A. "You should watch for throat infections, not ear infections."
   B. "Ear infections are much more common because germs can get into the ear from the open cleft in the palate."
   C. "Ear infections are caused by the same genetic problem that caused the cleft lip and palate."
   D. "This child is more prone to all types of infections because of a problem with immunity."

Chapter 37: Cleft Lip and Palate

Application Exercises Answer Key

Scenario: A mother has given birth to a newborn who has a unilateral cleft lip and palate. She gave birth to her first child 2 years ago. This child was born without a cleft lip/palate.

1. What initial therapeutic nursing intervention(s) is most appropriate following delivery?

   Support and encouragement for the family is an initial therapeutic intervention. Showing acceptance of the infant is also important. Pointing out several unique qualities or family resemblances is helpful in establishing other features other than the facial deformity. The family will also have many questions. Sitting with the family and answering questions shows a nursing presence. This also reassures the family that the newborn has a promising future.

2. How might the nursing care for this newborn/family differ from the nursing care provided to a newborn/family without a cleft lip/palate?

   Bonding between a newborn and parents usually takes place without difficulty. A newborn with a cleft lip/palate may present challenges due to the fact that the newborn is born with a physical defect and requires special care for feeding. This family may require special attention to assist with acceptance, which is a priority if bonding is to take place. This family will also need specialized discharge teaching to promote adequate intake of the newborn, prevention of infection, and preparation for surgical repair.

3. What discharge instructions are essential for the newborn's home care prior to discharge?

   Provide a quiet, calm environment for feeding. Hold the newborn upright while feeding to prevent choking. Burp the newborn frequently because the newborn swallows a lot of air while eating. If breastfeeding, place the breast fully into the newborn's mouth, making a seal. If bottle feeding, use a specialized nipple or a large syringe attached to rubber tubing. Instill the formula slowly, observing that the newborn is swallowing. Do not be afraid if milk comes through the newborn's nose. This is okay because the cleft palate opens directly into the nasal cavity. Don't tire the newborn. Eating can be difficult and stressful. Limit feeding times to 20 to 30 min. Also, teach parents to observe for ear infections and encourage speech attempts and any activities that will increase bonding, such as cuddling or talking to the newborn.

4. The newborn's cleft lip is surgically repaired. List several teaching points that the nurse can provide the family when they are observing the newborn for possible signs of infection.

Redness, swelling, purulent drainage at the surgical site; increased irritability; loss of appetite; and/or fever

5. An infant has received surgery for a cleft palate. Which of the following nursing interventions should the nurse provide for the infant's family regarding prevention of damage to the surgical site? (Select all that apply.)

   X   **Maintain pain management.**

_____ Remove any packing from inside the infant's mouth whenever it becomes soiled.

_____ Use a cotton-tipped swab to clean the inside of the infant's mouth.

   X   **Use elbow restraints.**

   X   **Give the infant soft finger foods.**

Pain management is important to prevent the infant from attempting to pick at an incision site. It is also effective in preventing crying and fussing, which could also damage the site. Elbow restraints prevent the child from sticking objects inside the mouth. Giving finger foods avoids the possibility of using forks or other hard objects that might disturb the surgical site. If packing is in place, parents should not pull it out unless specifically told to do so. Using a swab in the infant's mouth could damage the surgical site.

6. A mother of a child with cleft lip and palate asks the nurse why she has specifically been told to observe for signs of ear infection. Which of the following responses by the nurse is appropriate?

A. "You should watch for throat infections, not ear infections."

B. "Ear infections are much more common because germs can get into the ear from the open cleft in the palate."

C. "Ear infections are caused by the same genetic problem that caused the cleft lip and palate."

D. "This child is more prone to all types of infections because of a problem with immunity."

Because of the open cleft inside the mouth, bacteria can easily move directly up to the middle ear through the eustachian tube, causing risk of frequent infection. Throat infections are no more common with these children than with children who do not have cleft lip/palate. Ear infections are not caused by a genetic problem and these children are not immunosuppressed.

Unit 2   Nursing Care of Children with System Disorders
Section: Nursing Care of Children with Endocrine Disorders

Chapter 38:   **Diabetes Mellitus**
                Contributor: Diana Rupert, MSN, RN, ABD

 **NCLEX-RN® Connections:**

Learning Objective: Review and apply knowledge within "**Diabetes Mellitus**" in readiness for performance of the following nursing activities as outlined by the NCLEX-RN® test plan:

Δ   Assist with relevant laboratory, diagnostic, and therapeutic procedures within the nursing role, including:

  • Client preparation for the procedure.

  • Client teaching (before and following the procedure).

  • Accurate collection of specimens.

  • Evaluation of the child's response to the procedure.

  • Planning and implementing body system-specific interventions as appropriate.

  • Monitoring and taking actions to prevent or minimize the risk of complications.

  • Accurate interpretation of procedure results.

Δ   Perform and document appropriate assessments based on the child's problem.

Δ   Apply knowledge of pathophysiology to planning care for clients with specific alterations in body systems, including recognizing associated signs and symptoms.

Δ   Interpret data that need to be reported immediately.

Δ   Monitor therapeutic devices (drainage/irrigating devices, chest tubes), if inserted, for proper functioning.

Δ   Explore resources, make referrals, collaborate with interdisciplinary team, and ensure continuity of client care.

Δ   Evaluate plans of care for multiple clients and revise plan as needed based on priorities of care and promotion of recovery.

Δ   Provide the child/family teaching regarding management of the child's health problem.

Δ   Recognize/respond to emergency situations, and evaluate/document the client's response to emergency interventions.

Key Points

Δ   Diabetes mellitus is a metabolic disease in which there is an absolute or relative deficiency of insulin. This disease is due to the body's inability to produce or use insulin.

Δ   Classifications include:

- Type 1 – destruction of pancreatic beta cells resulting in an absolute insulin deficiency

- Type 2 – deficiency of insulin production and insulin resistance

Δ   The deficiency of insulin results in:

- Dysfunction of carbohydrate, protein, and fat metabolism. This leads to the metabolic complications of diabetes mellitus (hypoglycemia and hyperglycemia).

- Development of macrovascular, microvascular, and neurological changes. This leads to the long-term complications of diabetes mellitus (delayed wound healing, peripheral neuropathy, and retinopathy).

Key Factors

Δ   The etiology of type 1 and type 2 diabetes mellitus is multifactorial.

- The beta cell destruction in type 1 diabetes mellitus is due to a combination of genetic, immunologic, viral, and environmental factors. The onset is usually before age 30.

- Type 2 diabetes mellitus is often due to the development of resistance to insulin as a result of obesity, physical inactivity, high triglycerides (greater than 250 mg/dL), and/or hypertension.

Assessment

Δ   Nursing history information should include:

- The child's past and present health status.

- Presence of classic signs of hyperglycemia, which include polyuria, polyphagia, and polydipsia, weight loss, fatigue, and malaise.

- The child's dietary practices and exercise patterns.

- The child's self-monitoring blood glucose skill proficiency.

- The child's self medication administration proficiency.

- Sleep patterns and presence of nocturia.

- Reports of vision changes, infection, acute illness, neuropathies, and/or pain.

Δ   Physical assessment should include:

- Current blood glucose level.

- Baseline height and weight.

- I&O.

- Skin integrity and healing status of any wounds.

- Funduscopic exam to detect retinopathy.

- Neurological exam to detect neurosensory changes (e.g., decreased sensation).

- Podiatric exam to assess condition of feet.

- Signs and symptoms of blood glucose alterations.

  ◊   Hypoglycemia – blood glucose level less than 60 mg/dL

Autonomic Nervous System Responses – occur rapidly	Impaired Cerebral Function – gradual onset
• Hunger, lightheadedness, shakiness • Nausea • Anxiety, irritability • Pale, cool skin • Diaphoresis • Irritability • Respirations normal or shallow • Tachycardia and palpitations	• Strange or unusual feelings • Decreasing level of consciousness • Difficulty in thinking and inability to concentrate • Change in emotional behavior • Slurred speech • Headache, blurred vision • Seizures leading to coma

  ◊   Hyperglycemia – blood glucose level greater than 250 mg/dL

    °   Thirst

    °   Frequent urination

    °   Hunger

    °   Skin that is warm, dry, and flushed with poor turgor

    °   Dry mucous membranes

    °   Soft eyeballs

    °   Weakness

    °   Malaise

    °   Rapid, weak pulse; hypotension

    °   Rapid, deep respirations (with acetone/fruity odor due to ketones)

Diagnostic Procedures and Nursing Interventions

Δ   Diagnostic Criteria

- Symptoms of diabetes mellitus plus random (without regard to last meal) plasma glucose concentration of greater than 200 mg/dL

- Fasting (8 hr) blood glucose greater than 126 mg/dL

  ◊ Instruct the child not to consume any food or drink (with the exception of water) 8 hr prior to the blood draw.

- Two-hour glucose greater than 200 mg/dL with an oral glucose tolerance test after 10 to 12 hr fasting

  ◊ Instruct the child to eat a balanced diet for 3 days prior to the test and then fast for 10 to 12 hr prior to the test.

  ◊ A fasting blood glucose will be taken at the start of the test and then the child is to consume a specified amount of glucose. Blood glucose levels are drawn every 30 min for 2 hr. Assess the child for signs of hypoglycemia.

Δ   Glycosylated Hemoglobin (HbA1c)

- Normal HbA1c levels are usually between 4 to 6%. Children with diabetes mellitus should have HbA1c levels of about 7.5%. Acceptable levels may vary based on individual differences. HbA1c levels are the best indicator of the child's average blood glucose level for the past 120 days. HbA1c assists in evaluating treatment effectiveness and compliance.

- Blood samples can be taken without regard to food intake or time of day.

Δ   BUN, creatinine, 24-hr creatinine clearance to detect nephropathy

Δ   Urinalysis and culture and sensitivity are used to detect presence of bacteria, microalbuminuria, proteinuria, glucose, and ketones.

NANDA Nursing Diagnoses

Δ   Fatigue

Δ   Risk for infection

Δ   Deficient knowledge

Δ   Imbalanced nutrition: less than body requirements

Δ   Imbalanced nutrition: more than body requirements

Δ   Effective therapeutic regimen management

Nursing Interventions

△ Monitor blood glucose as ordered.

△ Administer insulin as prescribed. Know onset, peak, and duration, and monitor the child for signs of hypoglycemia.

Insulin	For meal time doses, administer	Onset	Peak	Duration
Lispro insulin (Humalog)	15 min ac.	Rapid 15 to 30 min	½ to 2.5 hr	Short, rapid-acting (3 to 6.5 hr)
Aspart insulin (NovoLog)	5 to 10 min ac.	Rapid 10 to 20 min	1 to 3 hr	Short, rapid-acting (3 to 5 hr)
Regular insulin (Humulin R, Novolin R)	30 min ac.	30 to 60 min	1 to 5 hr	Short, slower-acting (6 to10 hr)
NPH insulin (Humulin-N, Novolin-N)	two times/day (same time).	1 to 2 hr	6 to 14 hr	Intermediate (16 to 24 hr)
Glargine insulin (Lantus)	one time/day (same time).	70 min	None	Long (24 hr)

△ Initial child/family teaching of self-administration of insulin should include:

- Rotating injection sites (prevents lipohypertrophy) within one anatomic site (prevents day-to-day changes in absorption rates).

- Cleaning injection site with soap and warm water. Allow to dry before injection. Avoid use of alcohol.

- Injecting insulin at a 90° angle (45° if thin). Aspirating for blood is not necessary.

- Drawing up the shorter-acting insulin into the syringe first and then the longer-acting insulin (reduces risk of introducing longer-acting insulin into the shorter-acting insulin vial) when mixing rapid- or short-acting insulin with a longer-acting insulin.

- Using appropriate alternate injection mechanisms such as a syringe-loaded injector.

- Using an insulin pump if the child is a candidate.

- Observing the child perform self-administration of the insulin.

△ Nutritional Management

- Dietary intake should be sufficient to meet growth and development needs of the child.

- Attempt to maintain normal blood glucose levels to prevent development of complications.

- Plan meals to achieve appropriate timing of food intake, activity, onset and peak of insulin. Calories and food composition should be similar each day.

- Consider the child's personal, cultural, and religious food preferences. Allow for flexibility.

- There is no need for special foods or supplements.

- Encourage use of sugar substitutes in moderation.

Δ   Self Blood Glucose Monitoring

- Teach the child/family appropriate technique for obtaining samples, recording and responding to results, and correct handling of supplies and equipment.

- Assist the child/family to develop schedule for checking blood glucose levels.

- Maintain appropriate activity level

    ◊   Encourage planned exercise so insulin needs may be predicted.

    ◊   Teach child to be aware of energy needs with spontaneous periods of exercise. Increase complex carbohydrate snacks with increased exercise. Decrease snacks when exercise is decreased.

Δ   Teach the child/family measures to take in response to hypoglycemia symptoms (occur most often before meals and at time of insulin peak).

- Follow guidelines outlined by the primary care provider/diabetes mellitus educator.

- Guidelines may include:

    ◊   Stopping activity and sitting down.

    ◊   Checking blood glucose level.

    ◊   Treating the child with 15 g of carbohydrates.

    ◊   Rechecking the child's blood glucose in 15 min.

    ◊   Giving 15 g of carbohydrates if the child's blood glucose is still low.

    ◊   Rechecking the child's blood glucose in 15 min.

        °   If blood glucose is within normal limits, the child should eat a snack of 7 g protein, such 2 graham crackers and 8 oz of milk (if the next meal is more than 1 hr away).

        °   If blood glucose is still below 70 mg/dL, the child should receive medical care.

- Examples of foods that contain 15 g of carbohydrates include 4 oz of orange juice, 2 oz of grape juice, 8 oz of milk, and glucose tablets per manufacturer's suggestion. Use of commercial products, such as glucose tablets, can provide a more predictable response.

- If the child is unconscious or unable to swallow, administer 1 mg of glucagon SC or IM (repeat in 10 min if still unconscious) and notify the primary care provider or go to the local emergency department.

Δ   Teach the child/family measures to take in response to hyperglycemia.

- Encourage oral fluid intake.

- Administer insulin as prescribed.

- Restrict exercise when blood glucose levels are greater than 250 mg/dL.

- Test urine for ketones and report if abnormal.

- Consult the primary care provider if symptoms progress.

Δ   Teach the child/family guidelines to follow when sick.

- Monitor blood glucose every 4 hr.

- Continue to take insulin or oral antidiabetic agents.

- Consume 8 oz of sugar-free noncaffeinated liquid every hour to prevent dehydration.

- Meet carbohydrate needs through solid food if possible. If not, consume liquids equal to usual carbohydrate content.

- Test urine for ketones and report if abnormal (should be negative to small).

- Tell the child to rest.

- Call the primary care provider if:

  ◊   Blood glucose is greater than 250 mg/dL.

  ◊   Ketones are moderate or large.

  ◊   Fever is higher than 38.9° C (102° F), does not respond to acetaminophen (Tylenol), and/or lasts more than 12 hr.

  ◊   Child feels groggy and/or confused.

  ◊   Child experiences rapid breathing.

  ◊   Child vomits more than once.

  ◊   Diarrhea occurs more than five times or for longer than 24 hr.

  ◊   Child is unable to retain liquids.

  ◊   Illness lasts longer than 2 days.

Δ   Encourage child to wear Medic Alert bracelet or necklace.

Δ   Refer the child who is newly diagnosed with diabetes mellitus to a diabetes mellitus educator for comprehensive education in diabetes mellitus management.

Complications and Nursing Implications

Δ   Diabetic Ketoacidosis (DKA)

- Causes of DKA include insufficient insulin (usually failure to take appropriate dose), acute stress as from trauma or stress, and poor management of acute illness.

- Signs and symptoms of DKA

  ◊ Elevated blood glucose level

  ◊ Ketosis – Kussmaul respirations (hyperventilation seen as increased rate and depth), nausea, vomiting, and abdominal pain

  ◊ Dehydration and/or electrolyte loss – polyuria, polydipsia; flushed, dry skin, dry mucous membranes; fever, increasing restlessness, confusion; decreased level of consciousness; and lethargy leading to coma

- Rapid nursing assessment of DKA and preparation for emergency treatment includes:

  ◊ Treating the child in an ICU with continuous cardiac monitoring.

  ◊ Obtaining the child's laboratory work, including blood glucose level, electrolytes, and ABGs. Do not administer potassium until serum potassium levels are known.

  ◊ Giving the child fluids and electrolytes (potassium) to treat dehydration and electrolyte imbalances. Replacement is usually slow. Give fluids and electrolytes over 24 to 48 hr to prevent cerebral edema.

  ◊ Give continuous IV infusion of low-dose insulin to control blood glucose levels.

Δ   Support family during DKA crisis.

Δ   Once the child is stable, nursing implications also include teaching family early signs of DKA and the importance of seeking medical attention.

Primary Reference:

Hockenberry, M., Wilson, D., & Winkelstein, M. (2005). *Wong's essentials of pediatric nursing care.* (7th ed.). St. Louis, MO: Mosby.

Additional Resources:

For information about diabetes mellitus, go to the American Diabetes Association Web site, *www.diabetes.org.*

Ignatavicius, D. D., & Workman, M. L. (2006). *Medical-surgical nursing* (5th ed.). St. Louis, MO: Saunders.

NANDA International (2004). *NANDA nursing diagnoses: Definitions and classification 2005-2006.* Philadelphia: NANDA.

Chapter 38: Diabetes Mellitus

Application Exercises

1. A nurse is reviewing sick day management with a parent of a child with type 1 diabetes mellitus. Which of the following should the nurse include in the teaching? (Select all that apply.)

_____ Monitor blood glucose every 4 hr.

_____ Discontinue taking insulin until feeling better.

_____ Drink 8 oz of fruit juice every hour.

_____ Test urine for ketones.

_____ Call primary care provider if blood glucose is greater than 250 mg/dL.

2. Place the following steps used to treat hypoglycemia detected by low blood glucose level in the correct order.

_____ Recheck blood glucose in 15 min.

_____ Treat with 15 g carbohydrates.

_____ If still low, give 15 g more of carbohydrates.

_____ Stop activity and sit down.

_____ Recheck blood glucose in 15 min.

3. A child with type 1 diabetes mellitus is taking twice-daily insulin injections consisting of a combination of lispro (Humalog) and NPH insulin. The child eats breakfast at 8 a.m. daily. At what time should the child inject morning insulin? Provide rationale.

4. When providing health teaching to a group of adolescents with diabetes mellitus, a nurse teaches them to observe for signs and symptoms of hypoglycemia. For which of the following should the adolescents be alert to detect hypoglycemia? (Select all that apply.)

_____ Frequent urination

_____ Increased energy level

_____ Nausea

_____ Nervousness and irritability

_____ Sweating and pallor

_____ Deep, rapid, and labored respirations

5. When providing health teaching to a group of adolescents with type 1 diabetes mellitus, a nurse instructs them that a hypoglycemic reaction can occur because of

    A. too much glucose in the body.

    B. eating too much junk food.

    C. exercising strenuously.

    D. not enough insulin in the body.

6. A nurse is caring for a child with type 1 diabetes mellitus who has been taking insulin for 3 months. Which of the following diagnostic studies will the provider most likely order to determine how well the child's diabetes mellitus is being managed?

    A. Morning fasting blood glucose

    B. 2-hr oral glucose tolerance test

    C. Hb1Ac

    D. Diary of the child's daily blood glucoses

7. When teaching a child newly diagnosed with type 1 diabetes mellitus, a nurse should place the highest priority on information regarding

    A. weight loss measures.

    B. self-monitoring of blood glucose.

    C. need to reduce physical activity.

    D. elimination of sugar from the diet.

8. During a scheduled exam, a child's Hb1Ac reading is 9%. The child has had type 1 diabetes mellitus for 1 year. Which of the following actions should the nurse take?

    A. Assess signs of infection and child's intake for the past 24 hr.

    B. Explore the child's general dietary patterns for the past 3 months.

    C. Review the parents' understanding of diabetic foot care.

    D. Immediately administer child's rapid-acting insulin dose.

Chapter 38: Diabetes Mellitus

Application Exercises Answer Key

1. A nurse is reviewing sick day management with a parent of a child with type 1 diabetes mellitus. Which of the following should the nurse include in the teaching? (Select all that apply.)

  __X__ **Monitor blood glucose every 4 hr.**
  _____ Discontinue taking insulin until feeling better.
  _____ Drink 8 oz of fruit juice every hour.
  __X__ **Test urine for ketones.**
  __X__ **Call primary care provider if blood glucose is greater than 250 mg/dL.**

During acute illness it is very important to check blood glucose levels frequently to identify hyperglycemia. Urine should be checked for ketones because presence of ketones is an indication that proteins and fats are being broken down for energy and this can result in diabetic ketoacidosis. The primary care provider should be notified if blood glucose level exceeds 250 mg/dL, as this may require a change in insulin dosage. Insulin should not be discontinued because acute illness results in hyperglycemia even if intake has decreased. Eight ounces of sugar-free noncaffeinated liquid should be consumed to prevent dehydration. Fruit juice is high in carbohydrates and can contribute to hyperglycemia.

2. Place the following steps used to treat hypoglycemia detected by low blood glucose level in the correct order.

  __3__ Recheck blood glucose in 15 min.
  __2__ Treat with 15 g carbohydrates.
  __4__ If still low, give 15 g more of carbohydrates.
  __1__ Stop activity and sit down.
  __5__ Recheck blood glucose in 15 min.

3. A child with type 1 diabetes mellitus is taking twice-daily insulin injections consisting of a combination of lispro (Humalog) and NPH insulin. The child eats breakfast at 8 a.m. daily. At what time should the child inject morning insulin? Provide rationale.

The child should inject the insulin between 7:45 and 7:50 a.m. because lispro insulin begins to act within 10 to 15 min after injection.

4. When providing health teaching to a group of adolescents with diabetes mellitus, a nurse teaches them to observe for signs and symptoms of hypoglycemia. For which of the following should the adolescents be alert to detect hypoglycemia? (Select all that apply.)

_____ Frequent urination

_____ Increased energy level

__X__ **Nausea**

__X__ **Nervousness and irritability**

__X__ **Sweating and pallor**

_____ Deep, rapid, and labored respirations

Signs/symptoms of hypoglycemia include nausea, nervousness/irritability, sweating and pale skin. Frequent urination and deep, rapid, labored respirations (Kussmaul respirations) are signs of hyperglycemia. Increased energy level is not seen in either hypo- or hyperglycemia.

5. When providing health teaching to a group of adolescents with type 1 diabetes mellitus, a nurse instructs them that a hypoglycemic reaction can occur because of

A. too much glucose in the body.

B. eating too much junk food.

C. exercising strenuously.

D. not enough insulin in the body.

Strenuous exercise, eating too little food, and injecting too much insulin can cause hypoglycemia. The other three options cause hyperglycemia.

6. A nurse is caring for a child with type 1 diabetes mellitus who has been taking insulin for 3 months. Which of the following diagnostic studies will the provider most likely order to determine how well the child's diabetes mellitus is being managed?

A. Morning fasting blood glucose

B. 2-hr oral glucose tolerance test

C. Hb1Ac

D. Diary of the child's daily blood glucoses

The Hb1Ac level reflects the average blood glucose levels during the previous 2 to 3 months. It is very useful in assessing overall control of blood glucose levels. The morning fasting blood glucose only gives information about that particular morning's glucose levels. The glucose tolerance test can be used in diagnosis of diabetes mellitus but not in management of the disorder. The diary of blood glucoses may be somewhat helpful, but is not as useful to assess control of diabetes mellitus as the Hb1Ac level.

7. When teaching a child newly diagnosed with type 1 diabetes mellitus, a nurse should place the highest priority on information regarding

    A. weight loss measures.

    B. self-monitoring of blood glucose.

    C. need to reduce physical activity.

    D. elimination of sugar from the diet.

The priority should be to teach self-monitoring of blood glucose in order to better maintain stable glucose levels and prevent injury from hypo or hyperglycemia. Dietary teaching is also important; however, elimination of all sugar from the diet is not a goal and the amount of sugars a child can eat is individualized. Weight loss measures are important for children with type 2 diabetes mellitus. Reduction in physical activity is not necessary for most children with diabetes mellitus.

8. During a scheduled exam, a child's Hb1Ac level is 9%. The child has had type 1 diabetes mellitus for 1 year. Which of the following actions should the nurse take?

    A. Assess signs of infection and child's intake for the past 24 hr.

    B. Explore the child's general dietary patterns for the past 3 months.

    C. Review the parents' understanding of diabetic foot care.

    D. Immediately administer child's rapid-acting insulin dose.

An elevated Hb1Ac means that the average blood glucose level is higher than it should be. Acceptable Hb1Ac levels for a child with diabetes mellitus are around 7.5%. Since this test analyzes the child's blood glucose levels for the past 2 to 3 months, intake and infection over the past 24 hr would not be assessed by this test. The parents' understanding of diabetic foot care has nothing to do with this test. Whether or not the child requires insulin at this point in time is determined by a single blood glucose test rather than Hb1Ac results.

Unit 2   Nursing Care of Children with System Disorders

Section: Nursing Care of Children with Endocrine Disorders

Chapter 39:   Growth Hormone Deficiency

Contributor: Diana Rupert, MSN, RN, ABD

 NCLEX-RN® Connections:

Learning Objective: Review and apply knowledge within "**Growth Hormone Deficiency**" in readiness for performance of the following nursing activities as outlined by the NCLEX-RN® test plan:

Δ   Assist with relevant laboratory, diagnostic, and therapeutic procedures within the nursing role, including:

- Client preparation for the procedure.

- Client teaching (before and following the procedure).

- Accurate collection of specimens.

- Evaluation of the child's response to the procedure.

- Planning and implementing body system-specific interventions as appropriate.

- Monitoring and taking actions to prevent or minimize the risk of complications.

- Accurate interpretation of procedure results.

Δ   Perform and document appropriate assessments based on the child's problem.

Δ   Apply knowledge of pathophysiology to planning care for clients with specific alterations in body systems, including recognizing associated signs and symptoms.

Δ   Interpret data that need to be reported immediately.

Δ   Monitor therapeutic devices (drainage/irrigating devices, chest tubes), if inserted, for proper functioning.

Δ   Explore resources, make referrals, collaborate with interdisciplinary team, and ensure continuity of client care.

Δ   Evaluate plans of care for multiple clients and revise plan as needed based on priorities of care and promotion of recovery.

Δ   Provide the child/family teaching regarding management of the child's health problem.

Δ   Recognize/respond to emergency situations, and evaluate/document the client's response to emergency interventions.

Key Points

Δ   Human growth hormone (GH), somatotropin, is a naturally occurring substance that is secreted by the pituitary gland, which is the master gland of the body and located in the brain

Δ   GH is important for normal growth, development, and cellular metabolism.

Δ   A deficiency in GH prevents somatic growth throughout the body.

Δ   Other hormones that work with GH to control metabolic processes include adrenocorticotropic hormone (ACTH), thyroid stimulating hormone (TSH), and the gonadotropins (e.g., follicle-stimulating hormone [FSH] and luteinizing hormone [LH]).

Δ   Hypopituitarism is the diminished or deficient secretion of pituitary hormones (primarily GH). Consequences of the condition depend on the degree of the deficiency.

Δ   The child with hypopituitarism is normal at birth but his growth pattern will demonstrate progressive deviation from the norm. This may start in infancy.

Δ   Achondroplasia, unlike GH deficiency, is a genetic disorder that causes nonproportional (short-limbed) dwarfism.

- Besides short stature, achondroplasia causes a relatively long trunk with shortened upper parts of arms and legs, large head with prominent forehead, flattened bridge of the nose, shortened hands and fingers, and decreased muscle tone.

- These children tend to have physical disabilities such as scoliosis, breathing problems (due to small chests), and lower back pain.

- Achondroplasia is not successfully treated with GH.

Key Factors

Δ   Deficiency of GH may be due to structural factors (e.g. tumors, trauma, structural defects, surgery).

Δ   Heredity disorders may cause GH deficiency.

Δ   GH deficiency is frequently associated with other pituitary hormone deficiencies such as deficiencies of TSH or ACTH.

Δ   Most often, GH deficiencies are idiopathic.

Δ   Short stature occurs when a child who was in normal range for weight and length at birth begins to deviate from the normal growth curve. Short stature may be familial, a result of hormone deficiency, nutritional deficiencies, medications, long-term stress, and/or chronic illness (e.g., asthma, congenital heart disease, cystic fibrosis).

Assessment

Δ   Take family assessment including growth patterns of parents and siblings.

Δ   Obtain the child's history of any chronic illnesses.

Δ   Short stature is usually evident after the child's first year of life. Until then, children are normally proportioned and well-nourished.

Δ   Primary teeth usually appear at appropriate age. Permanent teeth are delayed, malpositioned, and often overcrowded.

Δ   The height of a child is more affected than weight. Bone age usually matches height age.

Δ   Children under age 3 are usually measured at least every 6 months, and children over 3, every year. If there is any concern about growth, measurements may be made as often as every 3 months until a growth pattern becomes clear.

Δ   The child's height and weight are measured and marked on a growth chart as part of every visit to the primary care provider.

Δ   Evaluation of the growth curve

   •   Accurately obtain and plot height and weight measurements.

   •   Assess height velocity or height over time.

   •   Determine height-to-weight relationship.

   •   Project target height in context of genetic potential.

Δ   Assess skeletal maturity by comparing epiphyseal centers on x-ray to age-appropriate published standards.

Δ   Take a psychosocial assessment related to self-esteem issues.

   •   Body image

   •   Willingness or capability to participate in activities such as sports due to a smaller stature

   •   Seclusion and loneliness, self-imposed, or related to peers' perception of size

   •   Behaviors appropriate for chronologic age

Diagnostic Procedures and Nursing Interventions

Δ   Plasma insulin-like growth factor – 1(IGF-1) levels

- IGF-1 test is used to diagnose abnormalities of growth and assess the function of the pituitary gland.

- Results of this test are interpreted based on the child's age, gender, and reference range of the individual laboratory where the test is taken.

- IGF-1 levels assist to determine GH status in the child's body.

- The child should fast the night before the test.

Δ   GH stimulation/GH Suppression Testing

- GH suppression is tested by having the child drink a high-glucose solution, and then blood samples are taken at set time intervals to measure the suppressive effect of the glucose on GH.

- GH stimulation is tested by administering IV insulin, arginine, or glucagon, blood samples are taken at set time intervals to measure the release of GH.

- The child should refrain from strenuous activity and food/fluids 10 to 12 hr prior to the test.

Δ   Radiologic Assessments

- Assess the child's skeletal maturity by comparing epiphyseal centers on an x-ray to age-appropriate published standards.

- General skeletal survey in children under 3 years, or survey of hands and wrists in older children, provides information about growth as well as epiphyseal function.

Δ   Magnetic resonance imaging (MRI) identifies tumors or other structural defects.

NANDA Nursing Diagnoses

Δ   Disturbed body image

Δ   Ineffective coping

Δ   Delayed growth and development

Δ   Risk for disproportionate growth

Δ   Powerlessness

Nursing Interventions

Δ   Maintain growth records.

Δ   Assess and monitor effectiveness of GH replacement. GH is supplied by recombinant DNA technology.

Δ   Obtain measurements at start of therapy.

Δ   Monitor bone age annually and growth rates every 3 to 6 months during therapy for evidence of hormone effectiveness.

Δ   Provide the child/family teaching regarding GH replacement therapy.

- No significant side effects are known when GH replacement therapy is used in appropriate dose for GH deficiency. Positive effects on self-esteem may be seen.

- GH will assist with muscle growth development.

- GH is usually administered 6 to 7 days a week by subcutaneous injection.

- GH is usually continued until bone maturation takes place. This may be 16 years of age or older for boys and 14 years of age or older for girls.

- Children with GH deficiency in childhood should be evaluated in early adulthood to determine the need for continued replacement therapy.

Δ   Administer other hormone replacements if prescribed (e.g., thyroid hormone).

Δ   Provide support to the child/family regarding psychosocial concerns (e.g., altered body image, depression). Reassure the child/family that there are no cognitive delays or deficits.

Δ   Stress the importance of maintaining realistic expectations based on the child's age and abilities.

Complications and Nursing Implications

Δ   Complications of GH deficiency without hormone replacement are a disruption in vertical growth, delayed epiphyseal closure, retarded bone age, delayed sexual development, and premature aging later in life.

- Early identification of GH deficiency

- Appropriate support and education to facilitate success of GH replacement therapy

Primary Reference:

Hockenberry, M., Wilson, D., & Winkelstein, M. (2005). *Wong's essentials of pediatric nursing care*. (7th ed.). St. Louis, MO: Mosby.

Additional Resources:

Keep Kids Healthy, LLC. (2003, July). *Short stature*. Retrieved February 7, 2007, from http://www.keepkidshealthy.com/welcome/conditions/short_stature.html

Lab Tests Online. (2004, December). *IGF-1*. Retrieved February 6, 2007, from http://www.labtestsonline.org/understanding/analytes/igf1/test.html

NANDA International (2004). *NANDA nursing diagnoses: Definitions and classification 2005-2006*. Philadelphia: NANDA.

Nemours Foundation. (2004, October). *Growth problems*. Retrieved February 7, 2007, from http://www.kidshealth.org/teen/diseases_conditions/growth/growth_hormone.html

Nemours Foundation. (2005, October). *Dwarfism*. Retrieved February 7, 2007, from http://www.kidshealth.org/parent/growth/growth/dwarfism.html

Van Voorhees, B. W. (2006, June). *Medical encyclopedia: Growth hormone deficiency*. Retrieved February 7, 2007, from http://www.nlm.nih.gov/medlineplus/ency/article/001176.htm

Pescovitz, O. H., Rogol, A., & Rosenfeld, R. (Eds.). (2003, December). *Get the facts: Growth hormone issues in children and adults*. Retrieved February 8, 2007, from http://www.hormone.org/pdf/GHIssuesinChildrenandAdults.pdf

Chapter 39: Growth Hormone Deficiency

Application Exercises

1. A nurse is asking a 12-year-old child with GH deficiency to draw a picture of herself playing with children on a playground. Identify potential characteristics in the child's picture that represent a positive self-esteem and characteristics that the nurse might identify as poor self-esteem in this child.

2. Compose a head-to-toe assessment for a 12-year-old child newly diagnosed with GH deficiency.

3. During which of the following periods of growth and development should a nurse anticipate behavioral problems from a child with untreated GH deficiency?

   A. Infant

   B. Preschooler

   C. School-age child

   D. Adolescent

4. Match the following diagnostic tests below with their findings related to growth disorders.

   _____ X-rays of wrist and hand   A. Determines GH level

   _____ IGF-1   B. Identifies pituitary gland tumor

   _____ MRI   C. Determines bone age

   _____ GH stimulation/suppression test D. Measures effect of glucose on GH

5. A parent of a 9-year-old child with GH deficiency asks the nurse how long his son will need to take injections for his growth problem. Which of the following responses by the nurse is most appropriate?

   A. "Injections are usually continued until age 10 for girls and age 12 for boys."

   B. "Injections need to continue until the child reaches the fifth percentile on the growth chart."

   C. "Injections should continue until bone maturation is complete, usually between 14 and 16 years of age."

   D. "The injections will need to be administered throughout the child's entire life."

Chapter 39: Growth Hormone Deficiency

Application Exercises Answer Key

1. A nurse is asking a 12-year-old child with GH deficiency to draw a picture of herself playing with children on a playground. Identify potential characteristics in the child's picture that represent a positive self-esteem and characteristics that the nurse might identify as poor self-esteem in this child.

   Positive characteristics include:

   Δ   **Child playing with other children.**

   Δ   **Child smiling**

   Δ   **Interaction between children.**

   Δ   **True height discrepancy.**

   Δ   **Bright, colorful picture.**

   Negative characteristics include:

   Δ   **Child standing off to the side while other children are playing.**

   Δ   **Drawing indicates teasing and/or ridicule.**

   Δ   **Child appears much smaller than others.**

   Δ   **Dark picture that is scribbled.**

2. Compose a head-to-toe assessment for a 12-year-old child newly diagnosed with GH deficiency.

   The child is of normal intelligence. Alert and oriented. Skin warm and dry. Few eruptions of permanent teeth. Mouth appears crowded with teeth in areas. Lungs clear. Heart rate regular. Abdomen soft. Bowel sounds noted in all quadrants. Stature is less than the third percentile on the growth chart. Skeletal proportions are normal for age. Appropriate sexual development noted. Activity level appropriate for age.

   Rationale: The child with GH deficiency typically has a normal intelligence, normal activity level, and a normal physical assessment with the few exceptions noted, such as delay in permanent tooth eruption, and overcrowding of teeth in mouth. Stature is typically below the third to fifth percentile for age. Sexual development may or may not be delayed.

3. During which of the following periods of growth and development should a nurse anticipate behavioral problems from a child with untreated GH deficiency?

    A. Infant

    B. Preschooler

    C. School-age child

    D. Adolescent

Emotional problems are not uncommon near puberty when smallness in stature becomes increasingly apparent in comparison with peers. Social situations may become difficult as the adolescent may be teased or ridiculed. Height discrepancy has been significantly correlated with emotional adjustment problems. Height discrepancy is not an issue for the child during infancy. Preschool and school-age children do not have as much difference in height as the adolescent.

4. Match the following diagnostic tests below with their findings related to growth disorders.

  C X-rays of wrist and hand   A. Determines GH level

  A IGF-1   B. Identifies pituitary gland tumor

  B MRI   C. Determines bone age

  D GH stimulation/suppression test   D. Measures effect of glucose on GH

5. A parent of a 9-year-old child with GH deficiency asks the nurse how long his son will need to take injections for his growth problem. Which of the following responses by the nurse is most appropriate?

    A. "Injections are usually continued until age 10 for girls and age 12 for boys."

    B. "Injections need to continue until the child reaches the fifth percentile on the growth chart."

    C. "Injections should be continued until bone maturation is complete, usually between 14 and 16 years of age."

    D. "The injections will need to be administered throughout the child's entire life."

GH replacement continues until the endocrinologist determines that the child's bone maturation is complete. This usually occurs around age 14 for females and age 16 for males. However, all clients should be assessed on an individual basis to determine adequate growth. Percentiles of growth on the growth chart are not used to determine when therapy is complete. GH treatments should not continue after the child's bone growth is complete. Nonetheless, the child with GH deficiency should be re-evaluated in young adulthood to determine the need for GH replacement.

Unit 2   Nursing Care of Children with System Disorders
Section: Nursing Care of Children with Genitourinary/Reproductive Disorders/Diseases

Chapter 40:   Genitourinary Tract Defects and Enuresis
                Contributor: Michele Hinds, PhD, RN

 NCLEX-RN® Connections:

> **Learning Objective**: Review and apply knowledge within "**Genitourinary Tract Defects and Enuresis**" in readiness for performance of the following nursing activities as outlined by the NCLEX-RN® test plan:
>
> Δ   Assist with relevant laboratory, diagnostic, and therapeutic procedures within the nursing role, including:
>
> - Client preparation for the procedure.
> - Client teaching (before and following the procedure).
> - Accurate collection of specimens.
> - Evaluation of the child's response to the procedure.
> - Planning and implementing body system-specific interventions as appropriate.
> - Monitoring and taking actions to prevent or minimize the risk of complications.
> - Accurate interpretation of procedure results.
> - Perform and document appropriate assessments based on the child's problem.
> - Apply knowledge of pathophysiology to planning care for clients with specific alterations in body systems, including recognizing associated signs and symptoms.
> - Interpret data that need to be reported immediately.
> - Monitor therapeutic devices (drainage/irrigating devices, chest tubes), if inserted, for proper functioning.
> - Explore resources, make referrals, collaborate with interdisciplinary team, and ensure continuity of client care.
> - Evaluate plans of care for multiple clients and revise plan as needed based on priorities of care and promotion of recovery.
> - Provide the child/family teaching regarding management of the child's health problem.
> - Recognize/respond to emergency situations, and evaluate/document the client's response to emergency interventions.

Key Points

- Δ Bladder exstrophy is the protrusion of the bladder through an abdominal opening.

- Δ Hypospadias is the location of the urethral meatus below the glans penis or on the ventral surface of the penis.

- Δ Chordee is a ventral curvature of the penis that is often associated with hypospadias.

- Δ Epispadias is the location of the urethral meatus on the dorsal side of the penis.

- Δ Phimosis is the narrow opening of the preputial opening of the foreskin that prevents the foreskin from retracting over the glans penis.

- Δ Cryptorchidism is the failure of one or both testicles to descend through the inguinal canal.

  - A history of prolonged cryptorchidism is related to formation of testicular cancer later in life.

  - Infertility can also be a problem later in life.

- Δ Hydrocele is abnormal fluid in the scrotum.

- Δ Ambiguous genitalia are congenital malformations that prevent identification of a child's sex.

- Δ Enuresis is uncontrolled urination, usually during sleep, after the child is beyond age at which bladder control is achieved.

Key Factors

- Δ Children become aware of and are very interested in the genital area, normality of genital function, and gender differences between the ages of 3 and 6 years. Due to this, repair of structural defects should be done before age 3 if possible to minimize damage to body image.

- Δ Exstrophy is the result of failure of the abdominal wall and other underlying structures to fuse in utero.

- Δ Males may experience exstrophy, epispadias, undescended testes, short penis and an inguinal hernia together due to the lack of abdominal wall and structural fusion.

- Δ Chordee is caused by fibrous bands on the penis that causes the glans penis to be pulled ventrally.

- Δ Ambiguous genitalia may be caused by any disturbance of the chromosomal complement, embryogenesis, or biochemical development.

- Δ Enuresis has no clear etiology, but may be influenced by heredity, neuromuscular bladder functioning, or emotional factors.

- Uncontrolled urination must occur at least twice a week for at least 3 months, and the child must be at least 5 years of age before enuresis is diagnosed.

- Enuresis may be the result of failure of the kidneys to concentrate urine during sleep due to lack of antidiuretic hormone.

Assessment

Δ   Structural Defects

- Nursing history should include pregnancy history, family perception of the child's defect, family support, and coping.

- A physical assessment should be done to identify defect and evaluate skin integrity. Defect may be visible by observation or need for palpation such as with cryptorchidism.

Δ   Enuresis

- History of dryness at night

- History of chronic or acute illness such as urinary tract infection, diabetes mellitus, or neurologic defects

- History of emotional stress

- Family history of enuresis

- Fluid intake, especially at night

- Family's perception of enuresis

- Family coping

- Child's perception of enuresis

- Child's self-esteem

- Child's coping, support

Diagnostic Procedures and Nursing Interventions

Δ   Chromosome analysis, ultrasonography, radiographic contrast studies, biochemical tests, and laparotomy or gonad biopsy may be used to determine the sex of a child with ambiguous genitalia.

- Chromosome analysis determines the genetic karyotype.

- Ultrasonography and radiographic contrast studies determine the presence or absence of genital and urinary structures.

- Biochemical tests may detect adrenal cortical syndromes.

- Laparotomy or gonad biopsy is used for a definite diagnosis of the sex of a child.

NANDA Nursing Diagnoses

- Anxiety

- Disturbed body image

- Ineffective coping

- Risk for infection

- Impaired skin integrity

- Disturbed sleep pattern

- Risk for social isolation

- Impaired urinary elimination

Therapeutic Procedures and Nursing Interventions

Δ   Explain to the family that enuresis is not a behavioral problem and should not be punished.

Δ   Help parents identify ways to improve the child's self-image related to enuresis.

Δ   Structural defects will be treated with surgical intervention. The earlier the interventions, the less emotional trauma for the child/family.

Δ   The goal of most structural defect repairs is to preserve or create normal urinary function.

Condition	Surgical Procedure
Bladder exstrophy	• Staged repair • Bladder closure, pelvic bone separation corrected, and inguinal herniorrhaphy in neonate period • Epispadias repair and creation of urethral sphincter between 3 to 5 years • Subsequent surgeries for reconstruction may be needed
Hypospadias	May use foreskin to create skin flap that reaches the tip of the penis
Epispadias	Lengthening of penis and urethra and possibly reconstruction of the bladder neck
Chordee	Release of fibrous bands that cause chordee
Cryptorchidism	Orchiopexy
Phimosis	Circumcision
Ambiguous genitalia	Surgical reconstruction as appropriate

Δ   Prepare the child/family for surgical procedures.

- Explain procedures at the appropriate level for both child and parents.

- Help the child understand that surgery is not a punishment, and it will not mutilate the body.

Δ   Provide postoperative care.

- Use an appropriate pain assessment tool.

- Administer pain medication as prescribed.

- Provide wound care.

- Observe for signs of infection.

Δ   Enuresis may be treated through conditioning therapy, retention control training, or medication therapy.

- Conditioning therapy involves a wire pad that is placed in the underpants of the child and is attached to a buzzer or bell. When urine is detected by the pad, the buzzer or bell rings, waking the child, so the child may continue urination in the toilet.

- Retention control training involves having the child drink fluid and holding the urine as long as the child can tolerate. Pelvic muscle exercises are practiced throughout the day to help with bladder control.

- Medication therapy involves using one of the following classifications of medications:

  ◊ Tricyclic antidepressants.

  ◊ Antidiuretics.

  ◊ Antispasmodics.

- Medication therapy may be tried for a period of time, then the child is weaned off the therapy.

Δ   The child/parents need to understand that therapies for enuresis may be helpful for a short time, but may not be a cure. Support the child/parents in their decisions.

Δ   Explain to the family that enuresis is not a behavioral problem and that the child should not be punished.

Δ   Help parents identify ways to improve the child's self-image related to enuresis.

Complications and Nursing Implications

     Δ   Infection

         •   Observe and teach family to observe for signs of infection including fever, skin inflammation, foul urine odor, cloudy urine, and/or urinary frequency.

     Δ   Psychologic problems (e.g., poor self-esteem, body image, social isolation, fears)

         •   Support child/family by listening to concerns and correcting misperceptions.

Primary Reference:

Hockenberry, M. J., Wilson, D. & Winkelstein, M. L. (2005). *Wong's Essentials of Pediatric Nursing.* (7th ed.). St. Louis: Mosby.

Additional Resources:

NANDA International (2004). *NANDA nursing diagnoses: Definitions and classification 2005-2006.* Philadelphia: NANDA.

Chapter 40: Genitourinary Tract Defects and Enuresis

Application Exercises

Scenario: A 6-year-old child who has been bladder trained without enuresis since age 4 has begun having accidents both at night and occasionally during the day. The child's parents are very concerned and ask the nurse what could be wrong. They have been trying to deal with the situation by withholding fluids from the child after 4 p.m. daily, but this has proved unsuccessful.

1. List several nursing diagnoses appropriate for this situation.

2. Which of the following should be ruled out as possible cause(s) of this child's enuresis? (Select all that apply.)

_____ Glomerulonephritis

_____ Urinary tract infection

_____ New onset of diabetes mellitus

_____ Epispadias

_____ Bladder exstrophy

3. Match the structural genitourinary disorders with their definition.

_____ Hypospadias
_____ Epispadias

_____ Phimosis
_____ Bladder exstrophy
_____ Cryptorchidism
_____ Chordee
_____ Hydrocele

A. Ventral curvature of the penis
B. Narrowed opening in urinary meatus preventing retraction of the foreskin over the glans penis
C. Failure of one or both testicles to descend into the scrotum
D. Collection of fluid in the scrotal sac
E. Urethral meatus is located on ventral side of glans penis
F. Eversion of bladder through lower abdominal wall
G. Urethral meatus located on dorsal side of glans penis

4. True or False: Failure to repair hypospadias can lead to testicular cancer later in life.

5. True or False: Multiple surgeries will be required for a child with bladder exstrophy to repair damage to the bladder and pelvic area.

Chapter 40: Genitourinary Tract Defects and Enuresis

Application Exercises Answer Key

Scenario: A 6-year-old child who has been bladder trained without enuresis since age 4 has begun having accidents both at night and occasionally during the day. The child's parents are very concerned and ask the nurse what could be wrong. They have been trying to deal with the situation by withholding fluids from the child after 4 p.m. daily, but this has proved unsuccessful.

1. List several nursing diagnoses appropriate for this situation.

   Anxiety

   Disturbed body image

   Risk for infection

   Social isolation

2. Which of the following should be ruled out as possible cause(s) of this child's enuresis? (Select all that apply.)

   _____ Glomerulonephritis

   __X__ **Urinary tract infection**

   __X__ **New onset of diabetes mellitus**

   _____ Epispadias

   _____ Bladder exstrophy

   Both urinary tract infection and the onset of juvenile onset diabetes mellitus could be causes for enuresis. Glomerulonephritis does not lead to enuresis. Epispadias is found in boys only. Bladder exstrophy is a serious structural defect present at birth; therefore, it would not be a newly-diagnosed problem in this child.

3. Match the structural genitourinary disorders with their definition.

E Hypospadias

G Epispadias

B Phimosis

F Bladder exstrophy

C Cryptorchidism

A Chordee

D Hydrocele

A. Ventral curvature of the penis

B. Narrowed opening in urinary meatus preventing retraction of the foreskin over the glans penis

C. Failure of one or both testicles to descend into the scrotum

D. Collection of fluid in the scrotal sac

E. Urethral meatus is located on ventral side of glans penis

F. Eversion of bladder through lower abdominal wall

G. Urethral meatus located on dorsal side of glans penis

4. True or False: Failure to repair hypospadias can lead to testicular cancer later in life.

False. Cryptorchidism (undescended testicle) may cause testicular cancer later in life if not repaired. That is not the case with hypospadias, which is when the urethral meatus is located below the glans penis or on the ventral surface of the penis.

5. True or False: Multiple surgeries will be required for a child with bladder exstrophy to repair damage to the bladder and pelvic area.

True. Bladder exstrophy is a serious congenital defect that requires multiple surgeries over several years to repair.

Unit 2
Section:

Nursing Care of Children with System Disorders
Nursing Care of Children with Genitourinary/Reproductive Disorders/Diseases

Chapter 41:   Urinary Tract Infection
Contributor: Glenda J. Bondurant, MSN, RN

 NCLEX-RN® Connections:

Learning Objective: Review and apply knowledge within **"Urinary Tract Infection"** in readiness for performance of the following nursing activities as outlined by the NCLEX-RN® test plan:

Δ   Assist with relevant laboratory, diagnostic, and therapeutic procedures within the nursing role, including:

- Client preparation for the procedure.

- Client teaching (before and following the procedure).

- Accurate collection of specimens.

- Evaluation of the child's response to the procedure.

- Planning and implementing body system-specific interventions as appropriate.

- Monitoring and taking actions to prevent or minimize the risk of complications.

- Accurate interpretation of procedure results.

Δ   Perform and document appropriate assessments based on the child's problem.

Δ   Apply knowledge of pathophysiology to planning care for clients with specific alterations in body systems, including recognizing associated signs and symptoms.

Δ   Interpret data that need to be reported immediately.

Δ   Monitor therapeutic devices, if inserted, for proper functioning.

Δ   Explore resources, make referrals, collaborate with interdisciplinary team, and ensure continuity of client care.

Δ   Evaluate plans of care for multiple clients and revise plan as needed based on priorities of care and promotion of recovery.

Δ   Provide the child/family teaching regarding management of the child's health problem.

Δ   Recognize/respond to emergency situations, and evaluate/document the client's response to emergency interventions.

📖 **Key Points**

Δ Urinary tract infection (UTI) refers to an infection in any portion of the lower urinary tract (e.g., cystitis, urethritis).

Δ Upper UTI refers to conditions such as pyelonephritis.

Δ Untreated UTIs may lead to urosepsis, which can lead to septic shock and death.

Key Factors

Δ UTI causative organisms include *Escherichia coli* (most common), *Proteus, Pseudomonas, Klebsiella,* or *Staphylococcus aureus.*

Δ Risk Factors

- Urinary conditions (congenital anomalies, stasis, calculi, and residual urine)

- Reflux along urinary system – most specifically at vesicoureteral junction

- Increased sexual activity in adolescents may lead to UTIs

- Sexual abuse

- Short urethra in females and its close proximity to the rectum predisposes them to UTI

- Other risks factors include:

  ◊ Synthetic, tight underwear, and wet bathing suits.

  ◊ Frequent submersion into baths (bubble baths) or hot tubs.

  ◊ During adolescence, hormonal influences within the vaginal flora, the frequent use of feminine hygiene sprays, tampons, and/or sanitary napkins.

- Chronic disease (e.g., diabetes mellitus, cerebral palsy)

Assessment

Δ Signs and Symptoms

- Fever greater than 39.4° C (103° F)

- Urinary frequency with voiding of small amounts, urgency, and **nocturia**

- Dysuria, bladder cramping, or spasms

- Perineal itching; reddened perineal area

- Warm sensation during urination

- Urethral discharge

- Cloudy or foul-smelling urine

- Hematuria (tea or cola-colored urine)

- Lower back or lower abdominal discomfort and tenderness over the bladder area

- Nausea and vomiting, and diarrhea

- Urinary incontinence in a child already toilet trained

- Reddened perineal area

- Infants

  ◊ Fever of unknown origin

  ◊ Irritability/fussiness

  ◊ Poor feeding

Diagnostic Procedures and Nursing Interventions

Δ Urinalysis and Urine Culture and Sensitivity

- Sterile catheterization and/or suprapubic aspiration is the most accurate method for obtaining urine for culture in infants and toddlers.

  ◊ Suprapubic aspiration for children younger than 2 years

    ° Requires consent

    ° Done by a physician

- If the child is old enough to cooperate, a clean-catch urine sample may be used. Attempt to obtain urine specimen first thing in the morning.

- The specimen for culture should be taken to the laboratory without delay. The specimen may be refrigerated for up to 24 hr if immediate culture is not possible.

- Expected findings

  ◊ Bacteria, sediment, WBCs, and RBCs

  ◊ Positive leukocyte esterase (85 to 90% specific)

  ◊ Positive nitrate (95% specific)

- Dipstick tests may be used to identify leukocyte esterase and nitrite before the culture is completed.

Δ Obtain WBC count and differential if urosepsis is suspected.

- A WBC count at or above $10,000/mm^3$ with a shift to the left indicates an increased number of immature cells in response to infection.

Δ Cystoscopy, voiding cystoureterography, intravenous pyelograms (IVP), and urodynamic tests may be used for complicated UTIs.

- Assess for allergy to iodine/shellfish if contrast medium is used.

- Sedation may be required for infants and young children. Assist the older child to remain quiet during the examinations.

- The child must be NPO after midnight in preparation for a cystoscopy and IVP. IVP requires bowel preparation.

- Prepare the child if catheterization is necessary.

- Monitor the child after the procedure according to facility protocol. Monitoring usually requires obtaining frequent vital signs during immediate postprocedure period.

Δ Rule out sexually transmitted diseases.

NANDA Nursing Diagnoses

Δ Impaired urinary elimination

Δ Deficient knowledge

Δ Acute pain

Δ Impaired skin integrity

Nursing interventions

Δ Encourage frequent voiding and complete emptying of the bladder.

Δ Encourage small, frequent meals including the child's favorite foods.

Δ Child/family education should include:

- Preparing the child for diagnostic tests.

- Completing all prescribed antibiotics even if symptoms are no longer present. Medications commonly used for treatment of UTIs include cefaclor (Ceclor), nitrofurantoin (Macrobid), or sulfamethoxazole with trimethoprim (Bactrim, Septra).

- Advising that certain urinary analgesics, such as phenazopyridine (Pyridium), will turn the urine orange.

- Recognizing signs and symptoms for future UTI.

- Preventing possible recurrence.
    - ◊ Wipe the perineal area from front to back for female infants. Teach toddler and preschool girls to do the same.
    - ◊ Retract and clean foreskin on male infants.
    - ◊ Keep underwear dry.
    - ◊ Maintain adequate hydration.

◊   Encourage frequent voiding.

◊   Encourage emptying of bladder.

◊   Avoid bubble baths.

Complications and Nursing Implications

Δ   Pyelonephritis

- Urinary reflux from the bladder into the ureters may contribute to pyelonephritis.

- Monitor for signs and symptoms (e.g., pain in back, groin, and/or flank, high fever, hematuria, vomiting).

- Reinforce teaching about prevention, early identification, and treatment of UTI.

Primary Reference:

Hockenberry, M., Wilson, D., & Winkelstein, M. (2005). *Wong's essentials of pediatric nursing care.* (7th ed.). St. Louis, MO: Mosby.

Additional Resources:

Mayo Foundation for Medical Education and Research. (2005). *Kidney infection.* Retrieved February 27, 2007, from http://www.mayoclinic.com/health/kidney-infection/DS00593

NANDA International (2004). *NANDA nursing diagnoses: Definitions and classification 2005-2006.* Philadelphia: NANDA.

WebMD. (n.d.). *Find a drug.* Retrieved February 14, 2007, from http://www.webmd.com/drugs/index-drugs.aspx

Chapter 41: Urinary Tract Infection

Application Exercises

Scenario: A 4-month-old infant is brought by her mother to the pediatric outpatient facility for the second time with a UTI. The primary care provider prescribes trimethoprim-sulfamethoxazole (Septra) one-half teaspoon by mouth twice a day. The infant is to return to the office in 1 week for follow-up. The infant is scheduled for a voiding cystourethrogram in 2 weeks.

1. The mother tells the nurse that she did not complete the infant's last round of antibiotics because she could not get the infant to swallow the medication. What can the nurse do to help her with this problem?

2. The mother asks what the purpose of the voiding cystourethrogram is. How should the nurse respond?

3. The mother asks if there is anything she could do to prevent another UTI. What other suggestions should the nurse give?

4. A 6-year-old child is admitted to an acute care unit with a diagnosis of possible UTI. Which of the following symptoms should the nurse expect to find during an initial assessment?

    A. Dysuria, thirst, light-colored urine, and ammonia odor in urine
    B. Dysuria, left-sided pain, foul odor to urine, and dark color to urine
    C. Polyuria, lower abdominal pain, yellow urine, and sweet odor to urine
    D. Oliguria, epigastric pain, yellow skin tones, and ammonia odor to breath

5. A nurse is preparing discharge teaching for the mother of a 6-year-old girl who had a severe UTI. Which of the following instructions are beneficial for the mother? (Select all that apply.)

    _____ Avoid bubble baths.
    _____ Change the child's bathing suit immediately after swimming.
    _____ Encourage the child to go to the bathroom every 6 hr.
    _____ Have the child wear cotton underpants rather than nylon.
    _____ Observe the child wiping back to front after voiding.

6. Which of the following orders should a nurse implement first for a child with a UTI?

        A. Ampicillin 250 mg IV q 12 hr

        B. Blood and urine culture

        C. Sitz bath PRN for pain

        D. Voiding cystourethrogram

Chapter 41: Urinary Tract Infection

Application Exercises Answer Key

Scenario: A 4-month-old infant is brought by her mother to the pediatric outpatient facility for the second time with a UTI. The primary care provider prescribes trimethoprim-sulfamethoxazole (Septra) one-half teaspoon by mouth twice a day. The infant is to return to the office in 1 week for follow-up. The infant is scheduled for a voiding cystourethrogram in 2 weeks.

1. The mother tells the nurse that she did not complete the infant's last round of antibiotics because she could not get the infant to swallow the medication. What can the nurse do to help her with this problem?

   The nurse must emphasize to the mother the importance of administering the entire medication to the infant. Methods of administering the medication to the infant include using a syringe to dribble the medication down the inside of the infant's cheeks, or on the back of the infant's tongue. Prior to feeding, place an empty nipple into the infant's mouth, then place the medication in the nipple and the child will naturally suck the medication down.

2. The mother asks what the purpose of the voiding cystourethrogram is. How should the nurse respond?

   The voiding cystourethrogram checks for problems of the urethra and bladder, specifically for problems with bladder emptying. Having two UTIs in such a short time is quite unusual for an infant; therefore, it is important to find out the cause of the infection.

3. The mother asks if there is anything she could do to prevent another UTI. What other suggestions should the nurse give?

   Cleaning the perineal area from front to back, not putting the child in a bubble bath, changing diapers when wet, and ensuring regular feedings can help prevent UTI. Another very important thing is to complete the full dose of antibiotics prescribed for this UTI.

4. A 6-year-old child is admitted to an acute care unit with a diagnosis of possible UTI. Which of the following symptoms should the nurse expect to find during an initial assessment?

      A. Dysuria, thirst, light-colored urine, and ammonia odor in urine

      B. Dysuria, left-sided pain, foul odor to urine, and dark color to urine

      C. Polyuria, lower abdominal pain, yellow urine, and sweet odor to urine

      D. Oliguria, epigastric pain, yellow skin tones, and ammonia odor to breath

Painful urination with left flank pain, foul odor in urine, and dark color are symptoms of UTI. Light-colored urine and ammonia odor in urine are normal. Polyuria and sweet odor are indicative of diabetes mellitus. Oliguria, epigastric pain, yellow skin tones, and ammonia odor to breath are all signs of renal failure, not UTI.

5. A nurse is preparing discharge teaching for the mother of a 6-year-old girl who had a severe UTI. Which of the following instructions are beneficial for the mother? (Select all that apply.)

      __X__ **Avoid bubble baths.**

      __X__ **Change the child's bathing suit immediately after swimming.**

      _____ Encourage the child to go to the bathroom every 6 hr.

      __X__ **Have the child wear cotton underpants rather than nylon.**

      _____ Observe the child wiping back to front after voiding.

Bubble baths should not be used (or used rarely) with a child prone to UTIs. The wet lining of a bathing suit can foster a site for bacterial growth; therefore, wet clothing should be changed as soon as possible. Cotton underwear keeps the perineal area drier than nylon, preventing bacterial growth. Parents should encourage the child to go to the bathroom every 2 to 4 hr to prevent urine stasis. The perineal area should be wiped from front to back; otherwise, bacteria is being introduced into the urinary meatus.

6. Which of the following orders should a nurse implement first for a child with a UTI?

      A. Ampicillin 250 mg IV q 12 hr

      B. Blood and urine culture

      C. Sitz bath PRN for pain

      D. Voiding cystourethrogram

Blood and urine culture need to be collected prior to initiation of antibiotic therapy. Voiding cystourethrogram is typically scheduled with the resolution of a UTI. A sitz bath is only needed for comfort and is not the highest priority.

Unit 2   Nursing Care of Children with System Disorders
Section: Nursing Care of Children with Genitourinary/Reproductive Disorders/Diseases

Chapter 42:   Glomerular Disease
                Contributor: Glenda J. Bondurant, MSN, RN

 NCLEX-RN® Connections:

Learning Objective: Review and apply knowledge within "**Glomerular Disease**" in readiness for performance of the following nursing activities as outlined by the NCLEX-RN® test plan:

Δ   Assist with relevant laboratory, diagnostic, and therapeutic procedures within the nursing role, including:

  • Client preparation for the procedure.

  • Client teaching (before and following the procedure).

  • Accurate collection of specimens.

  • Evaluation of the child's response to the procedure.

  • Planning and implementing body system-specific interventions as appropriate.

  • Monitoring and taking actions to prevent or minimize the risk of complications.

  • Accurate interpretation of procedure results.

Δ   Perform and document appropriate assessments based on the child's problem.

Δ   Apply knowledge of pathophysiology to planning care for clients with specific alterations in body systems, including recognizing associated signs and symptoms.

Δ   Interpret data that need to be reported immediately.

Δ   Monitor therapeutic devices (drainage/irrigating devices, chest tubes), if inserted, for proper functioning.

Δ   Explore resources, make referrals, collaborate with interdisciplinary team, and ensure continuity of client care.

Δ   Evaluate plans of care for multiple clients and revise plan as needed based on priorities of care and promotion of recovery.

Δ   Provide the child/family teaching regarding management of the child's health problem.

Δ   Recognize/respond to emergency situations, and evaluate/document the client's response to emergency interventions.

Glomerulonephritis

 Key Points

Δ   Glomerulonephritis is an inflammation of the glomerular capillaries, usually following a streptococcal infection. It is an immune complex disease, not an infection of the kidney.

Δ   Glomerulonephritis may be acute, latent, or chronic.

Δ   Acute Glomerulonephritis (AGN)

   •   Insoluble immune complexes develop and become trapped in the glomerular tissue producing swelling and capillary cell death.

   •   This may result in:

      ◊   Decreases in glomerular filtration rate.

      ◊   Hematuria.

      ◊   Fluid retention.

      ◊   Decreased urinary output.

   •   Renal manifestations usually occur 10 to 21 days after infection.

   •   Prognosis varies depending upon specific cause, but spontaneous recovery generally occurs after the acute illness.

   •   Acute poststreptococcal glomerulonephritis (APSGN) is one form of AGN and is the most common noninfectious renal disease in childhood.

   •   APSGN affects children mainly between the ages of 6 and 7.

Key Factors

Δ   Risk Factors

   •   Immunological reactions

      ◊   Primary infection with Group A β-hemolytic streptococcal infection (GABHS) (most common)

      ◊   Systemic lupus erythematosus

   •   Vascular injury (hypertension)

   •   Metabolic disease (diabetes mellitus)

   •   Nephrotoxic medications

   •   Excessively high-protein and high-sodium diets

Diagnostic Procedures

Δ Urinalysis – proteinuria, hematuria, cell debris (red cells and casts), increased urine specific gravity (greater than 1.025)

Δ Serum BUN – **elevated**: 100 to 200 mg/dL; normal range is 5 to 18 mg/dL

Δ Serum creatinine – **elevated**: greater than 6 mg/dL; normal range is 0.2 to 1.0 mg/dL

Δ Creatinine clearance – **decreased**: 50 mL/min; normal range is 89 to 137 mL/min

Δ Electrolytes – hyperkalemia, hypermagnesemia, and dilutional hyponatremia if urine output is decreased

Δ Throat culture to identify possible streptococcus infection (usually negative by the time of diagnosis)

Δ **Antistreptolysin-O (ASO) titer** – positive indicator for the presence of streptococcal antibodies

Δ Presence of antihyaluronidase (AHase), antideoxyribonuclease B (ADNase-B), and streptozyme antibodies

Δ Serum complement (C3) – decreased; increases as recovery takes place

Δ Erythrocyte sedimentation rate (ESR) – **elevated;** indicates active inflammatory response; normal range is 0 to 15 mm/hr

Δ WBC – **elevated**; indicates inflammation and presence of active streptococcal infection

Δ Chest x-ray is used to identify pulmonary complications.

• Pulmonary edema

• Cardiac enlargement

• Pleural effusions

Δ X-ray of kidney, ureter, bladder (KUB) is used to detect structural abnormalities such as atrophy.

Assessment

Δ   Nursing History

- Recent upper respiratory infection or streptococcal infection

- Vague reports by younger child

- Reports of fatigue, abdominal pain, headaches, back pain, painful urination, and anorexia/nausea, from older children

Δ   Signs and Symptoms (characteristic of systemic circulatory overload)

- Renal symptoms

  ◊   Decreased urine output

  ◊   Smoky or tea-colored urine (hematuria)

  ◊   Proteinuria (3+ or 4+)

- Fluid volume excess symptoms

  ◊   Shortness of breath

  ◊   Orthopnea

  ◊   Bibasilar rales

  ◊   Periorbital edema

  ◊   Facial edema worse in the morning but then spreads to extremities and abdomen with progression of day

  ◊   Mild to severe hypertension

- Child appears ill and is lethargic, irritable, pale, and has activity intolerance

Nephrotic Syndrome

 Key Points

Δ   Nephrotic syndrome is a group of symptoms, not a disease. It is the most common presentation of glomerular injury in children.

Δ   Glomerular capillaries are damaged from immune complex deposits, nephrotoxic antibodies, or nonimmunological insults.

Δ   Damaged glomerular capillaries are permeable to serum proteins, resulting in decreased serum osmotic pressure.

Δ   Nephrotic syndrome is characterized by proteinuria, hypoalbuminemia, and edema.

Key Factors

Δ   Causes/Risk Factors

- Minimal change nephrotic syndrome (MCNS) accounts for 80% of the cases of nephrotic syndrome.

  ◊ Peak incidence is between 2 and 7 years, although it may occur in older children

  ◊ Cause is unknown but may have a multifactorial etiology (e.g., immune-mediated, biochemical)

- Two other types of this disorder include:

  ◊ Secondary nephrotic syndrome, which occurs after or is associated with glomerular damage due to a known cause (e.g., AIDS, hepatitis, tuberculosis, renal vein thrombosis, malignancies, malaria, sickle cell disease, medication toxicity).

  ◊ Congenital nephrotic syndrome, which is an inherited disorder.

Assessment

Δ   Signs and Symptoms

- Weight gain with poor appetite, possibly anorexia, nausea, and vomiting

- Edema (periorbital) is worse in morning and decreases as the day progresses

- Ascites and dependent edema

- Dark, frothy urine, decreased urine output

- Blood pressure may be normal or hypotensive

- Irritability, malaise, activity intolerance, fatigue

Diagnostic Procedures

Δ   Urinalysis/24-hr Urine Collection

- Protein as high as 3+ or 4+ (greater than 3.5 g in 24 hr) (proteinuria)

- Casts

- Increased specific gravity

- Color change

Δ   Serum Chemistry

- Serum albumin – less than 2.5 g/dL (hypoalbuminemia)

- Serum lipid levels – elevated triglycerides, low-density, and very low-density lipoproteins (hyperlipidemia)

- Elevated cholesterol – greater than 200 mg/dL
- Elevated Hgb, Hct, platelets (hemoconcentration)
- Elevated sodium
- BUN – greater than 20 mg/dL (azotemia)
- Creatinine – greater than 1.2 mg/dL

Δ Kidney Biopsy

- Minimal to extensive damage
- Fatty deposits in tubules
- Epithelium changes
- Glomerular sclerosis
- Immunoglobulins in capillary walls

Glomerulonephritis/Nephrotic Syndrome

NANDA Nursing Diagnoses

Δ Activity intolerance

Δ Disturbed body image

Δ Excess fluid volume

Δ Risk for infection

Δ Deficient knowledge

Δ Imbalanced nutrition: less than body requirements

Δ Impaired tissue integrity

Δ Ineffective tissue perfusion

Nursing Interventions

Δ Monitor I&O. Assess color, specific gravity, and presence of protein in urine.

Δ Monitor daily weights and abdominal girth if ascites present.

Δ Assess respiratory system for fluid overload (e.g., crackles, dyspnea)

Δ   Monitor vital signs.

- Monitor for hypertension with AGN.

  ◊   Administer antihypertensives as prescribed.

  ◊   Administer diuretics as prescribed.

- Monitor for hypotension with nephrotic syndrome.

Δ   Implement seizure precautions if condition indicates.

Δ   Encourage adequate nutritional intake within restriction guidelines. Sodium, fluids, and foods high in potassium may be restricted for the child with hypertension and edema.

- Encourage lowering sodium intake (no salt added diet) and avoid foods high in sodium (e.g., salted snacks, french fries).

- Adjust protein intake according to protein loss in urine over 24 hr.

- Provide high biologic value protein (lean meat, fish, poultry, dairy).

- Provide small, frequent feedings because of the child's loss of appetite.

- Refer the child for dietary consultation if indicated.

Δ   Monitor skin for breakdown areas.

Δ   Prevent pressure sores.

- Frequently turn and reposition the child.

- Keep the child's skin dry.

- Pad bony prominences.

- Elevate edematous body parts.

Δ   Administer medications as prescribed, which include:

- Diuretics and antihypertensives to control blood pressure.

- 25% albumin as prescribed in nephrotic syndrome.

- Prednisone for nephrotic syndrome at 2 mg/kg/day. This dose will be continued for 7 to 21 days (based on response) and then tapered with decreasing doses until discontinued.

- Cyclophosphamide (Cytoxan) or chlorambucil (Leukeran) may be prescribed for children who cannot tolerate prednisone or who have repeated relapse of MCNS.

Δ   Determine tolerance for activity. Provide for frequent rest periods.

Δ   Provide for age-appropriate diversional activity.

Δ   Cluster care to facilitate tolerance of activity.

Δ   Monitor and prevent infection.

- Turn, cough, and deep breathe to prevent pulmonary involvement.

- Monitor vital signs for changes secondary to infection.

- Maintain good handwashing.

- Administer antibiotic therapy as prescribed.

Δ   Provide emotional support.

Δ   Home Care Instructions

- Allow the child to verbalize feelings related to body image.

- Follow appropriate dietary management.

- Provide for adequate rest.

- Regard the need for follow-up care. The child should be seen by the primary care provider weekly for several weeks and then monthly until the disease is fully resolved.

- Adhere to strategies to decrease risk of infection (e.g., good handwashing, up-to-date immunizations, avoidance of infected persons).

- Observe for side effects of prednisone, which include weight gain, increased appetite, and/or infection.

Complications and Nursing Implications

Δ   Renal Failure

- Repeated episodes of glomerulonephritis that go untreated or partially treated could result in chronic renal failure.

- Without control of the disease process, nephrotic syndrome progresses over time to chronic renal failure.

- Teach parents to observe for signs of renal failure, which include oliguria, edema, and/or drowsiness.

- Reinforce parental teaching regarding seeking early treatment, especially if signs of renal failure are present.

Δ   Sepsis/Infection

- Partially treated precipitating streptococcal infections could lead to septicemia.

- Untreated or partially treated glomerulonephritis could lead to septicemia.

- Steroid therapy for nephrotic syndrome may make the child vulnerable to infection.

- Prevention of sepsis

    ◊   Early recognition

    ◊   Completion of antibiotic therapy

Primary Reference:

Hockenberry, M., Wilson, D., & Winkelstein, M. (2005). *Wong's essentials of pediatric nursing care.* (7th ed.). St. Louis, MO: Mosby.

Additional Resources:

NANDA International (2004). *NANDA nursing diagnoses: Definitions and classification 2005-2006.* Philadelphia: NANDA.

WebMD. (n.d.). Find a drug. Retrieved February 9, 2007, from http://www.webmd.com/drugs/index-drugs.aspx

Chapter 42: Glomerular Disease

Application Exercises

Scenario: A child with glomerulonephritis is admitted to the pediatric ICU for overnight observation. During admission, the child presents with the following assessment findings.

Vital signs	Diagnostic laboratory values
Blood pressure 150/90 mm Hg	2+ proteinuria
Heart rate 108/min	Specific gravity 1.022
Respiratory rate 30/min	+ streptococcal antibody
Temperature 38.1° C (100.6° F)	CBC – WNL
	2+ hematuria

Physical Assessment Findings

Δ   Periorbital edema, midtibial edema, 2+ pitting pedal edema

Δ   Lungs with crackles ⅓ up from bases

Δ S_3 on cardiac assessment

Δ   Weight 20 kg

1. During the admission nursing assessment, the child's parent tells the nurse that her child has gained 10 lb in the last week. How much fluid has this child gained? What does this information tell the nurse about the potential degree of renal complications?

2. What nursing diagnosis will receive priority?

3. What interventions should the nurse include in the child's plan of care?

4. List other nursing diagnoses that the ICU nurse should consider.

5. A nurse is assigned to care for a child admitted with glomerulonephritis. Which of the following assessment findings indicates a need to call the primary care provider?

    A. Specific gravity decrease from 1.022 to 1.020

    B. Crackles in the bases bilaterally

    C. Absence of an S_3 on auscultation

    D. Weight gain of 0.91 kg (2 lb) overnight

6. A child is admitted with glomerulonephritis. The nurse should expect to see a recent _____ infection in the history from the mother.

7. A child is admitted with nephrotic syndrome. Which of the following classic symptoms should the nurse observe for in this child?

    A. Hypertension, hyponatremia, hemoconcentration

    B. Hypernatremia, hypoalbuminemia, hyperlipidemia

    C. Hematuria, hypoaldosteronemia, hypernatremia

    D. Hemodilution, hyperalbuminemia, hypoproteinuria

8. A parent of a child with excess fluid volume and weeping skin tells the nurse he would like to be more involved in the child's care. Which of the following should the nurse encourage the parent to do?

    A. Administer the IV Lasix under the supervision of the nurse.

    B. Read to the child from the bedside chair.

    C. Reposition the child every 30 min.

    D. Assist in changing the linens as they become wet.

9. A toddler with nephrotic syndrome has a platelet count of 700,000 mm^3. For which of the following signs and symptoms should the nurse monitor?

    A. Thrombosis

    B. Bruising

    C. Pulmonary congestion

    D. Cardiac enlargement

Chapter 42: Glomerular Disease

Application Exercises Answer Key

Scenario: A child with glomerulonephritis is admitted to the pediatric ICU for overnight observation. During admission, the child presents with the following assessment findings.

Vital signs

Blood pressure 150/90 mm Hg

Heart rate 108/min

Respiratory rate 30/min

Temperature 38.1° C (100.6° F)

Diagnostic laboratory values

2+ proteinuria

Specific gravity 1.022

+ streptococcal antibody

CBC – WNL

2+ hematuria

Physical Assessment Findings

Δ   Periorbital edema, midtibial edema, 2+ pitting pedal edema

Δ   Lungs with crackles ⅓ up from bases

Δ S_3 on cardiac assessment

Δ   Weight 20 kg

1. During the admission nursing assessment the child's parent tells the nurse that her child has gained 10 lb in the last week. How much fluid has this child gained? What does this information tell the nurse about the potential degree of renal complications?

   The child has gained 10 lb. This is 4.545 kg. 1 kg = 1 L; therefore, this child has gained 4.5 L of fluid in a week. This is an indicator that the kidneys are not functioning at full capacity and cannot excrete the excessive fluid.

2. What nursing diagnosis will receive priority?

   Excess fluid volume

3. What interventions should the nurse include in the child's plan of care?

Assess for signs and symptoms of excess fluid volume.

Assess crackles, dyspnea, retractions, and cough.

Monitor I&O.

Monitor daily weights.

Monitor vital signs.

Monitor for hypertension.

Administer antihypertensives as prescribed.

Administer diuretics as prescribed.

Monitor urine output for:

    a.   Color.

    b.   Specific gravity as ordered.

    c.   Protein dipsticks as ordered.

Implement fluid restrictions as ordered.

Limit sodium intake with diet as ordered.

4. List other nursing diagnoses that the ICU nurse should consider.

Activity intolerance

Disturbed body image

Deficient knowledge

Imbalanced nutrition: less than body requirements

Impaired tissue integrity

Ineffective tissue perfusion

Risk for infection

5. A nurse is assigned to care for a child admitted with glomerulonephritis. Which of the following assessment findings indicates a need to call the primary care provider?

    A. Specific gravity decrease from 1.022 to 1.020

    B. Crackles in the bases bilaterally

    C. Absence of an S_3 on auscultation

    D. Weight gain of 0.91 kg (2 lb) overnight

The weight gain is an indictor of fluid retention, which is a cause for concern. The decrease in specific gravity and the absence of S_3 are all indicators of a positive change in the child. The presence of crackles in the bases does not have enough detail to determine if this is a change for the better or for the worse.

6. A child is admitted with glomerulonephritis. The nurse should expect to see a recent _____ infection in the history from the mother.

Streptococcal. Typically, a streptococcal infection precedes the majority of cases of acute glomerulonephritis. Other infections that can cause glomerulonephritis include pneumococcal infections and viral infections.

7. A child is admitted with nephrotic syndrome. Which of the following classic symptoms should the nurse observe for in this child?

    A. Hypertension, hyponatremia, hemoconcentration

    B. Hypernatremia, hypoalbuminemia, hyperlipidemia

    C. Hematuria, hypoaldosteronemia, hypernatremia

    D. Hemodilution, hyperalbuminemia, hypoproteinuria

The child with nephrotic syndrome is experiencing increased permeability at the basement membrane. This child is losing albumin leading to hypoalbuminemia. The child is hemoconcentrated, resulting in hypernatremia and hyperlipidemia. Option A is incorrect because hypotension is more likely to occur than hypertension, and hemoconcentration leads to hypernatremia, not hyponatremia. None of the choices in option C or D are correct.

8. A parent of a child with excess fluid volume and weeping skin tells the nurse he would like to be more involved in the child's care. Which of the following should the nurse encourage the parent to do?

> A. Administer the IV Lasix under the supervision of the nurse.
>
> B. Read to the child from the bedside chair.
>
> C. Reposition the child every 30 min.
>
> **D. Assist in changing the linens as they become wet.**

This child needs parental cuddling, not reading from the bedside chair. The parent does not need to reposition the child every 30 min, but he does need to keep the child as dry as possible; this will require frequent movement of the child. The parent should not administer the IV medication.

9. A toddler with nephrotic syndrome has a platelet count of 700,000 mm^3. For which of the following signs and symptoms should the nurse monitor?

> **A. Thrombosis**
>
> B. Bruising
>
> C. Pulmonary congestion
>
> D. Cardiac enlargement

The toddler is at risk for developing a clot that could lead to phlebitis, stroke, and/or myocardial infarction (normal thrombocyte count is 150,000 to 400,000 mm^3). The increase in thrombocytes will not increase the risk of bleeding, cardiac enlargement, or pulmonary edema.

Unit 2   Nursing Care of Children with System Disorders
Section: Nursing Care of Children with Neurosensory Disorders

Chapter 43:   Meningitis
Contributor: Glenda J. Bondurant, MSN, RN

 **NCLEX-RN® Connections:**

Learning Objective: Review and apply knowledge within "**Meningitis**" in readiness for performance of the following nursing activities as outlined by the NCLEX-RN® test plan:

Δ   Inform the child/family of appropriate immunization schedules.

Δ   Provide and instruct the child/family regarding appropriate infection control interventions.

Δ   Assist with relevant laboratory, diagnostic, and therapeutic procedures within the nursing role, including:

   •   Client preparation and teaching for the procedure.

   •   Accurate collection of specimens.

   •   Evaluation of the child's response to the procedure.

   •   Planning and implementing body system-specific interventions as appropriate.

   •   Monitoring and taking actions to prevent or minimize the risk of complications.

   •   Accurate interpretation of procedure results.

Δ   Perform and document appropriate assessments based on the child's problem.

Δ   Apply knowledge of pathophysiology to planning care for clients with specific alterations in body systems, including recognizing associated signs and symptoms.

Δ   Interpret data that need to be reported immediately.

Δ   Monitor therapeutic devices if inserted, for proper functioning.

Δ   Explore resources, make referrals, collaborate with interdisciplinary team, and ensure continuity of client care.

Δ   Evaluate plans of care for multiple clients and revise plan as needed based on priorities of care and promotion of recovery.

Δ   Provide the child/family teaching regarding management of the child's health problem.

Δ   Recognize/respond to emergency situations, and evaluate/document the client's response to emergency interventions.

Key Points

Δ   Meningitis is an inflammation of the meninges, which are the membranes that protect the brain and spinal cord.

Δ   Viral or aseptic, meningitis is the most common form of meningitis and commonly resolves without treatment.

Δ   Bacterial, or septic, meningitis is a contagious infection with a high mortality rate. The prognosis depends on the supportive care given to the child.

Key Factors

Δ   Risk Factors for Viral Meningitis

 •   Viral illnesses (e.g., mumps, measles, herpes)

Δ   Risk Factors for Bacterial Meningitis

 •   Upper respiratory infections (e.g., otitis media, tonsillitis) caused by bacterial agents (e.g., *Neisseria meningitides* [meningococcal], *Streptococcus pneumonia* [pneumococcal], *Haemophilus influenzae*, *Escherichia coli*)

 •   Immunosuppression

 •   Injuries that provide direct access to cerebrospinal fluid (e.g., skull fracture, penetrating head wound)

 •   Overcrowded living conditions, such as college dorms

Assessment

Δ   Signs and Symptoms

 •   2 years through adolescence

   ◊   Excruciating, unrelenting headache

   ◊   Irritability and restlessness may progress to drowsiness, stupor, and coma

   ◊   Nausea and vomiting

   ◊   Fever and chills

   ◊   Photophobia

   ◊   Nuchal rigidity that may advance to opisthotonos

   ◊   Positive Brudzinski's sign (flexion of extremities occurring with deliberate flexion of the child's neck)

   ◊   Positive Kernig's sign (resistance to extension of the child's leg from a flexed position)

   ◊   Seizures (may be first sign)

- 2 months to 2 years – do not usually show classic signs
    - ◊ High-pitched cry
    - ◊ Seizures with high-pitched cry
    - ◊ Fever
    - ◊ Poor feeding and vomiting
    - ◊ Extremely irritable
    - ◊ Bulging fontanels
    - ◊ Nuchal rigidity not always present
- Neonates
    - ◊ Clinical signs are vague and nonspecific, making diagnosis very difficult
    - ◊ Nuchal rigidity not usually present
    - ◊ Vomiting
    - ◊ Poor muscle tone
    - ◊ Irritability and drowsiness
    - ◊ Irregular respirations and possibly apnea
- Specific to bacterial organism
    - ◊ *S. pneumonia* – draining ear
    - ◊ *N. meningitides* – red macular rash
    - ◊ *N. meningitides* and *H. influenzae* – involvement of joints

Diagnostic Procedures and Nursing Interventions

Δ   Cerebrospinal fluid (CSF) analysis is the most definitive diagnostic procedure.

- Collect CSF with a lumbar puncture (performed by a primary care provider, usually a physician).
    - ◊ Have the child empty his bladder.
    - ◊ Place the child in the fetal position and assist in maintaining position. May need to use distraction.
    - ◊ Sedate the child if necessary with fentanyl (Sublimaze) and midazolam (Versed).
    - ◊ Clean the child's skin prior to injection of a local anesthetic. If time allows, apply a eutectic mixture of local anesthetics (EMLA [lidocaine/prilocaine]) over the area between L3 and L5 60 min prior to the procedure.
    - ◊ Insert the needle into the subarachnoid space.
    - ◊ Pressure readings are taken but may be difficult to obtain if the child is crying.

◊ Collect three to five test tubes of CSF.

◊ Remove the needle, apply pressure, and cover the injection site with a dressing.

◊ Appropriately label specimens and deliver them to the laboratory.

- The child should remain in bed for 4 to 8 hr in a flat position to prevent leakage and a resulting spinal headache. This may not be possible for an infant, toddler, or preschooler.

- Monitor the site for hematoma and/or infection.

- Results indicative of meningitis

  ◊ Appearance of CSF: cloudy (bacterial) or clear (viral)

  ◊ Elevated WBC

  ◊ Elevated protein

  ◊ Decreased glucose (bacterial)

  ◊ Elevated CSF pressure

Δ Perform a blood culture and sensitivity to identify an appropriate broad-spectrum antibiotic.

Δ A CT scan or an MRI may be performed to identify increased ICP and/or an abscess.

NANDA Nursing Diagnoses

Δ Acute pain

Δ Imbalanced nutrition: less than body requirements

Δ Anxiety

Δ Social isolation

Δ Ineffective tissue perfusion (cerebral)

Δ Deficient fluid volume

Nursing Interventions

Δ Isolate the child as soon as meningitis is suspected. Isolation usually is in the ICU.

Δ Initiate and maintain isolation precautions per facility protocol. Continue for 24 hr after the first antibiotic has been administered.

Δ Continue frequent monitoring of vital signs, urine output, fluid status, pain level, neurological status, and head circumference (for infants).

Δ Initiate IV fluids to maintain hydration. Continue fluid and electrolyte replacement as indicated by laboratory values.

Δ   Administer prescribed medications.

• Administer antibiotics for bacterial infections per IV route. Length of therapy is determined by the child's condition and CSF results (e.g., normal blood glucose levels, negative culture). May be as long as 10 days.

• Administer dexamethasone (Decadron) to prevent neurological complications in bacterial meningitis.

• Anticonvulsants – phenytoin (Dilantin)

• Analgesics – nonopioid to avoid masking changes in the level of consciousness

Δ   Maintain NPO status if the child has a decreased level of consciousness. As the child's condition improves, advance to clear liquids and then a diet as tolerated by the child.

Δ   Decrease environmental stimuli.

• Provide for a quiet environment.

• Minimize the child's exposure to bright light (natural and electric).

Δ   Provide for comfort.

• Keep the child's room cool.

• Position the child without a pillow and slightly elevate the head of the bed. The child may prefer the side-lying position to take pressure off of his neck.

Δ   Maintain safety (e.g., keep bed in low position, take seizure precautions).

Δ   Keep the family informed of the child's condition.

Δ   Prevention of future episodes

• Early/complete treatment for upper respiratory infections

• Hib vaccine in children younger than 5 years

Complications and Nursing Implications

Δ   Increased ICP (possibly leading to brain damage)

• Monitor for signs of increased intracranial pressure.

◊ Infants – bulging or tense fontanels, increased head circumference, high-pitched cry, distended scalp veins, irritability, bradycardia, and respiratory changes

◊ Children – increased irritability, headache, nausea, vomiting, diplopia, seizures, bradycardia, and respiratory changes

• Provide interventions to reduce ICP (e.g., positioning, avoidance of coughing and straining)

Primary Reference:

Hockenberry, M., Wilson, D., & Winkelstein, M. (2005). *Wong's essentials of pediatric nursing care*. (7th ed.). St. Louis, MO: Mosby.

Additional Resources:

NANDA International (2004). *NANDA nursing diagnoses: Definitions and classification 2005-2006*. Philadelphia: NANDA.

Chapter 43: Meningitis

Application Exercises

Scenario: A mother brings her 6-month-old child to the emergency department. Four days ago the infant was diagnosed with otitis media. Now the mother says her infant is lethargic and cries constantly when held. The infant has not eaten in 8 hr and only ate 2 oz with the last feeding.

1. What interventions should the emergency department nurse anticipate after assessing the child?

2. When performing the initial assessment, the nurse found that when the infant's head was flexed his knees and hips also flexed. The nurse should document this finding as

    A. Kernig's sign.

    B. Nuchal rigidity.

    C. Brudzinski's sign.

    D. Cushing's reflex.

3. A 3-year-old child with meningitis is documented as having photophobia. Which of the following interventions is most effective in minimizing this symptom?

    A. Avoid using the TV.

    B. Keep the volume down on the radio.

    C. Bandage both eyes temporarily.

    D. Elevate the head of the bed.

4. Which of the following vaccines protect infants from bacterial meningitis? (Select all that apply.)

    _____ IPV (inactivated polio vaccine)

    _____ PCV (pneumococcal vaccine)

    _____ DTaP (diphtheria and tetanus toxoids and pertussis)

    _____ Hib (*Haemophilus influenzae* type B vaccine)

    _____ TIV (trivalent inactivated influenza vaccine)

Chapter 43: Meningitis

Application Exercises Answer Key

Scenario: A mother brings her 6-month-old child to the emergency department. Four days ago the infant was diagnosed with otitis media. Now the mother says her infant is lethargic and cries constantly when held. The infant has not eaten in 8 hr and only ate 2 oz with the last feeding.

1. What interventions should the emergency department nurse anticipate after assessing the child?

   After the assessment, the nurse should suspect meningitis; therefore, she should isolate the child from others in the facility. The nurse should also be prepared to initiate IV access and to assist with performance of a lumbar puncture.

2. When performing the initial assessment, the nurse found that when the infant's head was flexed his knees and hips also flexed. The nurse should document this finding as

   A. Kernig's sign.
   B. Nuchal rigidity.
   C. Brudzinski's sign.
   D. Cushing's reflex.

   Brudzinski's sign is the flexion of the hips and knees when the child's head is purposefully flexed. Kernig's sign is the pain associated with extending the knee when the hip is flexed. Nuchal rigidity is resistance of the neck to passive range of motion. Cushing's reflex is a late neurological sign of increased intracranial pressure in which there is increased blood pressure with widened pulse pressure and bradycardia.

3. A 3-year-old child with meningitis is documented as having photophobia. Which of the following interventions is most effective in minimizing this symptom?

> **A. Avoid using the TV.**
> B. Keep the volume down on the radio.
> C. Bandage both eyes temporarily.
> D. Elevate the head of the bed.

Photophobia is an abnormal sensitivity to light. This is best prevented by using minimal light, such as by keeping the TV off. Regulating the volume of sounds would not affect light sensitivity. Bandaging both eyes would be extremely irritating to the child. Elevating the head of the bed is an effective comfort measure for the child with meningitis, but it has no effect on photophobia.

4. Which of the following vaccines protect infants from bacterial meningitis? (Select all that apply.)

> _____ IPV (inactivated polio vaccine)
> __X__ **PCV (pneumococcal vaccine)**
> _____ DTaP (diphtheria and tetanus toxoids and pertussis)
> __X__ **Hib (*Haemophilus influenzae* type B vaccine)**
> _____ TIV (trivalent inactivated influenza vaccine)

Immunizing infants beginning at age 2 months with Hib and PCV protects them from common types of bacterial meningitis. IPV, DTaP, and TIV vaccines will not prevent bacterial meningitis.

Unit 2   Nursing Care of Children with System Disorders

Section: Nursing Care of Children with Neurosensory Disorders

Chapter 44:   Reye Syndrome

Contributor: Glenda J. Bondurant, MSN, RN

 **NCLEX-RN® Connections:**

> **Learning Objective**: Review and apply knowledge within "**Reye Syndrome**" in readiness for performance of the following nursing activities as outlined by the NCLEX-RN® test plan:
>
> Δ Assist with relevant laboratory, diagnostic, and therapeutic procedures within the nursing role, including:
>
> - Client preparation for the procedure.
>
> - Client teaching (before and following the procedure).
>
> - Accurate collection of specimens.
>
> - Evaluation of the child's response to the procedure.
>
> - Planning and implementing body system-specific interventions as appropriate.
>
> - Monitoring and taking actions to prevent or minimize the risk of complications.
>
> - Accurate interpretation of procedure results.
>
> Δ Perform and document appropriate assessments based on the child's problem.
>
> Δ Apply knowledge of pathophysiology to planning care for clients with specific alterations in body systems, including recognizing associated signs and symptoms.
>
> Δ Interpret data that need to be reported immediately.
>
> Δ Monitor therapeutic devices (drainage/irrigating devices, chest tubes), if inserted, for proper functioning.
>
> Δ Explore resources, make referrals, collaborate with interdisciplinary team, and ensure continuity of client care.
>
> Δ Evaluate plans of care for multiple clients and revise plan as needed based on priorities of care and promotion of recovery.
>
> Δ Provide the child/family teaching regarding management of the child's health problem.
>
> Δ Recognize/respond to emergency situations, and evaluate/document the client's response to emergency interventions.

Key Points

Δ Reye syndrome is a life-threatening disease that leads to multisystem failure. Reye syndrome primarily affects the liver and brain, causing:

- Liver dysfunction.
  ◊ Bleeding and poor blood clotting
  ◊ Elevated liver enzymes
  ◊ Elevated ammonia levels
- Cerebral edema (with increased intracranial pressure).
  ◊ Lethargy progressing to coma
  ◊ Potential for cerebral herniation
- Hypoglycemia.
- Shock.

Key Factors

Δ The cause of Reye syndrome is unknown. However, research has revealed an association between using aspirin (salicylate) products for treating viral infections and the development of Reye syndrome.

- It may occur without the use of aspirin products; however, the incidence of Reye syndrome has decreased since the link of salicylates and viral disorders became known in 1980.

- The surgeon general and many other health organizations recommend not giving aspirin to children under the age of 19 for any fever-causing illness.

Δ Peak incidence occurs in January, February, and March. The symptoms most often appear at the end of a viral illness (e.g., viral upper respiratory infection, varicella) but may occur earlier in the illness.

Δ Reye syndrome has been mistaken for a variety of other disorders including encephalitis, meningitis, poisoning, sudden infant death syndrome (SIDS), diabetes mellitus, and psychiatric illness.

Δ The prognosis for Reye syndrome is best with early recognition and treatment.

Assessment

Δ Obtain history of recent viral illness.

Δ The infant may present with diarrhea (without vomiting), hyperventilation, episodes of apnea and seizures, and/or elevated liver enzymes with jaundice.

△ The older child may present with vomiting (usually without diarrhea) after a viral illness, lethargy, elevated liver enzymes without jaundice, and/or irrational behavior.

△ Reye syndrome presents in five clinical stages. Each stage contains intensified signs and symptoms of the previous stage.

Stage	Manifestations
I	• Lethargy • Vomiting • Anorexia • Early liver dysfunction • Brisk pupillary reaction • Able to follow commands
II	• Confusion/disorientation/delirium • Combativeness • Hyperventilation • Hyperactive reflexes • Pupillary response sluggish • Responds to painful stimuli
III	• Coma/obtunded • Seizures • Decorticate (extension)
IV	• Deeper coma • Decerebrate (flexion) • Fixed, large pupils, and loss of corneal reflexes • Brainstem dysfunction • Minimal liver dysfunction
V	• Loss of deep tendon reflexes • Flaccidity • Seizures • Respiratory arrest

Diagnostic Procedures and Nursing Interventions

△ Tests performed to determine diagnosis may include:

• Liver biopsy.

◊ Adhere to NPO prior to procedure.

◊ Obtain consent form.

◊ Monitor for hemorrhage postprocedure.

◊ Apply pressure dressing.

◊ Assess vital signs frequently postprocedure.

- Lumbar puncture – to collect CSF to rule out meningitis as cause of symptoms (performed by a primary care provider, usually a physician)

  ◊ Have the child empty his bladder.

  ◊ Place the child in the fetal position and assist in maintaining position. May need to use distraction.

  ◊ Sedate the child if necessary with fentanyl (Sublimaze) and midazolam (Versed).

  ◊ Clean the child's skin prior to injection of a local anesthetic. If time allows, apply a eutectic mixture of local anesthetics (EMLA [lidocaine/prilocaine]) over the area between L3 and L5 60 min prior to the procedure.

  ◊ Insert the needle into the subarachnoid space.

  ◊ Pressure readings are taken but may be difficult to obtain if the child is crying.

  ◊ Collect three to five test tubes of CSF.

  ◊ Remove the needle, apply pressure, and cover the injection site with a dressing.

  ◊ Appropriately label specimens and deliver them to the laboratory.

Δ Additional blood studies include:

- Liver enzymes (e.g., alanine aminotransferase [ALT], aspartate aminotransferase [AST]): elevated.

- Serum ammonia level: elevated.

- Serum electrolytes and blood glucose to identity fluid and electrolyte imbalances and hypoglycemia.

- CBC may indicate low Hgb, Hct, and platelets.

- Coagulation times may be extended.

NANDA Nursing Diagnoses

Δ Anxiety

Δ Ineffective breathing patterns

Δ Acute confusion

Δ Deficient fluid volume

Δ Impaired gas exchange

Δ Interrupted family processes

Δ Anticipatory grieving

Δ Risk for injury

Δ Deficient knowledge

Δ Nausea

Δ Ineffective tissue perfusion

Nursing Interventions

Δ Maintain hydration.

- Administer IV fluids as prescribed.

- Maintain accurate I&O.

- Insert urinary catheter as ordered.

- Position the child midline with the head of the bed elevated 15 to 30°.

Δ To decrease cerebral swelling, administer an osmotic diuretic, such as mannitol (Osmitrol), as prescribed. Monitor the child for increased intracranial pressure.

Δ Administer other prescribed medications, such as insulin, to increase glucose metabolism and corticosteroids to decrease brain inflammation.

Δ Monitor appropriateness of coagulation.

- Note unexplained or prolonged bleeding.

- Apply pressure after procedures.

- Prepare to administer vitamin K.

Δ Monitor pain status and response to painful stimuli. Administer pain medications when appropriate.

Δ Insert nasogastric tube as ordered.

Δ Assist with intubation and maintain ventilator if required.

Δ Maintain Swan-Ganz catheter if needed for CVP and cardiac output monitoring.

Δ Take seizure precautions.

Δ Keep the family informed of the child's status.

Δ Provide private time for the family to be with the child if death is imminent.

Δ Contact support for the family.

Δ   Future Prevention of Reye Syndrome

   •   Teach parents to avoid giving salicylates for pain or fever in children.

   •   Teach parents to read labels of over-the-counter medications for presence of salicylates.

Complications and Nursing Implications

Δ   Neurological Sequelae

   •   Neurological complications may include speech and/or hearing impairment, cerebral palsy, paralysis, and/or developmental delays based on length and severity of illness.

   •   Explain the child's condition and needs to the family.

   •   Help the family identify support services for home care.

Δ   Death

   •   Support the family in grief.

   •   Contact spiritual support as appropriate.

Primary Reference:

Hockenberry, M., Wilson, D., & Winkelstein, M. (2005). *Wong's essentials of pediatric nursing care*. (7th ed.). St. Louis, MO: Mosby.

Additional Resources:

NANDA International (2004). *NANDA nursing diagnoses: Definitions and classification 2005-2006*. Philadelphia: NANDA.

National Reye's Syndrome Foundation. (2007). *Emergency room information*. Retrieved February 8, 2007, from http://www.reyessyndrome.org/

National Institute of Neurological Disorders and Stroke. (2006, January). *NINDS Reye's syndrome information page*. Retrieved February 8, 2007, from http://www.ninds.nih.gov/disorders/reyes_syndrome/reyes_syndrome.htm#What_is

CNN.com. (2005, November, 17). *Reye's syndrome*. Retrieved February 18, 2007, from http://www.cnn.com/HEALTH/library/DS/00142.html

Chapter 44: Reye Syndrome

Application Exercises

Scenario: A 6-year-old child is brought by her parent to the emergency department with lethargy, extreme confusion, combative behavior, dyspnea, and multiple small bruises covering her body. Her vital signs are temperature 38.2° C (100.8° F), pulse 132/min, respirations 42/min, and blood pressure 90/40 mm Hg. Diagnostic laboratory results reveal increased bleeding times, decreased platelet count, and elevated liver enzymes and serum ammonia levels. The child's oxygen saturation is 88% and her pupils are equal but slow to react to light.

1. What is the priority nursing diagnosis at the time of admission?

2. What priority interventions should the nurse take at this time secondary to the priority nursing diagnosis?

3. What is the primary concern when interpreting the vital signs?

4. What interventions should the nurse prepare to do for the above concern?

5. A child is admitted with possible Reye syndrome. Which of the following factors in the child's health history might be supportive of this diagnosis?

    A. Recent history of urinary tract infection
    B. Recent history of bacterial otitis media
    C. Recent episode of gastroenteritis
    D. Recent episode of *Haemophilus influenzae* meningitis

6. Which of the following positions is the most effective in preventing a further increase in pressure for a child with increased intracranial pressure?

    A. Left side-lying, head flexed, knees drawn up
    B. Trendelenburg position
    C. Fowler's position
    D. Supine with 30° head elevation

7. Which of the following manifestations are indicative of Stage II of Reye syndrome? (Select all that apply.)

_____ Coma

_____ Fixed pupils

_____ Hyperventilation

_____ Combativeness

_____ Hyperactive deep tendon reflexes

Chapter 44: Reye Syndrome

Application Exercises Answer Key

Scenario: A 6-year-old child is brought by her parent to the emergency department with lethargy, extreme confusion, combative behavior, dyspnea, and multiple small bruises covering her body. Her vital signs are temperature 38.2° C (100.8° F), pulse 132/min, respirations 42/min, and blood pressure 90/40 mm Hg. Diagnostic laboratory results reveal increased bleeding times, decreased platelet count, and elevated liver enzymes and serum ammonia levels. The child's oxygen saturation is 88% and her pupils are equal but slow to react to light.

1. What is the priority nursing diagnosis at the time of admission?

   The priority nursing diagnosis is the child's impaired gas exchange. The child's respirations are very rapid, oxygen saturation is decreased, and she has dyspnea, lethargy, and confusion.

2. What priority interventions should the nurse take at this time secondary to the priority nursing diagnosis?

   The nurse should assess the child's respiratory function, monitoring pulse oximetry, maintaining airway, elevating the head of the bed, administering oxygen by nasal cannula, preparing for intubation, and maintaining the head at midline.

3. What is the primary concern when interpreting the vital signs?

   The nurse should be primarily concerned about the child going into shock. This potential complication evidenced by the child's decreased blood pressure and elevated pulse and respirations.

4. What interventions should the nurse prepare to do for the above concern?

   Initiate IV access and administer IV fluids and medications as prescribed; monitor vital signs and I&O. Prepare to insert a Foley catheter and to assist with insertion of a Swan-Ganz catheter to monitor cardiac output.

5. A child is admitted with possible Reye syndrome. Which of the following factors in the child's health history might be supportive of this diagnosis?

    A. Recent history of urinary tract infection

    B. Recent history of bacterial otitis media

    C. Recent episode of gastroenteritis

    D. Recent episode of *Haemophilus influenzae* meningitis

Gastroenteritis is the only recent illness mentioned that is related to a viral episode. The other choices are caused by bacterial infections.

6. Which of the following positions is the most effective in preventing a further increase in pressure for a child with increased intracranial pressure?

    A. Left side-lying, head flexed, knees drawn up

    B. Trendelenburg position

    C. Fowler's position

    D. Supine with 30° head elevation

When treating a child with increased intracranial pressure, the best position to place the child in is midline with the head of the bed elevated to 15 to 30°. Left side-lying with head flexed and knees drawn up is the position most often used during a lumbar puncture. Trendelenburg position with legs higher than the head may be used for the child in shock. Fowler's position could be a position of choice for the child in respiratory distress.

7. Which of the following manifestations are indicative of Stage II of Reye syndrome? (Select all that apply.)

    _____ Coma

    _____ Fixed pupils

    __X__ Hyperventilation

    __X__ Combativeness

    __X__ Hyperactive deep tendon reflexes

Stage II symptoms include confusion/disorientation/delirium, combativeness, hyperventilation, hyperactive reflexes, sluggish pupillary response, and an ability to respond to painful stimuli. The first two choices are symptoms in later stages of Reye syndrome.

Key Points

Δ   Cerebral palsy (CP) is the most common permanent disability in children.

Δ   CP is a nonprogressive impairment of motor function control, especially muscle control and coordination.

Δ   CP may cause abnormal perception and sensation; visual, hearing, and speech impairments; seizures; and cognitive disabilities.

Δ   Depending on the severity of the disability, the child may not be diagnosed until up to 3 years of age, even if brain injury occurs before or at the time of birth.

Δ   CP manifests differently in each child. Many children with CP are able to perform most or all developmental tasks, and more than half will be able to work outside the home as adults. Others will require complete care for their entire lives.

Key Factors

Δ   CP results from brain injuries or anoxia in utero or during delivery.

Δ   Brain anomalies and/or postnatal injury may also be a cause for CP.

•   Postnatal injury includes cerebral infections, head trauma (e.g., shaken baby syndrome), and/or anoxia to the brain.

Δ   Risk factors include:

•   Premature birth.

•   Multiple birth.

•   Low birth weight.

•   Inability of the placenta to provide the developing fetus with oxygen and nutrients.

•   RH or ABO blood type incompatibility between mother and infant.

•   Maternal infection with rubella or other viral diseases in early pregnancy.

•   Maternal bacterial infection while pregnant.

•   Prolonged loss of oxygen during the birthing process.

•   Severe jaundice shortly after birth.

Δ   Early warning signs that may later be diagnosed as CP include:

•   3-month-old with poor head control or who does not smile.

•   Stiff arms or legs during infancy and early childhood. The infant/child may push away or arch his back.

- A floppy or limp body in infants.

- An inability to sit up without support (8-month-old infant).

- Use of one side of the body to play or move about (infant/child).

- Feeding difficulties (e.g., moving food from side to side with tongue, inability to swallow safely).

Δ CP is classified based on clinical manifestations.

- Spastic

- Dyskinetic/athetoid

- Ataxic

- Mixed type/dystonic

Assessment

Δ Obtain prenatal history for maternal trauma, illness, and/or infection.

Δ Nursing history should include questions related to: history of seizures, nutritional intake, impairments of vision, hearing and/or speech, pain, respiratory distress, ability to control secretions, and ability to control bladder and bowel function.

Δ Physical assessment

- Inspect the child's general appearance, skin color, and affect.

- Assess motor function, looking for the presence of muscle tightness or spasticity, involuntary movements, and disturbance in gait or mobility.

- Assess for ability to swallow food safely (without aspiration/choking difficulties) and nutritional status.

- Identify problems with speech, sensation, and perception.

- Evaluate cognitive development and abilities.

- Assess skin integrity for pressure sores if paralysis is present and/or braces are worn.

- Assess gastrostomy site if the child is tube fed.

Δ   Assessments for Specific Types of CP

Classification	Manifestations
Spastic: • Causes hypertonicity with poor control of motion, balance, and posture. • Impairs fine and gross motor skills.	
Hemiplegia/hemiparesis	• Affects the arm and hand on one side of the body. Hemiplegia/hemiparesis can also affect the leg on that same side. • Often causes affected limbs to be shorter and thinner. • May cause scoliosis. • Delays the ability to walk in children. Children may walk on tips of toes because of tight heel tendons. • May cause seizures. • Will delay speech, but intelligence is usually normal.
Diplegia/diparesis	• Predominantly causes muscle stiffness in the legs. The child's hands may also be clumsy. • Causes deep tendon reflexes to become hyperactive. • Causes toes to point up. Tightness in certain leg muscles makes the legs move like the arms of a scissor (scissor walking). • Does not interfere with the child's intelligence or language skills.
Quadriplegia/quadriparesis	• Is the most severe form of CP and is often associated with moderate-to-severe mental retardation due to widespread brain damage or significant brain malformations. • Causes severe limb stiffness with a floppy neck. • Causes seizures. The child may be unable to walk. • Will interfere with the child's ability to speak. The child is often hard to understand.
Dyskinetic/athetoid • Causes involuntary abnormal movements. • Causes slow and uncontrollable writhing movements of the hands, feet, arms, and/or legs. • Hyperactive facial muscles cause the child to frown and possibly to drool. • May impair speech.	
Ataxic • Will affect the child's balance and depth perception, causing poor coordination and unsteady, wide-based gait. • Will cause the child to experience difficulty with quick or precise movements (e.g., writing, buttoning a shirt).	

Δ Evaluate need for hearing and speech evaluation.

Δ Assess the child's body image and level of self-esteem.

Δ Determine extent of family coping and support.

Δ Assess family awareness of available resources.

Diagnostic Procedures and Nursing Interventions

Δ CT scan is used to evaluate brain areas that are underdeveloped, cysts, and/or other physical problems. Sedation may be necessary.

Δ MRI is used to evaluate structures or abnormal areas located near bone. Sedation may be necessary.

Δ A cranial ultrasound may be needed. Explain the procedure to the child's parents and encourage them to go to radiology with the child if appropriate.

Δ Screen the child for metabolic defects.

NANDA Nursing Diagnoses

Δ Risk for aspiration

Δ Disturbed body image

Δ Caregiver role strain

Δ Risk for delayed development

Δ Risk for infection

Δ Risk for injury (falls, seizures)

Δ Imbalanced nutrition: less than body requirements

Δ Impaired physical mobility

Δ Risk for impaired skin integrity

Δ Impaired swallowing

Nursing Interventions

Δ Determine and approach the child at appropriate developmental level.

Δ Communicate with the child directly but include parents as needed.

Δ Include the family in physical care of the hospitalized child with cerebral palsy.

• Ask the family about routine care and encourage them to provide if appropriate.

- Encourage the family to help verify the child's needs if communication is impaired.

Δ Maintain an open airway by elevating the head of the child's bed (especially important if the child has increased oral secretions).

Δ Ensure adequate nutrition.

- Determine the child's ability to take oral nutrition.

- Provide foods that are similar to food eaten at home when possible.

- Ascertain correct positioning for feeding the child, using head positioning and manual jaw control methods as needed.

- Administer feedings through gastric tubes if ordered.

- Maintain weight/height chart.

- Assess for the possibility of aspiration for children who are severely disabled.

Δ Maintain skin integrity by turning the child to keep pressure off bony prominences.

Δ Keep skin clean and dry.

Δ Work with physical therapist to promote decreased spasticity of muscles in children with spastic CP.

Δ Promote independence with self-care activities as much as possible.

Δ Administer medications as prescribed.

- Medications for muscle spasm, such as baclofen (Lioresal)

- Anti-seizure medications used by about 40% of children with spastic CP (carbamazepine [Tegretol], valproic acid [Depakote], phenytoin [Dilantin])

Δ Coordinate care with other professionals, such as speech therapists, physical and recreational therapists, education specialists, and/or medical specialists.

Δ Work to increase self-esteem and body image through capitalizing on the child's abilities and by helping others accept the child for his strengths and assets.

Δ Help the child to use electronic devices for speech and other types of communication.

Δ   Educate and reinforce home care for the child.

- Feeding schedule and techniques if changed since hospitalization
- Medication administration
- Developmental stimulation
- Wound care if needed

Δ   Help the family identify resources needed, such as respite care.

Δ   Connect the family with area support groups for CP.

Therapeutic Procedures and Nursing Interventions

Δ   Surgical intervention may be needed for tendon release to correct contractures or other spastic deformities.

Δ   The insertion of feeding tubes may be necessary.

- Prepare the child/family for the procedure. This includes explaining the procedure and anticipated postoperative care.

Complications and Nursing Implications

Δ   Aspiration of Oral Secretions

- Keep the child's head elevated.
- Keep suction available if copious oral secretions are present or the child has difficulty with swallowing food and/or fluids.

Δ   Risk for injury related to disability

- Make sure the child's bed rails are raised to prevent falls from bed.
- Pad side rails and wheelchair arms to prevent injury.
- Secure the child in mobility devices such as wheelchairs.
- Encourage the child to receive adequate rest to prevent injury at times of fatigue.
- Encourage the use of helmets, seat belts, and other safety equipment.

Primary Reference:

Hockenberry, M., Wilson, D., & Winkelstein, M. (2005). *Wong's essentials of pediatric nursing care.* (7th ed.). St. Louis, MO: Mosby.

Additional Resources:

For information about cerebral palsy, go to the United Cerebral Palsy (UCP) Web site, *www.ucp.org.*

National Institute of Neurological Disorders and Stroke. (2007, February, 14). *NINDS spasticity information page.* Retrieved February 15, 2007, from http://www.ninds.nih.gov/disorders/spasticity/spasticity.htm

NANDA International (2004). *NANDA nursing diagnoses: Definitions and classification 2005-2006.* Philadelphia: NANDA.

Chapter 45: Cerebral Palsy

Application Exercises

Scenario: A 3-year-old child diagnosed with spastic quadriplegia due to cerebral palsy is admitted to the pediatric acute care facility with pneumonia. This is the child's third bout of pneumonia in the past year. The child uses a wheelchair and has involuntary movements of both arms and spasms of both legs when passive range of motion is attempted. He makes unintelligible attempts at speech, although his parents can understand some of what he's trying to communicate. His tongue moves continually within his mouth and it takes about 1 hr to feed him. Weight charts show him at the fifth percentile for weight in his age group.

1. What is the probable cause of this child's recurrent pneumonia?

2. List three high priority nursing diagnoses for this child.

3. The child has a gastrostomy tube in place for feedings during his hospitalization. He is receiving bolus feedings of 60 mL over 20 min every 2 hr during the day. How should the nurse manage these feedings to be sure the stomach is emptying well and the child is not at risk to aspirate excess feeding?

4. List at least two safety precautions that should be taken with this child to prevent injury while he is hospitalized. Give a rationale for each precaution.

5. Lack of which of the following is a warning sign of cerebral palsy in a 3-month-old infant?

    A. Crawling

    B. Sitting up without assistance

    C. Holding head upright

    D. Babbling simple words

6. Match the type of cerebral palsy with its correct description.

_____ Hemiplegia/hemiparesis

_____ Diplegia/diparesis

_____ Quadriplegia/quadriparesis

_____ Dyskinetic/athetoid

_____ Ataxic

A. Will cause the child to experience difficulty with quick or precise movements (e.g., writing, buttoning a shirt)

B. Causes slow and uncontrollable writhing movements of the hands, feet, arms, and/or legs

C. Delays the ability to walk in children (may walk on tips of toes because of tight heel tendons)

D. Tightness in certain leg muscles makes the legs move like the arms of a scissor (scissor walking)

E. Will interfere with the child's ability to speak (child often hard to understand)

Chapter 45: Cerebral Palsy

Application Exercises Answer Key

Scenario: A 3-year-old child diagnosed with spastic quadriplegia due to cerebral palsy is admitted to the pediatric acute care facility with pneumonia. This is the child's third bout of pneumonia in the past year. The child uses a wheelchair and has involuntary movements of both arms and spasms of both legs when passive range of motion is attempted. He makes unintelligible attempts at speech, although his parents can understand some of what he's trying to communicate. His tongue moves continually within his mouth and it takes about 1 hr to feed him. Weight charts show him at the fifth percentile for weight in his age group.

1. What is the probable cause of this child's recurrent pneumonia?

   From the assessment data it seems that aspiration pneumonia is the likely cause. The child's tongue moves continually, which makes chewing and swallowing difficult. It takes a long time to feed him, and he is in a low weight percentile for his age.

2. List three high priority nursing diagnoses for this child.

   Any of the following could be considered high priority at this time. However, the first four are especially important.

   Risk for aspiration

   Risk for infection

   Impaired swallowing

   Imbalanced nutrition: less than body requirements

   Risk for delayed development

   Impaired physical mobility

3. The child has a gastrostomy tube in place for feedings during his hospitalization. He is receiving bolus feedings of 60 mL over 20 min every 2 hr during the day. How should the nurse manage these feedings to be sure the stomach is emptying well and the child is not at risk to aspirate excess feeding?

Aspirate and measure stomach contents before feeding to ascertain the amount left in the stomach. If residuals are more than the amount set by the primary care provider or nutritionist, based on the size of the child, do not continue feeding. Refeed stomach contents aspirated per facility protocol. Elevate the head of the child's bed at least 30° to prevent movement of feeding up through the esophagus and into the airway. Check weight daily to see how the child is progressing.

4. List at least two safety precautions that should be taken with this child to prevent injury while he is hospitalized. Give a rationale for each precaution.

Pad side rails, wheelchair rails, and other hard objects that the child could hit and be injured by due to involuntary movements of arms.

Position the child carefully and reposition frequently to prevent pressure ulcers on skin due to the child being unable to make purposeful movements. Check the child frequently to assure he is safe in a bed or wheelchair.

5. Lack of which of the following is a warning sign of cerebral palsy in a 3-month-old infant?

    A. Crawling

    B. Sitting up without assistance

    C. Holding head upright

    D. Babbling simple words

Head control is a physical task that a 3-month-old child should have mastered, and lack of mastery may mean that cerebral palsy is present. The infant will not yet be able to perform the other tasks mentioned here because all of them occur later in infancy.

6. Match the type of cerebral palsy with its correct description.

C Hemiplegia/hemiparesis

D Diplegia/diparesis

E Quadriplegia/quadriparesis

B Dyskinetic/athetoid

A Ataxic

A. Will cause the child to experience difficulty with quick or precise movements (e.g., writing, buttoning a shirt)

B. Causes slow and uncontrollable writhing movements of the hands, feet, arms, and/or legs

C. Delays the ability to walk in children (may walk on tips of toes because of tight heel tendons)

D. Tightness in certain leg muscles makes the legs move like the arms of a scissor (scissor walking)

E. Will interfere with the child's ability to speak (child often hard to understand)

Unit 2   Nursing Care of Children with System Disorders

Section: Nursing Care of Children with Neurosensory Disorders

Chapter 46:   Spina Bifida

                Contributor: Michele Hinds, PhD, RN

 NCLEX-RN® Connections:

Learning Objective: Review and apply knowledge within "**Spina Bifida**" in readiness for performance of the following nursing activities as outlined by the NCLEX-RN® test plan:

Δ   Assist with relevant laboratory, diagnostic, and therapeutic procedures within the nursing role, including:

•   Client preparation for the procedure.

•   Client teaching (before and following the procedure).

•   Accurate collection of specimens.

•   Evaluation of the child's response to the procedure.

•   Planning and implementing body system-specific interventions as appropriate.

•   Monitoring and taking actions to prevent or minimize the risk of complications.

•   Accurate interpretation of procedure results.

Δ   Perform and document appropriate assessments based on the child's problem.

Δ   Apply knowledge of pathophysiology to planning care for clients with specific alterations in body systems, including recognizing associated signs and symptoms.

Δ   Interpret data that need to be reported immediately.

Δ   Monitor therapeutic devices (drainage/irrigating devices, chest tubes), if inserted, for proper functioning.

Δ   Explore resources, make referrals, collaborate with interdisciplinary team, and ensure continuity of client care.

Δ   Evaluate plans of care for multiple clients and revise plan as needed based on priorities of care and promotion of recovery.

Δ   Provide the child/family teaching regarding management of the child's health problem.

Δ   Recognize/respond to emergency situations, and evaluate/document the client's response to emergency interventions.

📖 Key Points

Δ   In spina bifida, a neural tube defect presents at birth, affecting the CNS and osseous spine.

Δ   The term spina bifida is usually used to refer to myelomeningocele, a visible defect in the spine with a saclike protrusion at any level of the spinal column at the midline of the back.

   •   The sac contains meninges, spinal fluid, and nerves.

Δ   The degree of neurologic dysfunction is determined by the level of sac protrusion and tissue involved.

Δ   Other, less severe spinal defects may occur and are usually not symptomatic because nerves are not displaced and nerve damage does not occur.

   •   In spina bifida occulta there is a defect in the bony spine invisible to the eye with no manifestations or problems.

   •   In meningocele the spinal defect and the sac-like protrusion are present, but only spinal fluid and meninges are present in the sac. After the sac is repaired, no further symptoms are usually seen since spinal nerves are not damaged.

Δ   Depending on level of spinal injury, the child may use a wheelchair due to paralysis or may have decreased sensation of extremities.

Δ   All children with myelomeningocele have bowel and bladder incontinence problems. This is expected and is due to decreased enervation in the sacral area of the cord, which is responsible for bowel and bladder function.

Δ   Hydrocephalus (increased intracranial pressure caused by inability of cerebral spinal fluid [CSF] to drain from the cranium normally) is found in many children with myelomeningocele.

   •   Hydrocephalus is related to a malformation of the brain called Chiari's malformation. This malformation pulls the brain stem downward toward the spinal column.

   •   In about ⅓ of children, shunt placement is needed to prevent symptoms of hydrocephalus.

   •   Chiari's malformation may also cause breathing and feeding difficulties in infants and balance/coordination problems and arm spasms in older children.

Key Factors

Δ   Neural tube defect is caused by the failure of the neural tube to close in the first 3 to 5 weeks of gestation.

Δ   Neural tube defect has been linked to insufficient folic acid in the maternal diet.

- Up to 70% of cases of spina bifida are thought to be preventable if women of childbearing age take 400 mcg of folic acid daily before becoming pregnant.

Δ The other 30% of cases of spina bifida have an unknown etiology, but are thought to be caused by some combination of genetics and environmental causes.

Assessment

Δ Assess prenatal and family history of neural tube defects.

Δ Physical assessment includes:

- Inspecting the sac at birth to determine whether it is intact.

- Inspecting the lumbosacral area for dimpling. This may indicate spina bifida occulta.

- Noting the infant's ability to move extremities and other mobility impairments. Impairments will present depending on level of spinal injury – from complete paralysis to slightly decreased sensation in lower extremities.

- Assessing for an increase in head circumference, which may increase rapidly with hydrocephalus until normal cranial growth is reached.

- Assessing for headache and orthopedic pain using an appropriate assessment tool.

- Assessing skin integrity for pressure sores caused by decreased sensation in the affected trunk and extremities.

- Identifying allergies. Specifically assess for latex allergy. (Latex allergy may occur in up to 80% of children.)

- Assessing cognitive development. This may be permanently delayed in some children.

- Assessing bladder/bowel functioning in preschool children. Functioning is permanently affected in all children with spina bifida.

- Monitoring for manifestations of infection, including elevation of body temperature, nausea, vomiting, and fatigue.

- Assessing for self-esteem and body image disturbances, which arise due to bowel and bladder incontinence, use of mobility aids, inability to keep up with peers, and other physical and social problems.

Δ Assess family knowledge and available resources.

Δ Assess family coping and support.

Diagnostic Procedures

Δ   Maternal serum can be tested for serum alpha-fetoprotein levels between 15 and 20 weeks gestation. Elevated levels will require further testing, such as an amniocentesis.

Δ   An amniocentesis is performed to test amniotic fluid for levels of alpha-fetoprotein. Elevated levels may indicate neural tube defects.

Δ   MRI, ultrasound, CT, and myelography may be used to determine brain and spinal cord involvement.

Δ   Laboratory studies may be used to determine causative pathogens for meningitis or UTI.

NANDA Nursing Diagnoses

Δ   Disturbed body image

Δ   Bowel incontinence

Δ   Caregiver role strain

Δ   Risk for infection

Δ   Risk for latex allergy response

Δ   Imbalanced nutrition: more than body requirements

Δ   Impaired physical mobility

Δ   Toileting self-care deficit

Δ   Impaired skin integrity

Δ   Impaired urinary elimination

Δ   Reflex urinary incontinence

Nursing Interventions

Δ   Monitor head circumference for signs of increasing intracranial pressure or shunt failure.

Δ   Monitor for elevations in body temperature.

Δ   Use an appropriate pain assessment tool.

Δ   Use nonlatex gloves, catheters, and other equipment to decrease the risk of latex allergy.

Δ   Promote skin integrity.

- Keep skin clean and dry.

- Keep pressure off bony prominences.

- Reposition the child hourly.

Δ Provide range of motion to legs. This may be passive or active depending on disability.

Δ Work with child/family on bladder control measures.

- Teach clean, intermittent self-catheterization when the child reaches school age.

- Work with the family on other strategies for acceptable bladder care, such as incontinence supplies and condom catheters.

- Note color, clarity, odor, and amount of urine. Monitor for UTI.

Δ Monitor bowel function for constipation and incontinence.

- Avoid rectal temperatures due to irritation of rectal sphincter.

- Administer laxatives or enemas to assist bowel function as ordered.

Δ Teach principles of nutrition and work with the family to prevent obesity.

Therapeutic Procedures and Nursing Interventions

Δ Elective cesarean birth may reduce motor dysfunction caused by myelomeningocele.

Δ Early surgical closure of an open myelomeningocele sac prevents injury and infection.

- The exposed sac should be covered with a sterile, moist (NS), nonadherent dressing until surgery.

- The sac should be protected from injury by placing the neonate in a prone position until surgery.

Δ If hydrocephalus develops, a surgical shunt should be inserted.

- Postoperatively, measure the infant's head circumference and abdominal girth.

- Observe for signs of increased intracranial pressure (e.g., high-pitched cry, bulging fontanels, vomiting, irritability).

Δ Other surgical procedures performed for children with spina bifida as they grow from infancy include:

- Bladder surgery, which is done to manage bladder dysfunction (either spasms or flaccidity) that occurs with practically all infants who had spina bifida.

- Various orthopedic surgeries to correct such problems as clubfoot, scoliosis, and other malformations of the feet and legs.

Δ   Recurring neurosurgery to replace shunts that have failed due to infection or blockages.

Complications and Nursing Implications

Δ   Infection

- Assess for fever, headache, nausea and vomiting, fatigue, and/or lethargy.

- Obtain blood and urine cultures as ordered.

- Administer ordered antibiotics.

Δ   Skin ulceration

- Monitor skin for redness and breakdown.

- Reposition frequently to prevent pressure on bony prominences.

- Teach the child/family to monitor skin integrity.

Δ   Increased Intracranial Pressure

- Signs and symptoms include:

    ◊ Infancy – high-pitched cry, lethargy, vomiting, bulging fontanels, and/or widening cranial suture lines.

    ◊ Childhood – headache, lethargy, nausea, vomiting, decreased school performance of learned tasks, decreased level of consciousness, seizures, and/or increased blood pressure with widened pulse pressure and bradycardia (signs of Cushing's reflex).

- Interventions to prevent an increase in intracranial pressure include:

    ◊ Using gentle movements when performing range-of-motion exercises.

    ◊ Minimizing environmental stressors (e.g., noise, frequent visitors).

    ◊ Appropriately controlling pain.

Primary Reference:

Hockenberry, M., Wilson, D., & Winkelstein, M. (2005). *Wong's essentials of pediatric nursing care*. (7th ed.). St. Louis, MO: Mosby.

Additional Resources:

Hydrocephalus Association. (2002). *Hydrocephalus in infants and children*. Retrieved February 13, 2007, from http://www.hydroassoc.org/information/infant.html

NANDA International (2004). *NANDA nursing diagnoses: Definitions and classification 2005-2006*. Philadelphia: NANDA.

Spina Bifida Association. (2006). *Frequently asked questions about spina bifida*. Retrieved February 13, 2007, from http://www.sbaa.org/site/c.gpILKXOEJqG/b.2021103/k.87E7/FAQ_about_SB.htm

Spina Bifida Association. (2006). *Prevention*. Retrieved February 13, 2007, from http://www.sbaa.org/site/c.gpILKXOEJqG/b.2021051/k.3037/Prevention.htm

The Nemours Foundation. (2005, July). *Prenatal tests*. Retrieved February 28, 2007, from http://kidshealth.org/parent/system/medical/prenatal_tests.html

Chapter 46: Spina Bifida

Application Exercises

1. A woman who is pregnant is undergoing an amniocentesis. During the test, elevated levels of AFP are found. What further diagnostic tests will be performed?

2. An infant is born with a myelomeningocele at the high lumbar level. What nursing assessments and interventions should the nurse prepare for after the child is born and before the infant's initial surgery to repair the defect?

3. A 6-year-old child with spina bifida (myelomeningocele) is not yet toilet trained for either bowel or bladder. Nursing interventions for this child are based on the knowledge that the child with spina bifida

   A. has intellectual delays that may delay the ability to toilet train her.
   B. cannot be toilet trained because she is in a wheelchair and has difficulty using the toilet.
   C. has decreased enervation to bowel and bladder and requires special strategies to manage bowel and bladder function.
   D. has difficulty with toilet training due to the inability to coordinate the use of her arms and legs.

4. True or False: A child with spina bifida should be instructed in intermittent bladder catheterization using a clean latex catheter.

5. True or False: A priority nursing diagnosis for a child who sits in a wheelchair all day is risk for impaired skin integrity.

6. A school-age child with spina bifida has a shunt in place for hydrocephalus. Which of the following signs and symptoms are manifestations of increased intracranial pressure? (Select all that apply.)

   _____ Fever
   _____ Hypotension
   _____ Headache
   _____ Lethargy
   _____ Bulging anterior fontanel
   _____ Seizures
   _____ Change in school performance

Chapter 46: Spina Bifida

Application Exercises Answer Key

1. A woman who is pregnant is undergoing an amniocentesis. During the test, elevated levels of AFP are found. What further diagnostic tests will be performed?

   If alpha-fetoprotein levels are elevated in amniotic fluid, the primary care provider will order an MRI, CT scan, radiograph, or other test to determine what type of neural tube defect the fetus might have.

2. An infant is born with a myelomeningocele at the high lumbar level. What nursing assessments and interventions should the nurse prepare for after the child is born and before the infant's initial surgery to repair the defect?

   Protect the sac over the infant's spinal cord with a clear sterile dressing and avoid pressure to the area. Place the infant in prone position until surgery is performed. Observe for signs of hydrocephalus by monitoring for bulging fontanels and measuring serial head circumference. Monitor the infant's skin integrity and prevent pressure sores, observe the infant's ability to move extremities, and take the infant's temperature (may indicate infection).

3. A 6-year-old child with spina bifida (myelomeningocele) is not yet toilet trained for either bowel or bladder. Nursing interventions for this child are based on the knowledge that the child with spina bifida

   A. has intellectual delays that may delay the ability to toilet train her.

   B. cannot be toilet trained because she is in a wheelchair and has difficulty using the toilet.

   C. has decreased enervation to bowel and bladder and requires special strategies to manage bowel and bladder function.

   D. has difficulty with toilet training due to the inability to coordinate the use of her arms and legs.

   Decreased enervation, caused by damage to the spinal cord above the area that affects bowel and bladder control (lower sacral area), is present in all children with spina bifida. The child will require special strategies to manage bowel and bladder control. Intellectual delays occur in some children with spina bifida, but these are not the cause of toilet training problems. Being in a wheelchair or having coordination problems are not the cause of the child's bowel and bladder difficulties.

4. True or False: A child with spina bifida should be instructed in intermittent bladder catheterization using a clean latex catheter.

False. Although the child may learn to catheterize himself intermittently, it is important to use a nonlatex catheter due to the child's potential risk for latex allergy.

5. True or False: A priority nursing diagnosis for a child who sits in a wheelchair all day is risk for impaired skin integrity.

True. Due to decreased sensation, the child with paralysis who sits in a wheelchair is at very high risk for pressure ulcers.

6. A school-age child with spina bifida has a shunt in place for hydrocephalus. Which of the following signs and symptoms are manifestations of increased intracranial pressure? (Select all that apply.)

    _____ Fever

    _____ Hypotension

    _X_ Headache

    _X_ Lethargy

    _____ Bulging anterior fontanel

    _X_ Seizures

    _X_ Change in school performance

Headache, lethargy, seizures, change in school performance or personality, and nausea/ vomiting are some of the manifestations of increased intracranial pressure (ICP). Body temperature changes are not a sign of increased ICP. Hypertension and widening pulse pressure may be signs of increased ICP, but hypotension is not. The anterior fontanel should be closed in children after 18 months.

Unit 2   **Nursing Care of Children with System Disorders**

Section: Nursing Care of Children with Neurosensory Disorders

Chapter 47:   **Seizures**

Contributor: Glenda J. Bondurant, MSN, RN

 NCLEX-RN® Connections:

> **Learning Objective**: Review and apply knowledge within "**Seizures**" in readiness for performance of the following nursing activities as outlined by the NCLEX-RN® test plan:
>
> Δ   Assist with relevant laboratory, diagnostic, and therapeutic procedures within the nursing role, including:
>
> • Client preparation for the procedure.
>
> • Client teaching (before and following the procedure).
>
> • Accurate collection of specimens.
>
> • Evaluation of the child's response to the procedure.
>
> • Planning and implementing body system-specific interventions as appropriate.
>
> • Monitoring and taking actions to prevent or minimize the risk of complications.
>
> • Accurate interpretation of procedure results.
>
> Δ   Perform and document appropriate assessments based on the child's problem.
>
> Δ   Apply knowledge of pathophysiology to planning care for clients with specific alterations in body systems, including recognizing associated signs and symptoms.
>
> Δ   Interpret data that need to be reported immediately.
>
> Δ   Monitor therapeutic devices (drainage/irrigating devices, chest tubes), if inserted, for proper functioning.
>
> Δ   Explore resources, make referrals, collaborate with interdisciplinary team, and ensure continuity of client care.
>
> Δ   Evaluate plans of care for multiple clients and revise plan as needed based on priorities of care and promotion of recovery.
>
> Δ   Provide the child/family teaching regarding management of the child's health problem.
>
> Δ   Recognize/respond to emergency situations, and evaluate/document the client's response to emergency interventions.

📖 **Key Points**

Δ A seizure is an episode of uncontrolled electrical discharges within the CNS. The seizure is initiated by the activity of a cluster of overly excitable neurons (a focus).

Δ This abnormal electrical discharge may cause disturbances in motor and sensory function, autonomic function of the viscera, level of consciousness, and behavior.

Δ A seizure disorder (epilepsy) is a chronic syndrome characterized by persistent but intermittent episodes of seizure activity.

Δ Seizures are classified as neurologic emergencies in all triage systems. Sustained untreated seizures can result in hypoxia, cardiac dysrhythmias, and lactic acidosis.

Key Factors

Δ A genetic predisposition may attribute to the development of epilepsy.

Δ Epilepsy can be idiopathic (no known cause) or secondary to another condition, which may include:

- Acute febrile state (most common between 6 months and 3 years).

    ◊ Temperature is usually above 38.8° C (101.8° F), and usually seizures usually occur during the rise in temperature.

- Head trauma.

- Cerebral edema.

- Abrupt cessation of antiepileptic medications (AEDs).

- Infection.

- Metabolic disorder (e.g., hypoglycemia).

- Exposure to toxins.

- Brain tumor.

- Hypoxia.

- Acute drug and alcohol withdrawal.

- Fluid and electrolyte imbalances.

Δ Triggering factors may include:

- Increased physical activity.

- Stress.

- Fatigue.

- Alcohol.

- Caffeine.

- Some chemicals

Assessment

Δ   Obtaining an assessment of a child with a seizure disorder includes information gathered from the child, family members, and health care providers. It is important to have information about the child before, during, and after the seizure.

Δ   History questions should include:

- Onset, duration, and frequency of seizure activity.

- Exposure to medications or poisons prior to the seizure.

- Reports of not feeling well or feeling "odd" just before the seizure.

- Reports of headache, nausea, and/or muscle pain.

- Occurrence of vomiting, fever, and incontinence of stool and/or urine.

- Description of any abnormal sensations experienced before, during, or after the seizure.

- Recall of the seizure.

Δ   Objective Findings to Assess

Seizure Phase	Postictal Phase

• Description of seizure activity to include onset, duration, and preseizure behavior
• Description of motor activity to include type of motor activity present (e.g., tonic-clonic movements, automatisms), location of movement, change of location, unilateral or bilateral, and whether or not the child fell
• Skin – may be pale, flushed, and/or cyanotic
• Level of consciousness – change or loss
• Eyes – dilation or constriction of pupils or deviation of eyes to one side
• Respiratory effort – any apnea, dyspnea, or foaming/frothing at the mouth
• Bowel or bladder incontinence
	• How long the phase lasts (may last up to several hours)
	• Level of consciousness:
	  ◊ When does the child regain consciousness?
	  ◊ Is the child hard to awaken and keep semiconscious for a period of time?
	  ◊ Does the child sleep for several hours after an episode, but is conscious when awakened?
	• Motor function – Gross motor movement may be uncoordinated with difficulty with fine motor control.
	• Speech may be slow, slurred.
	• Vision – The child may have difficulties focusing.
	• Orientation – The child may be confused for several hours.
	• Note any injury such as bruises, lacerations, and/or scrapes.

Δ   Classification of Seizures and the Associated Specific Manifestations

Seizure Classification	Manifestations
Febrile seizures	Generalized body response lasting less than 5 min
Partial (focal) seizures – simple	• No loss of consciousness • Isolated loss of motor control • Autonomic response: sweating, vomiting, and flushing • Sensory response: paresthesia and hearing/vision alteration • Sense of anxiety/fear
Partial (focal) seizures – complex	• Impaired consciousness with amnesia • Staring • Lip smacking or chewing
Generalized – absence (formerly petit mal)	• Loss of consciousness for very short time, usually 5 to 10 sec or less than a min • Staring, lip smacking or chewing, eye fluttering • Abrupt start and stop (no aura) • Typical report of daydreaming • May occur several times a day
Generalized – tonic-clonic (formerly grand mal)	• Usually proceeded by aura • Tonic phase: rigidity of muscles, apnea/cyanosis, incontinence, and pupils fixed and dilated • Clonic phase: alternating contraction and relaxation, hyperventilation with relaxation, rigidity with contraction, and drooling • Lasts no longer than 1 to 2 min • Postictal phase – may last several hours; the child may have no memory of events preceding seizure and actual seizure event
Status epilepticus	• Generalized seizure lasting for more than 10 min • A series of seizures that occur over a 20- to 30-min period • Requires emergency management and can be life-threatening

Δ   Determine family understanding of seizure management.

Δ   Assess family support and coping.

Diagnostic Procedures and Nursing Interventions

Δ   Electroencephalogram (EEG) records electrical activity and identifies the origin of seizure activity. Client instruction includes:

- **Abstaining from caffeine** for 8 hr prior to the test.

- Washing hair before (no oils, sprays) and after the procedure (to remove electrode glue).

- Asking the child to lie still on the examining table.

- Asking the child to look at flashes of a strobe light.

- Withholding sleep prior to test and possibly inducing it during test.

Δ   Various laboratory and diagnostic tests used to identify or rule out potential causes of seizures include:

- Magnetic resonance imaging (MRI), computed tomography (CT) scan/computed axial tomography (CAT) scan, positron emission tomography (PET) scan, and skull x-ray.

- Serum electrolytes and blood glucose level.

- Toxicology screening of blood and urine.

- Lumbar puncture for cerebrospinal fluid analysis (performed by a primary care provider, usually a physician).

  ◊   Have the child empty his bladder.

  ◊   Place the child in the fetal position and assist in maintaining position. May need to use distraction.

  ◊   Sedate the child if necessary with fentanyl (Sublimaze) and midazolam (Versed).

  ◊   Clean the child's skin prior to injection of a local anesthetic. If time allows, apply a eutectic mixture of local anesthetics (EMLA [lidocaine/prilocaine]) over the area between L3 and L5 60 min prior to the procedure.

  ◊   Insert the needle into the subarachnoid space.

  ◊   Pressure readings are taken but may be difficult to obtain if the child is crying.

  ◊   Collect three to five test tubes of CSF.

  ◊   Remove the needle, apply pressure, and cover the injection site with a dressing.

  ◊   Appropriately label specimens and deliver them to the laboratory.

Δ   Therapeutic medication levels are measured to evaluate the effectiveness of pharmacological management of seizures.

NANDA Nursing Diagnoses

Δ   Ineffective airway clearance

Δ   Ineffective coping

Δ   Risk for injury

Δ   Readiness for enhanced knowledge

Δ   Social isolation

Δ   Ineffective tissue perfusion

Nursing Interventions

Δ   Maintain a quiet environment.

Δ   Implement precautionary measures.

- Assess and monitor vital signs and oxygen saturation.

- Establish IV access.

- Treat elevated temperature with prescribed antipyretics.

Δ   Provide a safe environment prior to a seizure.

- Pad side rails on admission.

- Set bed in lowest position.

- Remove sharp/harmful objects.

- Have oxygen, airway, and suctioning equipment on standby.

Δ   Maintain patent airway during a seizure.

- Loosen tight clothing.

- Turn the child to side-lying position to prevent aspiration.

- Do not insert objects into the mouth.

Δ   Provide for safety during the seizure.

- Keep padded side rails in up position.

- Assist the child to the floor if standing when seizure starts.

- Do not restrain the child.

- Do not insert objects into the child's mouth, attempt to hold his tongue, and/or open his jaw (may damage teeth, lips, and tongue).

- Refrain from giving liquids during or just after a seizure.

Δ Management during the postictal phase includes:

- Assessing and monitoring vital signs and performing neurological checks.

- Allowing the child to rest/sleep, preferably in a side-lying position.

- Performing suctioning and administering oxygen if indicated.

- Reorienting and calming the child, who may be agitated.

- Maintaining seizure precautions.

- Documentation should include:

  ◊ Precipitating factors.

  ◊ Onset and duration.

  ◊ Type of muscular activity during the seizure(s).

  ◊ Injury.

  ◊ Postictal assessment.

Δ Pharmacological management includes:

- Diazepam (Valium) (may be given rectally) or lorazepam (Ativan) may be given during seizure activity.

- Oral medications for long-term management include:

  ◊ Phenytoin (Dilantin), carbamazepine (Tegretol), valproic acid (Depakene), gabapentin (Neurontin), and lamotrigine (Lamictal) for partial and/or generalized seizures.

  ◊ Ethosuximide (Zarontin) and valproic acid for absence seizures.

- Monitoring for therapeutic level with each medication.

Δ Provide the child/family education regarding seizure management. Instructions include:

- Stressing the importance of monitoring AED medication levels and maintaining therapeutic medication levels.

- Taking medications as prescribed. Do not decrease dosage or discontinue medication without primary care provider instructions.

- Wearing a Medic Alert bracelet or necklace at all times.

- Observing for potential side effects of medications (e.g., sedation, headaches, dizziness, nausea/vomiting, gingival hyperplasia, bleeding gums, photosensitivity).

- Avoiding precipitating factors if possible.

- Practicing good oral hygiene.

- Maintaining normal activities as much as possible.

Complications and Nursing Implications

Δ   Aspiration

- Turn the child to the side and suction as needed.

Δ   Status epilepticus

- Status epilepticus is a potential complication of all seizure disorders.

- Establish airway, provide oxygen, ensure IV access, perform ECG monitoring, and monitor ABG results.

- Administer diazepam (Valium) or lorazepam (Ativan) as prescribed along with a loading dose followed by a continuous infusion of phenytoin (Dilantin).

Primary Reference:

Hockenberry, M., Wilson, D., Winkelstein, M. (2005). *Wong's essentials of pediatric nursing care*. (7th ed.). St. Louis, MO: Mosby.

Additional Resources:

Ignatavicius, D. D., & Workman, M. L. (2006). *Medical-surgical nursing* (5th ed.). St. Louis, MO: Saunders.

NANDA International (2004). *NANDA nursing diagnoses: Definitions and classification 2005-2006*. Philadelphia: NANDA.

Chapter 47: Seizures

Application Exercises

Scenario: A 15-year-old adolescent is admitted to the hospital after a seizure. The adolescent, who is lethargic, has no previous history of seizures. The adolescent's father tells the nurse that he heard the adolescent grunting in her bedroom, and when he entered, the adolescent's arms and legs were thrashing around and she was blue. He tells the nurse that this lasted less than 1 min, and because the adolescent was difficult to arouse afterward, he called 911. The nurse obtains the adolescent's laboratory work, which reveals normal CBC and electrolytes and a serum glucose of 65 mg/dL. Urinalysis drug screen results are pending.

1. What should the nurse do to prepare the room for admission of this child?

2. The adolescent calls the nurse on the intercom and tells her she is having a strange feeling. The nurse then hears a grunting sound. When the nurse arrives in the adolescent's room, she notes the child having a tonic-clonic seizure. What should the nurse do next?

3. What should the nurse do when the adolescent's seizure stops?

4. The adolescent is discharged with a prescription for phenytoin (Dilantin). Which of the following statements by the father indicates that discharge teaching has been effective?

    A. "I need to administer her medicine in the morning and evening."
    B. "I will keep the annual appointment for follow-up on her medication."
    C. "I will be sure to encourage good oral care and regular dental visits."
    D. "I can allow her to stop taking the medication after 6 weeks, as long there are no seizures."

5. A single seizure lasting at least 10 min or a series of seizures lasting 20 to 30 min is called _____.

6. Match each type of seizure below with its definition.

_____ Tonic-clonic

_____ Absence seizure

_____ Febrile seizure

_____ Complex partial seizure

A. Occurs with temperatures greater than 38.8° C (101.8° F)

B. Generalized movement of all extremities

C. Decreased consciousness with staring, lip smacking, and chewing during the seizure

D. 5- to 10-sec loss of consciousness that looks like daydreaming

Chapter 47: Seizures

Application Exercises Answer Key

Scenario: A 15-year-old adolescent is admitted to the hospital after a seizure. The adolescent, who is lethargic, has no previous history of seizures. The adolescent's father tells the nurse that he heard the adolescent grunting in her bedroom, and when he entered, the adolescent's arms and legs were thrashing around and she was blue. He tells the nurse that this lasted less than 1 min, and because the adolescent was difficult to arouse afterward, he called 911. The nurse obtains the adolescent's laboratory work, which reveals normal CBC and electrolytes and a serum glucose of 65 mg/dL. Urinalysis drug screen results are pending.

1. What should the nurse do to prepare the room for admission of this child?

   Place the bed in a low position, pad the side rails, place suction in the room, and have oxygen ready. The child should be admitted to the first available room that is closest to the nurses' station.

2. The adolescent calls the nurse on the intercom and tells her she is having a strange feeling. The nurse then hears a grunting sound. When the nurse arrives in the adolescent's room, she notes the child having a tonic-clonic seizure. What should the nurse do next?

   The nurse should time the seizure, assess what parts of the adolescent's body are moving, assess the adolescent's respiratory effort and color changes, ensure the bed is in low position, move all items away from the child, and turn on the suction and oxygen. If the adolescent has IV access, administer AEDs as prescribed.

3. What should the nurse do when the adolescent's seizure stops?

   Note the time, assess airway, suction as needed, position her on her side, assess for respiratory effort, apply oxygen, obtain vital signs, assess for any other injuries, stay with the adolescent to provide reassurance, ensure the primary care provider is notified, and administer medications as prescribed.

4. The adolescent is discharged with a prescription for phenytoin (Dilantin). Which of the following statements by the father indicates that discharge teaching has been effective?

    A. "I need to administer her medicine in the morning and evening."

    B. "I will keep the annual appointment for follow-up on her medication."

    C. "I will be sure to encourage good oral care and regular dental visits."

    D. "I can allow her to stop taking the medication after 6 weeks, as long there are no seizures."

Phenytoin can lead to gingival problems; therefore, good oral care and regular dental visits are important. The next appointment with the primary care provider will most likely be within a few weeks. Medications need to be given at specific times and should not be stopped for any reason.

5. A single seizure lasting at least 10 min or a series of seizures lasting 20 to 30 min is called

_____.

Status epilepticus

6. Match each type of seizure below with its definition.

B	Tonic-clonic	A. Occurs with temperatures greater than 38.8° C (101.8° F)
D	Absence seizure	B. Generalized movement of all extremities
A	Febrile seizure	C. Decreased consciousness with staring, lip smacking, and chewing during the seizure
C	Complex partial seizure	D. 5- to 10-sec loss of consciousness that looks like daydreaming

Unit 2   Nursing Care of Children with System Disorders
Section: Nursing Care of Children with Neurosensory Disorders

Chapter 48:   Head Injury
Contributor: Glenda J. Bondurant, MSN, RN

 NCLEX-RN® Connections:

> **Learning Objective**: Review and apply knowledge within "**Head Injury**" in readiness for performance of the following nursing activities as outlined by the NCLEX-RN® test plan:
>
> Δ   Assist with relevant laboratory, diagnostic, and therapeutic procedures within the nursing role, including:
>
> - Client preparation for the procedure.
>
> - Client teaching (before and following the procedure).
>
> - Accurate collection of specimens.
>
> - Evaluation of the child's response to the procedure.
>
> - Planning and implementing body system-specific interventions as appropriate.
>
> - Monitoring and taking actions to prevent or minimize the risk of complications.
>
> - Accurate interpretation of procedure results.
>
> Δ   Perform and document appropriate assessments based on the child's problem.
>
> Δ   Apply knowledge of pathophysiology to planning care for clients with specific alterations in body systems, including recognizing associated signs and symptoms.
>
> Δ   Interpret data that need to be reported immediately.
>
> Δ   Monitor therapeutic devices (drainage/irrigating devices, chest tubes), if inserted, for proper functioning.
>
> Δ   Explore resources, make referrals, collaborate with interdisciplinary team, and ensure continuity of client care.
>
> Δ   Evaluate plans of care for multiple clients and revise plan as needed based on priorities of care and promotion of recovery.
>
> Δ   Provide the child/family teaching regarding management of the child's health problem.
>
> Δ   Recognize/respond to emergency situations, and evaluate/document the client's response to emergency interventions.

📖 Key Points

Δ A head injury is one that causes pathologic damage to the scalp, skull, and/or brain as a result of a mechanical blow.

Δ Severity is related to location, depth, and physiological response of the brain to the injury.

Δ Types and Manifestations of Head Injury

Injury	Manifestations
Concussion	• Confusion to brief loss of consciousness after a mechanical blow to the head • Transient and reversible • Possible amnesia about injury
Closed injury	• Skin and skull integrity maintained after blow to head • Possible presence of damage to underlying tissue
Contusion	Bruise to brain tissue
Intracranial hematoma	• A blood clot within the skull can result in increased intracranial pressure. • Intracranial hematoma is usually a result of a skull fracture and venous and/or arterial tear. • Epidural hematoma occurs between the skull and the dura. • Subdural hematoma is bleeding between the dura and the brain.
Fractures	• Break in the skull • May cause tearing of the meninges • Linear fracture – lines of fracture reflecting the site, velocity of impact, and strength of bone • Depressed fractures – bone usually broken into pieces and pushed toward the brain • Compound fractures – skin laceration that is deep enough to see fractured bone • Basal skull fractures – hemorrhage around both eyes (raccoon eyes), nasal hemorrhage, and bruising of the neck under and posterior to ear (Battle's sign) • Diastatic fractures – cranial sutures separated with dural tear

Key Factors

Δ Head injuries in children are often caused by falls, motor vehicle injuries, or bicycle injuries.

Δ Risk Factors

• Lack of supervision

- Poor/absent safety practice

- Improper use of safety devices (e.g., helmets, seat belts)

Assessment

Δ   Obtain history of events leading up to the injury, reports of dizziness, headache, diplopia, and/or vomiting.

Δ   Physical Assessment

- Assess respiratory status noting rate, effort, breath sounds, and O_2 saturation.

- Assess level of consciousness including loss of consciousness. Changes in level of consciousness are the earliest indications of neurological deterioration.

- Assess site of injury for bleeding.

- Identify alcohol or drug use at time of injury (can mask increased ICP) for adolescents.

- Assess for amnesia (loss of memory) before or after injury.

- Observe for:

  ◊   Cerebrospinal fluid (CSF) leakage from the nose and ears (halo sign – yellow stain surrounded by blood, test positive for glucose).

  ◊   Changes in behavior – irritability, restlessness, agitation.

  ◊   Cushing reflex (severe hypertension with a widened pulse pressure and bradycardia) – late sign of increased ICP.

  ◊   Posturing

    °   Decorticate (dysfunction of the cerebral cortex) demonstrates the arms, wrists, and fingers flexed and bent inward onto the chest, and legs extended and adducted.

    °   Decerebrate (dysfunction at the midbrain) demonstrates a backward arching of the head, arms and legs rigidly extended, and toes pointing downward.

    °   Flaccidity demonstrates no muscle tone.

- Assess pupillary changes (PERRLA, pinpoint, fixed/nonresponsive, dilated).

- Assess for seizures.

- Assess for signs of infection (nuchal rigidity with meningitis).

- Perform Glasgow Coma Scale (GCS) rating (15 normal; 3 = deep coma) as part of complete neurological assessment.

Glasgow Coma Scale			
Eye Opening Response (E)	Verbal Response (V)	Motor Response (M)	
4 = Spontaneous	5 = Normal conversation	6 = Normal	
3 = To Voice	4 = Disoriented conversation	5 = Localizes to pain	
2 = To Pain	3 = Words, but not coherent	4 = Withdraws to pain	
1 = None	2 = No words, only sounds	3 = Decorticate posture	
	1 = None	2 = Decerebrate	
		1 = None	
E Score	V Score	M Score	E + V + M = Total Score

Diagnostic Procedures

Δ   ABGs are used to assess oxygen status.

Δ   CT/CAT scan(s) are used to assess the location (epidural, subdural) and extent of the head injury.

Δ   Intracranial pressure (ICP) monitoring

• Intraventricular, subarachnoid, epidural, and/or subdural

• Pose risk of infection

• Normal ICP level = 10 to 15 mm Hg

NANDA Nursing Diagnoses

Δ   Ineffective breathing pattern

Δ   Ineffective airway clearance

Δ   Disturbed body image

Δ   Risk for infection

Δ   Acute pain

Δ   Impaired skin integrity

Δ   Ineffective tissue perfusion

Nursing Interventions

Δ   Maintain a patent airway. Prepare for or provide mechanical ventilation as indicated. Keep suction and oxygen at bedside for emergency use.

Δ   Maintain stability of neck and spine until radiologic evidence indicates that neck and spine are not injured.

Δ   Elevate head of bed to 30° to avoid extreme flexion or extension. Maintain head in midline neutral position to reduce ICP and to promote venous drainage.

Δ   Frequently assess and report changes of (as frequently as every 15 min if indicated):

- Vital signs and pulse oximetry.
- Neurological status.
- Pupillary response.
- Motor activity.
- Verbal responses.
- Sensory perception.

Δ   Determine appropriate response to pain in a child with altered level of consciousness.

- Fentanyl (Sublimaze), midazolam (Versed), and vecuronium (Norcuron) may be administered by continuous IV infusion as paralyzing agents.
- Administer pain medications as prescribed. Morphine sulfate and codeine may be used, but careful monitoring of level of consciousness is required.

Δ   Monitor fluid and electrolyte values.

Δ   Insert indwelling urinary catheter and monitor I&O.

Δ   Provide adequate fluid to maintain cerebral perfusion.

Δ   Maintain fluid control to prevent further increase in ICP.

Δ   Provide nutritional support (enteral nutrition).

Δ   Administer mannitol (Osmitrol), an osmotic diuretic for cerebral edema, as prescribed.

Δ   Administer antiepileptic agents (may be prophylactically) as prescribed.

Δ   Implement seizure precautions.

Δ   Instruct the child to avoid coughing and blowing nose (increases ICP).

Δ   Report presence of CSF from nose or ears to the provider.

Δ   Provide a calm, restful environment (limit visitors, minimize noise).

Δ   Use energy conservation measures, and alternate activities with rest periods.

Δ   Implement measures to prevent complications of immobility (Turn every 2 hr, and use footboard and splints).

Δ   Involve the child/family in care as appropriate.

Δ   Observe the child/family interaction.

Δ   Encourage the child's independence during convalescence.

Δ   Report to appropriate agencies any inconsistencies between injury and child/family story of how injuries were sustained (possible abuse investigation).

Δ   Family Education

- Prepare the child/family for rehabilitation care when ordered.

- Educate the child/family about equipment and interventions.

- Encourage parent participation/involvement in child's level of comfort.

- Recommend support groups for the child/family.

- Provide for quiet times for child.

- Organize interdisciplinary meetings with the child/family to include:

  ◊ Mutual goal setting.

  ◊ Case management.

  ◊ Updating of plan of care.

  ◊ Financial/social support.

- Instruct parents to observe for change in the child's status if discharged home. Signs and symptoms to report include:

  ◊ Changes in level of consciousness, lethargy, and/or somnolence.

  ◊ Behavior changes, agitation, and/or confusion.

  ◊ Headache.

  ◊ Vomiting.

  ◊ Change in vision.

  ◊ Seizures.

  ◊ Change in mobility.

Therapeutic Procedures and Nursing Interventions

Δ   Surgical Intervention

- The child/family requires clear explanations regarding surgical intervention, especially if it is an emergency.

- Consent is needed for surgery.

- Postoperative care includes wound care and frequent neurological assessment.

Δ   Suturing of Scalp and Dural Lacerations

- Use of topical gels such as lidocaine, epinephrine, and tetracaine (LET) provide noninvasive anesthesia.

- The child may need to be restrained for suturing.

- The child may need sedation.

Complications and Nursing Implications

Δ   Brain Herniation – downward shift of brain tissue due to cerebral edema

- Signs include fixed dilated pupils, deteriorating level of consciousness, Cheyne-Stokes respirations (CSR), hemodynamic instability, and abnormal posturing.

- Elevate head of bed to 30°.

- Administer mannitol (Osmitrol) as prescribed.

- Provide mechanical ventilation.

- Frequently monitor and report changes in level of consciousness and respiratory status.

Primary Reference:

Hockenberry, M., Wilson, D., Winkelstein, M. (2005). *Wong's essentials of pediatric nursing care.* (7th ed.). St. Louis, MO: Mosby.

Additional Resources:

Ignatavicius, D. D., & Workman, M. L. (2006). *Medical-surgical nursing.* (5th ed.). St. Louis, MO: Saunders.

NANDA International (2004). *NANDA nursing diagnoses: Definitions and classification 2005-2006.* Philadelphia: NANDA.

Smeltzer, S. C., & Bare, B. G. (2003). *Brunner and Suddarth's textbook of medical-surgical nursing.* (10th ed.). Philadelphia: Lippincott, Williams & Wilkins.

Chapter 48: Head Injury

Application Exercises

Scenario: A 9-year-old child is found by her parent lying on the sidewalk next to her bicycle. The child is bleeding profusely at the base of her skull. Blood is found in each ear. Emergency medical services transport the child to the hospital. Upon arrival to the emergency department, the child is unresponsive with respirations of 10/min, heart rate 50/min, blood pressure 136/40 mm Hg, and temperature 36.7° C (98° F).

1. What priority interventions should the emergency department staff take?

2. List two priority nursing diagnoses for this child with supporting data for each.

3. What is the purpose of each of the following tests ordered by the primary care provider: CBC, CT scan, electrolytes, coagulation studies, ABGs, type and cross match?

4. Which of the following sets of vital signs is indicative of Cushing's reflex in a 6-year-old child?

    A. Temperature 37.2° C (99° F), pulse 100/min, respiratory rate 22/min, and blood pressure 100/70 mm Hg

    B. Temperature 37.9° C (100.2° F), pulse 140/min, respiratory rate 26/min, and blood pressure 60/30 mm Hg

    C. Temperature 35.6° C (96° F), pulse 50/min, respiratory rate 18/min, and blood pressure 80/50 mm Hg

    D. Temperature 37.8° C (100° F), pulse 64/min, respiratory rate 20/min, and blood pressure 140/40 mm Hg

5. A nurse is stimulating a child who has head trauma. During the stimulation, the nurse observes the child extending his arms and legs, and his toes are pointing downward. What posture is the child demonstrating?

6. A child who has a concussion is being discharged home with her parent. Which of the following statements by the parent indicates a need for further teaching?

    A. "I will keep him awake all night to make sure there is no change."

    B. "I should call the hospital if I cannot arouse him."

    C. "His pupils should remain equal and get smaller when I shine a light into them."

    D. "I should call the doctor if he starts to vomit."

7. A 6-month-old infant is admitted to the pediatric critical care unit with a basilar skull fracture. Which of the following assessment findings should the nurse expect? (Select all that apply.)

    _____ Two black eyes

    _____ Nuchal rigidity

    _____ Split cranial sutures

    _____ Bruising of neck posterior to infant's ear

    _____ Nosebleed

8. A child has sustained a fall from a window. Her father finds her completely unconscious and not speaking or moving. What should her Glasgow Coma Scale score be?

    A. 3

    B. 5

    C. 10

    D. 15

Chapter 48: Head Injury

Application Exercises Answer Key

Scenario: A 9-year-old child is found by her parent lying on the sidewalk next to her bicycle. The child is bleeding profusely at the base of her skull. Blood is found in each ear. Emergency medical services transport the child to the hospital. Upon arrival to the emergency department, the child is unresponsive with respirations of 10/min, heart rate 50/min, blood pressure 136/40 mm Hg, and temperature 36.7° C (98° F).

1. What priority interventions should the emergency department staff take?

The emergency department staff will assess and manage the child's airway and prepare for intubation. The child will be placed on continuous monitoring for cardiac assessment, frequent vital signs, and pulse oximetry. IV access should be initiated and anticipation of administration of an antibiotic.

2. List two priority nursing diagnoses for this child with supporting data for each.

Nursing Diagnosis	Supporting Data
Ineffective tissue perfusion (cerebral) related to bleeding second to head injury	Vital functions of the brain, such as effective respiratory rate and heart rate, are compromised, with respirations of 10/min and heart rate 50/min.
Ineffective breathing pattern related to head injury	Respiratory rate of 10/min is too low for a child of this age who has sustained a trauma.

3. What is the purpose of each of the following tests ordered by the primary care provider: CBC, CT scan, electrolytes, coagulation studies, ABGs, type and cross match?

CBC establishes a baseline and identifies if excessive blood loss has occurred.

CT scan determines the extent and location of cranial injury.

Electrolytes establish a baseline and determine if compromise has occurred.

Coagulation studies establish a baseline for the child, who will be taken to surgery and who is already bleeding. Bleeding disorders could also result from the injury.

ABGs will signify whether or not the child is at risk for respiratory compromise. The primary care provider will need to know if intubation is required and how to set the ventilator.

Type and cross match will determine blood type in order to make transfusion available for the child if it is needed prior to or during surgery.

4. Which of the following sets of vital signs is indicative of Cushing's reflex in a 6-year-old child?

    A. Temperature 37.2° C (99° F), pulse 100/min, respiratory rate 22/min, and blood pressure 100/70 mm Hg

    B. Temperature 37.9° C (100.2° F), pulse 140/min, respiratory rate 26/min, and blood pressure 60/30 mm Hg

    C. Temperature 35.6° C (96° F), pulse 50/min, respiratory rate 18/min, and blood pressure 80/50 mm Hg

    D. Temperature 37.8° C (100° F), pulse 64/min, respiratory rate 20/min, and blood pressure 140/40 mm Hg

Signs of Cushing's reflex include bradycardia, systolic hypertension, and widening pulse pressure, which are all present in the correct answer. Respirations are not part of Cushing's triad, although Cheyne-Stokes respirations often occur along with the other three symptoms. Temperature is not part of the triad.

5. A nurse is stimulating a child who has head trauma. During the stimulation, the nurse observes the child extending his arms and legs, and his toes are pointing downward. What posture is the child demonstrating?

The child is demonstrating decerebrate posturing, which is indicative of dysfunction at the midbrain and is characterized by extension and rotation of the arms and backward arching of the head.

6. A child who has a concussion is being discharged home with her parent. Which of the following statements by the parent indicates a need for further teaching?

A. "I will keep him awake all night to make sure there is no change."

B. "I should call the hospital if I cannot arouse him."

C. "His pupils should remain equal and get smaller when I shine a light into them."

D. "I should call the doctor if he starts to vomit."

The child should be allowed to sleep, but the parents need to arouse him on a regular basis. An inability to arouse the child, dilated pupils that do not constrict, or the onset of vomiting can indicate increased intracranial pressure.

7. A 6-month-old infant is admitted to the pediatric critical care unit with a basilar skull fracture. Which of the following assessment findings should the nurse expect? (Select all that apply.)

__X__ Two black eyes

_____ Nuchal rigidity

_____ Split cranial sutures

__X__ Bruising of neck posterior to infant's ear

__X__ Nosebleed

Signs of a basilar skull fracture include raccoon eyes (both blackened), Battle's sign (bruising of neck posterior to ear), and bleeding from the nose. Nuchal rigidity, which is a painful and rigid neck, is caused by meningitis. Split cranial sutures are seen in a diastatic skull fracture.

8. A child has sustained a fall from a window. Her father finds her completely unconscious and not speaking or moving. What should her Glasgow Coma Scale score be?

A. 3

B. 5

C. 10

D. 15

This child's GCS would be the lowest possible score: 3. A score of 5 would indicate either some abnormal posture (such as decorticate or decerebrate) or that she opened her eyes or had some sort of a verbal response. A score of 10 or 15 would indicate that the child had some type of eye, verbal, and motor response.

Unit 2   Nursing Care of Children with System Disorders
Section: Nursing Care of Children with Neurosensory Disorders

Chapter 49:   Sensory Disorders-Visual and Hearing Impairments
               Contributor: Glenda J. Bondurant, MSN, RN

 NCLEX-RN® Connections:

Learning Objective: Review and apply knowledge within "**Sensory Disorders-Visual and Hearing Impairments**" in readiness for performance of the following nursing activities as outlined by the NCLEX-RN® test plan:

Δ   Assist with relevant laboratory, diagnostic, and therapeutic procedures within the nursing role, including:

  •   Client preparation for the procedure.

  •   Client teaching (before and following the procedure).

  •   Accurate collection of specimens.

  •   Evaluation of the child's response to the procedure.

  •   Planning and implementing body system-specific interventions as appropriate.

  •   Monitoring and taking actions to prevent or minimize the risk of complications.

  •   Accurate interpretation of procedure results.

Δ   Perform and document appropriate assessments based on the child's problem.

Δ   Apply knowledge of pathophysiology to planning care for clients with specific alterations in body systems, including recognizing associated signs and symptoms.

Δ   Interpret data that need to be reported immediately.

Δ   Monitor therapeutic devices (drainage/irrigating devices, chest tubes), if inserted, for proper functioning.

Δ   Explore resources, make referrals, collaborate with interdisciplinary team, and ensure continuity of client care.

Δ   Evaluate plans of care for multiple clients and revise plan as needed based on priorities of care and promotion of recovery.

Δ   Provide the child/family teaching regarding management of the child's health problem.

Δ   Recognize/respond to emergency situations, and evaluate/document the client's response to emergency interventions.

Key Points

Δ   Common types of visual impairment in children include strabismus (misalignment of eyes), refractive errors (nearsightedness, farsightedness, astigmatism), and amblyopia (decreased acuity in one eye).

Δ   Children may also experience cataracts and glaucoma.

Δ   Hearing impairments affect the ability to clearly process linguistic sounds and impact speech.

Key Factors

Δ   Strabismus is a misalignment of visual axis caused by muscle weakness that can be present in one or both eyes. The child has an inability to focus on a single image (sees image twice).

Δ   Hearing defects can be caused by a variety of conditions including anatomic malformation, maternal ingestion of toxic substances during pregnancy, perinatal asphyxia, perinatal infection, chronic ear infection, and/or ototoxic medications.

Δ   Hearing defects are associated with chronic conditions such as Down syndrome and/or cerebral palsy.

Δ   Hearing defects include:

- Conductive losses involving interference of sound transmission, which is most often a result of otitis media.

- Sensorineural losses involving interference of the transmission along the nerve pathways. Most of them are a result of congenital defects or secondary to acquired conditions (e.g., infection, ototoxic medications, exposure to constant noise – as in NICU).

- Central auditory imperception involving all other hearing losses (e.g., aphasia, agnosia [inability to interpret sounds]).

Assessment

Δ   Visual screening using age-appropriate tools (E Snellen chart used for children who cannot read; alphabet Snellen chart used for children who can read)

Δ   Corneal light reflex – may be asymmetrical

Δ   Cover/uncover test – one eye may deviate outward or inward

Δ   Alteration in visual judgment

Δ   Headache

Δ   Dizziness

Δ   Photophobia

Δ   Inability to focus

Δ   Squints or closes one eye to focus

Δ   Auditory Assessment

- Infants lack of startle reflex

- Failure to respond to noise

- Absence of vocalization

- Delayed verbal development

- Older children speak in monotone

- Need for repeated conversation

- Speak loudly for situation

Δ   Determination of how the child perceives self and the sensory alteration

Therapeutic Procedures

Δ   Surgical intervention for correction of strabismus shortens the eye muscle and allows for realignment of eye

Δ   Use a hearing aid for conductive loss.

Δ   Provide surgical intervention such as cochlear implants for sensorineural loss.

NANDA Nursing Diagnoses

Δ   Disturbed body image

Δ   Delayed growth and development

Δ   Risk for injury

Δ   Disturbed sensory perception

Nursing Interventions

Δ   Maintain normal to bright lighting for the child when reading, writing, or any activity that requires close vision.

Δ   Monitor for signs of eye strain (e.g., squinting, closing one eye).

Δ   Patch unaffected eye as prescribed.

Δ   Assess gait/balance for instability.

Δ   Adjust environment for physiological symptoms.

Δ   Identify safety hazards.

Δ   Educate child/family regarding home care for strabismus.

- Determine knowledge level/understanding.
- Emphasize importance of keeping all appointments.
- Identify symptoms of eye strain.
- Patch eye(s) if prescribed.

Δ   Use an interpreter when working with a child who is hearing impaired, always remembering to talk to the child, not the interpreter.

Δ   Encourage parents to participate in programs that aid in auditory communication.

Δ   If the child wears a hearing aid, instruct the parents to store batteries in a safe place that is out of reach.

Δ   Teach the child not to remove batteries without adult supervision.

Δ   Help the family identify community resources for their hearing-impaired child.

Δ   Encourage the family to work with the child's school to meet educational needs.

Δ   Teach the child/family to avoid further damage and hearing loss.

- Avoid exposing the child to hazardous noise.
- Encourage wearing ear protection if the child cannot avoid loud environmental noise.

Complications and Nursing Implications

Δ   Delayed Growth and Development

- Visual and hearing impairment may prevent the child from appropriate speech and motor development.

- Identify the impairment early.

- Encourage self-care and optimal independence.

- Assist the family to obtain and access appropriate assistive devices.

Primary Reference:

Hockenberry, M., Wilson, D., Winkelstein, M. (2005). *Wong's essentials of pediatric nursing care.* (7th ed.). St. Louis, MO: Mosby.

Additional Resources:

Hain, T. C. (2006, September). *Congenital deafness.* Retrieved February 14, 2007, from http://www.dizziness-and-balance.com/disorders/hearing/cong_hearing.html

Isaacson, J. E. & Vora, N. M. (2003, September 15). Differential diagnosis and treatment of hearing loss. *American Family Physician, 68*(6), 1125-1132. Retrieved February 14, 2007, from http://www.aafp.org/afp/20030915/1125.html

NANDA International (2004). *NANDA nursing diagnoses: Definitions and classification 2005-2006.* Philadelphia: NANDA.

Chapter 49: Sensory Disorders

Application Exercises

Scenario: A school health nurse is performing a vision clinic for kindergarten children. He has set up an area to use the E Snellen vision chart for each student and to do a visual assessment.

1. Explain why the nurse should use the E Snellen chart to test vision in kindergarten children.

2. A teacher tells the nurse that one of her students has a lazy eye. Upon assessment, the nurse notices the child's left eye moves inward and downward as the right eye remains centered. What should the nurse recommend to the child's parent?

3. What suggestions could the nurse make to the child's teacher to assist the child in learning?

4. For which of the following children would strabismus be a normal finding?

    A. 5 month old

    B. 10 month old

    C. 3 year old

    D. 10 year old

5. The parents of a 7-year-old child with strabismus are trying to help their child with school work. Which of the following strategies will assist this child to complete homework? (Select all that apply.)

    _____ Perform the work on a computer with a 15-inch monitor.

    _____ Work at a desk using a well-placed desk lamp.

    _____ Do the work immediately after school.

    _____ Provide minimal distractions.

    _____ Read the assignment to the child without letting him see the paper.

6. While observing a classroom of students, a school nurse notices the following signs in a child. Which of these signs are indicative of strabismus? (Select all that apply.)

_____ Laying the head down beside the work and writing

_____ Moving the head around over the work and squinting

_____ Covering one eye while reading

_____ Positioning the work further away from the eyes

_____ Frequent blinking

7. A mother is talking to a community health nurse about her child's hearing problem. The mother tells the nurse that her child was fine until about 2 days ago when the child said he had constant "tickling" in his right ear and was unable to hear out of it. The nurse suspects conductive hearing loss. Which of the following factors is a cause for conductive hearing loss? (Select all that apply.)

_____ Congenital nerve damage in the inner ear

_____ A foreign body, such as a bug, lodged in the ear canal

_____ Middle ear infection

_____ External ear canal infection

_____ Exposure to noise from explosion

_____ Excess ear wax

Chapter 49: Sensory Disorders

Application Exercises Answer Key

Scenario: A school health nurse is performing a vision clinic for kindergarten children. He has set up an area to use the E Snellen vision chart for each student and to do a visual assessment.

1. Explain why the nurse should use the E Snellen chart to test vision in kindergarten children.

   A kindergarten student may or may not be able to distinguish the letters of the alphabet yet. They should all be able to distinguish directions by pointing after brief instructions from the nurse.

2. A teacher tells the nurse that one of her students has a lazy eye. Upon assessment, the nurse notices the child's left eye moves inward and downward as the right eye remains centered. What should the nurse recommend to the child's parent?

   The child needs to visit the primary care provider, who can then make a referral to an ophthalmologist.

3. What suggestions could the nurse make to the child's teacher to assist the child in learning?

   Ensure that the child sits close to the front of the classroom, has a well-lit environment for working, and is provided with printed materials, such as homework assignments, that are clearly printed.

4. For which of the following children would strabismus be a normal finding?

   A. 5 month old
   B. 10 month old
   C. 3 year old
   D. 10 year old

   Strabismus is normal up until the age of 6 months.

5. The parents of a 7-year-old child with strabismus are trying to help their child with school work. Which of the following strategies will assist this child to complete homework? (Select all that apply.)

_____ Perform the work on a computer with a 15-inch monitor.

__X__ **Work at a desk using a well-placed desk lamp.**

_____ Do the work immediately after school.

__X__ **Provide minimal distractions.**

_____ Read the assignment to the child without letting him see the paper.

It is important for the child to have bright lighting and minimal distractions when doing school work. The child needs time to rest the eyes from reading for a period of time after school. The 15-inch monitor could cause strain on the eyes. Reading the assignment might be helpful, but it is important for the child to see the assignment.

6. While observing a classroom of students, a school nurse notices the following signs in a child. Which of these signs are indicative of strabismus? (Select all that apply.)

_____ Laying the head down beside the work and writing

__X__ **Moving the head around over the work and squinting**

__X__ **Covering one eye while reading**

_____ Positioning the work further away from the eyes

_____ Frequent blinking

The child with strabismus attempts to minimize the double vision that is occurring. The best way to do this is by squinting. This will allow the objects to focus into one another. The child might also cover one eye so that the object is only seen once. Laying the head down beside the work while writing, and positioning the work further away from the eyes, have no significance for the child with strabismus. Frequent blinking is a sign of myopia (nearsightedness).

7. A mother is talking to a community health nurse about her child's hearing problem. The mother tells the nurse that her child was fine until about 2 days ago when the child said he had constant "tickling" in his right ear and was unable to hear out of it. The nurse suspects conductive hearing loss. Which of the following factors is a cause for conductive hearing loss? (Select all that apply.)

_____ Congenital nerve damage in the inner ear

__X__ **A foreign body, such as a bug, lodged in the ear canal**

__X__ **Middle ear infection**

__X__ **External ear canal infection**

_____ Exposure to noise from explosion

__X__ **Excess ear wax**

All the problems mentioned could cause conductive hearing loss, except for congenital nerve damage in the inner ear and exposure to loud noise, which are both causes of sensorineural hearing loss.

Unit 2   Nursing care of Children with System Disorders
Section: Nursing Care of Children with Musculoskeletal Disorders

Chapter 50: **Musculoskeletal Congenital Disorders**
            Contributor: Candyce F. Antley, MN, RN

 NCLEX-RN® Connections:

Learning Objective: Review and apply knowledge within "**Musculoskeletal Congenital Disorders**" in readiness for performance of the following nursing activities as outlined by the NCLEX-RN® test plan:

Δ   Assist with relevant laboratory, diagnostic, and therapeutic procedures within the nursing role, including:

   • Client preparation for the procedure.

   • Client teaching (before and following the procedure).

   • Accurate collection of specimens.

   • Evaluation of the child's response to the procedure.

   • Planning and implementing body system-specific interventions as appropriate.

   • Monitoring and taking actions to prevent or minimize the risk of complications.

   • Accurate interpretation of procedure results.

Δ   Perform and document appropriate assessments based on the child's problem.

Δ   Apply knowledge of pathophysiology to planning care for clients with specific alterations in body systems, including recognizing associated signs and symptoms.

Δ   Interpret data that need to be reported immediately.

Δ   Monitor therapeutic devices (drainage/irrigating devices, chest tubes), if inserted, for proper functioning.

Δ   Explore resources, make referrals, collaborate with interdisciplinary team, and ensure continuity of client care.

Δ   Evaluate plans of care for multiple clients and revise plan as needed based on priorities of care and promotion of recovery.

Δ   Provide the child/family teaching regarding management of the child's health problem.

Δ   Recognize/respond to emergency situations, and evaluate/document the client's response to emergency interventions.

Key Points

Δ   **Clubfoot** is a complex deformity of the ankle and foot.

  •   Clubfoot occurs in every 1 to 2 births per 1,000 live births.

  •   Clubfoot affects boys twice as often as girls.

  •   Bilateral clubfoot occurs in 50% of diagnosed cases.

  •   Congenital clubfoot may occur as an isolated defect or is diagnosed in association with other disorders, including cerebral palsy and spina bifida.

Δ   **Developmental dysplasia of the hip (DDH)** is abnormal development of the hip structures.

  •   DDH may be identified during prenatal or postnatal periods or early in childhood.

  •   DDH occurs more frequently in girls than in boys.

Δ   **Scoliosis** is a complex deformity of the spine that also affects the ribs.

  •   Scoliosis is characterized by a lateral curvature of the spine and spinal rotation that causes rib asymmetry.

  •   Scoliosis is diagnosed if the curvature of the spine is greater than 10°. A 10° or less curvature is usually attributed to posture.

  •   Not all curvatures of the spine are scoliosis. A curve less than 10° may be a postural variation.

  •   Idiopathic scoliosis is the most common form of scoliosis.

Key Factors

Δ   The cause of clubfoot and DDH is unknown.

  •   Clubfoot may be related to abnormal embryonic development.

  •   Certain cases of clubfoot are related to abnormal positioning and restricted movement while in utero.

  •   Clubfoot is classified as positional (intrauterine crowding) or syndromic (associated with other deformities).

  •   Clubfoot may be associated with increased risk of developmental dysplasia of the hip.

  •   Variations of the deformity and manifestation(s) may be in one or both feet.

Deformity Name	Manifestations
Talipes equinovarus (most common)	Plantar flexion (feet bending inward)
Talipes calcaneus	Dorsiflexion of feet
Talipes equinus	Plantar flexion of feet
Talipes varus	Inversion of feet (toes pointing toward midline)
Talipes valgus	Eversion of feet (toes pointing laterally)

Δ **DDH** may be affected by family history, gender, birth order, intrauterine position, and/or laxity of a joint.

- Predisposing factors include intrauterine placement, mechanical situations (e.g., size of infant, multiple births, breech presentation), and genetic factors.

Δ **Scoliosis** can be congenital, idiopathic, or acquired (result of neuromuscular disorders).

- Scoliosis may be present at birth or occur in early childhood. The common age of onset is during the preadolescent growth spurt.

- Scoliosis may have a genetic link.

- Idiopathic structural scoliosis begins with a right thoracic and left lumbar deformity that causes the ribs on the concave side to be forced together and the ribs on the convex side to be widely separated.

- Compromised lung expansion occurs if the curve is not corrected.

Assessment

Δ General assessment includes:

- Obtaining a genetic, pregnancy, and birth history.

- Assessing pain level using appropriate tool.

- Assessing the infant or child's motor ability.

- Determining child/family coping.

Δ Assessment for clubfoot includes:

- Noting the position and appearance of the foot or feet.

- Determining whether or not the defect will result in a rigid or nonrigid deformity.

Δ Assessment for DDH includes:

- Asymmetrical gluteal and thigh folds.

- Limited abduction of hips.

- Shorter femur on affected side.

- Positive Ortolani's and Barlow tests in children up to 3 months of age.

  ◊ Involves manipulation of hip by skilled examiner

  ◊ In positive tests, the affected hip can be moved from socket (Barlow test) and then reduced back into socket (Ortolani's test) by manipulation of the joint through adduction

- DDH can be assessed by observing posture and gait (for children able to walk).

  ◊ Trendelenburg sign – abnormal downward tilting of pelvis on the unaffected side when bearing weight on the affected side

  ◊ Waddling gait or abnormal lordosis of spine if bilateral dislocation

Δ Assessment for scoliosis includes:

- Conducting screenings that begin during preadolescence for boys and girls.

  ◊ Observe the child from the back, wearing underwear only.

  ◊ Have child bend over at waist with arms hanging down.

  ◊ Observe for asymmetry in scapula, ribs, flanks, shoulders, and hips.

  ◊ Use scoliometer to measure degree of curvature.

- History of poorly fitting slacks or skirts.

- Noting the degree of curvature of the spine.

- Assessing ease of chest movement during respirations.

- Noting depth, rate, and rhythm of respirations.

Diagnostic Procedures

Δ Clubfoot may be diagnosed by prenatal ultrasound.

- After birth, a radiograph is used to determine bone placement and tissue involved for clubfoot.

Δ DDH diagnosis uses ultrasound at 2 weeks of age to determine the cartilaginous head of the femur.

- Infants older than 4 months may be diagnosed with DDH using a radiographic exam.

Δ Diagnosis of scoliosis

- Radiograph of child in standing position to measure the curve

- Magnetic resonance imaging (MRI) to determine any other pathology

- Computed tomography (CT) scan

NANDA Nursing Diagnoses

- Δ   Disturbed body image

- Δ   Ineffective breathing pattern

- Δ   Acute pain

- Δ   Impaired physical mobility

- Δ   Risk for impaired skin integrity

- Δ   Ineffective therapeutic regimen management

Nursing Interventions

- Δ   Interventions for the Child With Clubfoot or DDH

  - Encourage parents to hold and cuddle the child.

  - Administer analgesics for pain as appropriate.

  - Explain the condition and expected course of treatment.

  - Emphasize the necessity of follow-up care.

  - Suggest keeping favorite items within the child's reach.

  - Perform neurovascular and skin integrity checks after cast placement.

  - Advise parents to use a stroller that will provide support to the cast.

  - Educate parents on use of seatbelt with spica cast (immobilizes part or all of one or more extremities and part or all of the child's trunk).

Therapeutic Procedures and Nursing Interventions

- Δ   Clubfoot

  - Use manipulation and serial casting for severe clubfoot.

  - A minor deformity may correct spontaneously or through passive exercise.

- Δ   DDH

  - Use Pavlik harness for an infant from birth up to 5 or 6 months.

    - ◊   Pavlik harness is a noninvasive device for keeping hips in an abducted position continually in order to stabilize the femur in normal position flexed within acetabulum.

    - ◊   The infant will wear the harness continuously for 3 to 5 months.

    - ◊   The infant's family will require teaching regarding safe use of the harness and how to prevent skin breakdown in the infant.

Δ   A hip spica cast can be used for children older than 6 months of age. It can also be used in children whose hip(s) were not stabilized by use of the Pavlik harness.

Δ   The child may undergo either closed or open reduction prior to placement of a hip spica cast.

Δ   Educate the family about cast care.

- Position casts on pillows.

- Instruct the family to keep the cast(s) elevated until dry.

- Handle the casts with the palm of the hand until dry.

- Note color and temperature of toes on casted extremity.

- Instruct parents to give sponge baths to avoid wetting the cast.

- Use waterproof barrier around genital opening of spica cast to prevent soiling with urine or feces.

Δ   Surgical Intervention and Reduction for Both Clubfoot and DDH

- Prepare the infant and family for surgery.

- Assess pain using appropriate scale.

- Provide pain medication on a regular basis during the first 48 hr following surgery.

Δ   Therapeutic procedures for scoliosis include:

- Bracing and exercise.

  ◊   Mild scoliosis (curvature of 10 to 20°) is treated with exercise to strengthen muscles to the outside of the curve and stretch the muscles to the inside of the curve.

  ◊   Instruct the child/family about the importance of compliance.

  ◊   Brace may be decorated to make it more tolerable to adolescents.

  ◊   Reinforce teaching done by physical therapy.

  ◊   Monitor signs of skin breakdown in children wearing a brace.

  ◊   Instruct the child to wear the brace 23 out of 24 hr a day.

  ◊   Use exercise along with bracing to strengthen spinal and abdominal muscles.

- **Surgical intervention** is used to realign and fuse the spine for curves greater than 40°. This is accomplished with internal fixation systems (e.g., Harrington, Dwyer, Zielke) and then fusion of the realigned spine.

  ◊ Preoperative care includes extensive preoperative teaching to educate the adolescent and promote cooperation and participation in recovery.

    ° Obtain autologous blood donation.

    ° Type and cross match for blood as prescribed.

    ° Orient the adolescent/family to the ICU.

    ° Demonstrate log rolling that will be used after surgery.

    ° Demonstrate the respiratory therapy techniques that will be used postoperatively to reduce complications of anesthesia.

    ° Discuss medical terms unfamiliar to adolescent.

  ◊ Postoperative care includes:

    ° Taking a respiratory assessment.

    ° Maintaining chest tubes (used for anterior repair) and medicating for pain prior to removal of chest tubes.

    ° Assisting with respiratory therapy procedures.

    ° Managing pain using PCA as prescribed.

    ° Log rolling to prevent damage to spinal fusion.

    ° Preventing rubbing and pressure from brace.

    ° Providing skin care by keeping skin clean and dry.

    ° Providing wound care.

    ° Assessing bowel sounds and observing for paralytic ileus.

    ° Maintaining NG tube as ordered.

    ° Assessing for postoperative hemorrhage.

    ° Administering blood or autologous blood as ordered.

    ° Obtaining accurate I&O.

    ° Maintaining Foley catheter.

    ° Giving emotional encouragement.

  ◊ Emphasize the importance of proper positioning of the spine.

  ◊ Encourage independence in the adolescent with a brace or an adolescent following surgery.

◊ Encourage the adolescent to contact friends when able.

◊ Emphasize the necessity of follow-up care.

◊ Suggest that the adolescent work with a peer support group of adolescents that have had the surgery.

Complications and Nursing Interventions

Δ For Clubfoot and DDH

• Infection

◊ Monitor temperature.

◊ Keep cast dry.

◊ Reposition infant frequently.

◊ Maintain adequate hydration.

◊ Report any foul odor and irritability of infant.

◊ Keep appointments for cast changes.

Δ For Scoliosis Following Surgery

• Hemorrhage – Monitor vital signs, check for bleeding, and monitor sensation in extremities.

• Infection – Monitor vital signs, provide wound care as prescribed, and note drainage color and odor.

• Ileus – Monitor for absence of bowel sounds, abdominal distention, and ambulate the child as soon as he is able.

Primary Reference:

Hockenberry, M., Wilson, D., Winkelstein, M. (2005). *Wong's essentials of pediatric nursing care*. (7th ed.). St. Louis, MO: Mosby.

Additional Resources:

Ball, J. W., & Bindler, R. C. (2005). *Child health nursing: Partnering with children and families*. (1st ed.). Upper Saddle River, NJ: Prentice Hall.

French, L. M. & Dietz, F. R. (1999, July). Screening for developmental dysplasia of the hip. *The American Academy of Family Physicians*. Retrieved February 12, 2007, from http://www.aafp.org/afp/990700ap/177.html

NANDA International (2004). *NANDA nursing diagnoses: Definitions and classification 2005-2006*. Philadelphia: NANDA.

Chapter 50: Musculoskeletal Congenital Disorders

Application Exercises

Scenario: A 6-week-old infant is brought by a parent to the pediatric unit for the first in a series of serial castings for congenital bilateral clubfoot. The infant's parents are concerned about the casts breaking if they move him around after surgery. They also tell the nurse they are worried that he will never walk. His mother asks the nurse if something during birth caused her infant's bilateral clubfoot.

1. Discuss how the nurse should respond to the mother's concern.

2. What should the nurse teach the parents about cast care and home management following the casting procedure?

3. A 2-year-old child who walks but has difficulty keeping up with peers is being assessed for possible right DDH. Which of the following assessments should a nurse use to assess for DDH in this child?

    A. Barlow test

    B. Trendelenburg sign

    C. Manipulation of right foot and ankle

    D. Ortolani's test

4. A 13-month-old child is diagnosed with left hip dysplasia and is scheduled for surgery and application of a hip spica cast. The child's mother questions the nurse as to why a Pavlik harness is not being used. Which of the following responses by the nurse appropriately addresses the mother's question?

    A. "The Pavlik harness is used for children with scoliosis, not hip dysplasia."

    B. "The Pavlik harness is used for school-age children."

    C. "Your child's condition is too severe to use a Pavlik harness."

    D. "The Pavlik harness is only used for infants less than 6 months of age."

Scenario: A 15-year-old adolescent is admitted to the orthopedic unit for Harrington rod instrumentation due to a 45° curvature of the spine. The adolescent is angry and states that she will "look like a freak." Her mother verbalizes concern about her daughter having to go to intensive care following the surgery.

5. What should the nurse teach the adolescent/mother regarding postoperative care following surgery?

6. Which of the following are priority assessments for this adolescent admitted to the ICU from the OR following surgery? (Select all that apply.)

_____ Ability to eat a balanced diet

_____ Blood pressure and pulse

_____ Oxygen saturation

_____ Assessment for body image disturbance

_____ Neurovascular assessment

_____ Pain assessment

_____ Assessment for wound infection

7. What should the nurse monitor to assess neurovascular status in the postoperative period?

8. What can the nurse do to promote normal development and compliance during postoperative care?

Chapter 50: Musculoskeletal Congenital Disorders

Application Exercises Answer Key

Scenario: A 6-week-old infant is brought by a parent to the pediatric unit for the first in a series of serial castings for congenital bilateral clubfoot. The infant's parents are concerned about the casts breaking if they move him around after surgery. They also tell the nurse they are worried that he will never walk. His mother asks the nurse if something during birth caused her infant's bilateral clubfoot.

1. Discuss how the nurse should respond to the mother's concern.

There is no indication that clubfoot is caused by any prenatal behavior of the mother. Etiology of clubfoot is unknown at this time.

2. What should the nurse teach the parents about cast care and home management following the casting procedure?

The nurse should tell the parents that the casts will be safe to handle after they dry. However, the infant's legs will need to be supported. The parents need to know how to protect the child from skin breakdown and to assess for circulation problems. Instructions to prevent skin breakdown and assess for circulation problems include:

Δ **Noting color and temperature of infant's toes on casted extremity.**

Δ **Giving sponge baths to avoid wetting the cast.**

3. A 2-year-old child who walks but has difficulty keeping up with peers is being assessed for possible right DDH. Which of the following assessments should a nurse use to assess for DDH in this child?

A. Barlow test

B. Trendelenburg sign

C. Manipulation of right foot and ankle

D. Ortolani's test

Assessment for the Trendelenburg sign is used for a child with possible hip dysplasia who is walking. In Trendelenburg sign, the child bears weight on the affected leg while holding onto something for balance. The examiner observes from behind for abnormal downward tilting of the pelvis on the unaffected side. The Barlow and Ortolani tests for DDH are most useful for infants 2 to 3 months and involve manipulating the hip(s) to feel for instability. Manipulation of the foot and ankle is an assessment for clubfoot.

4. A 13-month-old child is diagnosed with left hip dysplasia and is scheduled for surgery and application of a hip spica cast. The child's mother questions the nurse as to why a Pavlik harness is not being used. Which of the following responses by the nurse appropriately addresses the mother's question?

    A. "The Pavlik harness is used for children with scoliosis, not hip dysplasia."

    B. "The Pavlik harness is used for school-age children."

    C. "Your child's condition is too severe to use a Pavlik harness."

    D. "The Pavlik harness is only used for infants less than 6 months of age."

Scenario: A 15-year-old adolescent is admitted to the orthopedic unit for Harrington rod instrumentation due to a 45° curvature of the spine. The adolescent is angry and states that she will "look like a freak." Her mother verbalizes concern about her daughter having to go to intensive care following the surgery.

---

5. What should the nurse teach the adolescent/mother regarding postoperative care following surgery?

    Log rolling, deep breathing, pain management, incentive spirometer, and skin care

6. Which of the following are priority assessments for this adolescent admitted to the ICU from the OR following surgery? (Select all that apply.)

    _____ Ability to eat a balanced diet

    _X_ Blood pressure and pulse

    _X_ Oxygen saturation

    _____ Assessment for body image disturbance

    _X_ Neurovascular assessment

    _X_ Pain assessment

    _____ Assessment for wound infection

Priority assessments in the immediate postoperative period include assessment of cardiovascular status (blood pressure and pulse), oxygen saturation, neurovascular assessment to assure blood flow to extremities, and pain level. The adolescent will be NPO until gastric motility returns; therefore, she is unable to eat a balanced diet at this time. Assessment of self-concept and presence of body image disturbance are not a priority until the adolescent is physically stable. Infection is not a priority assessment in the immediate postoperative period; however, it will begin to be important within the next several days.

7. What should the nurse monitor to assess neurovascular status in the postoperative period?

Monitor extremities for color, temperature, motion, sensation, and presence of pulses.

8. What can the nurse do to promote normal development and compliance during postoperative care?

It is important for the nurse to develop a trusting nurse-client relationship with the adolescent. This can be accomplished by encouraging the adolescent to verbalize concerns, validating these feelings and answering questions honestly and directly. In addition, encourage participation in the discharge planning and treatment, and discuss the outcome if compliance with the treatment plan is not followed. To promote normal development, the adolescent should be allowed to socialize with peers. Telephone calls and visits with friends are important as soon as the adolescent is stable and interested in receiving visitors.

Unit 2   Nursing Care of Children with System Disorders
Section: Nursing Care of Children with Musculoskeletal Disorders

Chapter 51:   **Fractures**
                Contributor: Candyce F. Antley, MN, RN

 **NCLEX-RN® Connections:**

Learning Objective: Review and apply knowledge within "**Fractures**" in readiness for performance of the following nursing activities as outlined by the NCLEX-RN® test plan:

Δ   Assist with relevant laboratory, diagnostic, and therapeutic procedures within the nursing role, including:

- Client preparation for the procedure.
- Client teaching (before and following the procedure).
- Accurate collection of specimens.
- Evaluation of the child's response to the procedure.
- Planning and implementing body system-specific interventions as appropriate.
- Monitoring and taking actions to prevent or minimize the risk of complications.
- Accurate interpretation of procedure results.

Δ   Perform and document appropriate assessments based on the child's problem.

Δ   Apply knowledge of pathophysiology to planning care for clients with specific alterations in body systems, including recognizing associated signs and symptoms.

Δ   Interpret data that need to be reported immediately.

Δ   Monitor therapeutic devices (drainage/irrigating devices, chest tubes), if inserted, for proper functioning.

Δ   Explore resources, make referrals, collaborate with interdisciplinary team, and ensure continuity of client care.

Δ   Evaluate plans of care for multiple clients and revise plan as needed based on priorities of care and promotion of recovery.

Δ   Provide the child/family teaching regarding management of the child's health problem.

Δ   Recognize/respond to emergency situations, and evaluate/document the client's response to emergency interventions.

📖 Key Points/Key Factors

Δ   **Common Types of Fractures**

- Bend – bone can be bent up to a 45° angle

- Buckle (torus) – bulge or raised area at fracture site

- Displaced – bone fragments are not in alignment

- Nondisplaced – bone fragments remain in alignment

- Oblique – fracture occurs at oblique angle

- Spiral – fracture occurs from twisting motion (common with physical abuse)

- Impacted – fractured bone is wedged inside opposite fractured fragment

- Greenstick – fracture in only one cortex of bone

Δ   **Common Fractures Sites**

- Upper extremity – clavicle, humerus, olecranon, radius, ulna, wrist, hand

- Lower extremity – femur, patella, tibia, fibula, ankle, foot

- Trunk – spine (compression), rib, sternum, pelvis

Δ   Children and older adults are more likely to experience fractures.

Δ   Bone healing and remodeling is faster in children than in adults.

Δ   Ordinary play activities and recreation place children at risk for injury (e.g., falls from climbing or running, trauma to bones from skateboarding, skiing, playing soccer, basketball).

Δ   Epiphyseal injuries may result in altered bone growth.

Δ   Radiographic evidence of previous fractures in various stages of healing may be the result of physical abuse.

Assessment

Δ   Obtain history of trauma, metabolic bone disorders, chronic conditions, and possible use of steroid therapy.

Δ   Signs and symptoms include:

- Crepitus – a grating sound created by the rubbing of bone fragments.

- Deformity – may observe internal rotation of extremity, shortened extremity, and visible bone with open fracture.

- Muscle spasms – occur from the pulling forces of the bone when not aligned.

- Edema – swelling from trauma.

- Ecchymosis – bleeding into underlying soft tissues from trauma.

- Loss of function.

Δ Neurovascular Assessment

Neurovascular Components	Early or Late Sign	Normal Findings	Symptoms to Report
Pain	Early	Pain relieved with analgesics, ice, and/or positioning	Increasing pain not relieved with elevation or pain medication
Paresthesia	Early	No numbness/tingling	Numbness or tingling, pins and needles sensation
Pallor	Early	• Capillary refill is brisk • Brisk = less than 3 sec • Skin is pink and pale	• Increased capillary refill time less than 3 sec • Blue fingers or toes
Polar	Late	Skin by touch is warm and dry	Cool/cold fingers or toes
Paralysis	Late	• Able to move fingers or toes • Able to plantar and dorsiflex ankle area not involved or restricted by cast	• Unable to move fingers or toes • Unable to plantar/dorsiflex ankle
Pulses	Late	Pulse distal to injury is palpable and strong	• Weak palpable pulses • Unable to palpate pulses • Pulse detected only with Doppler

Diagnostic Procedures

Δ Radiographic Assessment

- Use x-ray, computed tomography (CT) imaging scan, and/or magnetic resonance imagery (MRI).

- Identify type of fracture and location.

- Identify pathological fractures resulting from tumor or mass.

- Determine soft tissue damage.

- Bone scan is used to determine fracture complications/delayed healing.

NANDA Nursing Diagnoses

Δ   Health-seeking behaviors

Δ   Risk for infection

Δ   Acute pain

Δ   Impaired physical mobility

Δ   Risk for impaired skin integrity

Nursing Interventions

Δ   Provide emergency care at time of injury.

- Maintain ABCs.

- Monitor vital signs and neurological status.

- Assess neurovascular status of injured extremity.

- Position the child in supine position.

- Stabilize injured area, avoiding unnecessary movement.

- Elevate limb and apply ice.

- Give analgesics.

- Keep the child warm.

Δ   General nursing interventions include:

- Frequently assessing pain and following appropriate pain management, both pharmacologic and nonpharmacologic.

- Initiating and continuing neurovascular checks on a regular schedule. Report any change in status.

- Maintaining proper alignment.

- Promoting range of motion of fingers, toes, and unaffected extremities.

- Instructing the child/family regarding activity restrictions.

Δ   Cast Care

- Casting materials include:

  ◊ Plaster of paris casts are heavy, not water resistant, and can take 24 to 48 hr to dry.

  ◊ Synthetic fiberglass casts are light, water resistant, and dry very quickly (in 30 min).

- Prior to casting, the area is cleaned and dried. Tubular cotton-web roll is placed over the affected area to maintain skin integrity. The casting material is then applied.

- Position the child on a firm mattress. Use an overbed trapeze for an older child.

- Elevate cast above the level of the heart during the first 24 to 48 hr to prevent swelling.

- Apply ice for the first 24 hr to decrease swelling.

- Position the child so that dry air circulates around and under the cast for faster drying. This will also prevent pressure from changing the shape of the cast.

  ◊ Use gloves to touch the cast until the cast is completely dry.

  ◊ Do not use heat lamps or warm hair dryers.

- Turn the child frequently while supporting all extremities and joints.

- Instruct the child to keep the affected extremity supported (with a sling) or elevated when sitting.

- If wound is present, monitor the skin through the window that has been placed in an area of the cast to allow for skin inspection.

- Monitor for drainage on cast. Outline any drainage on the outside of the cast with a marker (and note date and time) so it can be monitored for any additional drainage.

- Assess general skin condition and area around cast edges.

- Provide routine skin care and thorough perineal care to maintain skin integrity.

- Use moleskin over any rough area of the cast that may rub against the child's skin.

- Instruct the child not to place any foreign objects under the cast to avoid trauma to the skin.

- Cover areas of the cast with plastic to avoid soiling from urine or feces.

- Assist with proper crutch fitting and reinforce proper use.

- Instruct the child to soak the extremity in warm water and then apply lotion after the cast has been removed.

Δ   Traction Care

- Traction uses a pulling force to promote and maintain alignment to the injured area. The counterforce can be applied by the child's body (straight or running traction) or by balanced weight attached to an over bed frame with weights, ropes, and/or pulleys (balanced suspension traction).

◊ Skin traction uses a pulling force that is applied by weights (may be used intermittently). The weights are attached by a rope to the client using tape, straps, boots, and/or cuffs. Examples include chin halter straps, Buck's traction (for hip fractures preoperatively), and Russell's traction (for tibia fracture).

◊ Skeletal traction uses a continuous pulling force that is applied directly to the bone by weights attached by a rope. The rope is directly attached to a rod/screw placed through the bone. Skeletal traction allows the child to change positions without interfering with the pull of the traction. Examples include 90° traction for fractures of the femur and Crutchfield tongs for cervical fractures.

- **Maintain body alignment** and realign if the child seems uncomfortable or reports pain.

- **Avoid lifting or removing weights**.

- Assure that **weights hang freely** and that pulley ropes are free of knots.

- Notify the primary care provider if the child experiences severe pain from muscle spasms unrelieved with medications and/or repositioning.

- Place an overbed trapeze to assist the child to move in bed.

- Remove sheets from the head of the bed to the foot and remake the bed in the same manner.

- **Routinely monitor the child's skin integrity** and document.

- Assess pin site for pain, redness, swelling, drainage, or odor. Provide pin care per facility protocol.

- Promote frequent position changing within restrictions of traction.

Δ Provide discharge instructions.

- Teach proper care of cast.

- Instruct the child not to put anything sharp under the cast. May use antipruritic (diphenhydramine HCl [Benadryl]) if necessary.

- Set physical restrictions.

- Instruct the parents in appropriate pain management.

- Report signs and symptoms of increasing pain, redness, inflammation and/or fever to the primary care provider.

Therapeutic Procedures

- Promote immobilization with a cast, splint/immobilizer, traction, or external fixation.

- Closed reduction is when a pulling force (e.g., traction, manual manipulation) is applied manually to realign the displaced fractured bone fragments. Once the fracture is reduced, immobilization is used to allow the bone to heal.

- Operative Procedures
    ◊ Open reduction internal fixation (ORIF)
    ◊ External fixation
    ◊ Bone grafting

Complications and Nursing Interventions

Δ Acute compartment syndrome is a buildup of pressure within muscle compartment(s) that can cause circulatory obstruction resulting in tissue ischemia and possibly necrosis.

- Signs and symptoms include:
    ◊ Unrelieved pain or pain out of proportion to the injury.
    ◊ Initial sensory alterations include paresthesias, pallor, and then diminished pulses.
- Notify the primary care provider immediately.
- Interventions to relieve pressure include loosening constricting bulky dressings and cutting (bivalving) cast.

Δ **Osteomyelitis** is inflammation within the bone secondary to a bacterial infection (more common with open fractures).

- Signs and symptoms include:
    ◊ Bone pain that worsens with movement.
    ◊ Initial erythema, edema, and fever may occur.
- Definitive diagnosis is done by taking a bone biopsy. Cultures are performed for detection of possible aerobic and anaerobic organisms.
- Interventions include a long course (3 months) of IV and oral antibiotic therapy. Surgical debridement may also be indicated. Unsuccessful treatment can result in amputation.

Primary Reference:

Hockenberry, M., Wilson, D., Winkelstein, M. (2005). *Wong's essentials of pediatric nursing care.* (7th ed.). St. Louis, MO: Mosby.

Additional Resources:

Ignatavicius, D. D., & Workman, M. L. (2006). *Medical-surgical nursing.* (5th ed.). St. Louis, MO: Saunders.

NANDA International (2004). *NANDA nursing diagnoses: Definitions and classification 2005-2006.* Philadelphia: NANDA.

Chapter 51: Fractures

Application Exercises

Scenario: An 8-year-old child is admitted to the hospital with a fractured right femur after falling off his skateboard. He is placed in balanced suspension traction with a pin in the distal portion of the femur. The skin around the site is red with a small amount of serosanguineous drainage. The right lower leg is pale and warm, pedal pulses are present, and capillary refill is 2 sec. His vital signs are within normal limits, he denies having numbness or tingling, and his pain is relieved with morphine sulfate.

1. Describe the proper body alignment for this child.

2. Explain what the nurse should do if she is unable to detect a dorsalis pedis pulse in the child's right leg.

3. Describe how the nurse should explain the care of the pin site to the child's parent.

4. After 3 weeks in the hospital, the child is discharged. His leg has been placed in a cast. Which of the following discharge instructions should the nurse provide the child and his parent regarding cast care? (Select all that apply.)

   _____ Wash the cast carefully if it becomes soiled.
   _____ Allow the cast to remain uncovered until it dries completely.
   _____ Support the wet cast carefully and avoid denting it.
   _____ Make sure nothing is placed inside the cast.
   _____ Check the child's leg frequently for signs of swelling.

5. Which of the following is an early sign of impaired neurovascular function in a child with an arm cast?

   A. Cool, cold fingers
   B. Pain
   C. Inability to detect a pulse distal to cast
   D. Inability to move distal extremity

6. True or False: To prevent swelling of a casted extremity, elevate the extremity above heart level and apply ice to the cast.

7. True or False: Increased pain, erythema, and fever are three signs that compartment syndrome is occurring within a casted extremity.

Chapter 51: Fractures

Application Exercises Answer Key

Scenario: An 8-year-old child is admitted to the hospital with a fractured right femur after falling off his skateboard. He is placed in balanced suspension traction with a pin in the distal portion of the femur. The skin around the site is red with a small amount of serosanguineous drainage. The right lower leg is pale and warm, pedal pulses are present, and capillary refill is 2 sec. His vital signs are within normal limits, he denies having numbness or tingling, and his pain is relieved with morphine sulfate.

---

1. Describe the proper body alignment for this child.

   The child should be lying in supine position. A flat pillow should be used to support his head. His hips should be aligned with his shoulders.

2. Explain what the nurse should do if she is unable to detect a dorsalis pedis pulse in the child's right leg.

   If a dorsalis pedis pulse is not detected, the nurse should feel for a posterior tibial pulse. If the posterior tibial pulse is unable to be located, she should continue moving up the child's body until a pulse is detected. The rest of the neurovascular assessment should be performed on both of the child's legs. In addition, the nurse should obtain a Doppler to assess for pulse. Then, she should contact the primary care provider regarding the assessment, including pulse(s) not detected. Physical therapy can also be contacted to assess the traction.

3. Describe how the nurse should explain the care of the pin site to the child's parent.

   Explain that the area will be inspected daily. Pin care may include cleaning around the pin site with sterile water, saline, or another ordered solution, and applying sterile gauze around the site. Some orthopedists prefer to let a scab form over the pin site and do not order pin care.

4. After 3 weeks in the hospital, the child is discharged. His leg has been placed in a cast. Which of the following discharge instructions should the nurse provide the child and his parent regarding cast care? (Select all that apply.)

   _____ Wash the cast carefully if it becomes soiled.

   _X_ Allow the cast to remain uncovered until it dries completely.

   _X_ Support the wet cast carefully and avoid denting it.

   _X_ Make sure nothing is placed inside the cast.

   _X_ Check the child's leg frequently for signs of swelling.

All the choices are correct except washing the cast. The cast should never be washed or wet down with any liquid because of the possibility of excoriation of the skin under the cast.

5. Which of the following is an early sign of impaired neurovascular function in a child with an arm cast?

   A. Cool, cold fingers

   B. Pain

   C. Inability to detect a pulse distal to cast

   D. Inability to move distal extremity

Pain, or an increase in pain, is an early sign of neurovascular function. Numbness/tingling (paresthesias) pale skin, and slowed capillary refill are other early signs. Cool or cold extremities, and inability to move the distal extremity are all late signs of impaired neurovascular function.

6. True or False: To prevent swelling of a casted extremity, elevate the extremity above heart level and apply ice to the cast.

True. Elevation and ice application both help to prevent swelling of the casted extremity.

7. True or False: Increased pain, erythema, and fever are three signs that compartment syndrome is occurring within a casted extremity.

False. Increased pain is a sign of compartment syndrome. Other signs include pallor, paresthesias, and absent pulses distal to cast. Erythema and fever are signs of infection such as osteomyelitis.

Unit 2   Nursing Care of Children with System Disorders
Section: Nursing Care of Children with Musculoskeletal Disorders

Chapter 52:   Chronic Neuromusculoskeletal Disorders
Contributor: Candyce F. Antley, MN, RN

 NCLEX-RN® Connections:

Learning Objective: Review and apply knowledge within "**Chronic Neuromusculoskeletal Disorders**" in readiness for performance of the following nursing activities as outlined by the NCLEX-RN® test plan:

Δ   Assist with relevant laboratory, diagnostic, and therapeutic procedures within the nursing role, including:

- Client preparation for the procedure.
- Client teaching (before and following the procedure).
- Accurate collection of specimens.
- Evaluation of the child's response to the procedure.
- Planning and implementing body system-specific interventions as appropriate.
- Monitoring and taking actions to prevent or minimize the risk of complications.
- Accurate interpretation of procedure results.

Δ   Perform and document appropriate assessments based on the child's problem.

Δ   Apply knowledge of pathophysiology to planning care for clients with specific alterations in body systems, including recognizing associated signs and symptoms.

Δ   Interpret data that need to be reported immediately.

Δ   Monitor therapeutic devices (drainage/irrigating devices, chest tubes), if inserted, for proper functioning.

Δ   Explore resources, make referrals, collaborate with interdisciplinary team, and ensure continuity of client care.

Δ   Evaluate plans of care for multiple clients and revise plan as needed based on priorities of care and promotion of recovery.

Δ   Provide the child/family teaching regarding management of the child's health problem.

Δ   Recognize/respond to emergency situations, and evaluate/document the client's response to emergency interventions.

Juvenile Idiopathic Arthritis

 Key Points

Δ   Juvenile idiopathic arthritis (JIA) is the current term for juvenile rheumatoid arthritis (JRA). Changes in the nomenclature have attempted to reflect the process of the disorder rather than the presence of rheumatoid factor, which is present in approximately 10% of affected children.

Δ   JIA/JRA is a group of chronic autoimmune inflammatory diseases affecting joints and other tissues. There is chronic inflammation of the synovium of the joints that leads to wearing down and damage to the articular cartilage.

Δ   Symptoms of arthritis begin prior to age 16 and last more than 6 weeks.

Δ   Peak incidence is between 1 and 3 years of age or between 8 and 10 years of age. JIA/JRA is diagnosed more often in girls than in boys.

Δ   Acute changes rarely occur after age 19.

Key Factors

Δ   The cause for JIA/JRA is unknown.

Δ   The child may experience an uneven and slow rate of growth.

Δ   The most common report is joint stiffness in the morning accompanied by joint swelling.

Δ   JIA/JRA is most common in the joints of the knees and hands.

Δ   Arthritis subsides over time in most cases, but may leave joints deformed.

Δ   Major sub-types of JIA/JRA

  •   Polyarticular – five or more joints involved

  •   Pauciarticular – four or fewer joints involved, greater risk for ciliary body and iris inflammation (uveitis)

  •   Systemic onset – any number of joints involved, but characterized by severe high fever, rash, pericarditis, hepatosplenomegaly, lymphadenopathy, and pleuritis

Assessment

Δ Obtain history of pain including onset, location, duration, intensity, and relief measures.

Δ Obtain the child's history of other illnesses.

Δ Signs and Symptoms

- Joint swelling, stiffness, redness

- Mobility limitations

- Fever

- Rash

- Chest discomfort with breathing

- Nodules under the skin

- Delayed growth and development

- Enlarged lymph nodes

- Visual changes

Diagnostic Procedures

Δ Diagnosis is made by ruling out other disorders. A determination will be based on age of onset before 16 years of age, involvement of one or more joints, and symptoms that last longer than 6 weeks.

Δ Radiographic studies may be used for baseline comparison. X-rays may demonstrate increased synovial fluid in the joint, which causes soft tissue swelling or widening of the joint. Later findings may include osteoporosis and narrowed joint spaces.

Δ Erythrocyte sedimentation rate (ESR) may or may not be elevated.

Δ CBC with differential may demonstrate elevated WBCs.

Δ Antinuclear antibodies (ANA) may help identify the child with a pauciarticular form, but ANA is not specific for arthritis.

Δ Rheumatoid factor is present in approximately 10% of children with JIA/JRA.

NANDA Nursing Diagnoses

Δ   Anxiety

Δ   Acute pain

Δ   Disturbed body image

Δ   Delayed growth and development

Δ   Impaired physical mobility

Δ   Impaired skin integrity

Nursing Interventions

Δ   Include the family in the child's care so they are prepared for home care.

Δ   Regularly evaluate the child's pain.

Δ   Encourage the child to rest acutely-inflamed joints.

  •   Splint knees, wrists, and hands for sleep to decrease pain and prevent flexion deformities.

  •   Provide firm mattress and discourage use of pillows under knees.

Δ   Administer medications as prescribed for pain and inflammation.

  •   Administer NSAIDs of choice to control pain and inflammation (e.g., naproxen, ibuprofen, tolmetin).

    ◊   Instruct the child to take NSAIDs with food to minimize gastric irritation.

  •   Use aspirin less frequently. Caution parents regarding use of aspirin during viral illness due to risk of Reye syndrome.

  •   Methotrexate is used when NSAIDs do not work alone.

    ◊   Monitor liver function tests and CBC regularly.

  •   Corticosteroids are used with life-threatening conditions such as uveitis and severe arthritis. They are administered at the lowest effective dose for short-term therapy and then discontinued by tapering the dose. An injection into the intraarticular space may provide effective pain relief.

  •   Etanercept, a tumor necrosis factor alpha-receptor blocker, is used when methotrexate is not effective. It is given twice each week subcutaneously.

Δ   Teach the child/family nonpharmacological pain management techniques (e.g., distraction, relaxation).

Δ   Apply heat or warm moist packs to the child's affected joints prior to exercise. Encourage warm baths.

Δ   Reinforce exercises prescribed by physical and occupational therapy. May include exercise in warm water pool.

Δ   Encourage full range-of-motion exercises when pain and inflammation have subsided.

Δ   Identify alternate ways for the child to meet developmental needs during periods of pain and inflammation.

Δ   Encourage self-care by allowing adequate time for completion.

Δ   Encourage a well-balanced diet high in fiber and adequate fluids to prevent constipation from immobility.

Δ   Encourage contact with peers.

Δ   Assist parents in obtaining accommodations in school.

Complications and Nursing Implications

Δ   Joint Deformity and Functional Disability

• Encourage the child/family to be compliant with the treatment regime.

• Encourage self-care and active participation in an exercise program.

• Advocate for the child when treatments are not producing expected results.

Muscular Dystrophy

 Key Points/Key Factors

Δ   Muscular dystrophy (MD) is a group of inherited disorders with progressive degeneration of symmetric skeletal muscle groups.

Δ   Loss of muscular strength is insidious.

Δ   Developmental milestones are likely met until onset of disease.

Δ   Onset of disease, pace of progression, and muscle group affected depends on type of MD.

Δ   Duchenne muscular dystrophy (DMD) is the most common form of MD. Inherited as an X-linked recessive trait, DMD has an onset between 3 and 5 years of age. Life expectancy for DMD reaches into early adulthood.

Δ   Management of DMD is symptomatic to assist with maintaining highest level of mobility and prevention of complications as disease progresses.

Assessment

Δ Obtain history of illnesses and maternal family history of MD.

Δ Signs and Symptoms

- Muscular weakness in lower extremities

- Muscular hypertrophy, especially in calves

- Mild delay in motor skill development

- Mobility with general muscle strength declining with time

- Unsteady, wide-based or waddling gait, loss of walking ability usually by age 12

- Difficulty riding tricycle, running, rising from seated position

- Mental delay with learning disabilities present in approximately 30% of children

- Heart and muscles used for respiration are affected late in disease

Δ Assess and Monitor

- Ability to perform activities of daily living (ADLs)

- Respiratory function, including depth, rhythm, and rate of respirations during sleep and daytime hours

- Cardiac function

- Child and family understanding of long-term effects

- Child and family coping and support

Diagnostic Procedures

Δ DNA analysis using peripheral blood or muscle tissue biopsy

Δ Serum creatine phosphokinase (CK) is very elevated

Δ Electromyography (EMG) may also be used

NANDA Nursing Diagnoses

Δ Activity intolerance

Δ Ineffective breathing pattern

Δ Caregiver role strain

Δ Ineffective coping

Δ Anticipatory grieving

Δ   Risk for infection

Δ   Impaired skin integrity

Nursing Interventions

Δ   Maintain optimal physical function for as long possible.

- Encourage the child to be independent for as long as possible and to perform ADLs.

- Perform range of motion exercises and provide appropriate physical activity. Include stretching exercises, strength and muscle training, and breathing exercises.

- Maintain proper body alignment and encourage the child to reposition self frequently to avoid skin breakdown.

- Apply splints and braces as prescribed.

Δ   Maintain respiratory functioning.

- Encourage use of incentive spirometry.

- Position to enhance expansion of lungs.

- Provide oxygen as ordered.

Δ   Encourage adequate fluid intake.

Δ   Encourage family to consider assistance with care as disease progresses (e.g., respite care, long-term care, home health care).

Δ   Facilitate discussion of end-of-life decisions when appropriate, including use of mechanical ventilation and feeding tubes.

Δ   Refer the child/family to support groups for MD.

Δ   Provide for genetic counseling for parents.

Therapeutic Procedures and Nursing Interventions

Δ   Surgical release of contractures

- Routine preoperative and postoperative care with emphasis on respiratory care

Complications and Nursing Implications

Δ   Respiratory Compromise

- Help the child turn hourly or more frequently.

- Encourage deep breathing and coughing.

- Use incentive spirometer to encourage deep breathing.

- Use intermittent positive pressure ventilation and mechanically-assisted cough devices if indicated.

- Discuss mechanical ventilation options with child/family.

- Administer antibiotics as prescribed.

Primary Reference:

Hockenberry, M., Wilson, D., Winkelstein, M. (2005). *Wong's essentials of pediatric nursing care*. (7th ed.). St. Louis, MO: Mosby.

Additional Sources:

Ball, J. W., & Bindler, R. C. (2005). *Child health nursing: Partnering with children and families*. (1st ed.). Upper Saddle River, NJ: Prentice Hall.

NANDA International (2004). *NANDA nursing diagnoses: Definitions and classification 2005-2006*. Philadelphia: NANDA.

Chapter 52: Chronic Neuromusculoskeletal Disorders

Application Exercises

Scenario: A child was diagnosed with Duchenne's muscular dystrophy 2 years ago. He is now confined to a wheelchair and often needs supplemental oxygen to maintain adequate oxygenation. He is admitted to the pediatric unit with bilateral bacterial pneumonia and is receiving intravenous antibiotics.

1. What assessments will be needed daily for this child?

2. What comfort measures need to be provided?

3. Duchenne's muscular dystrophy is inherited by _____.

Scenario: An adolescent with rheumatoid arthritis presents to the emergency department with acute inflammation of certain joints. She tells the nurse that she has been feeling weak and has difficulty maintaining her activities of daily living. During examination, the nurse notes that her wrists and knees are red, swollen, and tender with limited movement.

4. Identify assessment data needed during the course of treatment to help determine this adolescent's progress and readiness to be discharged.

5. The adolescent reports severe pain during her physical therapy (PT) exercises, and states she doesn't want to go back to PT again. Suggest an intervention to solve this problem.

    A. Medicate with morphine sulfate before PT.

    B. Use ice packs before PT to decrease inflammation.

    C. Take a warm bath or use warm packs before PT.

    D. Perform passive ROM for the adolescent before PT.

6. What measures can be taken to decrease pain and prevent deformity during sleep?

7. Describe ways to meet the adolescent's developmental needs.

Chapter 52: Chronic Neuromusculoskeletal Disorders

Application Exercises Answer Key

Scenario: A child was diagnosed with Duchenne's muscular dystrophy 2 years ago. He is now confined to a wheelchair and often needs supplemental oxygen to maintain adequate oxygenation. He is admitted to the pediatric unit with bilateral bacterial pneumonia and is receiving intravenous antibiotics.

1. What assessments will be needed daily for this child?

   Assess respiratory and cardiac status, mobility, fluid and electrolyte status, and skin integrity.

2. What comfort measures need to be provided?

   Support joints and extremities, turn frequently, and provide diversional activities appropriate for the child's age.

3. Duchenne's muscular dystrophy is inherited by _____.

   X-linked recessive trait. An X-linked trait means the mother of the child is the carrier of the disease.

Scenario: An adolescent with rheumatoid arthritis presents to the emergency department with acute inflammation of certain joints. She tells the nurse that she has been feeling weak and has difficulty maintaining her activities of daily living. During examination, the nurse notes that her wrists and knees are red, swollen, and tender with limited movement.

4. Identify assessment data needed during the course of treatment to help determine this adolescent's progress and readiness to be discharged.

   Assess range of motion, anatomical alignment of the extremities (presence of deformities), ability to perform ADLs, compliance with physical therapy, level of pain and success of pain relief measures, and knowledge of medications and their side effects.

5. The adolescent reports severe pain during her physical therapy (PT) exercises, and states she doesn't want to go back to PT again. Suggest an intervention to solve this problem.

    A. Medicate with morphine sulfate before PT.

    B. Use ice packs before PT to decrease inflammation.

    C. Take a warm bath or use warm packs before PT.

    D. Perform passive ROM for the adolescent before PT.

Use of warm or hot packs or baths before exercising can decrease joint pain during exercise. Medicating with a narcotic would not decrease inflammation, and NSAIDs are better medications for inflammation and joint pain. Ice tends to increase stiffness in joints. Performance of passive ROM before PT is not realistic and would not decrease pain and inflammation.

6. What measures can be taken to decrease pain and prevent deformity during sleep?

Splinting of knees, wrists and hands, and sleeping on a firm mattress without pillows under knees may help decrease pain and prevent flexion deformities.

7. Describe ways to meet the adolescent's developmental needs.

Encourage discussions regarding concerns about body image, encourage contact with peers, and explain the purpose of the prescribed treatment to maintain mobility and functioning.

Unit 3   Nursing Care of Children with Emergencies, Developmental Disorders, or Psychosocial Issues

Chapter 53:   Pediatric Emergencies

Contributors: Glenda J. Bondurant, MSN, RN

Michele Hinds, PhD, RN

 NCLEX-RN® Connections:

Learning Objective: Review and apply knowledge within **"Pediatric Emergencies"** in readiness for performance of the following nursing activities as outlined by the NCLEX-RN® test plan:

Δ   Recognize and respond to emergency situations including notification of the primary care provider.

Δ   Perform and document appropriate assessments based upon the child's problem.

Δ   Recognize signs and symptoms associated with specific alterations in body systems.

Δ   Interpret data that need to be reported immediately.

Δ   Monitor therapeutic devices (drainage/irrigating devices, chest tubes), if inserted, for proper functioning.

Δ   Coordinate continuity of care.

Δ   Promote and evaluate the child's progress toward recovery.

Δ   Provide client teaching regarding management of the child's health problem.

Δ   Evaluate and document the child's response to emergency interventions and complete the proper documentation.

Δ   Assess the child/family's response and fears related to loss.

Δ   Assist and support the child/family during resolution of suffering, grief, loss, dying, and bereavement.

Δ   Make appropriate referrals to resources to help adjust to loss/bereavement.

Key Points

Δ **Respiratory Emergencies**

- Respiratory failure occurs when there is diminished ability to maintain adequate oxygenation of blood. A manifestation of respiratory insufficiency is increased work of breathing.

- Respiratory arrest occurs when breathing completely stops.

- When respiratory distress is treated, or rescue breathing is started in a timely manner, infants and children are less likely than adults to have cardiac arrest.

Δ **Drowning** – asphyxiation while being submerged in fluid

- Near-drowning incidents are those in which the child has survived for 24 hr after being submerged in fluid.

- Drowning may occur in any standing body of water of at least 1-inch depth (e.g., bathtubs, toilets, buckets, pools, ponds, lakes).

Δ **Sudden Infant Death Syndrome (SIDS)**

- SIDS is the sudden, unpredictable, and undetectable death of an infant without an identified cause, even after investigation and autopsy.

- It is a major cause of death in infants from 1 month to 1 year.

- SIDS is not preventable, but risks may be reduced.

- Education about reducing the risk of SIDS is on the rise.

Δ **Poisoning** – ingestion of or exposure to toxic substances

- Most poisonings occur in the child's home or homes of relatives or friends.

- Poisonings may also occur in schools or health care facilities.

- Toxic substances leading to poisoning are usually ingested, but some may be inhaled.

- Using methods to prevent poisoning is vital.

Key Factors

Δ   Respiratory emergencies (e.g., respiratory failure, respiratory arrest)

- Airway obstruction prevents adequate air exchange. This obstruction can lead to respiratory failure or arrest if not corrected.

- Physiologic functional alterations include:

Functional Alteration	Possible Causes
Primary inefficient gas exchange	• Cerebral trauma • Brain tumors • Overdose of barbiturates, opioids, and/or benzodiazepines • Asphyxia • CNS infections (e.g., encephalitis)
Obstructive lung disease (increased resistance)	• Aspiration • Infection • Tumors • Anaphylaxis • Laryngospasm • Asthma
Restrictive lung disease	• Cystic fibrosis ◊ Pneumonia • Respiratory distress syndrome

Δ   Factors that contribute to the risk of **drowning or near-drowning** include:

- Age of the child.

  ◊   Drowning is the second leading cause of accidental death in children ages 1 to 14.

  ◊   Drowning is the leading cause of accidental injury-related death in children ages 1 to 4.

- Gender.

  ◊   Males are two times more likely to drown than females, and females are two times more likely to drown in a bathtub than males.

- Swimming ability (may be overconfident) or lack of ability.

- Lack of supervision. (Children can drown while being supervised.)

- Boating without life jackets.

- Diving into water.

Δ   **SIDS**

- Infant was apparently healthy.

- SIDS is not caused by suffocation, nor does it have an identifiable cause.

- Death is often associated with sleep and without signs of suffering.

- SIDS is a diagnosis of exclusion that is made only after every other cause of death is discarded.

- Risk factors include:

  ◊ Maternal health and behaviors during pregnancy.

    ° Age less than 20 years

    ° Alcohol, drug, and/or tobacco use

    ° Low weight gain during pregnancy

    ° Anemia

    ° Placental abnormalities

    ° Sexually transmitted disease or urinary tract infection

  ◊ Twins.

  ◊ Premature birth.

  ◊ Small for gestational age.

  ◊ Persistent apnea.

  ◊ Bronchopulmonary dysplasia.

  ◊ Family history of SIDS.

  ◊ Environmental risk factors.

    ° Low socioeconomic status

    ° Crowded living conditions

    ° Cold weather

    ° Use of soft items in crib (e.g., stuffed animals, blankets)

    ° Prone sleeping position

    ° Sleeping with others

Δ **Poisoning**

- Children who are younger than 6 years are more likely to ingest toxic substances due to their developmental level. (e.g., Infants explore their environment orally, Preschoolers imitate others.)

- Medications, household chemicals, plants, and heavy metals are sources of toxic ingestion.

- Acetaminophen (Tylenol) is the most common medication poisoning in children (Toxic dose is 150 mg/kg or higher.).

- Liquid corrosives cause more damage than granular corrosives.

- Immediate danger with hydrocarbon ingestion is aspiration.

- Lead may be ingested or small particles inhaled during renovations of areas with lead-based paint.

- Common toxic substances ingested by children include acetaminophen, aspirin, iron, hydrocarbons, corrosives, and/or lead.

Assessment

Δ   History of illnesses (chronic or acute)

Δ   History of events leading to respiratory emergency

Δ   Presence of allergies

Δ   Physical Assessment Findings for **Respiratory Emergencies**

- Color of skin – central or peripheral cyanosis indicative of hypoxia

- Heart rate/rhythm – tachycardia or bradycardia (severe sign of hypoxia)

- Respiratory effort, depth of respirations, tachypnea or bradypnea (severe sign of hypoxia), expiratory grunting, nasal flaring, and presence of retractions and area noted, such as intercostal (between ribs)

- Assessment for palpable pulses, capillary refill – greater than 2 sec indicates decreased perfusion

- Ability to talk (sentences or just single words)

- CNS symptoms ranging from restlessness and lethargy to coma (severe sign)

- Diaphoresis

- Signs of choking

    ◊   Universal choking sign (clutching neck with thumb and index finger)

    ◊   Inability to speak

    ◊   Weak, ineffective coughs

    ◊   High-pitched sounds or no sounds made while inhaling

    ◊   Dyspnea

    ◊   Cyanosis

Δ   Specific Assessment Factors for **Drowning/Near Drowning**

- History of event including location and time of submersion

- Salt water or nonsalt water drowning

- Warm or cold water drowning (bathtub versus cold lake)

- Body temperature for hypothermia

- Observation for bruises, spinal cord injury, or other physical injuries

- Respiratory assessment for drowning/near drowning – same as above assessment for respiratory emergencies

Δ   Assessment for **SIDS**

- History of events prior to finding infant

- History of illnesses

- Pregnancy and birth history

- Presence of risk factors

- Family coping and support

Δ   Assessment for **poisoning**

- History of chronic and acute illnesses

- List of medications or chemicals that the child may have been exposed to

- Number of pills or amount of liquid ingested

- Time of ingestion

- Physical response

  ◊   Respiratory rate, rhythm, and effort

  ◊   Heart rate and rhythm

  ◊   Level of consciousness

  ◊   Seizures

  ◊   Pupil size and response

  ◊   Swelling of facial area, especially lips and mouth

  ◊   Color of mucous membranes

  ◊   Peripheral pulses

  ◊   Diaphoretic or dry skin

  ◊   Presence or absence of bowel sounds

Δ   Manifestations of specific substances

Substance	Clinical Manifestations
Acetaminophen	• 2 to 4 hr after ingestion – nausea, vomiting, sweating, and pallor • 24 to 36 hr after ingestion – improvement in the child's condition • 36 hr to 7 days or longer (hepatic stage) – pain in upper right quadrant, confusion, stupor, jaundice, and coagulation disturbances • Final stage – death or gradual recovery
Aspirin (acetylsalicylic acid)	• Acute poisoning – nausea, vomiting, disorientation, diaphoresis, tachypnea, tinnitus, oliguria, lightheadedness, and seizures • Chronic poisoning – subtle version of acute manifestations, bleeding tendencies, dehydration, and seizures more severe than acute poisoning
Supplemental iron	• Initial period 30 min to 6 hr after ingestion – vomiting, hematemesis, diarrhea, gastric pain, and bloody stools • Latency period 2 to 12 hr after ingestion – improvement of the child's condition • Systemic toxicity period 4 to 24 hr after ingestion – metabolic acidosis, hyperglycemia, bleeding, fever, shock, and possible death • Hepatic injury period 48 to 96 hr – seizures or coma
Hydrocarbons (e.g., gasoline, kerosene, lighter fluid, paint thinner, turpentine)	• Gagging, choking, coughing, nausea, and vomiting • Lethargy, weakness, tachypnea, cyanosis, grunting, and retractions
Corrosives (e.g., household cleaners, batteries, denture cleaners, bleach)	• Pain and burning in mouth, throat, and stomach • Edematous lips, tongue, and pharynx with white mucous membranes • Violent vomiting with hemoptysis • Drooling • Anxiety • Shock
Lead	• Low-dose exposure – easily distracted, impulsivity, hyperactivity, impaired hearing, and mild intellectual difficulty • High-dose exposure – mental retardation, blindness, paralysis, coma, seizures, and death • Other manifestations – renal impairment, impaired calcium function, anemia

Diagnostic Procedures

Δ   Respiratory Emergencies (including near drowning)

• Arterial blood gases (ABGs) to confirm oxygenation level

• Chest radiographs to determine status of lungs with respiratory distress, near drowning

Δ   SIDS

- Investigation of death scene

- Autopsy

Δ   Poisoning Diagnosis

- Lead levels in blood

- CBC with differential to identify anemia

- Liver function tests to identify liver damage

- ABGs to assess oxygenation status

- Serum iron

- Acetaminophen serum levels

NANDA Nursing Diagnoses

Δ   **Respiratory Emergencies** and **Drowning**

- Ineffective airway clearance

- Ineffective coping

- Anxiety

- Risk for aspiration

- Ineffective breathing pattern

- Fear

- Impaired gas exchange

- Risk for dysfunctional grieving

- Deficient knowledge

- Impaired tissue perfusion

- Impaired spontaneous ventilation

Nursing Interventions

Δ   Interventions for the infant, child, or adolescent with respiratory arrest (collapse), including respiratory injuries, poisoning with respiratory arrest, and drowning/near drowning episodes include:

- Checking for responsiveness; if none, call out for help.

- Opening airway by head-tilt/chin lift or jaw thrust (if trauma suspected).

- Checking for breathing by looking, listening, and feeling.

- Giving two effective breaths at 1 sec for each breath;

  ◊ If available, use correct-sized bag/valve/mask with connected oxygen for rescue breathing.

  ◊ Watch the chest rise and fall to assess effectiveness.

- Checking for pulse – brachial or femoral for infants (up to 1 year); carotid or femoral for the child age 1 to adolescent.

- Beginning chest compressions at the rate of 100/min using the American Heart Association guidelines (if no pulse or severe bradycardia).

  ◊ Hand position is just below the nipple line for infants; use two fingers for chest compressions.

  ◊ Hand position is in the center of the chest between the nipples for children and adolescents; use either the heel of one hand or the heels of both hands placed one on top of the other – depends on size of the victim.

  ◊ Compress approximately ⅓ to ½ the depth of the victim's chest.

- If pulse is present but there are no respirations, continuing rescue breathing 12 to 20 breaths/min (one breath every 3 to 5 sec)

- For rescue breathing with chest compressions in infants and children, using a 15 to 2 ratio for a single rescuer and 30 to 2 ratio for two professional rescuers

- Calling 911 or activating EMS system after performing five cycles of CPR after finding an already-collapsed victim

Δ For Obstructed Airway

- With a responsive victim:

  ◊ Infant – Use combination of back blows and chest thrusts.

  ◊ Child and adolescent – Use abdominal thrusts (Heimlich maneuver).

- Remove obstruction or large debris, but do not reach into the mouth of an infant to prevent pushing obstruction farther down the throat.

- Place the recovered child (one who resumes breathing) into recovery position – on side with legs bent at knees to stabilize in place.

- Use a calm approach with the child/family.

- Administer oxygen as prescribed.

- Administer medications as prescribed (e.g., steroids for inflammation; bronchodilators such as albuterol [Proventil]; racemic epinephrine; and antibiotics), IV fluids, and emergency medications.

- Keep the family informed of the child's status.

Δ **SIDS**

- Reduction of risk for SIDS
    - ◊ Infant sleep position should be on back for sleep.
    - ◊ Prevent exposure to tobacco smoke.
    - ◊ Prevent overheating.
    - ◊ Use a firm, tight-fitting mattress in the infant's crib.
    - ◊ Remove pillows, quilts, and sheepskins from the crib during sleep.
    - ◊ Ensure that the infant's head is kept uncovered during sleep.
- Allow the infant's family an opportunity to express feelings.
- Provide private time for the family to be with the infant after death.
- Provide support.
- Encourage using a home monitoring system for future infants.
- Provide home monitoring for those at high risk, such as a remaining twin.
- Educate or reinforce proper sleeping position, crib environment, smoke-free environment, and the avoidance of overheating.
- Recommend support groups.
- Recommend counseling.

Δ **Poisoning**

- Protect airway.
    - ◊ Assist with intubation if needed, and observe symmetrical movement of the infant's chest.
    - ◊ Position the infant with the head of the bed slightly elevated unless contraindicated.
    - ◊ Keep emergency equipment (e.g., oral airway, suction catheter) at bedside.

Δ Apply cardiac respiratory monitor to the child.

Δ Monitor the infant's pulse oximetry.

Δ Insert IV and begin administering fluids as prescribed.

Δ Insert nasogastric tube as ordered.

Δ Insert indwelling urinary catheter and attach to urine bag.

Δ Monitor I&O.

Δ Administer specific antidote as prescribed.

Interventions for Specific Substances	
Substance	**Interventions**
Acetaminophen	• Acetylcysteine (Mucomyst) given orally
Aspirin (acetylsalicylic acid)	• Activated charcoal • Gastric lavage • Sodium bicarbonate • Oxygen and ventilation • Vitamin K
Supplemental iron	• Emesis or lavage • Chelation therapy using deferoxamine mesylate (Desferal)
Hydrocarbons (e.g., gasoline, kerosene, lighter fluid, paint thinner, turpentine)	• No induced vomiting • Intubation with cuffed endotracheal tube prior to any gastric decontamination • Treatment of chemical pneumonia
Corrosives (e.g., household cleaners, batteries, denture cleaners, bleach)	• Airway maintenance • NPO • No attempt to neutralize • No induced vomiting • Analgesics for pain
Lead	• Chelation therapy using calcium EDTA (calcium disodium versenate)

- Keep family informed of the child's condition and needs.

- Family safety education:

    ◊ Keep Poison Control Center (PCC) number by the telephone.

    ◊ Contact PCC before taking any action other than maintaining the child's airway.

    ◊ Do not give the child ipecac.

    ◊ Install childproof locks on cabinets containing potentially harmful substances (e.g., medications, alcohol, cleaning solutions, mouthwash, outdoor chemicals).

    ◊ Supervise the child when he is taking medication(s).

    ◊ Do not take medication in front of children.

    ◊ Discard unused medications.

    ◊ Keep plants out of the reach of the child.

    ◊ Eliminate lead-based paint in the home.

    ◊ Use nonmercury thermometers.

Δ Home care education to prevent drowning

- Encourage parents to lock toilet seats if toddler is at home.

- Do not leave the child unattended in the bathtub.

- Do not leave the child unattended in a swimming pool, even if the child has had swimming lessons.

- Make sure private pools have locking gates to prevent the child from wandering into the area.

- Have the child wear a life jacket while boating.

Therapeutic Procedures and Nursing Interventions

Δ For the child with respiratory emergencies, near drowning, and/or poisoning where airway is unstable and aspiration is likely:

- Intubation may be needed with placement on a ventilator.

- Assistance with positioning during intubation may be needed to reduce possibility for injury.

Complications and Nursing Implications

Δ Respiratory arrest from any cause including drowning, poisoning, and possible SIDS

- Initiate CPR.

Δ Death

- Allow private time for parents to be with the child.

- Support the parents.

Primary Reference:

Hockenberry, M., Wilson, D., Winkelstein, M. (2005). *Wong's essentials of pediatric nursing care*. (7th ed.). St. Louis, MO: Mosby.

Additional Resources:

American Heart Association. (n.d.). *American Heart Association 2005 Guidelines for CPR and ECC*. Retrieved May 10, 2006, from http://www.americanheart.org/presenter.jhtml?identifier=3035517

For information about SIDS, go to the National SIDS/Infant Death Resource Center Web site, *www.sidscenter.org*.

NANDA International (2004). *NANDA nursing diagnoses: Definitions and classification 2005-2006*. Philadelphia: NANDA.

Safe Kids USA. (n.d.). *Safety Tips*. Retrieved, March 2, 2007, from http://www.usa.safekids.org/tier2_rl.cfm?folder_id=166

WebMD. (2006, May). Iron *poisoning treatment*. Retrieved March 2, 2007, from http://firstaid.webmd.com/iron_poisoning_treatment_firstaid.htm

WebMD. (2004, June). *Chelating agents for lead poisoning*. Retrieved March 2, 2007, from http://children.webmd.com/Chelating-agents-for-lead-poisoning

Chapter 53: Pediatric Emergencies

Application Exercises

Scenario: A nurse in the emergency department is caring for the parents of an infant who has just died from SIDS.

1. The parents tell the nurse they found their infant in the corner of the crib blue and not breathing. Which of the following questions should the nurse ask the parents?

    A. "What did you do when you put her down for the evening?"

    B. "Why did you put the blanket in the bed with her?"

    C. "Could you tell me more about how you found her?"

    D. "Didn't you know how to do CPR?"

2. The mother becomes angry and begins yelling at the nurse. How should the nurse react?

3. The nurse returns to the room and is working toward closure with the parents. Explain what intervention is important at this time.

4. Match the following common causes of poisoning in children with the symptoms seen in poisoning with that substance.

    _____ Acetaminophen   A. Edema of lips, hemoptysis, drooling

    _____ Aspirin   B. Mental impairment, blindness

    _____ Lead   C. Liver failure occurring without treatment

    _____ Corrosive substances   D. Nausea/vomiting, ringing in ears, lightheadedness

5. A child who has swallowed paint thinner is brought to the emergency department by her parent. The child is lethargic, gagging, and cyanotic. Which of the following emergency interventions should the nurse implement?

    A. Induce vomiting with syrup of ipecac.

    B. Insert gastric tube and give activated charcoal.

    C. Prepare for intubation with cuffed endotracheal tube.

    D. Administer chelation therapy using deferoxamine mesylate.

6. A nurse finds an infant unconscious and completely unresponsive in her crib in the acute care facility. The nurse pushes the emergency call button on the wall. Place the next four interventions in the correct order.

_____ Give two rescue breaths using a bag/valve/mask.

_____ Check for a femoral pulse.

_____ Open the airway by tilting neck and lifting chin.

_____ Look, listen, and feel for breathing.

7. A nurse is giving rescue breathing to a child who experienced respiratory arrest. How can the nurse ascertain whether or not the rescue breathing is effective?

8. A nurse is speaking to a group of parents with toddlers. List several nursing instructions the nurse can provide to help the parents prevent accidental poisoning in their toddler.

Chapter 53: Pediatric Emergencies

Application Exercises Answer Key

Scenario: A nurse in the emergency department is caring for the parents of an infant who has just died from SIDS.

1. The parents tell the nurse they found their infant in the corner of the crib blue and not breathing. Which of the following questions should the nurse ask the parents?

> A. "What did you do when you put her down for the evening?"
> B. "Why did you put the blanket in the bed with her?"
> **C. "Could you tell me more about how you found her?"**
> D. "Didn't you know how to do CPR?"

This is the most open-ended question, and its purpose is to obtain information. The other questions are judgmental or accusatory and will serve no purpose.

2. The mother becomes angry and begins yelling at the nurse. How should the nurse react?

The nurse should acknowledge the mother's anger. The nurse then needs to ensure that a family member is present and leave the room for a few minutes. The nurse needs to recognize that the mother will shift back and forth in the stages of grief for at least a few days between denial and anger, and that these are normal stages of grieving.

3. The nurse returns to the room and is working toward closure with the parents. Explain what intervention is important at this time.

The nurse should offer the parents the opportunity to hold their infant. The nurse could prepare a box with locks of hair, a blanket, arm bands, or any other personal items belonging to the infant.

4. Match the following common causes of poisoning in children with the symptoms seen in poisoning with that substance.

__C__ Acetaminophen   A. Edema of lips, hemoptysis, drooling

__D__ Aspirin   B. Mental impairment, blindness

__B__ Lead   C. Liver failure occurring without treatment

__A__ Corrosive substances   D. Nausea/vomiting, ringing in ears, lightheadedness

5. A child who has swallowed paint thinner is brought to the emergency department by her parent. The child is lethargic, gagging, and cyanotic. Which of the following emergency interventions should the nurse implement?

      A. Induce vomiting with syrup of ipecac.

      B. Insert gastric tube and give activated charcoal.

      C. Prepare for intubation with cuffed endotracheal tube.

      D. Administer chelation therapy using deferoxamine mesylate.

The emergency treatment for poisoning with hydrocarbons, such as paint thinner, includes intubation to protect the airway before proceeding with gastric decontamination of the stomach. Vomiting should not be induced. Buffering the stomach with activated charcoal is not indicated. Chelation therapy with deferoxamine mesylate is a specific antidote for iron poisoning.

6. A nurse finds an infant unconscious and completely unresponsive in her crib in the acute care facility. The nurse pushes the emergency call button on the wall. Place the next four interventions in the correct order.

      __3__ Give two rescue breaths using a bag/valve/mask.

      __4__ Check for a femoral pulse.

      __1__ Open the airway by tilting neck and lifting chin.

      __2__ Look, listen, and feel for breathing.

The next intervention after assuring unresponsiveness and calling for help is to open the infant's airway. The neck tilt, chin lift method may be used if no trauma is suspected. With the airway open, the nurse can assess for breathing by looking, listening, and feeling. Giving rescue breathing should occur next, and checking a pulse is the next response.

7. A nurse is giving rescue breathing to a child who experienced respiratory arrest. How can the nurse ascertain whether or not the rescue breathing is effective?

The nurse should observe the child's chest rising and falling to assure that rescue breathing has been effective.

8. A nurse is speaking to a group of parents with toddlers. List several nursing instructions the nurse can provide to help the parents prevent accidental poisoning in their toddler.

Place childproof locks on cabinets containing potentially harmful substances (e.g., medications, alcohol, cleaning solutions, mouthwash, outdoor chemicals).

Supervise the child when he is taking medication(s).

Do not take medication in front of children.

Discard unused medications.

Keep plants out of the reach of small children.

Eliminate lead-based paint.

Use nonmercury thermometers.

Unit 3   Nursing Care of Children with Emergencies, Developmental Disorders, or Psychosocial Issues

Chapter 54:   Developmental Disorders

Contributor: Candyce F. Antley, MN, RN

 NCLEX-RN® Connections:

Learning Objective: Review and apply knowledge within "**Developmental Disorders**" in readiness for performance of the following nursing activities as outlined by the NCLEX-RN® test plan:

Δ   Recognize and document signs and symptoms of the child's problem.

Δ   Assess the child's developmental stage and modify approaches to care in alignment with the child's developmental stage.

Δ   Assess/evaluate the child with altered communication abilities, and intervene to promote effective adaptation.

Δ   Identify stressors that impact the child's behavior and use of behavioral interventions.

Δ   Plan and provide care based on the child's health alteration.

Δ   Use alternative methods for client communication as appropriate.

Δ   Provide client teaching regarding management of the child's health alteration, including modification of approaches to care in alignment with the child's developmental stage.

Δ   Use, monitor, and evaluate effectiveness of behavior/therapeutic interventions (e.g., contract, behavior modification) to assist the child with achieving and maintaining self-control of behavior.

Δ   Evaluate and document care given.

 Key Points

Δ   **Down syndrome** is the most common chromosomal abnormality.

- It occurs in one out of every 800 to 1,000 live births.

- Clinical manifestations of Down syndrome include:

  ◊   Possibility of multiple physical problems including congenital heart defects, thyroid dysfunction, congenital hypothyroidism, dysfunctional immune system, and high risk for leukemia.

◊ The presence of cognitive defects with an IQ range from moderate (35 to 50) to low average (90).

Δ **Autism** is a complex bioneurological developmental disorder of brain function.

- Onset is usually before age 3.

- There is a broad range of severity of intellectual and behavioral deficits.

Δ **Attention Deficit Hyperactivity Disorder (ADHD)** involves the inability to control behaviors requiring sustained attention.

- Inattention, impulsivity, and hyperactivity are characteristic behaviors of ADHD.

- ADHD is more common in males than females.

- Types of ADHD include:

   ◊ Combined type – most common.

   ◊ ADHD predominantly inattentive.

   ◊ ADHD predominantly hyperactive-impulsive.

- ADHD does not affect the life expectancy of the child.

Key Factors

Δ The exact etiology of Down syndrome is unknown. However, certain multifactorial associations (e.g., maternal age) can be a contributing factor.

- A woman who is 35 years or older is at greatest risk for giving birth to an infant with Down syndrome.

- Down syndrome occurs in one out of every 400 live births in women who are age 35. It occurs in one out of every 110 live births in women who are older than 40.

- More than 80% of those with Down syndrome live to at least 55 years.

Δ   Autism is a behavioral spectrum disorder diagnosed four times more often in boys than girls.

- Genetics may play a major role in diagnosing autism.

- Autism is caused by abnormalities in brain structures or functions.

- Physical difficulties experienced by the child with autism include sensory integration dysfunction, sleep disorders, digestive disorders, feeding disorders, epilepsy, and/or allergies.

- Functioning can range from poor (inability to perform self-care, inability to communicate and relate to others) to high (ability to function at near normal level).

Δ   **ADHD** may have a genetic link.

- Organic cause of ADHD is theorized to be related to function of brain chemicals.

- Environmental and dietary factors are unsubstantiated.

- Other disorders often accompanying ADHD include Tourette's syndrome, oppositional defiant disorder, learning disabilities, depression, anxiety, conduct disorder, and bipolar disorder.

- Inattentive or impulsive behavior may put the child at risk for injury.

- Behaviors associated with ADHD may receive negative attention from adults and peers.

- Key symptoms of ADHD include:

  ◊   Inattention.

  - Difficulty paying attention

  - Difficulty listening

  - Easily distracted

  ◊   Hyperactivity.

  - Fidgeting, inability to sit still

  - Running and climbing inappropriately

  - Difficulty playing quietly

  - Talking excessively

  ◊   Impulsivity.

  - Difficulty waiting for turns

  - Interruptive

  - Blurting out answers

Assessments

Δ   Down Syndrome

- Obtain nursing history of mother's pregnancy and birth history and genetic testing.

  ◊   Observe physical characteristics of Down syndrome:

    ° Small head.

    ° Flattened forehead.

    ° Low-set ears.

    ° Upward slant to the eyes.

    ° Protruding tongue.

    ° Hypotonia (decreased muscle tone).

    ° Transverse palmar crease.

    ° Underdeveloped nasal bone.

- Assess respiratory functioning due to poor muscle tone.

- Assess heart sounds for presence of a murmur.

- Note infant's ability to eat due to protruding tongue and mouth breathing.

- Assess for dry mucous membranes due to mouth breathing.

- Assess bowel functioning.

- Assessment of an older child includes height and weight; compare to appropriate growth chart.

- Assess cognitive development.

- Assess skin integrity due to tendency toward dry, rough, cracking skin.

- Determine family knowledge, coping, and support.

- Observe interaction and bonding between mother and infant.

- Assess parental feelings about having a child with Down syndrome.

Δ   **Autism**

- Obtain nursing history of mother's pregnancy and birth history.

- Obtain history of the child's sleep patterns and difficulties.

- Obtain history of allergies.

- Obtain history of feeding or digestive difficulties such as constipation.

  ◊   Assess eating habits that may be problematic such as refusing to eat, eating inedible objects, and/or throwing food.

- Assess for history of self-mutilation.

- Assess the child's cognitive development pattern – cognitive delays may be present.

- Assess all communication, verbal and nonverbal, reactions to sensory stimuli, social interaction, ability to make or maintain eye contact, and appropriateness of behaviors for age. Psychosocial manifestations for the child with autism include:

  ◊ Behavior – may demonstrate rigid adherence to routine, hand or finger flapping, clapping, rocking, swaying, head banging, hand biting, and/or preoccupation with certain repetitive activities.

  ◊ Social interaction – may show lack of responsiveness to and interest in others, lack of eye contact, failure to cuddle or be comforted, and/or lack of peer friendships.

  ◊ Communication – language delay, echolalia, and/or failure to imitate communication with others.

Δ **ADHD**

- Nursing history of mother's difficulties with pregnancy or birth, family history of ADHD, and chronic and/or acute illness

- Child's developmental history

- Medications taken on regular basis

- Effect of medications taken for ADHD (e.g., lack of appetite, inability to sleep, anger or aggression when medication wearing off)

- Nutritional assessment to include daily intake

- Sleep patterns (may be awake while family is sleeping)

- Daily activities

- Family stress

- Parents' perceptions about and level of tolerance of child's behaviors

- Teachers' perceptions of child's behaviors and performance

- Management strategies used at home and school

- Perception of self, school and friends, and preferred activities

Diagnostic Procedures

Δ **Down Syndrome**

- Conduct prenatal testing, such as amniocentesis, for chromosome analysis to confirm the genetic abnormality.

- Chromosome analysis should be done to confirm the genetic abnormality.

Δ **Autism** and **ADHD** may be suspected early in the child's life or after the child begins school.

- Diagnosis may be delayed several years after symptoms appear.

- Children are diagnosed through recognition of behavioral symptoms by learning specialists and/or primary health care providers.

- Prognosis for autism/ADHD is best when diagnosed as early as possible.

NANDA Nursing Diagnoses

Δ Risk for caregiver role strain

Δ Delayed growth and development

Δ Risk for infection

Δ Risk for injury

Δ Deficient knowledge

Δ Imbalanced nutrition: less than body requirements

Δ Risk for impaired parenting

Δ Risk for impaired parent/infant/child attachment

Δ Self-care deficits

Δ Chronic low self-esteem

Δ Risk for self-mutilation

Δ Sleep pattern disturbance

Δ Risk for impaired skin integrity

Δ Social isolation

Δ Impaired social interaction

Δ Impaired verbal communication

Nursing Interventions

Δ   **Down Syndrome**

- Swaddle the infant to maintain warmth and security.

- Explain to the parents that the infant's lack of clinging is a physical characteristic due to hypotonia, and not a sign of detachment.

- Encourage parents to change the infant's position frequently to help promote aeration of the lungs.

- Teach the parents the importance of food and fluids to maintain adequate nutrition.

- Emphasize the need to balance adequate nutrition. Poor feeding can result in obesity later in life.

- Teach family how to prevent physical complications.

  ◊   Avoid infection by engaging in good handwashing.

  ◊   Increase fiber in diet to avoid constipation.

  ◊   Encourage physical activity.

- Support the family at the time of diagnosis.

Δ   Advise parents to seek regular check-ups for their child.

Δ   Emphasize the child's strengths while being aware of limitations to ensure safety.

Δ   Identify and refer child/parents to support groups.

Δ   Interventions specific to **autism** include:

- Providing a stable environment.

- Determining and respecting the child's possibly negative response to tactile stimulation and physical contact.

- Slowly changing the needs of the child's environment if indicated.

- Encouraging parents to help provide care in the health facility when appropriate.

- Cautiously providing nutrition to engage the child in eating.

- Positively reinforcing the child for verbal communication attempts.

- Using helmets if the child engages in head banging.

- Carefully monitoring the child's behaviors to ensure safety.

- Modifying behavior when appropriate.

- Limiting self-stimulating and ritualistic behaviors by providing alternative play activities.

- Supporting parents in their role.

- Providing one-on-one interactions when working with the child.

- Monitoring for signs/symptoms of anxiety or distress. Prognosis for more normal development is enhanced by early intervention.

- Identifying desired behaviors and rewarding the child for them.

- Role modeling social skills.

- Role-playing situations involving conflict.

- Determining emotional and situational triggers.

- Encouraging parents to seek specialized education programs and support groups.

Δ Interventions for Children with **ADHD**

- Use a calm, firm, respectful approach with the child.

- Model the kind of attention desirable from the child.

- Obtain the child's attention before giving the child important information or directions.

- Set limits for acceptable behavior if needed.

- Praise the child for cooperation and attention.

- Plan physical activities through which the child can use energy.

- Administer medications, such as methylphenidate (Ritalin), as prescribed.

   ◊ Note behavioral changes related to dose and time of medication administration.

   ◊ Teach the child/family about medications prescribed to include dose and time medication given for maximum effect and side effects related to appetite, sleep, and behavior.

   ◊ Encourage small, frequent snacks if medication is suppressing the child's appetite.

   ◊ Stress the importance of locking medication in cabinet.

Δ Help the family identify ways to minimize excessive environmental distractions.

Δ Discuss ways for the family to implement behavioral management plans.

Δ Plan activities that provide opportunities for success.

Δ Provide emotional support to the child/parents.

Δ Encourage parents to work with school nurse and teachers to develop an individual plan for the child's needs.

Therapeutic Procedures and Nursing Interventions

Δ   **Down Syndrome**

- Surgical intervention of congenital anomalies such as cardiac defects

  ◊   Listen to concerns and discuss with parents ethical dilemmas regarding treatment for physical defects.

  ◊   Postoperative nursing care includes wound care, respiratory care to prevent infection, and pain management.

- Periodic thyroid function testing

Complications and Nursing Interventions

Δ   Respiratory infections are common in children with **Down syndrome** due to decreased muscle tone and poor drainage of mucous because of deformed nasal bone.

- Teach family good handwashing. Encourage frequent repositioning of the child to promote respiratory function.

- Teach parents to perform postural drainage and percussion if needed.

- Rinse the child's mouth with water after feeding and at other times of the day when dry. Mucous membranes are dry due to constant mouth breathing, which also increases the risk for respiratory infection.

- Encourage exercise in older children.

- Seek health care at earliest sign of infection.

- Follow antibiotic schedule when prescribed.

Primary Reference:

Hockenberry, M., Wilson, D., Winkelstein, M. (2005). *Wong's essentials of pediatric nursing care.* (7th ed.). St. Louis, MO: Mosby.

Additional Resources:

Ball, J. W., & Bindler, R. C. (2005). *Child health nursing: Partnering with children and families.* (1st ed.). Upper Saddle River, NJ: Prentice Hall.

For information about autism, go to the National Autism Association Web site, *www.nationalautismassociation.org.*

NANDA International (2004). *NANDA nursing diagnoses: Definitions and classification 2005-2006.* Philadelphia: NANDA.

Townsend, M. C. (2004). *Essentials of psychiatric mental health nursing.* (3rd ed.). Philadelphia: F. A. Davis Company.

Varcarolis, Carson, & Shoemaker. (2006). *Foundations of psychiatric mental health nursing: A clinical approach.* St. Louis, MO: Saunders.

Chapter 54: Developmental Disorders

Application Exercises

1. A 5-year-old child is brought to the primary care provider by his mother. The mother tells the provider that the child is unable to sit through meals and is easily distracted. At night, he gets up while the family is sleeping and wanders about the house. She also tells the provider that he is doing poorly in his kindergarten class due to his inability to concentrate on work. For which of the following should this child be evaluated?

   A. Mental retardation

   B. Down syndrome

   C. ADHD

   D. Autism

Scenario: The parents of a newborn diagnosed with Down syndrome ask the nurse, "How can we manage a child with so many problems? We've heard that children with Down syndrome will never be normal, will never be independent, and always die young!"

2. Discuss how the nurse should respond to the parents' fears.

3. How should the nurse respond if the parents ask, "Why did this happen to our baby?"

4. A nurse is discussing with the parents of a 3-month-old infant with Down syndrome ways to help prevent recurrent respiratory infections. Which of the following interventions should the nurse discuss with these parents? (Select all that apply.)

   _____ Practice frequent handwashing.

   _____ Keep infant in Fowler's position most of the time to prevent choking.

   _____ Use a bulb syringe to remove nasal mucous.

   _____ Keep the infant's mouth moist by rinsing frequently with water.

5. A nurse is assessing a 4-year-old child for signs of autism. The nurse should be alert for

   A. constant talking and impulsive behavior.

   B. poor language and interpersonal skills.

   C. frequent respiratory and urinary tract infections.

   D. constant clinging to parents and wanting to be cuddled.

6. A 9-year-old child with autism continually hits his head on his desk. During a planning conference with teachers, the school nurse has devised one outcome for the problem, which states that the child "will develop self-control measures to prevent the behavior." The nurse should evaluate this outcome to be met when the child

      A. wears his helmet continually to prevent injury.

      B. begins cutting his arm instead of banging his head.

      C. seeks out a staff member instead of head banging.

      D. is placed in a seat without a desk to prevent the unacceptable behavior.

7. Identify methods of home behavior modification appropriate for a 6-year-old child with ADHD who is completely disruptive in the evenings during dinner.

Chapter 54: Developmental Disorders

Application Exercises Answer Key

1. A 5-year-old child is brought to the primary care provider by his mother. The mother tells the provider that the child is unable to sit through meals and is easily distracted. At night, he gets up while the family is sleeping and wanders about the house. She also tells the provider that he is doing poorly in his kindergarten class due to his inability to concentrate on work. For which of the following should this child be evaluated?

> A. Mental retardation
>
> B. Down syndrome
>
> **C. ADHD**
>
> D. Autism

> **The child with ADHD is often easily distracted, sleeps poorly, and has difficulty concentrating. There is no specific evidence to support this child having mental retardation, Down syndrome (which almost always is diagnosed at birth), or autism.**

Scenario: The parents of a newborn diagnosed with Down syndrome ask the nurse, "How can we manage a child with so many problems? We've heard that children with Down syndrome will never be normal, will never be independent, and always die young!"

---

2. Discuss how the nurse should respond to the parents' fears.

> **The nurse should listen to the parent's fears and support their grief as she allows them to voice their shock, anger, and sadness. The nurse should be accepting of the child, and role model needed care for the parents. Avoid giving advice or information that may not be realistic (e.g., "I'm sure your child will be able to do okay in school."). Guide interested parents to available support groups and give them literature that they can read when able.**

3. How should the nurse respond if the parents ask, "Why did this happen to our baby?"

> **Explain that Down syndrome is a chromosomal defect. There isn't a way to predict this disorder, and nothing they did during pregnancy could have changed the outcome.**

---

4. A nurse is discussing with the parents of a 3-month-old infant with Down syndrome ways to help prevent recurrent respiratory infections. Which of the following interventions should the nurse discuss with these parents? (Select all that apply.)

   _X_   **Practice frequent handwashing.**

   _____   Keep infant in Fowler's position most of the time to prevent choking.

   _X_   **Use a bulb syringe to remove nasal mucous.**

   _X_   **Keep the infant's mouth moist by rinsing frequently with water.**

Prevention methods should include good handwashing, using a bulb syringe to remove nasal mucous, and keeping mucous membranes moist. It is also important to change the infant's position frequently to promote normal respiratory function; therefore, placing the infant in Fowler's position most of the time is not advised. The infant should lie and sit in a variety of positions.

5. A nurse is assessing a 4-year-old child for signs of autism. The nurse should be alert for

   A. constant talking and impulsive behavior.

   B. poor language and interpersonal skills.

   C. frequent respiratory and urinary tract infections.

   D. constant clinging to parents and wanting to be cuddled.

Children with autism have difficulty learning language skills, and failure to develop interpersonal relationships is also very common. Constant talking and impulsive behavior are common with ADHD. Frequent infections are likely to occur in Down syndrome due to some common physical characteristics, but these are not present in autism. The child with autism is more likely to refuse cuddling and holding than to require it constantly.

6. A 9-year-old child with autism continually hits his head on his desk. During a planning conference with teachers, the school nurse has devised one outcome for the problem, which states that the child "will develop self-control measures to prevent the behavior." The nurse should evaluate this outcome to be met when the child

    A. wears his helmet continually to prevent injury.

    B. begins cutting his arm instead of banging his head.

    C. seeks out a staff member instead of head banging.

    D. is placed in a seat without a desk to prevent the unacceptable behavior.

If the child seeks intervention to prevent the unacceptable behavior, it shows that he is using self-control to prevent self-mutilation. Wearing a helmet may be a good intervention for the outcome, but it does not demonstrate self-control. Exchanging one mutilation behavior for another is not acceptable. Placing a school-age child in a chair without a desk top is a form of punishment and is an unacceptable intervention.

7. Identify methods of home behavior modification appropriate for a 6-year-old child with ADHD who is completely disruptive in the evenings during dinner.

Determine if a successful reward system is in use by teachers at the school, and if so, it may be modified for home use.

Use a tangible system the child can actually see or hold, such as a wall chart or tokens, which can be turned in for rewards.

Allow the child to have input in planning if possible.

Teach parents to be consistent and patient.

Assist parents in setting realistic goals in incremental steps.

Encourage a reward for every attempt, especially at first.

Encourage decreased environmental stimuli when working on behavior modification.

Unit 3   Nursing Care of Children with Emergencies, Developmental Disorders,
                or Psychosocial Issues

Chapter 55:   Psychosocial Issues of Infants and Children
                Contributor: Candyce F. Antley, MN, RN

 NCLEX-RN® Connections:

Learning Objective: Review and apply knowledge within **"Psychosocial Issues of Infants and Children"** in readiness for performance of the following nursing activities as outlined by the NCLEX-RN® test plan:

Δ   Assess the child for psychosocial health risks and intervene appropriately.

Δ   Assess the developmental level of the child and compare with norms.

Δ   Assess the child/family for signs/symptoms of abuse or neglect (physical, psychological, or financial).

Δ   Follow facility policy for reporting child abuse, neglect, and/or injury.

Δ   Identify the child who has been abused/neglected or is at risk of being abused/neglected, and plan care and intervene appropriately.

Δ   Provide a safe environment, physical care, and emotional care for the child who has been a victim of violence.

Δ   Plan and provide care for the child with altered nutrition.

Δ   Assess and document the child's weight to evaluate nutritional goals.

Δ   Provide teaching regarding high-risk behaviors, appropriate infection control procedures, and expected outcomes of high-risk behaviors.

 Key Points

Δ   **Maltreatment of infants and children** is most often attributed to family violence within the home.

    • Family violence occurs across all economic and educational backgrounds and racial/ethnic groups.

    • Maltreatment of children is made up of several specific types of behaviors, which include:

        ◊ Physical violence – causes pain or harm, such as shaken baby syndrome (caused by violent shaking of infants).

        ◊ Sexual violence – is any situation where the victim does not give consent. This includes any sexual behavior toward a minor and dating violence among adolescents.

◊ Emotional violence – includes behavior that minimizes an individual's feelings of self-worth. This form of violence humiliates, threatens, or intimidates a child (e.g., continual angry and belittling verbal comments).

◊ Neglect – the failure to provide, which includes:

° Physical care (e.g., feeding).

° Emotional care and/or stimulation to allow an individual to develop normally (e.g., not speaking to a child).

° Denying education to a child (e.g., never enrolling a young child in school).

◊ Economic maltreatment includes depriving family members of resources and/or support.

• **All states have mandatory reporting laws that require nurses to report suspected abuse and there are civil and criminal penalties for NOT reporting.**

Δ **Failure to thrive** in infants or children is manifested as inadequate growth resulting from inability to obtain or use calories required for growth. It is usually described in an infant or child who falls below the fifth percentile for weight (and possibly for height) or has persistent weight loss.

Key Factors

Δ Child maltreatment factors that make abuse against children more likely to occur include:

• A child under 3 years of age.

• A child who is physically disabled, of an unwanted pregnancy, or has some other trait that makes him particularly vulnerable. Almost always, a child who is abused is perceived by the perpetrator as being different.

Δ Failure to thrive can be the result of an organic (physical) cause, a definable psychosocial cause unrelated to disease, or idiopathic, in which the cause is unknown.

• Factors related to an organic cause include cerebral palsy, chronic renal failure, congenital heart disease, and/or gastroesophageal reflux.

• Factors related to nonorganic failure to thrive (NFTT) may include:

◊ Lack of parental knowledge, parental neglect, or a disturbed maternal-child attachment.

◊ Poverty.

◊ Health or childrearing beliefs.

◊ Family stress.

◊ Feeding resistance.

◊ Insufficient breast milk.

Assessment

Δ   Conducting an assessment interview regarding injury to the child

- Conduct the interview about family abuse in private.

- Be direct, honest, and professional.

- Use language the child understands.

- Be understanding and attentive.

- Inform the child/parent/caregiver if a referral must be made to children or adult protective services, and explain the process.

- Assess safety and help reduce danger for the victim.

- Use questions that are open-ended and require a descriptive response. These questions are less threatening and elicit more relevant information.

Δ   Assessment of the child's behavior for **sexual abuse**

- Inappropriate knowledge of or interest in sexual acts

- Seductive behavior

- Avoids anything related to sexuality or own genitals and body

- Overly compliant or excessively aggressive with others

- Fear of a particular person or family member

Δ   Physical assessment of possible **physical child abuse**

- Infant

  ◊ Shaken baby syndrome – shaking may cause intracranial hemorrhage. Assess for respiratory distress, bulging fontanels, and increased head circumference. Retinal hemorrhage may also be present.

  ◊ Any bruising on an infant before 6 months of age can be deemed by the nurse as suspicious.

- Preschooler to adolescent

  ◊ Assess for unusual bruising on the abdomen, back, and/or buttocks. Bruising is common on arms and legs in these age groups.

  ◊ Assess the mechanism of injury, which may not be congruent with physical appearance of the injury. Many bruises at different stages of healing may indicate continued beatings. Observe for bruises or welts that have taken on the shape of a belt buckle or other objects.

  ◊ Observe for burns that appear glove- or stocking-like on hands or feet, which may indicate forced immersion into boiling water. Small round burns may be caused by lit cigarettes.

  ◊ Note fractures with unusual features, such as forearm spiral fractures, which could be caused by twisting the extremity forcefully. The presence of multiple fractures is suspicious.

◊   Check the child for head injuries. Assess the child's level of consciousness, making sure to note equal and reactive pupils. Also, monitor the child for nausea/vomiting.

Δ   Nursing assessments for **failure to thrive**

- Obtain health and nutritional history.

- Obtain baseline of height and weight and continue to monitor.

- Monitor activity level.

- Assess developmental milestones.

- Assess interaction patterns of caregiver including eye contact, affection shown for child, and communication with child.

- Observe the infant interacting with others. Observe for negative interactions. such as no eye contact, irritability, and pushing caregiver away.

- Observe for indications of hunger and satiety.

- Assess the child's ability to be soothed.

- Observe feeding/eating patterns.

Diagnostic Procedures

Δ   Radiographs

Δ   CT scan or MRI

Δ   CBC, urinalysis, and other tests for bleeding

Δ   Tests for STDs in children who have been sexually abused

NANDA Nursing Diagnoses

Δ   Ineffective coping

Δ   Ineffective denial

Δ   Family processes: interrupted

Δ   Dysfunctional family processes: alcoholism

Δ   Delayed growth and development

Δ   Ineffective infant feeding pattern

Δ   Risk for injury

Δ   Helplessness

Δ   Parenting impaired

Δ   Altered nutrition: less than body requirements

Nursing Interventions

Δ Interventions related to child abuse

- **Nurses have a legal responsibility and are mandated by law to report suspected or actual cases of child abuse.**

- Clearly and objectively document information obtained in the interview and during the physical assessment.

Δ Interventions for **failure to thrive** include:

- Observing parent-child interactions.

- Obtaining accurate weights and nutritional I&O.

- Acting as a role model and teacher for the parents.

  ◊ Teach parents to recognize and respond to the infant's cues of hunger.

  ◊ Help a mother who is breastfeeding with proper positioning, latching on, timing, and other techniques.

  ◊ Model proper formula feeding or solid food feeding for infant/child including positioning, eye contact, talking to child, and other interventions.

  ◊ Model to parents proper burping techniques for infant.

- Obtaining frequent growth measurements.

Complications and Nursing Implications

Δ Child Abuse

- Serious physical injury or death

- Developmental delays

- Risk for lifelong emotional damage

- Risk for perpetuation of child abuse in future generations

- All suspicions of abuse should be reported.

Primary Reference:

Hockenberry, M., Wilson, D., Winkelstein, M. (2005). *Wong's essentials of pediatric nursing care.* (7th ed.). St. Louis, MO: Mosby.

Additional Resources:

Agras, W. S. (2002, June, 7). *The eating disorders: Anorexia nervosa.* Retrieved November 19, 2006, from http://www.medscape.com/viewarticle/534480

Advocates for Youth. (2007). *Teen pregnancy prevention.* Retrieved February 16, 2007, from http://www.advocatesforyouth.org/teenpregnancy.htm

Advocates for Youth. (2007). *Dating violence and child abuse.* Retrieved February 16, 2007, from http://www.advocatesforyouth.org/violenceabuse.htm

Ball, J. W., & Bindler, R. C. (2006) *Child health nursing: Partnering with children and families.* (1st ed.). Upper Saddle River, NJ: Prentice Hall.

Centers for Disease Control and Prevention. (2006). *Sexually transmitted diseases treatment guidelines 2006: Diseases characterized by vaginal discharge.* Retrieved February 17, 2007, from http://www.cdc.gov/std/treatment/2006/vaginal-discharge.htm

de Benedictus, T., Jaffe, J., & Segal, J. (2007). *Child abuse: Types, signs, symptoms, causes, and help.* Retrieved February 16, 2007, from http://www.helpguide.org/mental/child_abuse_physical_emotional_sexual_neglect.htm#sexual

Littleton, L. Y., & Engebretson, J. C. (2005). *Maternity nursing care.* (1st ed.). Florence, KY: Thomson Delmar Learning.

Varcarolis, E. M., Carson, V. B., and Shoemaker, N. (2006). *Foundations of psychiatric mental health nursing: A clinical approach.* (5th ed.). St. Louis, MO: Saunders.

Chapter 55: Psychosocial Issues of Infants and Children

Application Exercises

Scenario: The first-time parents of a 3-month-old infant take her to the inpatient pediatric unit. The infant has a medical diagnosis of failure to thrive. She was healthy and in the 40th percentile at birth for height and weight. By her 2-month check-up she had dropped to the 10th percentile. Today she has dropped below the 5th percentile.

1. Explain what assessments are needed at this time.

2. The mother tells the nurse that she is bottle feeding. Which of the following feeding techniques should the nurse teach the mother? (Select all that apply.)

    _____ Simulate feeding environment in common dining room.

    _____ Maintain eye contact with the infant during feeding.

    _____ Burp the infant frequently during feeding.

    _____ Give the infant as much formula as she can hold during each feeding.

    _____ Develop a structured feeding routine.

3. A nurse is evaluating a family in which child abuse has occurred. Which of the following best indicates that the parents are making progress toward resolution of the violence?

    A. Parents plan weekly outings to the park.

    B. Parents are attending parenting classes.

    C. Parents report high expectations for their children.

    D. Parents relate an understanding of normal growth and development.

4. A nurse is assessing the family of a child brought in for severe injuries. Which of the following behaviors by the parents indicates probable abuse?

    A. Delay in seeking treatment for the child's injuries

    B. Detailed description of the events prior to the injuries

    C. Anxious, concerned attitude

    D. Encouraging the child to explain the injuries

Chapter 55: Psychosocial Issues of Infants and Children

Application Exercises Answer Key

Scenario: The first-time parents of a 3-month-old infant take her to the inpatient pediatric unit. The infant has a medical diagnosis of failure to thrive. She was healthy and in the 40th percentile at birth for height and weight. By her 2-month check-up she had dropped to the 10th percentile. Today she has dropped below the 5th percentile.

1. Explain what assessments are needed at this time.

> **The nurse should assess the infant's I&O, daily weight, feeding patterns, interaction with parents, activity level, and parental concerns.**

2. The mother tells the nurse that she is bottle feeding. Which of the following feeding techniques should the nurse teach the mother? (Select all that apply.)

_____ Simulate feeding environment in common dining room.

_X_ Maintain eye contact with the infant during feeding.

_X_ Burp the infant frequently during feeding.

_____ Give the infant as much formula as she can hold during each feeding.

_X_ Develop a structured feeding routine.

Maintaining good eye contact, burping the infant frequently, and developing a structured feeding routine are all feeding techniques that promote increased infant feeding. The nurse should also maintain a quiet environment, rather than a noisy, stimulating one. Rather than giving large amounts of formula, it is better to give smaller amounts more frequently to promote good digestion and weight gain.

3. A nurse is evaluating a family in which child abuse has occurred. Which of the following best indicates that the parents are making progress toward resolution of the violence?

      A. Parents plan weekly outings to the park.

      B. Parents are attending parenting classes.

      C. Parents report high expectations for their children.

      D. Parents relate an understanding of normal growth and development.

Relating an understanding of normal growth and development will be the best indicator that the family is progressing toward a resolution of violence. Understanding normal growth and development will help them understand what normal behavior is and how to treat their children appropriately. Planning weekly outings is a positive family activity and can improve family relationships, but the parents still need to know how to interact appropriately with their children. Attendance at parenting classes is an intervention toward meeting the outcome of understanding normal growth and development and better parenting techniques. High expectations of children may be unrealistic and cause the parents to become angry and could lead to violence.

4. A nurse is assessing the family of a child brought in for severe injuries. Which of the following behaviors by the parents indicates probable abuse?

      A. Delay in seeking treatment for the child's injuries

      B. Detailed description of the events prior to the injuries

      C. Anxious, concerned attitude

      D. Encouraging the child to explain the injuries

Parents who have injured a child may delay seeking treatment for the child. The other options are not indicative of probable abuse and are likely to occur when an accidental injury happens.

Unit 3   Nursing Care of Children with Emergencies, Developmental Disorders, or Psychosocial Issues

Chapter 56:   Psychosocial Issues of Adolescents

Contributor: Candyce F. Antley, MN, RN

 NCLEX-RN® Connections:

Learning Objective: Review and apply knowledge within "**Psychosocial Issues of Adolescents**" in readiness for performance of the following nursing activities as outlined by the NCLEX-RN® test plan:

Δ   Assess the adolescent for psychosocial health risks and intervene appropriately.

Δ   Assess the developmental level of the adolescent and compare with norms.

Δ   Plan and provide care for the adolescent with altered nutrition.

Δ   Assess and document the adolescent's weight to evaluate nutritional goals.

Δ   Provide teaching regarding high-risk behaviors, appropriate infection control procedures, and expected outcomes of high-risk behaviors.

Δ   Identify communicable diseases and the methods of organism transmission and report as appropriate.

Δ   Assess/evaluate the adolescent/family emotional response to pregnancy and the adolescent's acceptance of changes in body image.

Δ   Assess the pregnant adolescent's physiological status and identify any signs of prenatal complications.

Δ   Provide perinatal education, including teaching regarding nutritional needs.

 Key Points

Δ   Eating Disorders

•   Anorexia nervosa – extreme weight loss through severe dieting/extreme exercising or binging and purging

•   Bulimia nervosa – severe binging and purging in between intense dieting

•   Obesity – poor dietary habits with inadequate physical activity

Δ   **Adolescent Pregnancy**

- Pregnancy rates for 15- to 19-year-old adolescents in the United States have declined since 1990 due to the increased use of birth control and higher rates of abstinence; however, pregnancy, birth, and abortion rates are higher in this age group in the United States than in other industrialized nations.

- Morbidity for teenage pregnancy remains high.

Δ   **Sexually transmitted diseases (STDs)** are the most frequently occurring infectious diseases during adolescence.

Key Factors

Δ   **Eating disorders** commonly develop during adolescence (more prevalent in girls than in boys) due to a fear of being overweight, fad diets, and/or as a mechanism of maintaining control over some aspect of life.

Δ   Factors that contribute to the risk **of adolescent pregnancy** include:

- Having a mother who was a adolescent parent.

- Sex with an older partner.

- Improper use/no use of contraception.

- Poor living conditions.

- Poor school performance.

Δ   Adolescent girls and their infants are at an increased risk for:

- Premature labor.

- Low birth weight.

- High neonatal mortality.

- Pregnancy-induced hypertension.

Δ   Risks associated with adolescent pregnancy may be minimized with early, consistent prenatal care.

Δ   Factors related to **STDs**

- Behavioral risk factors include:

  ◊   Increased use of drugs and/or alcohol.

  ◊   Lack of condom use.

  ◊   Limited access to health care.

  ◊   Delay in seeking treatment out of fear.

  ◊   Sexual partners with high incidence of disease.

- Other factors include:

  ◊ Sexual assault, incest, and/or abuse.

  ◊ The adolescent girl's cervix has cells that are more susceptible to STDs (e.g., human papillomavirus [HPV], chlamydia).

  ◊ The adolescent has not had time to develop resistance to HPV and chlamydia.

Assessment

Δ Psychosocial Assessment for Eating Disorders

- Obtain the adolescent's developmental history and current mental status.

- Inquire about the adolescent's perception of the problem.

- Assess the adolescent's eating habits.

- Obtain the adolescent's history of dieting.

- Monitor methods of weight control (restricting, purging, exercising).

- Inquire about the adolescent's value attached to a specific shape and weight.

- Assess interpersonal and social functioning.

- The adolescent's personal history may reveal great difficulty with impulsivity as well as compulsivity.

- Family relationships are frequently chaotic and reflect a lack of nurturing.

- The adolescent's life may be described as unstable, with troublesome interpersonal relationships.

Δ The nurse should assess for cognitive distortions and address them through therapeutic communication. Examples of cognitive distortions include:

- Overgeneralizations – "The girls at school don't like me. I'm sure it's because I'm fat."

- All-or-nothing thinking – "If I eat any dessert, I'll gain fifty pounds."

- Catastrophizing – "My life is over if I gain weight."

- Personalization – "When I walk through the hospital hallway, I know everyone is looking at me."

- Emotional reasoning – "I know I look bad because I feel bloated."

Δ Physical Assessment for **Eating Disorders**

- The adolescent with anorexia nervosa may demonstrate:

  ◊ Low weight.

  ◊ Fine, downy hair (lanugo) on the face and back.

◊   Mottled, cool extremities and poor skin turgor.

◊   Low blood pressure with possible orthostatic hypotension.

◊   Decreased pulse and body temperature.

◊   Irregular heart rate (dysrhythmias noted on cardiac monitor).

•   The assessment of an adolescent with bulimia may demonstrate enlargement of the parotid glands with dental erosion and caries if the adolescent has been inducing vomiting. The adolescent may be of normal weight or slightly underweight.

Δ   **Antenatal Assessment** for the Pregnant Adolescent

•   Nursing history should include:

◊   Date of last menstrual cycle to determine estimated date of delivery.

◊   The adolescent's understanding of prenatal care.

◊   The adolescent's housing status during pregnancy (e.g., homeless, with a friend).

◊   Ability to rest/sleep.

◊   Activities and level of tolerance.

◊   Presence of nausea or vomiting.

◊   Medications taken, including use of alcohol or illegal drugs.

◊   Dietary and fluid intake.

◊   Sexual activity.

◊   Concerns about delivery.

◊   Determining the adolescent's intent to keep the infant or place it up for adoption. Also, ask the adolescent if she would like to view the infant following delivery.

◊   Financial concerns.

◊   Support and coping.

◊   Plan of care for infant.

•   Physical assessment should include:

◊   Serum iron levels (presence of anemia).

◊   Presence of edema.

◊   Vital signs – Monitor blood pressure for elevations.

◊   Urinalysis – Monitor for glucose and protein.

◊   Weight – Determine if weight gain has been appropriate (too little or too much).

◊   Measurements of uterine height after the first 12 weeks.

◊   Fetal heart sounds and fetal movements.

Δ   **Postpartal Assessment** of the Adolescent

- Vital signs, weight
- Vaginal discharge
- Hemorrhoids and wound care from episiotomy or vaginal tears
- Emotional status
- Mother-infant bonding
- Feeding abilities
  - ◊ Breastfeeding, infant latch on, let-down of milk
  - ◊ Maternal nutritional needs for breastfeeding
  - ◊ Bottle feeding, infant's ability to take bottle, technique used
- Knowledge of infant growth and development
- Living situation, including financial and emotional support
- Support for child care
- Plans for mother to finish school
- Plans for sexual activity and contraception

Δ   Assessment for **STDs** in the adolescent

- History of risk factors – substance abuse, unprotected sex, lack of health care
- Assessment for physical symptoms

Infection	Males	Females
Gonorrhea (*Neisseria gonorrhoeae*)	• Dysuria • Urinary frequency • Purulent discharge from urethra	• Abdominal pain • Purulent discharge from vagina • Abnormal menses • Pelvic inflammatory disease may develop if untreated
Chlamydia (*Chlamydia trachomatis*) generally asymptomatic	• Dysuria • Discharge from urethra	• Dysuria • Discharge from vagina • May lead to pelvic inflammatory disease
Vaginitis (*Trichomonas vaginalis*)	N/A	• Pruritus, edema, and discomfort of genitalia • Foul smelling, green vaginal or urethral discharge
Syphilis (*Treponema pallidum*)	Stage I • Chancre – open lesion • Localized lymphadenopathy Stage II • Rash on palms of hands • Patches in mouth • Sore throat • Generalized lymphadenopathy • Papules in area of contact (most commonly perineum) • Flu-like symptoms • Latent asymptomatic period Stage III • Tumors of skin, bone, liver • Irreversible CNS damage	
Herpes progenitalis (Genital herpes simplex infection [HSV])	• Small vesicles on genital area, buttocks, and thighs • Vesicles rupture leaving shallow, circular painful lesions	
Human papillomavirus (HPV)	• Warts on genitalia	

Diagnostic Procedures and Nursing Interventions

Δ Common **diagnostic procedures for eating disorders**

- Serum levels of electrolytes

    ◊ Hypokalemia (due to dehydration and purging [vomiting] in both anorexia and bulimia)

    ◊ Hyponatremia and hypochloremia are common in bulimia.

- CBC to detect anemia and leukopenia with lymphocytosis
- Abnormal liver function test with increased enzyme levels
- Elevated cholesterol
- Abnormal thyroid function tests
- Elevated carotene levels, which cause skin to appear yellow
- Decreased bone density (osteoporosis may occur)

Δ **Diagnostic Tests for the Pregnant Adolescent**

- Ultrasound of fetus
- Maternal serum alpha-fetoprotein (MSAFP)
  ◊ Provide teaching regarding the importance of this blood test.

Δ Diagnostic tests for **STDs** include:

- Pap smear for HPV.
- Serum venereal disease research laboratory (VDRL) for syphilis.
- Visual examination of blisters and blood testing for herpes (HSV).
- EIA (enzyme immunoassay) and the ELISA (enzyme-linked immunosorbent assay) HIV testing.
- For STD testing
  ◊ Assist with positioning and specimen collection.
  ◊ Conduct vaginal/cervical/urethral microscopic examination or culture for:
    ° Gonorrhea.
    ° Chlamydia.
    ° Vaginitis (including trichomoniasis and bacterial vaginosis).

NANDA Nursing Diagnoses

Δ Disturbed body image

Δ Ineffective coping

Δ Decisional conflict

Δ Ineffective health maintenance

Δ Health-seeking behaviors

Δ Deficient knowledge

Δ   Imbalanced nutrition: less than body requirements

Δ   Risk for impaired parent-infant attachment

Δ   Powerlessness

Δ   Chronic low self-esteem

Nursing Interventions

Δ   Nursing interventions for **eating disorders** include:

- Admission to a highly structured inpatient unit providing a therapeutic milieu in order to interrupt the binge-purge cycle and prevent the disordered eating behaviors.

- Establishing and maintaining trust through consistency and therapeutic communication.

- Careful monitoring of food intake, exercise patterns, and the attempt to purge after eating.

- Health teaching that focuses not only on the eating disorder, but on meal planning, use of relaxation techniques, maintenance of a healthy diet and exercise, self-care skills, coping skills, and the physical and emotional effects of bingeing and purging.

- Behavior modification to reward the adolescent for weight gain and positive behaviors.

- Group education and family therapy sessions.

- Medical stabilization (may be necessary for the adolescent with malnutrition and fluid/electrolyte imbalances).

Δ   Interventions for **the Pregnant Adolescent**

- Discuss signs and symptoms of pregnancy.

- Encourage the adolescent to ask questions.

- Provide written information about pregnancy and needed prenatal care.

- Explain a balanced diet and assist the adolescent in making healthy food choices for herself and the infant.

- Encourage consumption of adequate calories with emphasis on protein and iron.

- Emphasize the need to take prenatal vitamins.

- Encourage exercise balanced with adequate rest.

- Discuss alternatives relative to the pregnancy, such as adoption and keeping the infant. Encourage the adolescent to discuss her feelings, values, and needs related to pregnancy alternatives.

- Encourage talking about fears and concerns regarding pregnancy, telling parents, and telling the father of the infant.

- Offer to help her tell her parents, but reassure her about confidentiality if she refuses.

- Discuss STD prevention and methods of future birth control.

- Encourage adolescent to return to school if appropriate.

- Help the adolescent find peer support groups.

- Identify social agencies that may be helpful to the adolescent.

Δ   Nursing interventions for **STDs** in adolescents include:

- Approaching the adolescent in a nonjudgmental manner.

- Praising the adolescent for seeking treatment.

- Presenting the facts about the disease process.

- Discussing the transmission mechanism(s).

- Teaching and preventing future infections.

- Encouraging abstinence from intercourse during treatment.

- Using condoms.

- Treating complications if left untreated.

- Instructing the adolescent to take the entire dose of antibiotic medications for bacterial infections.

- Explaining the importance of notifying sexual contacts so they can be treated.

- Reporting STD case to local health department.

Complications

Δ   Eating Disorders

- Lifelong psychological disability may result.

- Severe physical disability and death may occur.

Δ   Pregnancy Complications

- Death of pregnant adolescent may occur with lack of antenatal care or delivery complications.

- Premature delivery, disability, and/or death of fetus/newborn may occur with substance abuse in pregnancy, lack of antenatal care, and/or severe nutritional deficits of mother.

Δ   STD complications may include:

- Transmission to fetus.

- Pelvic inflammatory disease, which may result in infertility in males and females.

- Permanent damage to reproductive tract in both females and males.

- Death, which may be attributed to late stage syphilis or HIV/AIDS.

Primary Reference:

Hockenberry, M., Wilson, D., Winkelstein, M. (2005). *Wong's essentials of pediatric nursing care.* (7th ed.). St. Louis, MO: Mosby.

Additional Resources:

Agras, W. S. (2002, June, 7). *The eating disorders: Anorexia nervosa.* Retrieved November 19, 2006, from http://www.medscape.com/viewarticle/534480

Advocates for Youth. (2007). *Teen pregnancy prevention.* Retrieved February 16, 2007, from http://www.advocatesforyouth.org/teenpregnancy.htm

Ball, J. W., & Bindler, R. C. (2006) *Child health nursing: Partnering with children and families.* (1st ed.). Upper Saddle River, NJ: Prentice Hall.

Centers for Disease Control and Prevention. (2006). *Sexually transmitted diseases treatment guidelines 2006: Diseases characterized by vaginal discharge.* Retrieved February 17, 2007, from http://www.cdc.gov/std/treatment/2006/vaginal-discharge.htm

Littleton, L. Y., & Engebretson, J. C. (2005). *Maternity nursing care.* (1st ed.). Florence, KY: Thomson Delmar Learning.

NANDA International (2004). *NANDA nursing diagnoses: Definitions and classification 2005-2006.* Philadelphia: NANDA.

Varcarolis, E. M., Carson, V. B., & Shoemaker, N. (2006). *Foundations of psychiatric mental health nursing: A clinical approach.* (5th ed.). St. Louis, MO: Saunders.

Chapter 56: Psychosocial Issues of Adolescents

Application Exercises

Scenario: An adolescent client presents to the emergency department because of recurrent nausea and vomiting for the past 2 months. After a physical examination, the provider tells the adolescent that she is 10 weeks pregnant. She becomes extremely upset and begins to cry. She tells the provider that she just broke up with her boyfriend and asks the provider not to tell her parents about the pregnancy.

1. The priority nursing diagnosis is _____.

2. Identify two reasons why the nurse should be concerned about this adolescent's nutrition.

3. How should the nurse respond in regard to this adolescent not wanting her parents to know about the pregnancy?

4. An adolescent with syphilis is not experiencing any symptoms. Which of the following statements by the adolescent indicates a need for more education?

    A. "I will take my antibiotic until it is gone."

    B. "I am not going to tell my sexual partners because they will think I am dirty."

    C. "I will be sure to keep all of my appointments with my doctor."

    D. "It is important that I use a condom when I have sex."

5. Which of the following is an appropriate short-term goal for an adolescent with an eating disorder?

    A. Weigh within the 50th percentile for age and height.

    B. Eat a well-balanced diet.

    C. Resolve conflicts with parents.

    D. Look at self in mirror each morning.

Chapter 56: Psychosocial Issues of Adolescents

Application Exercises Answer Key

Scenario: An adolescent client presents to the emergency department because of recurrent nausea and vomiting for the past 2 months. After a physical examination, the provider tells the adolescent that she is 10 weeks pregnant. She becomes extremely upset and begins to cry. She tells the provider that she just broke up with her boyfriend and asks the provider not to tell her parents about the pregnancy.

1. The priority nursing diagnosis is _____.

   Ineffective coping. This is the priority diagnosis due to the adolescent's physical and emotional changes.

2. Identify two reasons why the nurse should be concerned about this adolescent's nutrition.

   This adolescent has increased nutritional needs and will need to increase her caloric intake to provide for the fetus. The amount of nausea/vomiting she has experienced is unknown, but could be a concern. She is upset that her parents will find out that she is pregnant and might not want to change her eating patterns.

3. How should the nurse respond in regard to this adolescent not wanting her parents to know about the pregnancy?

   Encourage her to tell her parents to gain their support but inform her that confidentiality will be maintained if she refuses. Have her talk about how she will keep her parents from finding out about the pregnancy, especially as it progresses. Ask her if there is a close adult family friend she could confide in. Make a referral to social services to assist her in accessing available resources.

4. An adolescent with syphilis is not experiencing any symptoms. Which of the following statements by the adolescent indicates a need for more education?

> A. "I will take my antibiotic until it is gone."
>
> **B. "I am not going to tell my sexual partners because they will think I am dirty."**
>
> C. "I will be sure to keep all of my appointments with my doctor."
>
> D. "It is important that I use a condom when I have sex."

It is important that the adolescent inform sexual partners because they too could be asymptomatic and unaware of the presence of the infection and need for treatment. The other options are true and show comprehension of the problem.

5. Which of the following is an appropriate short-term goal for an adolescent with an eating disorder?

> A. Weigh within the 50ᵗʰ percentile for age and height.
>
> **B. Eat a well-balanced diet.**
>
> C. Resolve conflicts with parents.
>
> D. Look at self in mirror each morning.

A realistic, short-term goal focuses on making sure the adolescent eats a nutritious diet. Options A and C might be possible long-term goals. Option D is not a proper goal because the client may look at herself in the mirror and have a distorted view of what she sees.